Boarding School Juliet

To LOVE, or not to LOVE

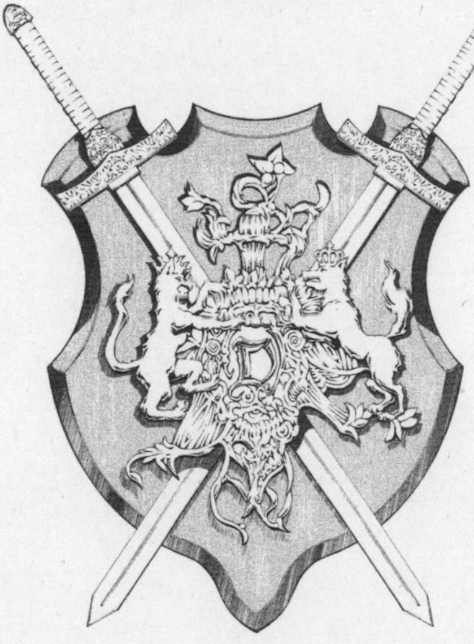

vol. 1

YOUSUKE KANEDA

contents

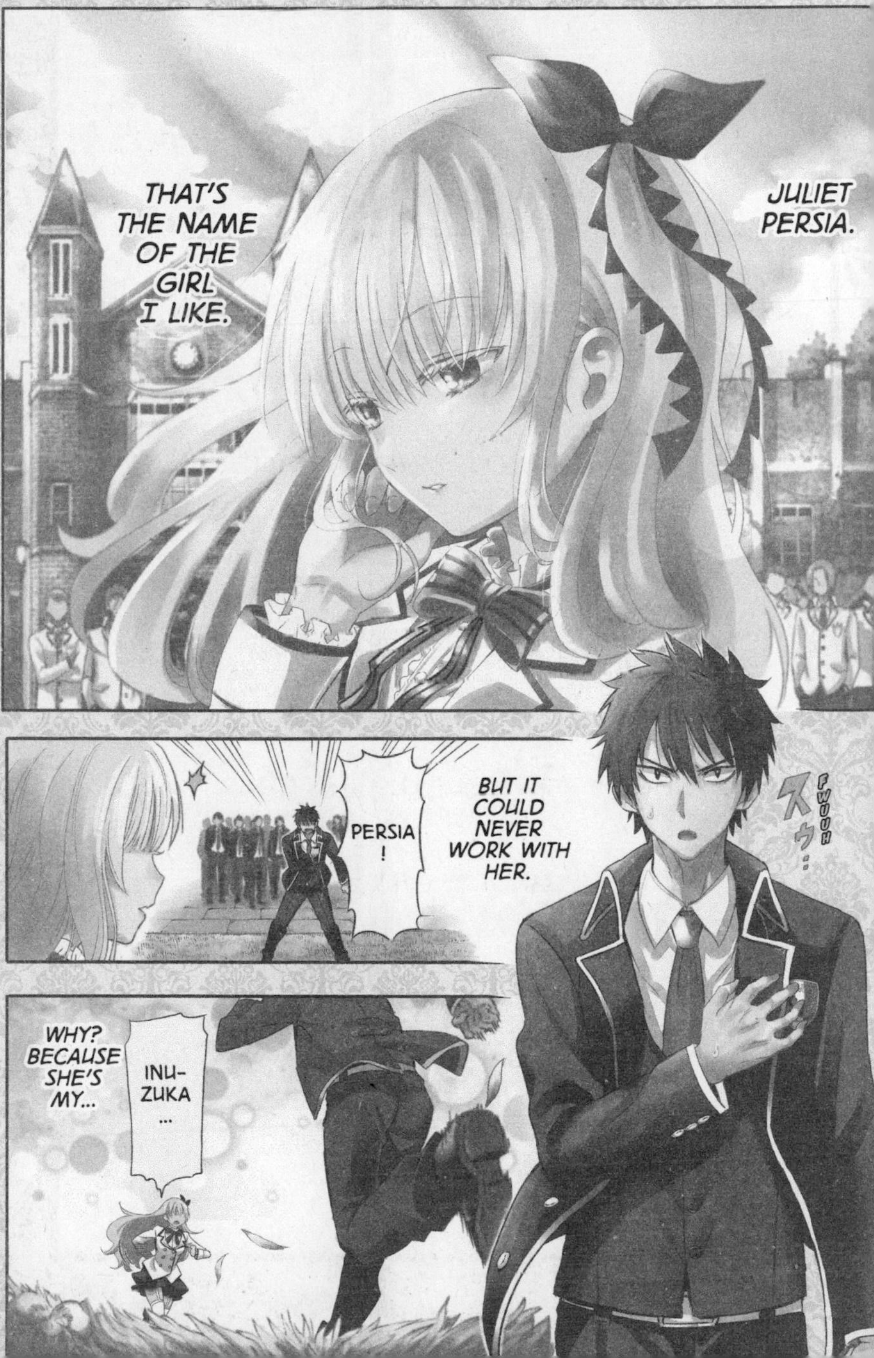
JULIET PERSIA.
THAT'S THE NAME OF THE GIRL I LIKE.
FWUUH
BUT IT COULD NEVER WORK WITH HER.
PERSIA!
INU-ZUKA...
WHY? BECAUSE SHE'S MY...

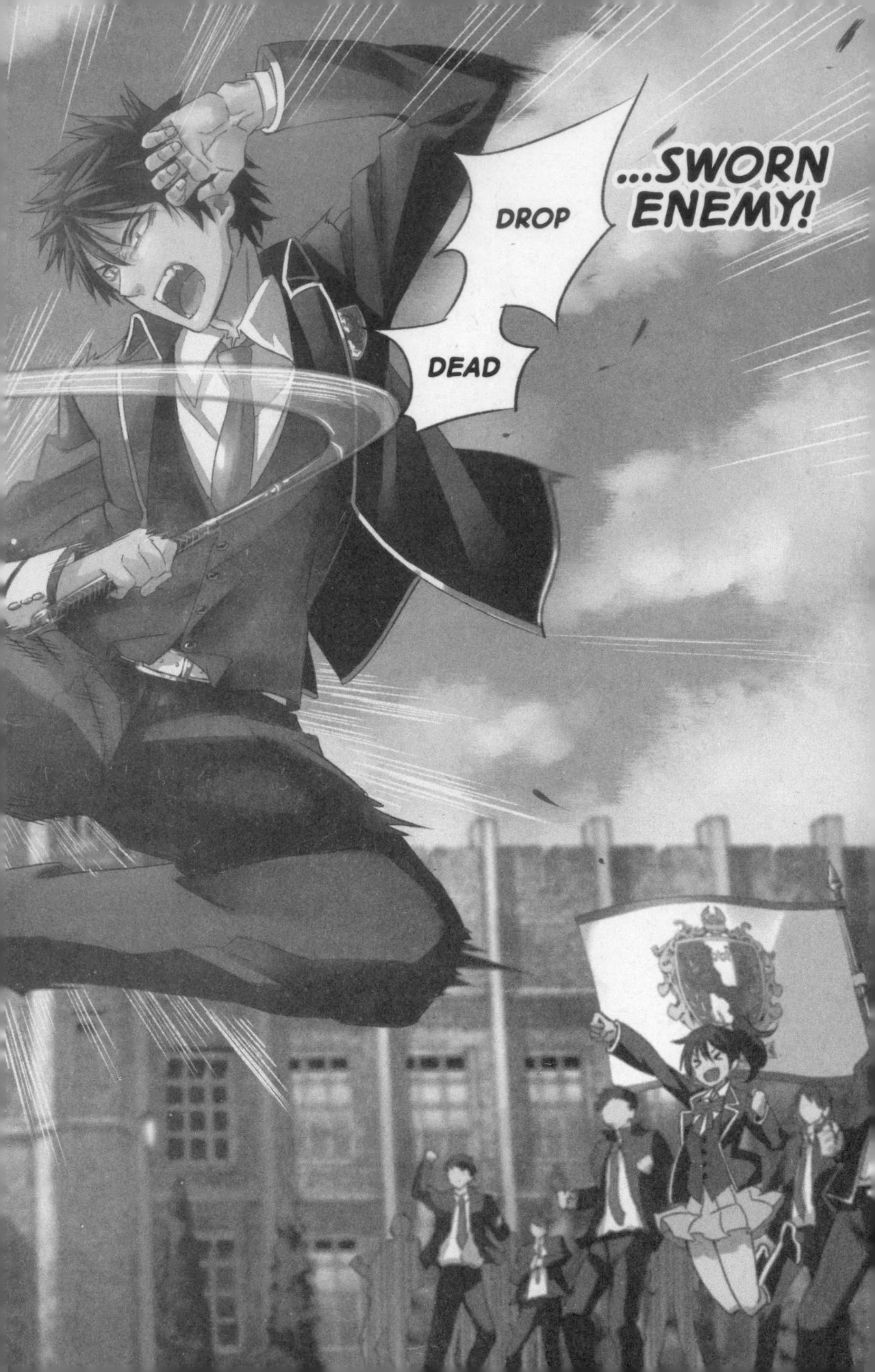
...SWORN ENEMY!
DROP DEAD

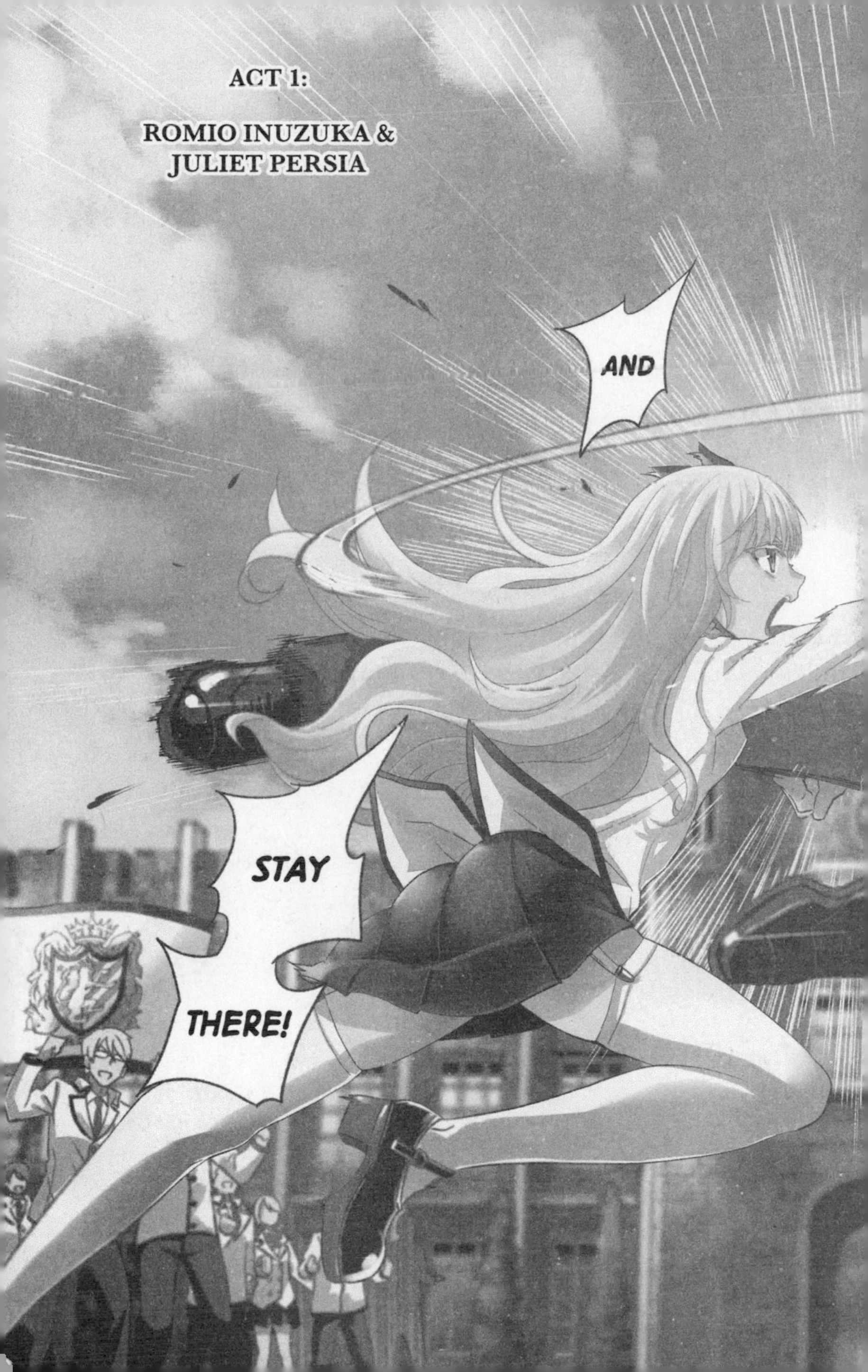
ACT 1:
ROMIO INUZUKA &
JULIET PERSIA
AND
STAY THERE!

Boarding
School *Juliet*

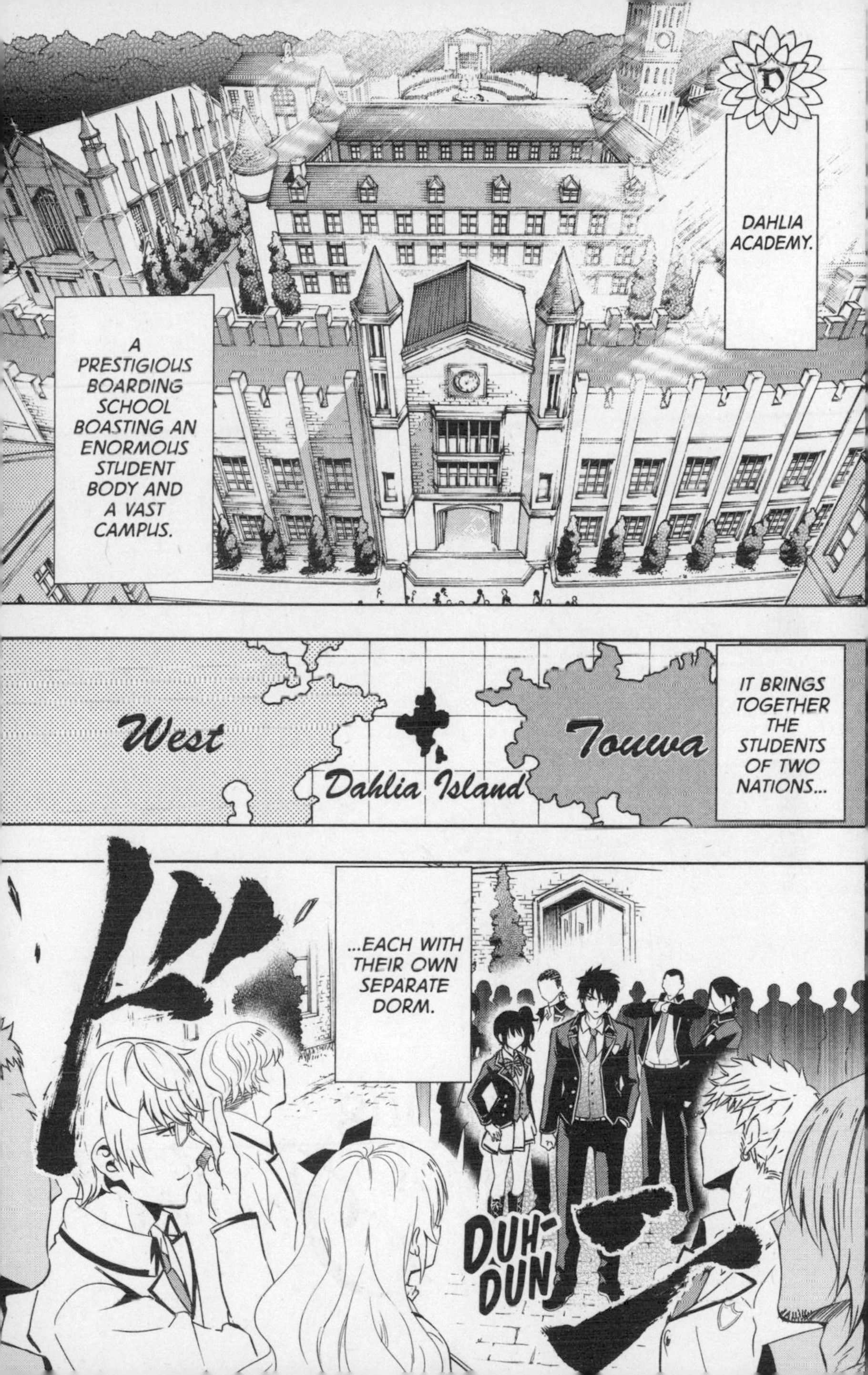
DAHLIA ACADEMY.
A PRESTIGIOUS BOARDING SCHOOL BOASTING AN ENORMOUS STUDENT BODY AND A VAST CAMPUS.
IT BRINGS TOGETHER THE STUDENTS OF TWO NATIONS...
Touwa
Dahlia Island
West
...EACH WITH THEIR OWN SEPARATE DORM.
DUH-DUN

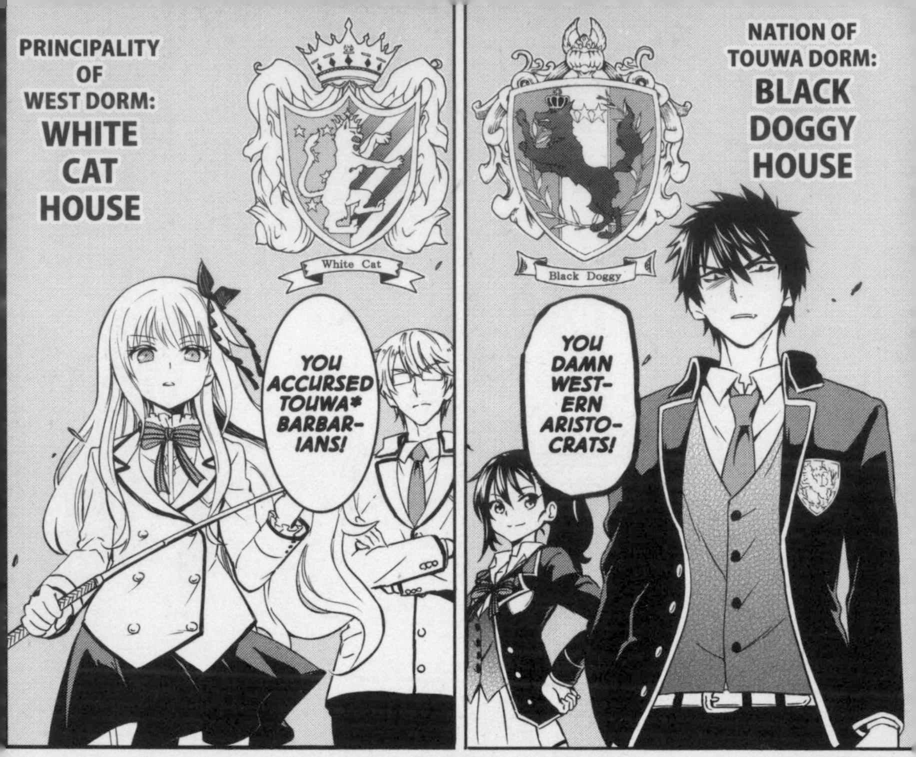
NATION OF TOUWA DORM: BLACK DOGGY HOUSE
Black Doggy
YOU DAMN WEST-ERN ARISTO-CRATS!
PRINCIPALITY OF WEST DORM: WHITE CAT HOUSE
White Cat
YOU ACCURSED TOUWA* BARBAR-IANS!

*The fantasy nation of Touwa is a stand-in for Japan—the kanji characters that make up the name mean "East" and "Japan/harmony."

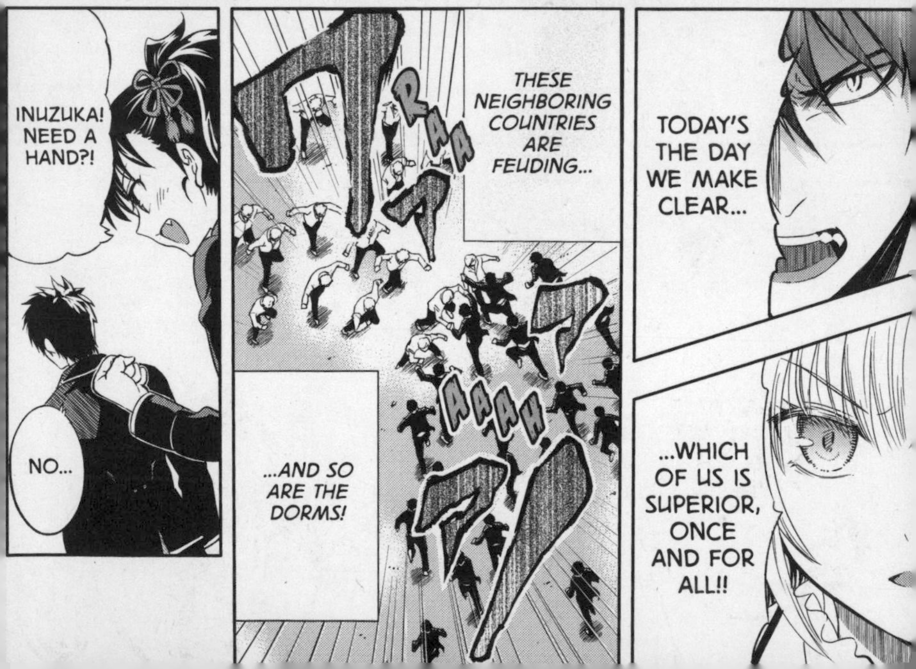
TODAY'S THE DAY WE MAKE CLEAR...
...WHICH OF US IS SUPERIOR, ONCE AND FOR ALL!!
THESE NEIGHBORING COUNTRIES ARE FEUDING...
RAAA
AAAAH
...AND SO ARE THE DORMS!
INUZUKA! NEED A HAND?!
NO...

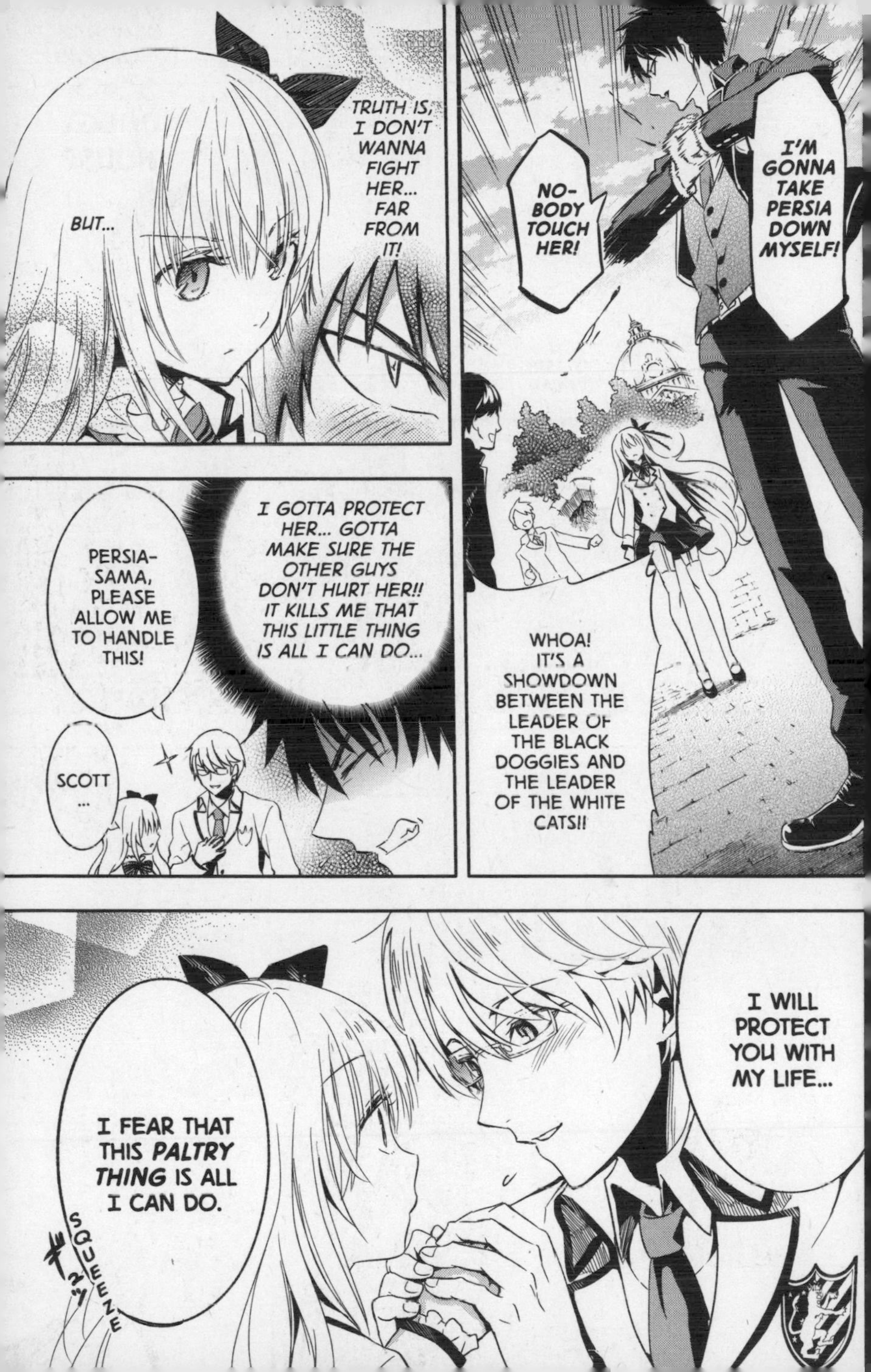
I'M GONNA TAKE PERSIA DOWN MYSELF!
NO-BODY TOUCH HER!
WHOA! IT'S A SHOWDOWN BETWEEN THE LEADER OF THE BLACK DOGGIES AND THE LEADER OF THE WHITE CATS!!
TRUTH IS, I DON'T WANNA FIGHT HER... FAR FROM IT!
BUT...
I GOTTA PROTECT HER... GOTTA MAKE SURE THE OTHER GUYS DON'T HURT HER!! IT KILLS ME THAT THIS LITTLE THING IS ALL I CAN DO...
PERSIA-SAMA, PLEASE ALLOW ME TO HANDLE THIS!
SCOTT ...
I WILL PROTECT YOU WITH MY LIFE...
I FEAR THAT THIS *PALTRY THING* IS ALL I CAN DO.
SQUEEZE

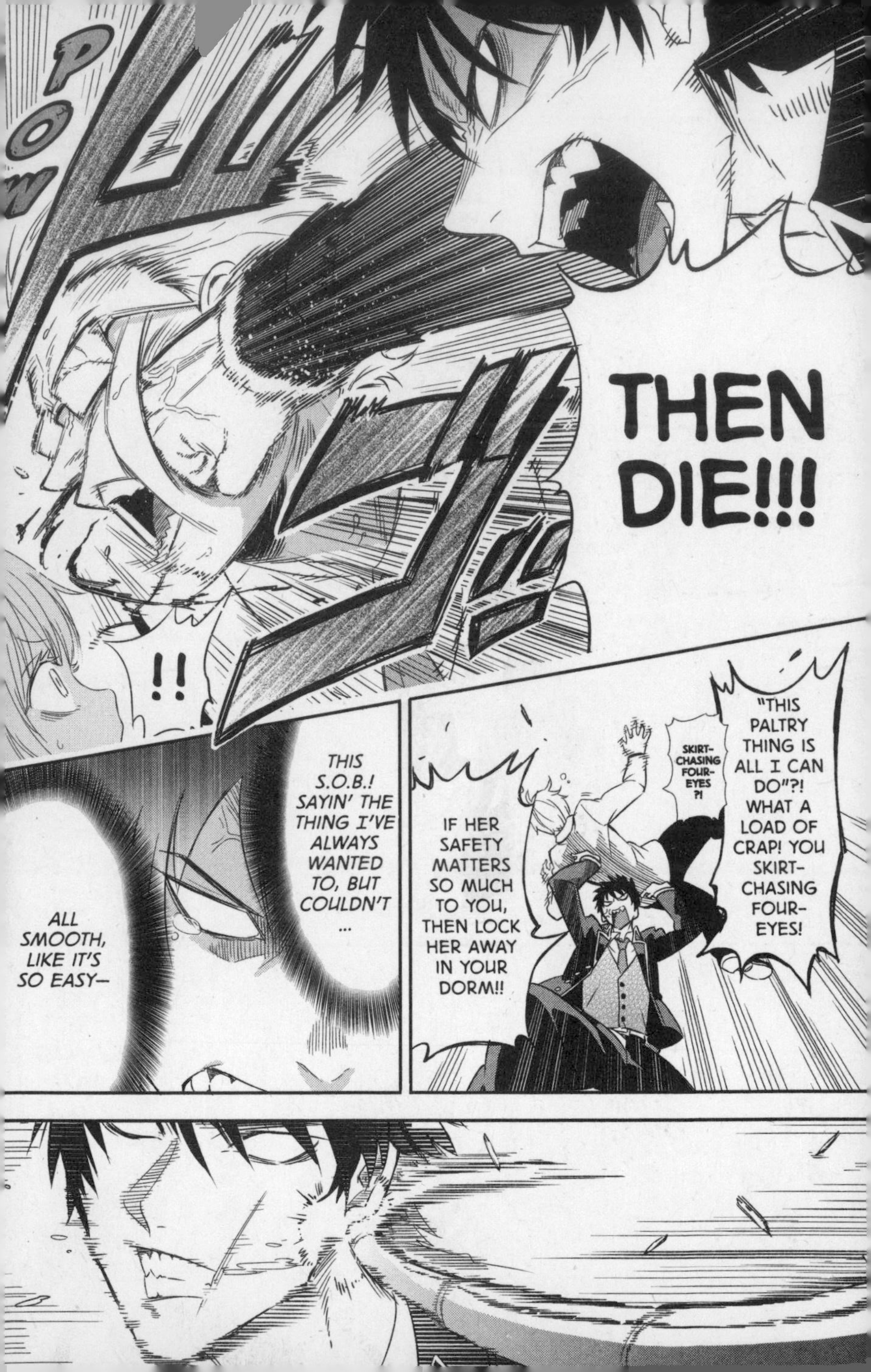
THEN DIE!!!
POW
!!
"THIS PALTRY THING IS ALL I CAN DO"?! WHAT A LOAD OF CRAP! YOU SKIRT-CHASING FOUR-EYES!
SKIRT-CHASING FOUR-EYES ?!
IF HER SAFETY MATTERS SO MUCH TO YOU, THEN LOCK HER AWAY IN YOUR DORM!!
THIS S.O.B.! SAYIN' THE THING I'VE ALWAYS WANTED TO, BUT COULDN'T ...
ALL SMOOTH, LIKE IT'S SO EASY—

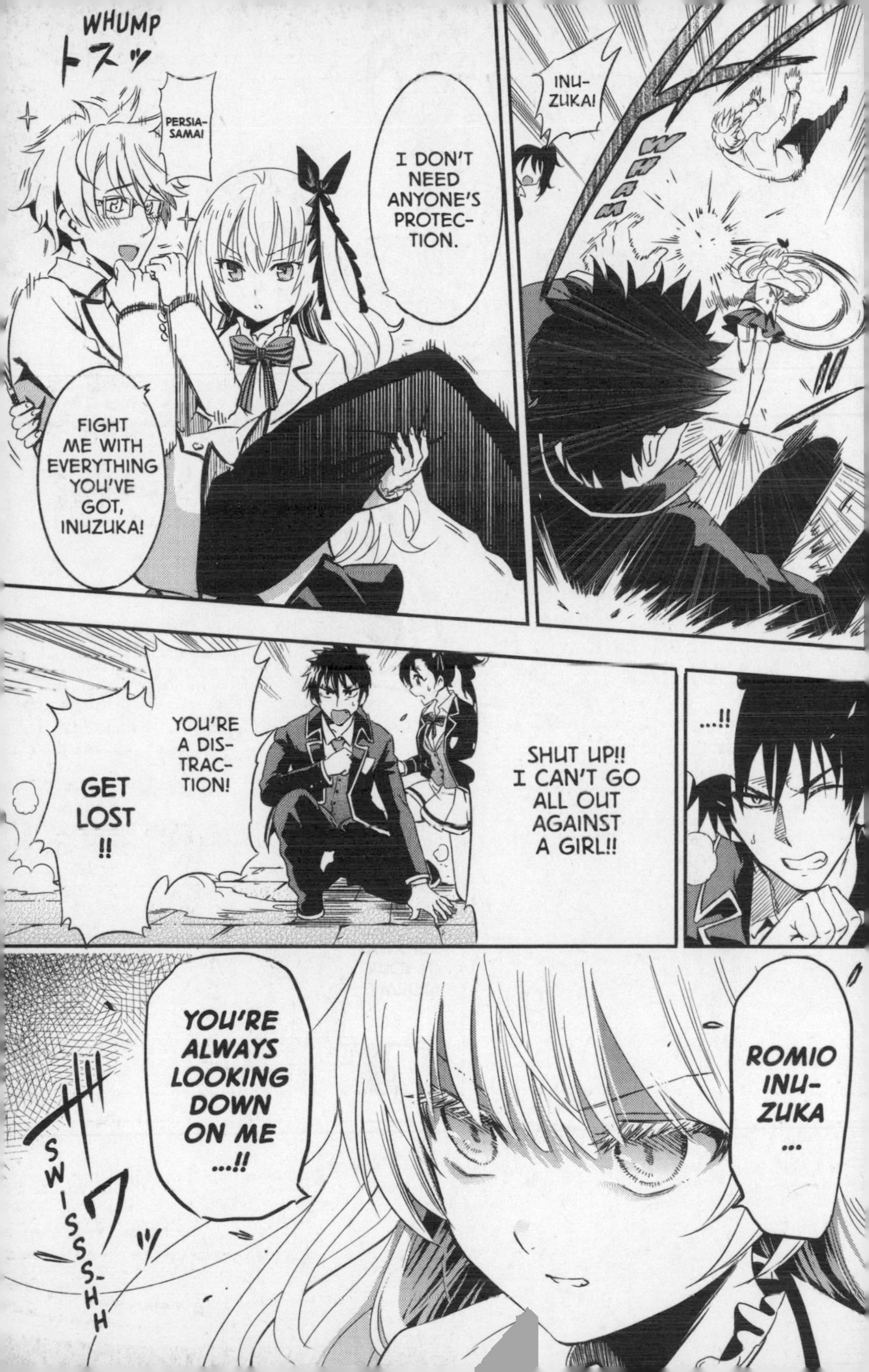
INU-ZUKA!
WHAM
I DON'T NEED ANYONE'S PROTEC-TION.
PERSIA-SAMA!
WHUMP
トスッ
FIGHT ME WITH EVERYTHING YOU'VE GOT, INUZUKA!
...!!
SHUT UP!! I CAN'T GO ALL OUT AGAINST A GIRL!!
YOU'RE A DIS-TRAC-TION!
GET LOST !!
ROMIO INU-ZUKA ...
YOU'RE ALWAYS LOOKING DOWN ON ME ...!!
SWISSSHH

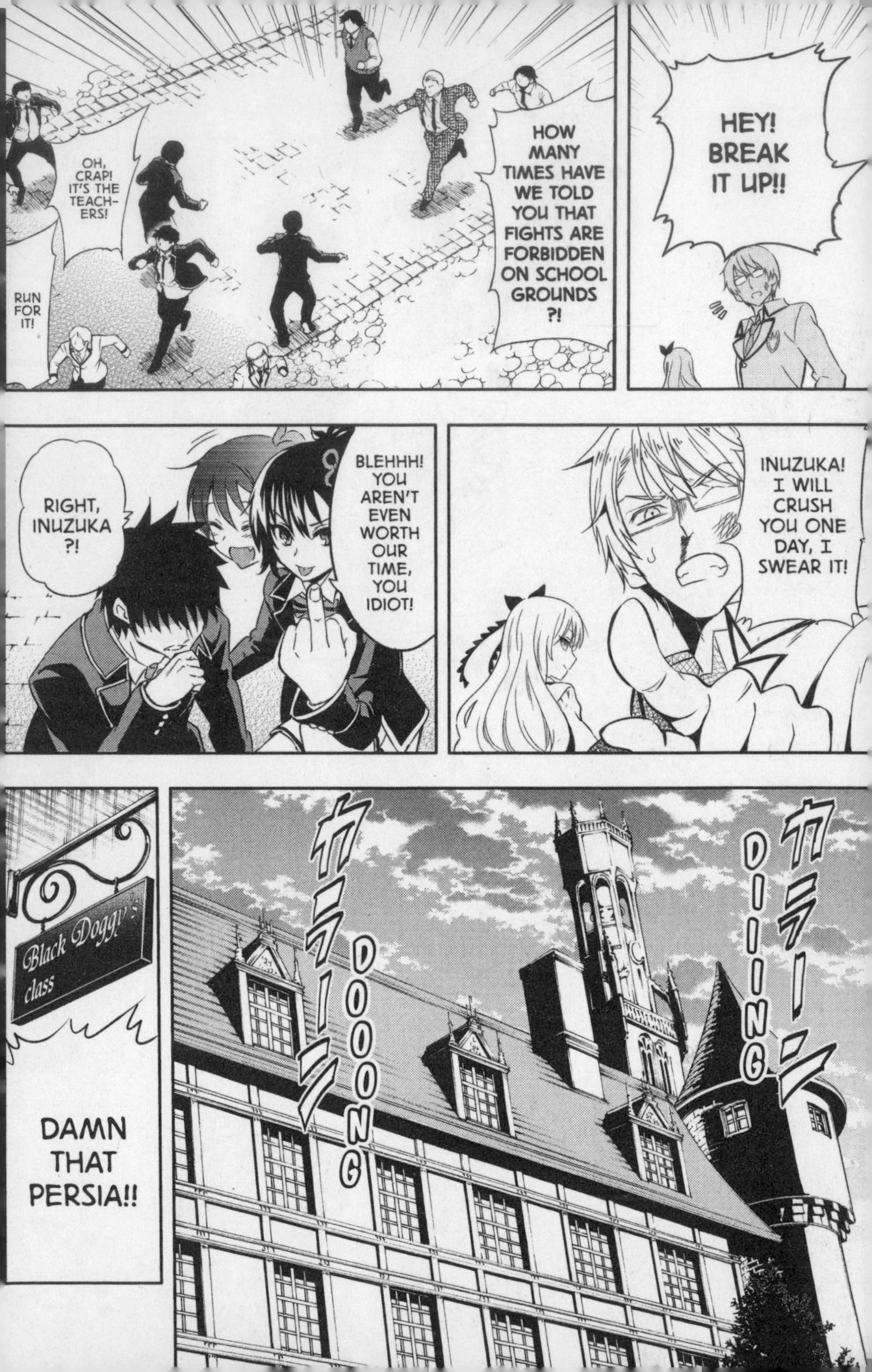
HEY! BREAK IT UP!!
HOW MANY TIMES HAVE WE TOLD YOU THAT FIGHTS ARE FORBIDDEN ON SCHOOL GROUNDS?!
OH, CRAP! IT'S THE TEACHERS!
RUN FOR IT!
INUZUKA! I WILL CRUSH YOU ONE DAY, I SWEAR IT!
BLEHHH! YOU AREN'T EVEN WORTH OUR TIME, YOU IDIOT!
RIGHT, INUZUKA?!
カラーン
DIIING
カラーン
DOOONG
Black Doggy's class
DAMN THAT PERSIA!!

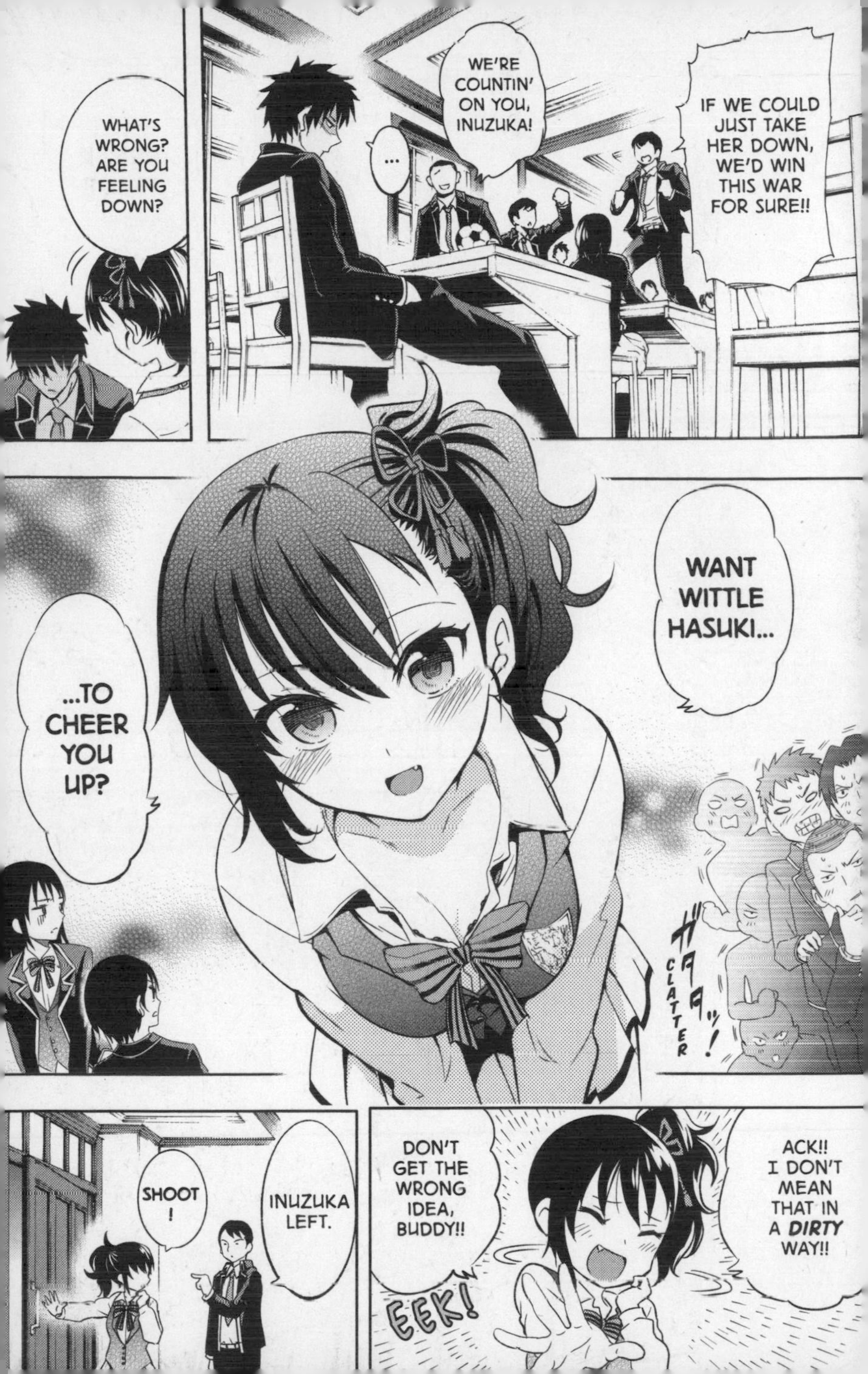
IF WE COULD JUST TAKE HER DOWN, WE'D WIN THIS WAR FOR SURE!!
WE'RE COUNTIN' ON YOU, INUZUKA!
...
WHAT'S WRONG? ARE YOU FEELING DOWN?
WANT WITTLE HASUKI...
...TO CHEER YOU UP?
CLATTER
ACK!! I DON'T MEAN THAT IN A *DIRTY* WAY!!
DON'T GET THE WRONG IDEA, BUDDY!!
EEK!
INUZUKA LEFT.
SHOOT!

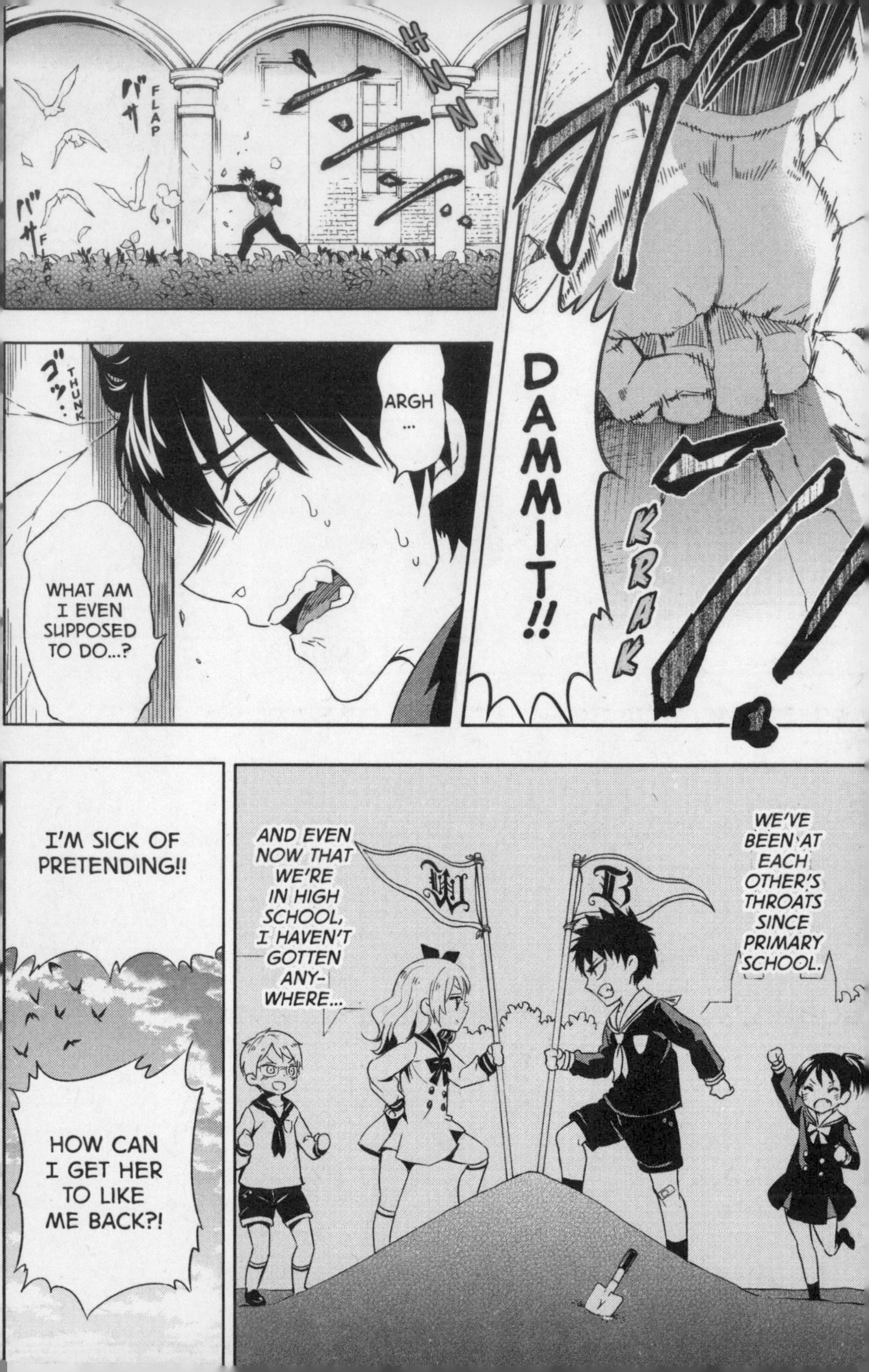
DAMMIT!!
KRAK
バサ
FLAP
バサ
FLAP
HNNNN
ゴッ…
THUNK
ARGH…
WHAT AM I EVEN SUPPOSED TO DO…?
WE'VE BEEN AT EACH OTHER'S THROATS SINCE PRIMARY SCHOOL.
AND EVEN NOW THAT WE'RE IN HIGH SCHOOL, I HAVEN'T GOTTEN ANY-WHERE…
I'M SICK OF PRETENDING!!
HOW CAN I GET HER TO LIKE ME BACK?!

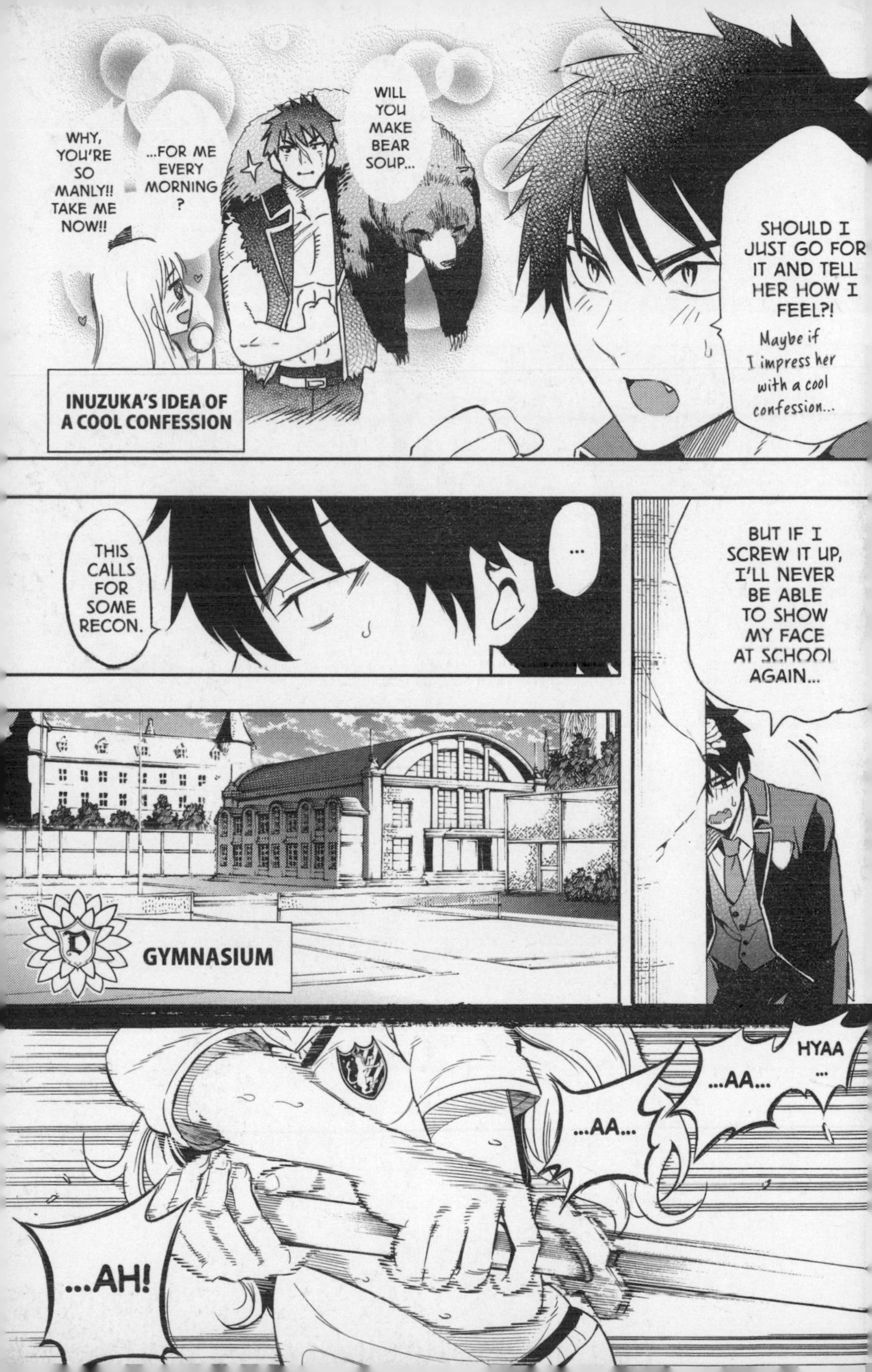
SHOULD I JUST GO FOR IT AND TELL HER HOW I FEEL?!
Maybe if I impress her with a cool confession...
WILL YOU MAKE BEAR SOUP...
...FOR ME EVERY MORNING ?
WHY, YOU'RE SO MANLY!! TAKE ME NOW!!
INUZUKA'S IDEA OF A COOL CONFESSION
BUT IF I SCREW IT UP, I'LL NEVER BE ABLE TO SHOW MY FACE AT SCHOOL AGAIN...
...
THIS CALLS FOR SOME RECON.
GYMNASIUM
HYAA ...
...AA...
...AA...
...AH!

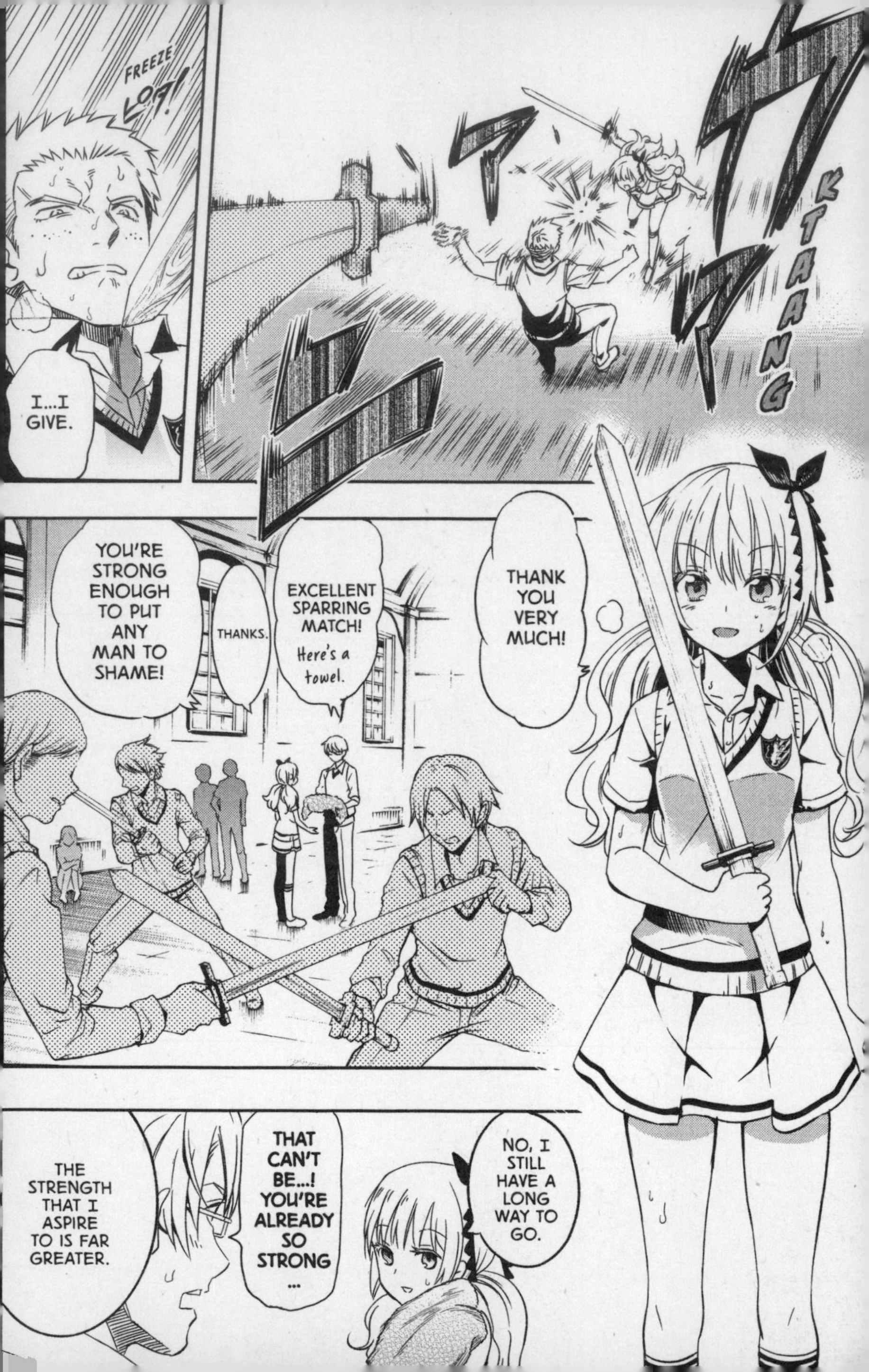
KTAANG
FREEZE
I...I GIVE.
THANK YOU VERY MUCH!
EXCELLENT SPARRING MATCH! Here's a towel.
THANKS.
YOU'RE STRONG ENOUGH TO PUT ANY MAN TO SHAME!
NO, I STILL HAVE A LONG WAY TO GO.
THAT CAN'T BE...! YOU'RE ALREADY SO STRONG...
THE STRENGTH THAT I ASPIRE TO IS FAR GREATER.

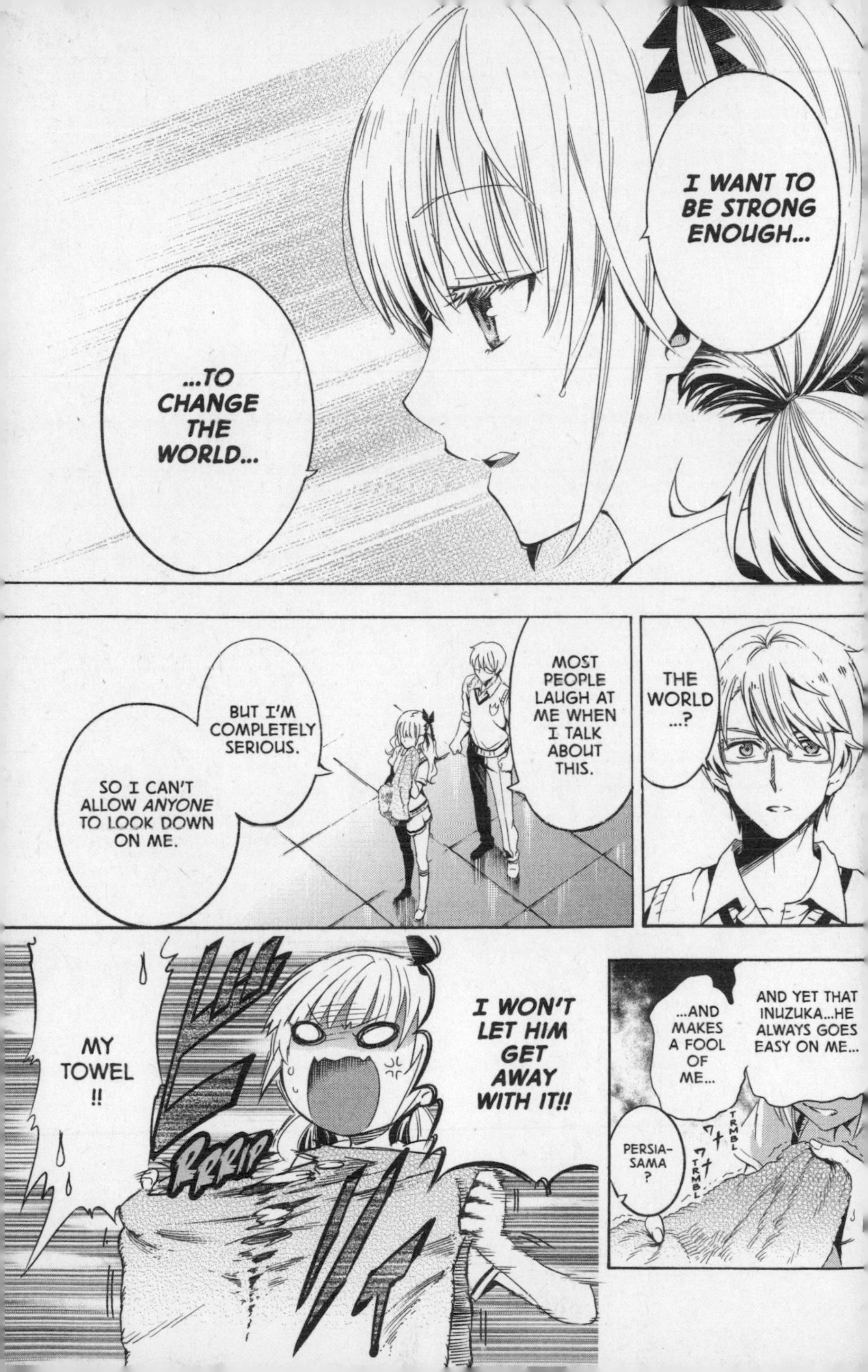
I WANT TO BE STRONG ENOUGH...
...TO CHANGE THE WORLD...
THE WORLD ...?
MOST PEOPLE LAUGH AT ME WHEN I TALK ABOUT THIS.
BUT I'M COMPLETELY SERIOUS.
SO I CAN'T ALLOW *ANYONE* TO LOOK DOWN ON ME.
AND YET THAT INUZUKA...HE ALWAYS GOES EASY ON ME...
...AND MAKES A FOOL OF ME...
TRMBL
TRMBL
PERSIA-SAMA ?
I WON'T LET HIM GET AWAY WITH IT!!
RRRIP
MY TOWEL !!

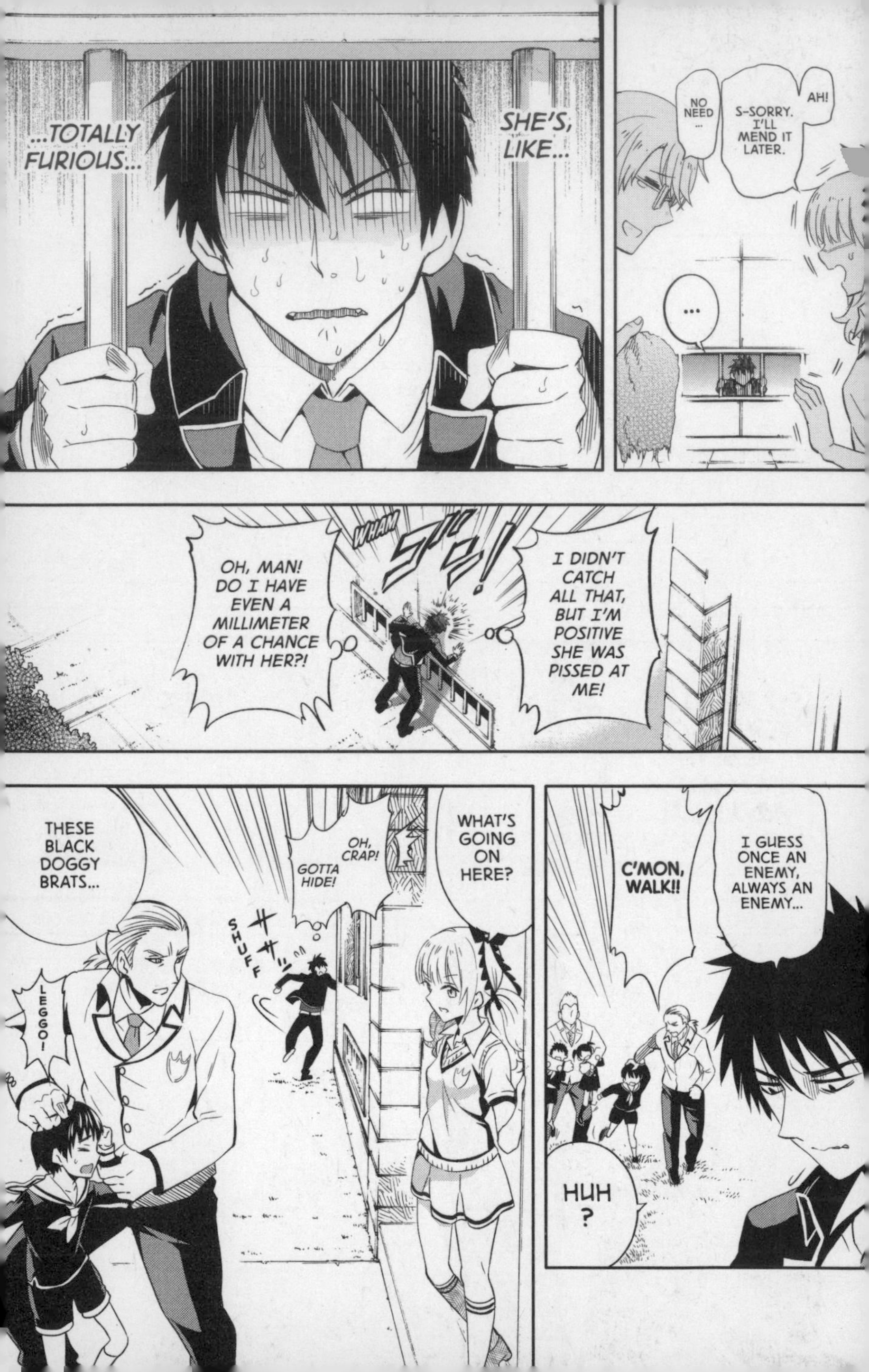
AH!
S-SORRY. I'LL MEND IT LATER.
NO NEED ...
...
SHE'S, LIKE...
...TOTALLY FURIOUS...
I DIDN'T CATCH ALL THAT, BUT I'M POSITIVE SHE WAS PISSED AT ME!
WHAM
OH, MAN! DO I HAVE EVEN A MILLIMETER OF A CHANCE WITH HER?!
I GUESS ONCE AN ENEMY, ALWAYS AN ENEMY...
C'MON, WALK!!
HUH?
WHAT'S GOING ON HERE?
OH, CRAP!
GOTTA HIDE!
SHUFF
THESE BLACK DOGGY BRATS...
LEGGO!

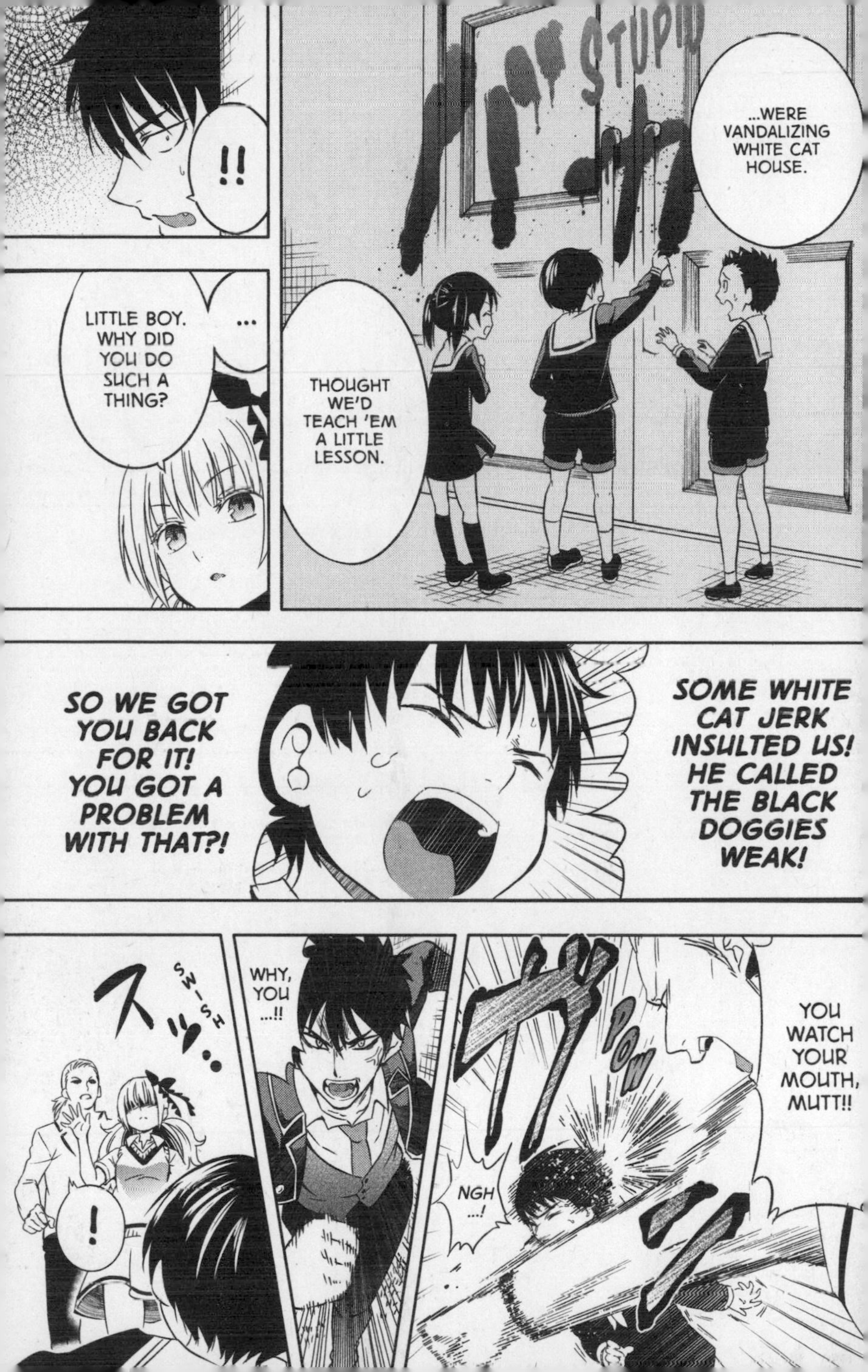
...WERE VANDALIZING WHITE CAT HOUSE.
THOUGHT WE'D TEACH 'EM A LITTLE LESSON.
!!
...
LITTLE BOY. WHY DID YOU DO SUCH A THING?
SOME WHITE CAT JERK INSULTED US! HE CALLED THE BLACK DOGGIES WEAK!
SO WE GOT YOU BACK FOR IT! YOU GOT A PROBLEM WITH THAT?!
YOU WATCH YOUR MOUTH, MUTT!!
POW
NGH ...!
WHY, YOU ...!!
SWISH
!

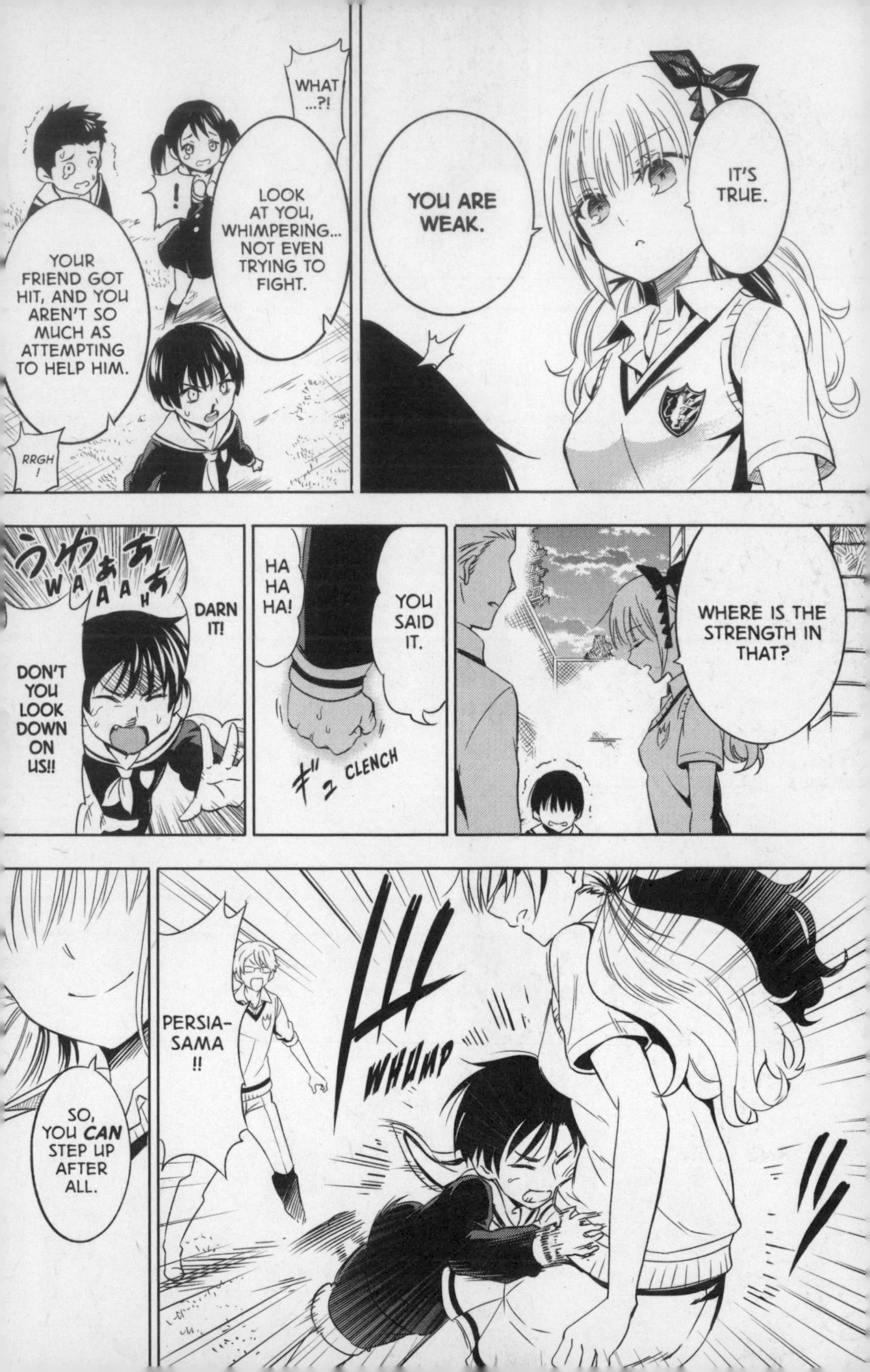
IT'S TRUE.
YOU ARE WEAK.
WHAT ...?!
LOOK AT YOU, WHIMPERING... NOT EVEN TRYING TO FIGHT.
!
YOUR FRIEND GOT HIT, AND YOU AREN'T SO MUCH AS ATTEMPTING TO HELP HIM.
RRGH!
WHERE IS THE STRENGTH IN THAT?
HA HA HA!
YOU SAID IT.
CLENCH
WAAAH
DARN IT!
DON'T YOU LOOK DOWN ON US!!
WHUMP
PERSIA-SAMA!!
SO, YOU CAN STEP UP AFTER ALL.

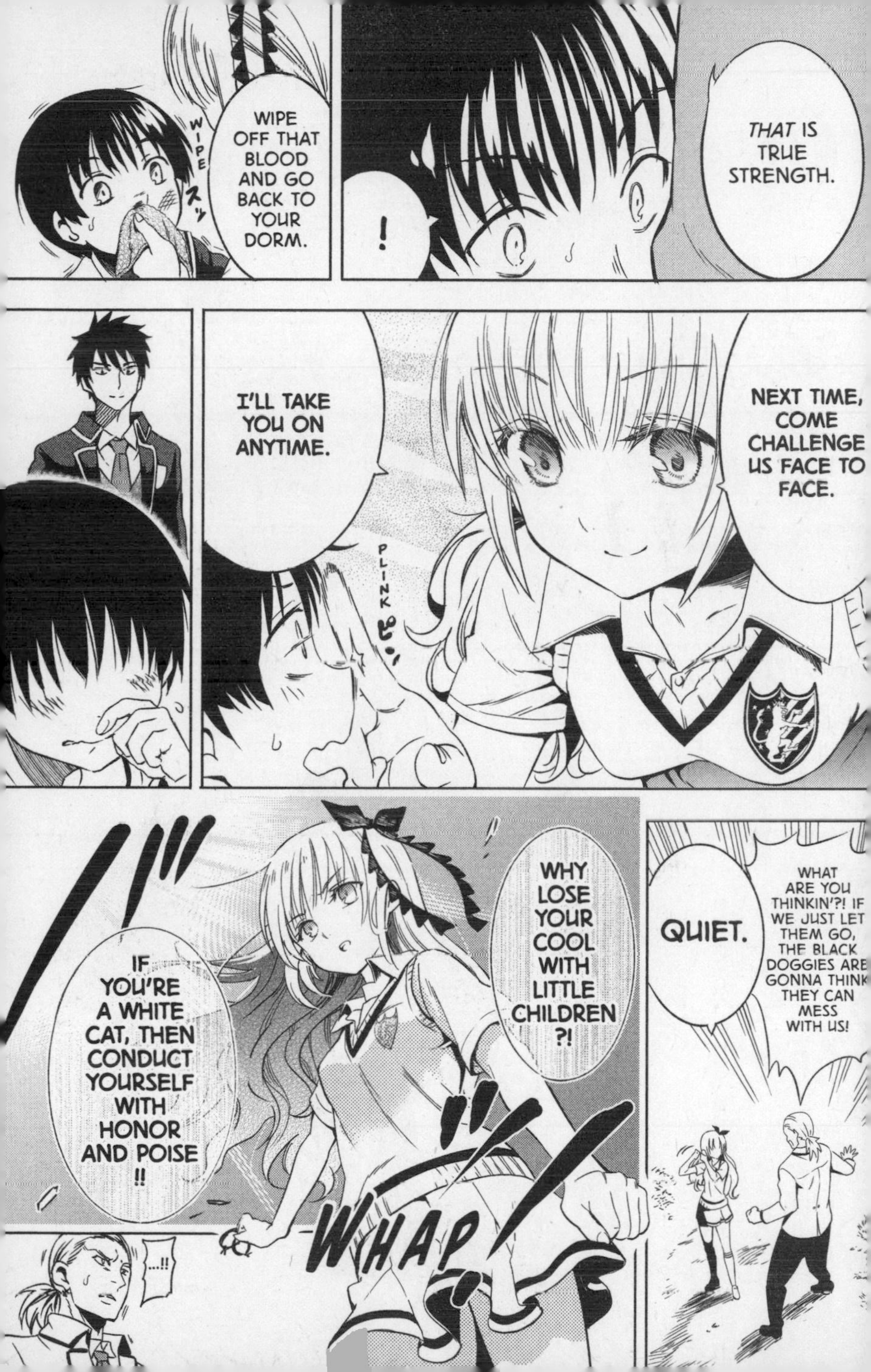
THAT IS TRUE STRENGTH.
!
WIPE OFF THAT BLOOD AND GO BACK TO YOUR DORM.
WIPE スッ
NEXT TIME, COME CHALLENGE US FACE TO FACE.
I'LL TAKE YOU ON ANYTIME.
PLINK ピッ
WHAT ARE YOU THINKIN'?! IF WE JUST LET THEM GO, THE BLACK DOGGIES ARE GONNA THINK THEY CAN MESS WITH US!
QUIET.
WHY LOSE YOUR COOL WITH LITTLE CHILDREN?!
IF YOU'RE A WHITE CAT, THEN CONDUCT YOURSELF WITH HONOR AND POISE!!
WHAP
...!!

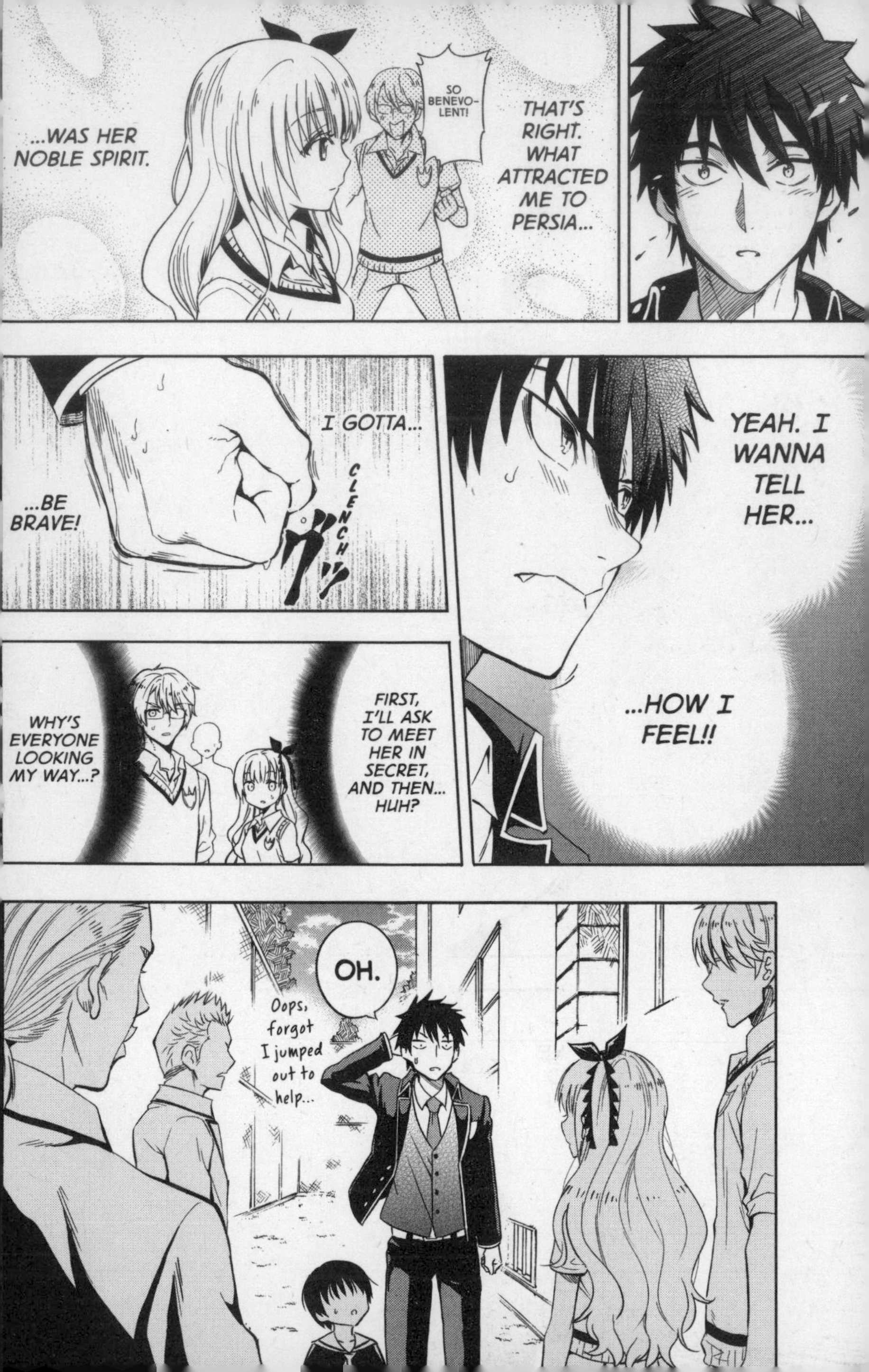
THAT'S RIGHT. WHAT ATTRACTED ME TO PERSIA...
SO BENEVOLENT!
...WAS HER NOBLE SPIRIT.
YEAH. I WANNA TELL HER...
...HOW I FEEL!!
I GOTTA...
CLENCH
...BE BRAVE!
FIRST, I'LL ASK TO MEET HER IN SECRET, AND THEN... HUH?
WHY'S EVERYONE LOOKING MY WAY...?
OH.
Oops, forgot I jumped out to help...

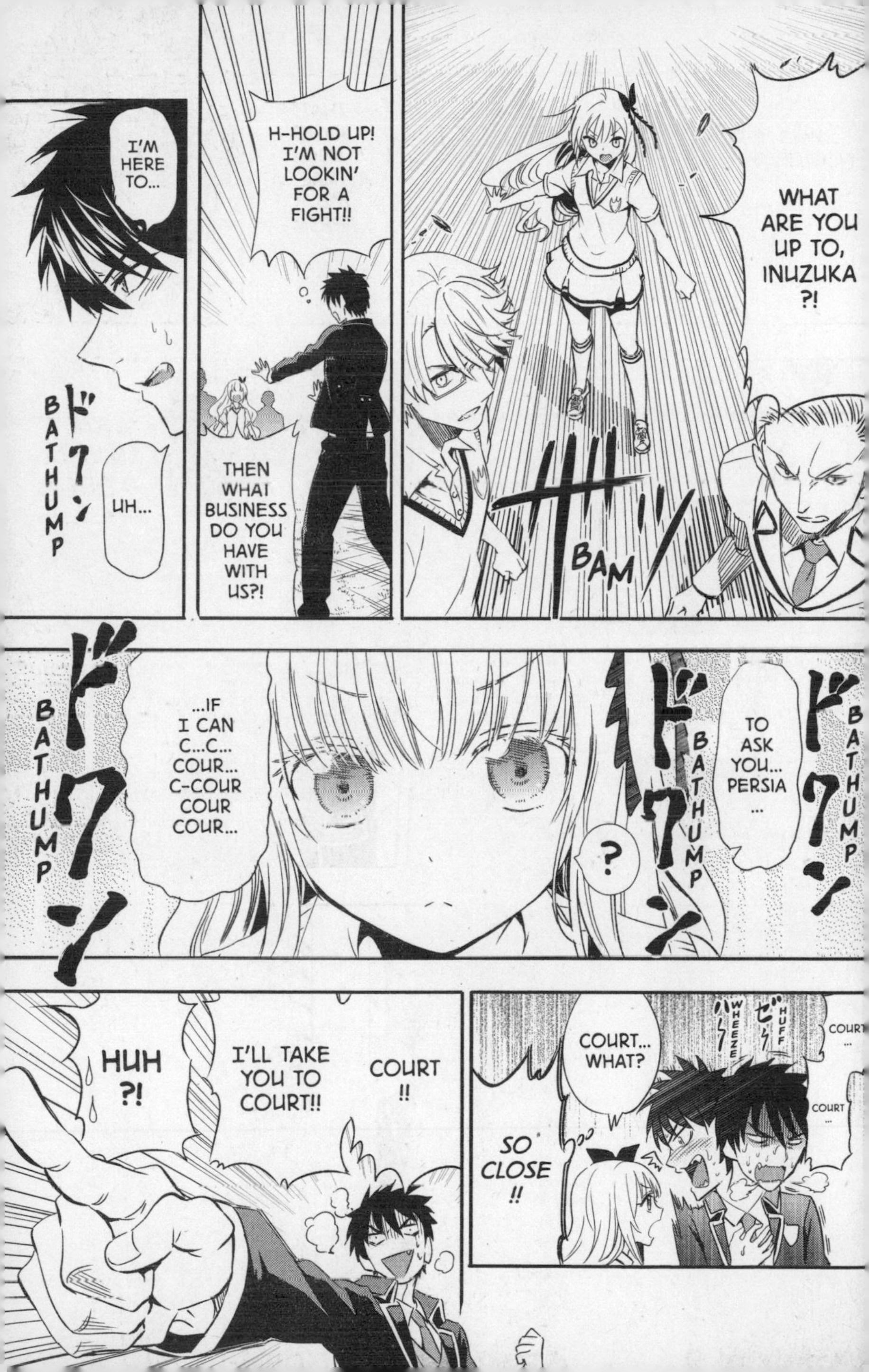
WHAT ARE YOU UP TO, INUZUKA?!
BAM
H-HOLD UP! I'M NOT LOOKIN' FOR A FIGHT!!
THEN WHAT BUSINESS DO YOU HAVE WITH US?!
I'M HERE TO...
UH...
BATHUMP
BATHUMP
TO ASK YOU... PERSIA...
BATHUMP
?
...IF I CAN C...C... COUR... C-COUR COUR COUR...
BATHUMP
COURT... WHAT?
HUFF
WHEEZE
COURT...
COURT...
SO CLOSE!!
COURT!!
I'LL TAKE YOU TO COURT!!
HUH?!

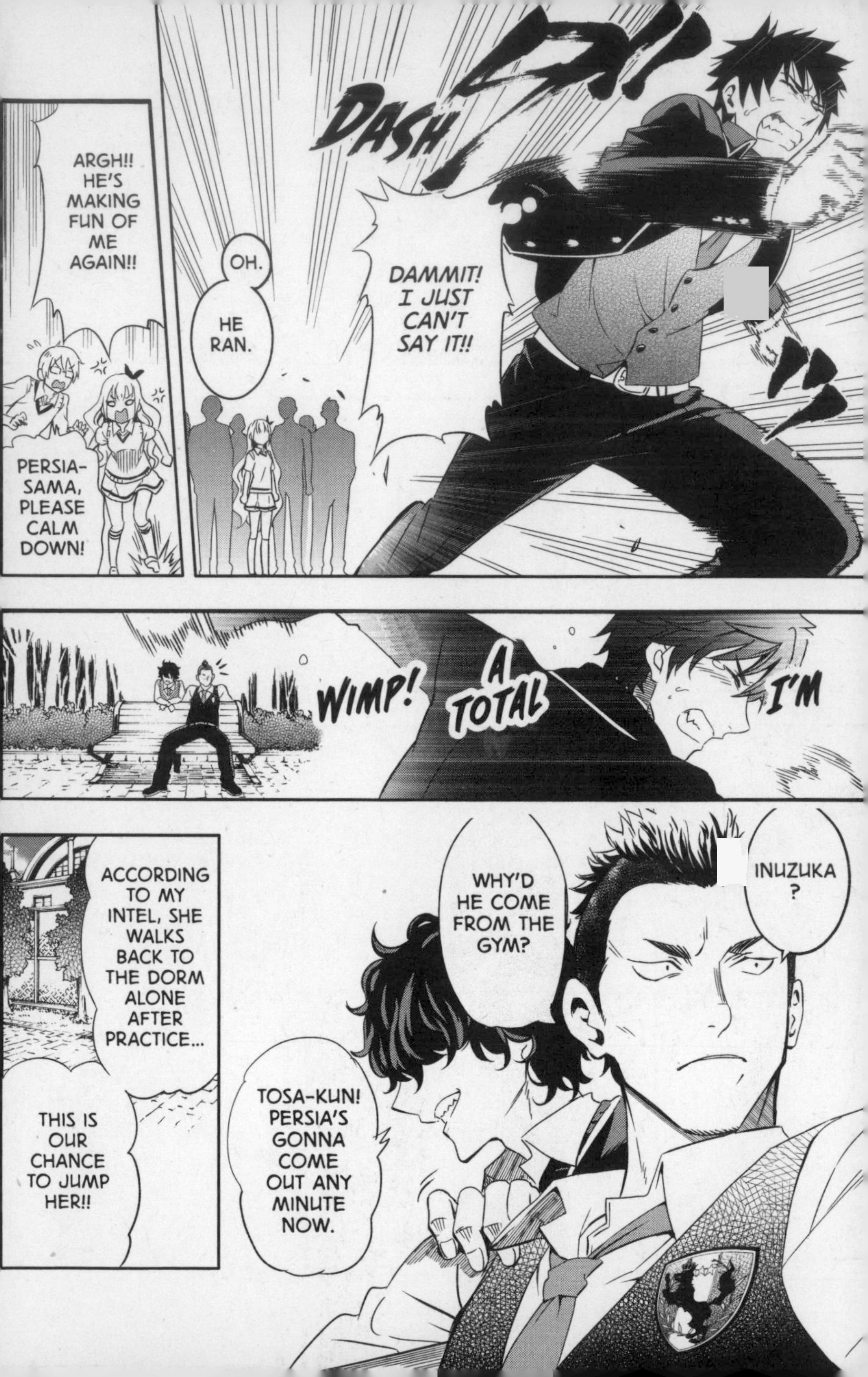
DASH
DAMMIT! I JUST CAN'T SAY IT!!
OH.
HE RAN.
ARGH!! HE'S MAKING FUN OF ME AGAIN!!
PERSIA-SAMA, PLEASE CALM DOWN!
I'M
A TOTAL
WIMP!
INUZUKA?
WHY'D HE COME FROM THE GYM?
TOSA-KUN! PERSIA'S GONNA COME OUT ANY MINUTE NOW.
ACCORDING TO MY INTEL, SHE WALKS BACK TO THE DORM ALONE AFTER PRACTICE...
THIS IS OUR CHANCE TO JUMP HER!!

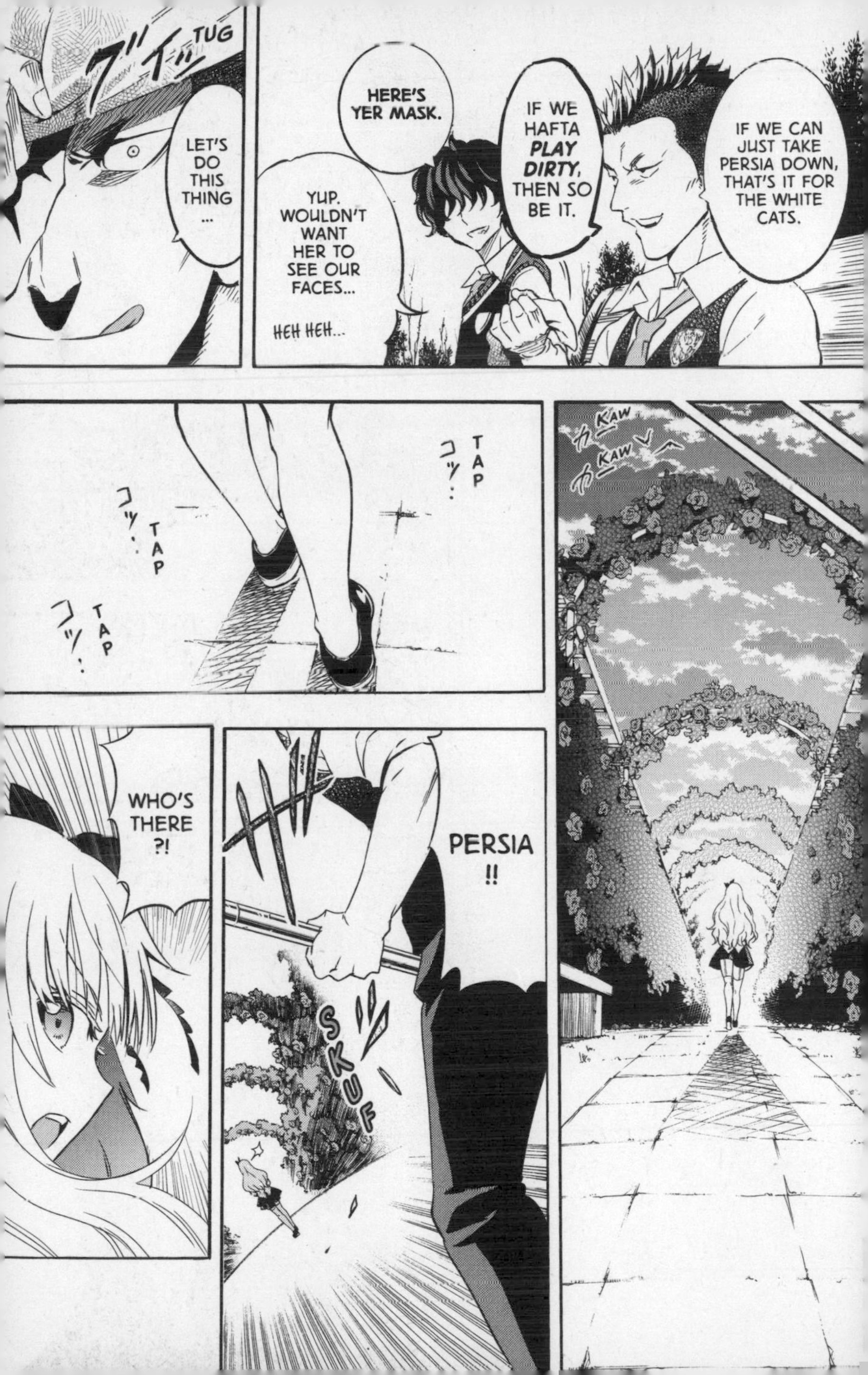
IF WE CAN JUST TAKE PERSIA DOWN, THAT'S IT FOR THE WHITE CATS.
IF WE HAFTA **PLAY DIRTY**, THEN SO BE IT.
HERE'S YER MASK.
YUP. WOULDN'T WANT HER TO SEE OUR FACES...
HEH HEH...
TUG
LET'S DO THIS THING ...
KAW
KAW
TAP
TAP
TAP
PERSIA !!
SKUF
WHO'S THERE ?!

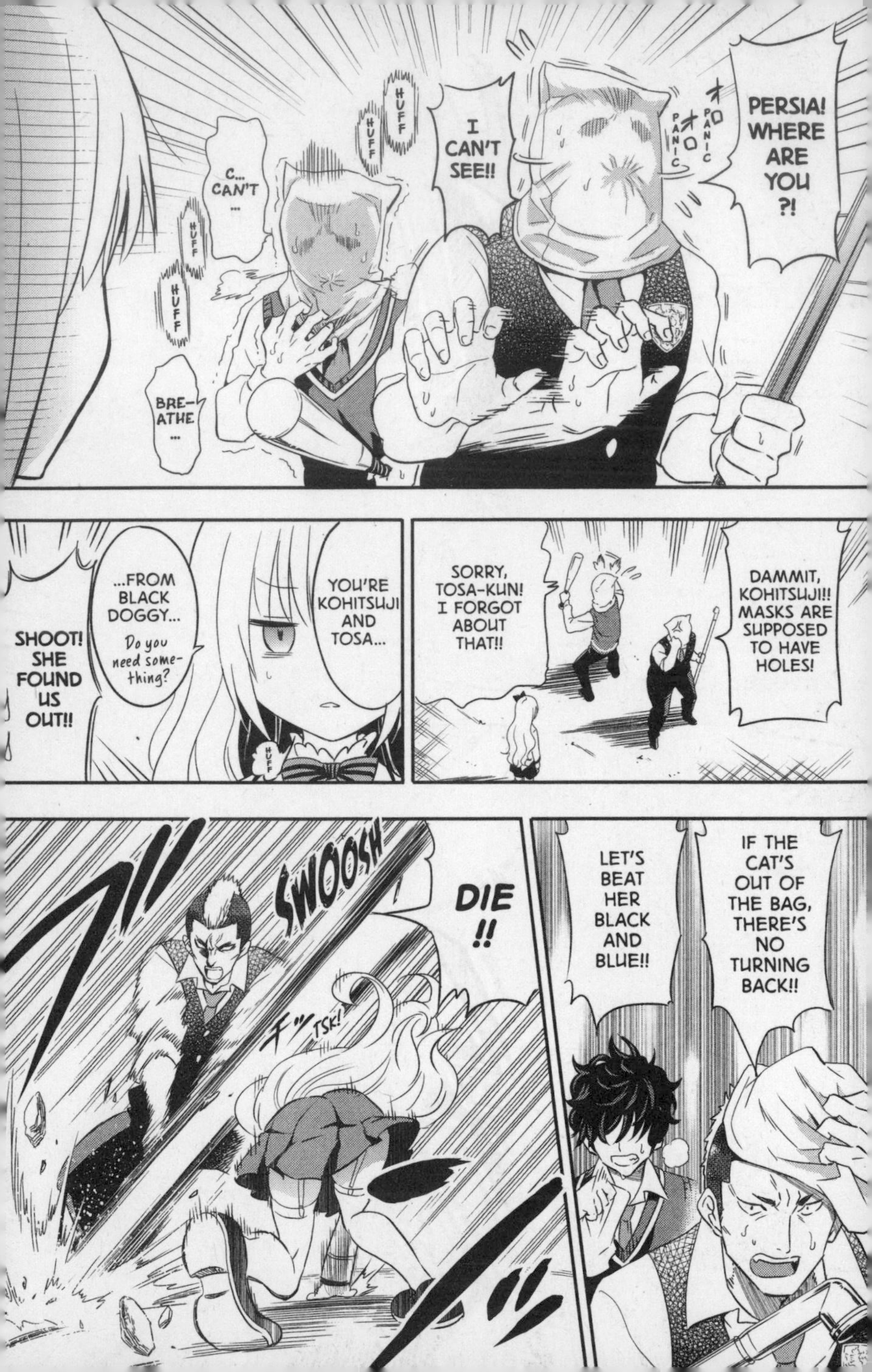
PERSIA! WHERE ARE YOU ?!
オロ オロ PANIC PANIC
I CAN'T SEE!!
HUFF HUFF
C... CAN'T ...
HUFF HUFF
BRE-ATHE ...
DAMMIT, KOHITSUJI!! MASKS ARE SUPPOSED TO HAVE HOLES!
SORRY, TOSA-KUN! I FORGOT ABOUT THAT!!
YOU'RE KOHITSUJI AND TOSA...
...FROM BLACK DOGGY...
Do you need some-thing?
HUFF
SHOOT! SHE FOUND US OUT!!
IF THE CAT'S OUT OF THE BAG, THERE'S NO TURNING BACK!!
LET'S BEAT HER BLACK AND BLUE!!
DIE !!
SWOOSH
チッ TSK!

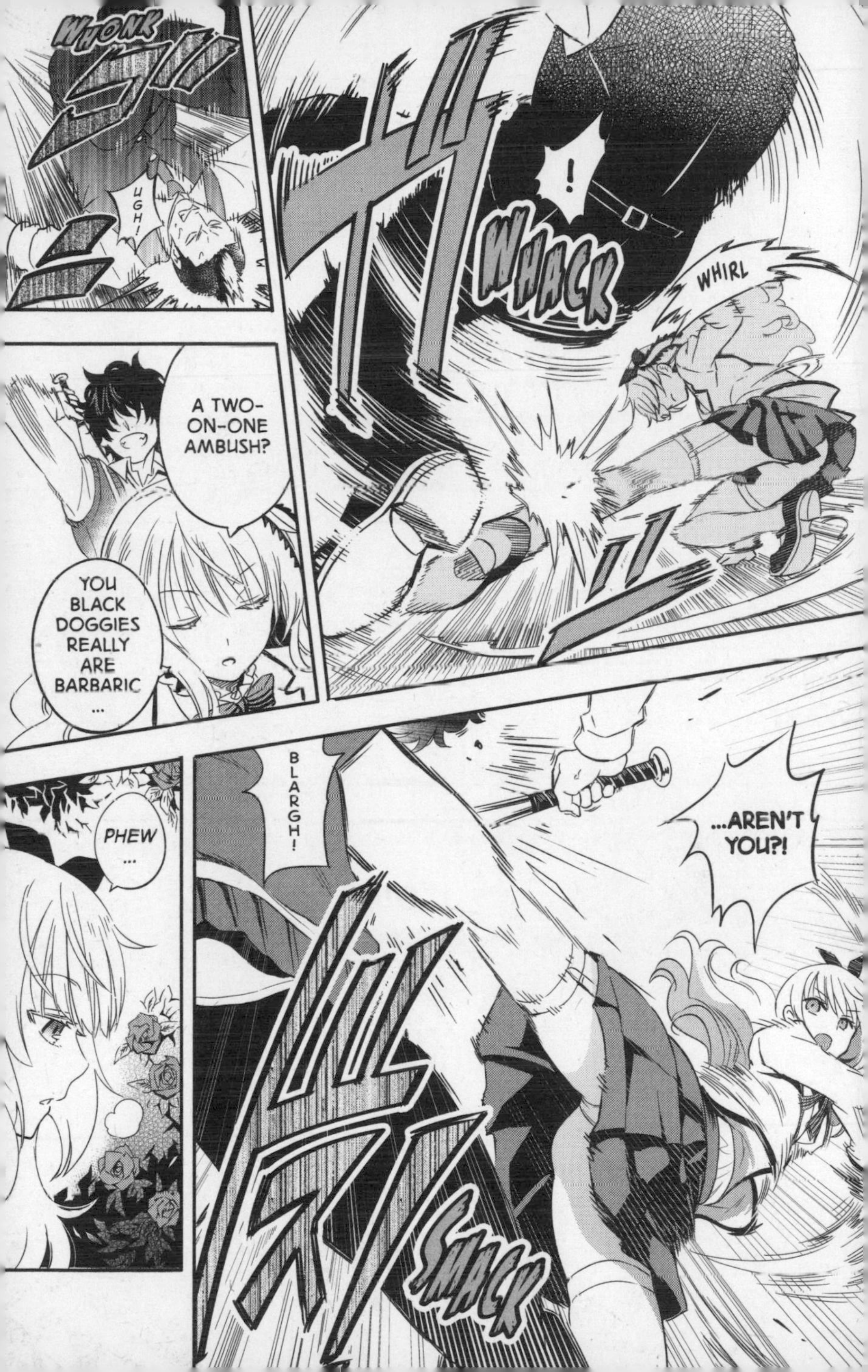
!
WHIRL
WHACK
WHONK
UGH!
A TWO-ON-ONE AMBUSH?
YOU BLACK DOGGIES REALLY ARE BARBARIC ...
...AREN'T YOU?!
BLARGH!
SMACK
PHEW ...

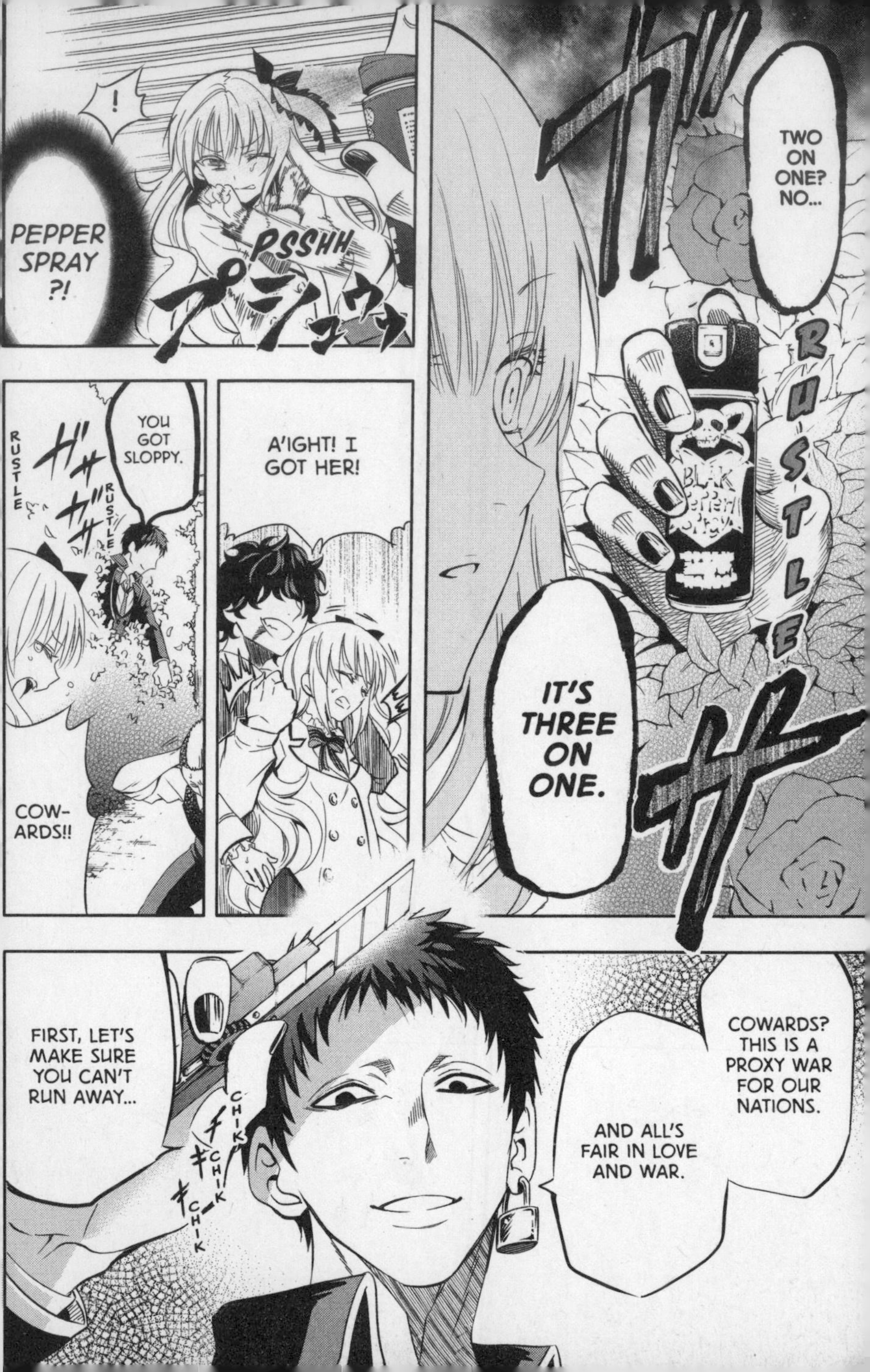
TWO ON ONE? NO...
RUSTLE
IT'S THREE ON ONE.
!
PEPPER SPRAY ?!
PSSHH
A'IGHT! I GOT HER!
YOU GOT SLOPPY.
RUSTLE
RUSTLE
COW-ARDS!!
COWARDS? THIS IS A PROXY WAR FOR OUR NATIONS.
AND ALL'S FAIR IN LOVE AND WAR.
CHIK
CHIK
CHIK
FIRST, LET'S MAKE SURE YOU CAN'T RUN AWAY...

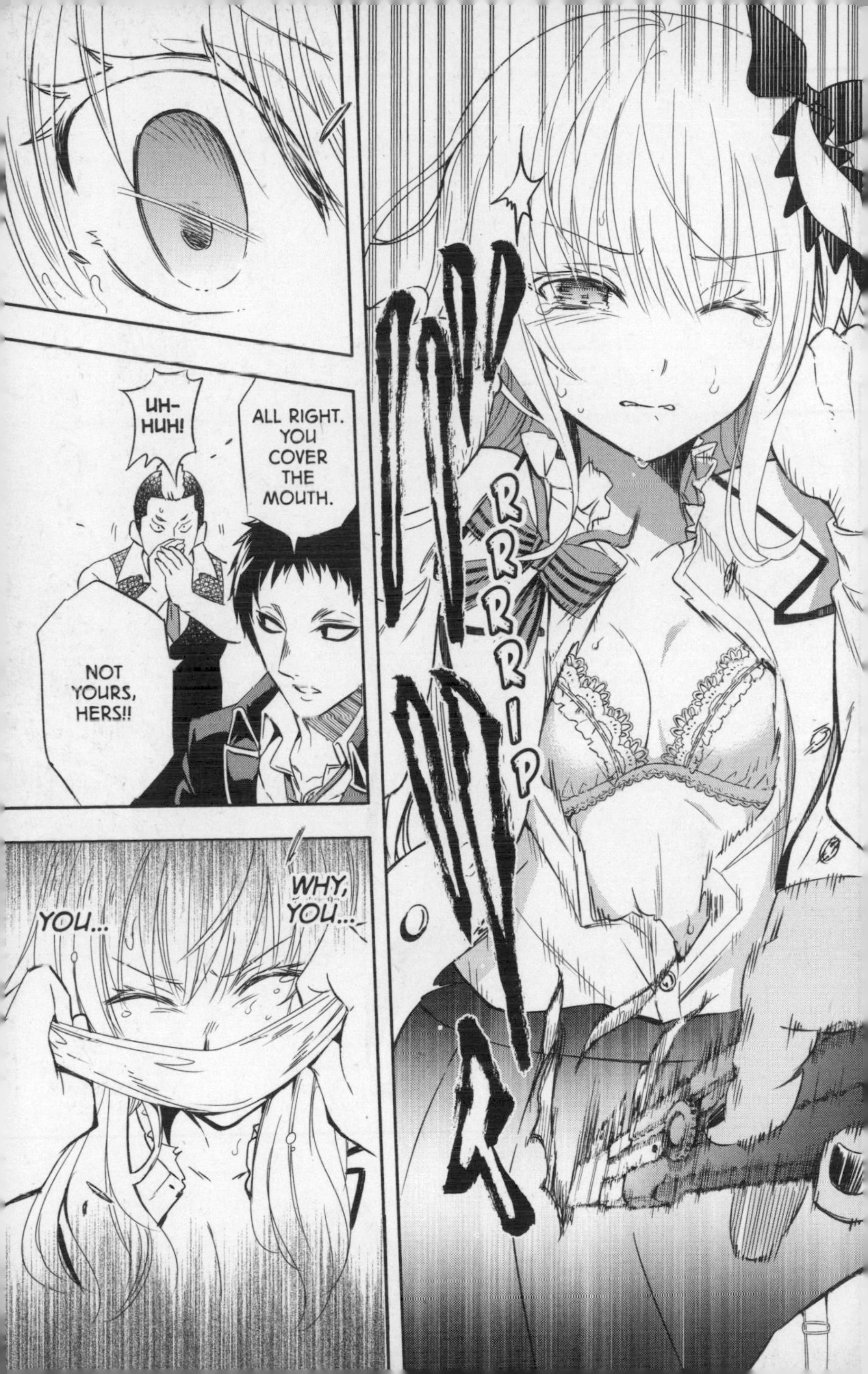
RRRRIP
ALL RIGHT. YOU COVER THE MOUTH.
UH-HUH!
NOT YOURS, HERS!!
WHY, YOU...
YOU...

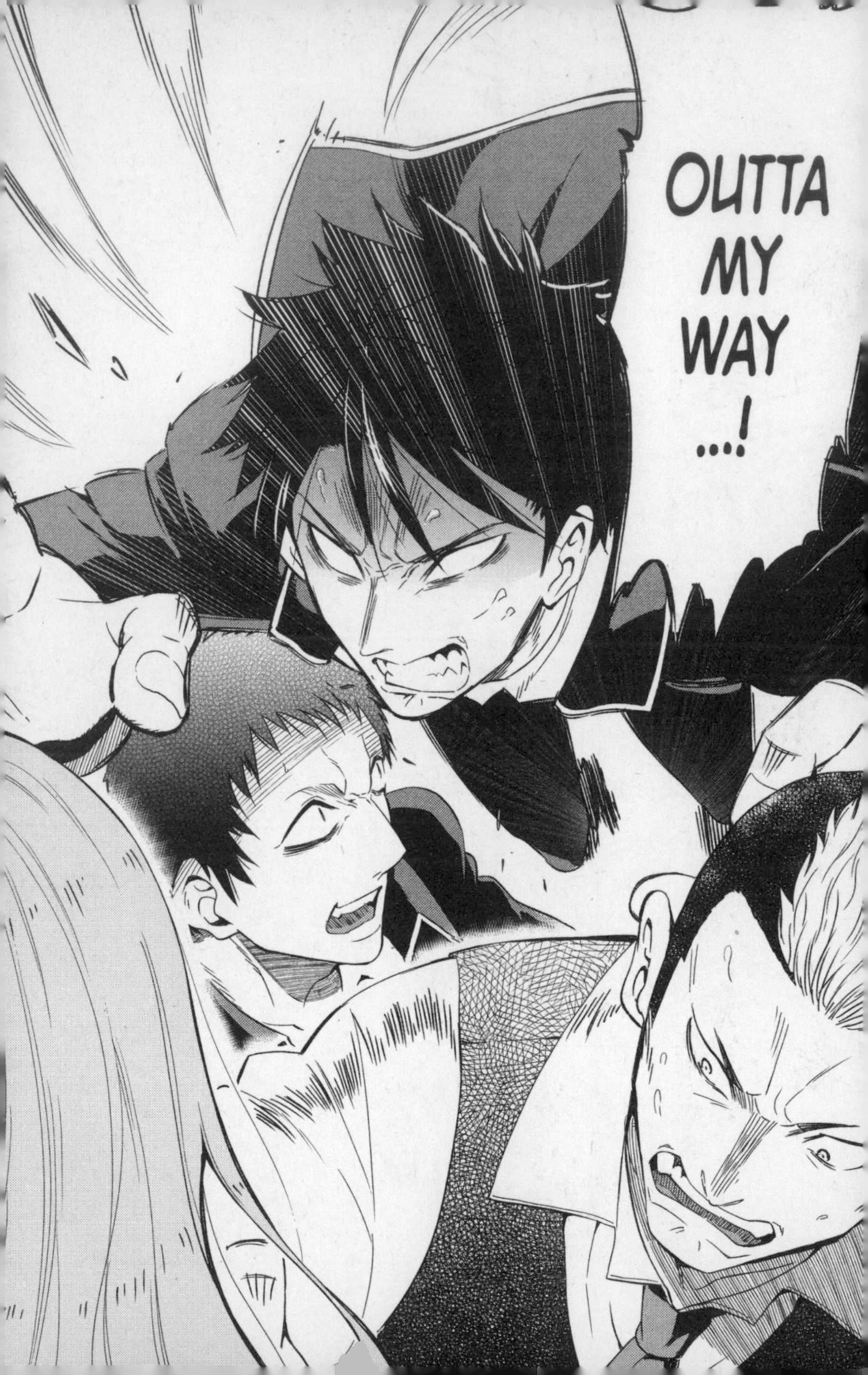
OUTTA MY WAY ...!

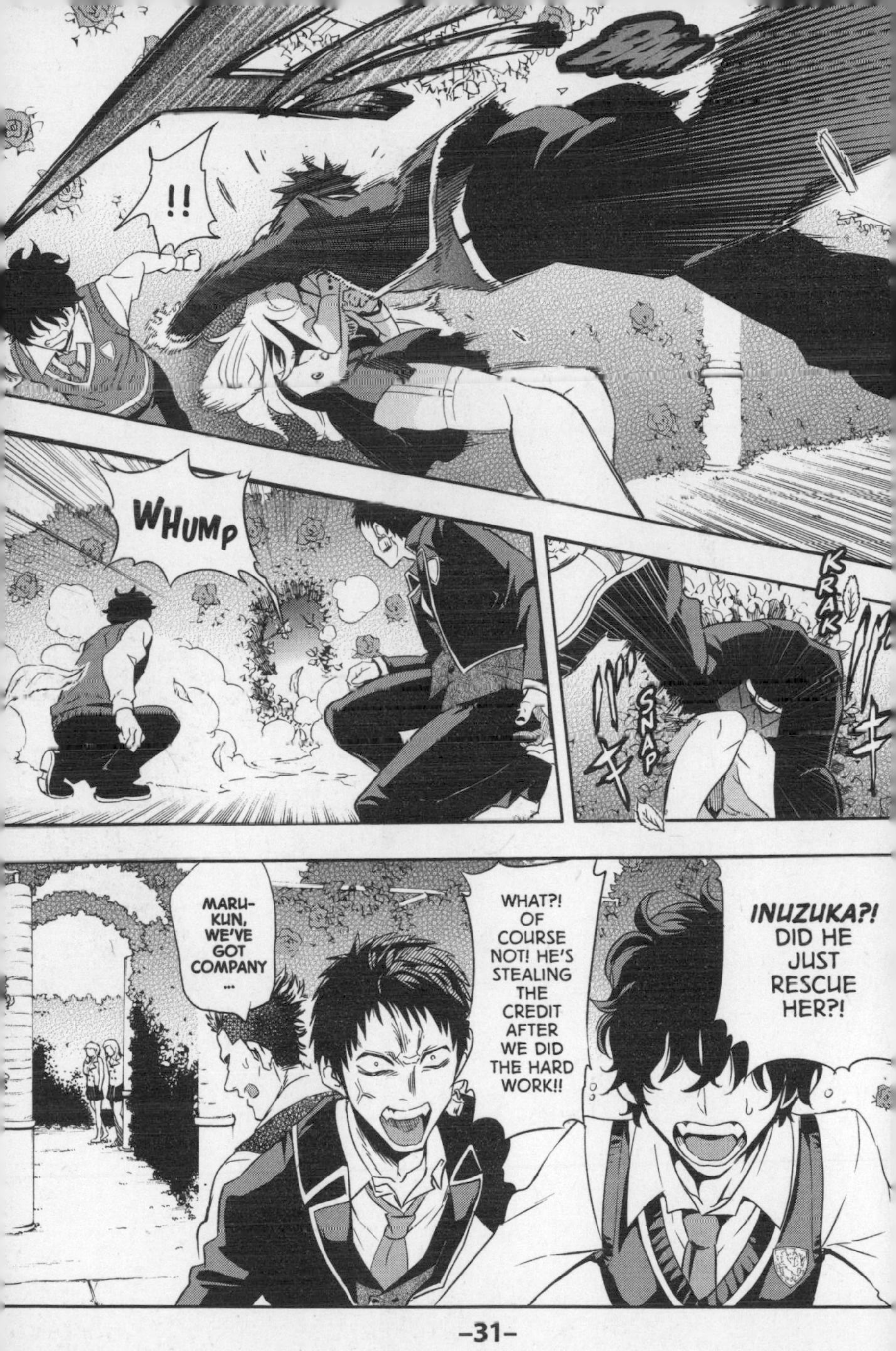
BAM
!!
KRAK
SNAP
WHUMP
INUZUKA?! DID HE JUST RESCUE HER?!
WHAT?! OF COURSE NOT! HE'S STEALING THE CREDIT AFTER WE DID THE HARD WORK!!
MARU-KUN, WE'VE GOT COMPANY ...

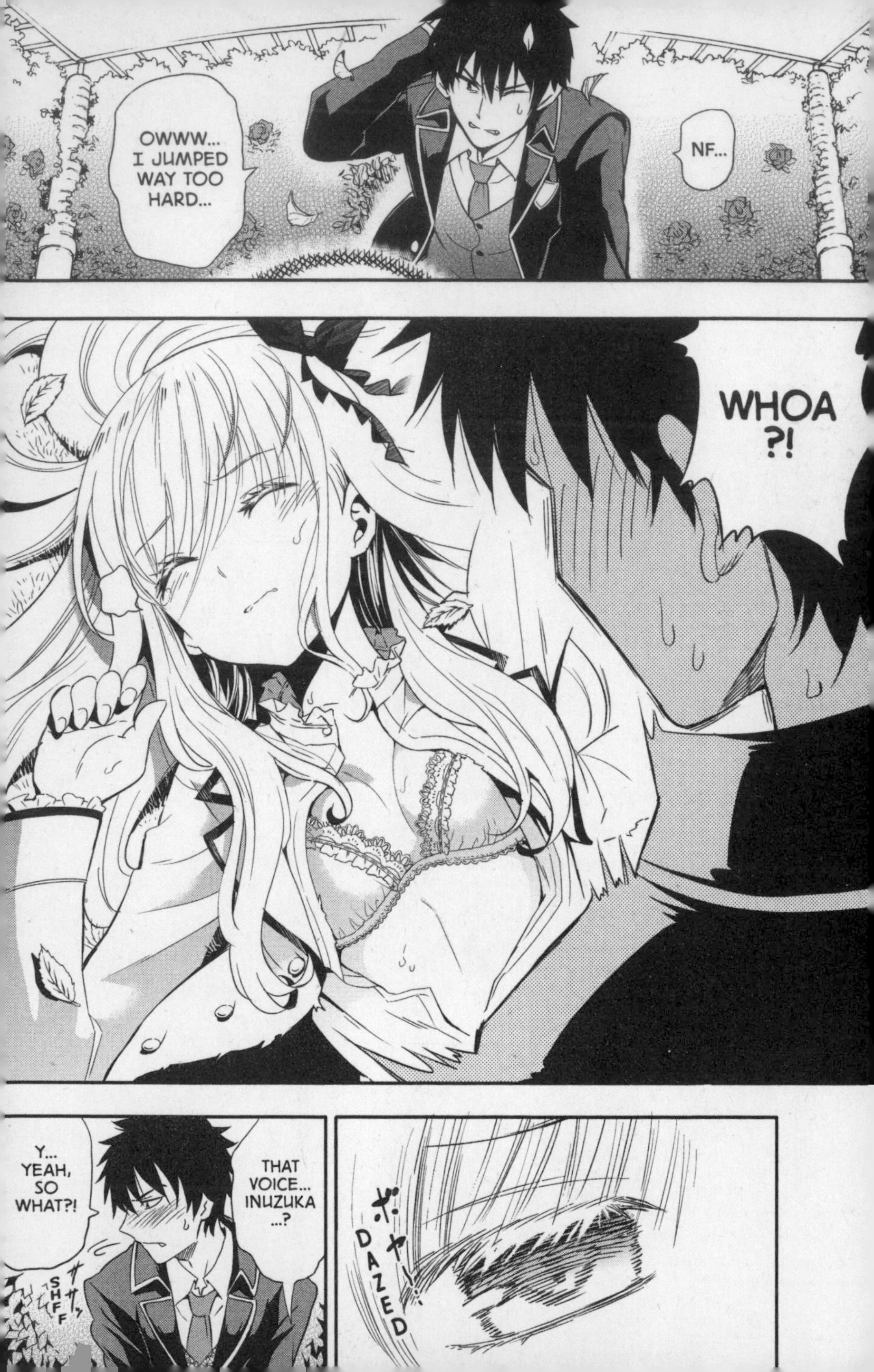
NF...
OWWW... I JUMPED WAY TOO HARD...
WHOA ?!
DAZED
THAT VOICE... INUZUKA ...?
Y... YEAH, SO WHAT?!
SHFF

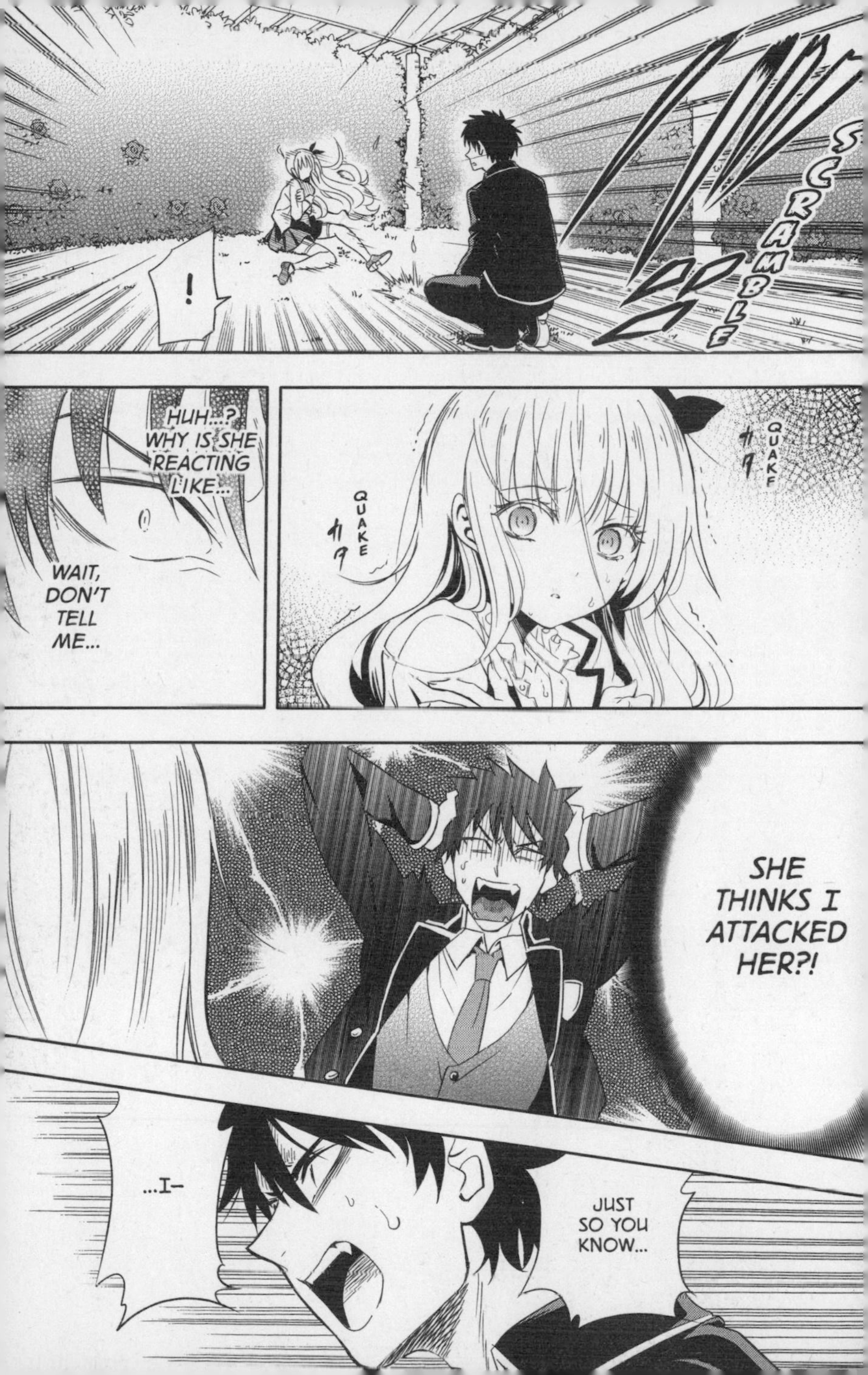
SCRAMBLE
!
カタ
QUAKF
カタ
QUAKE
HUH...? WHY IS SHE REACTING LIKE...
WAIT, DON'T TELL ME...
SHE THINKS I ATTACKED HER?!
JUST SO YOU KNOW...
...I–

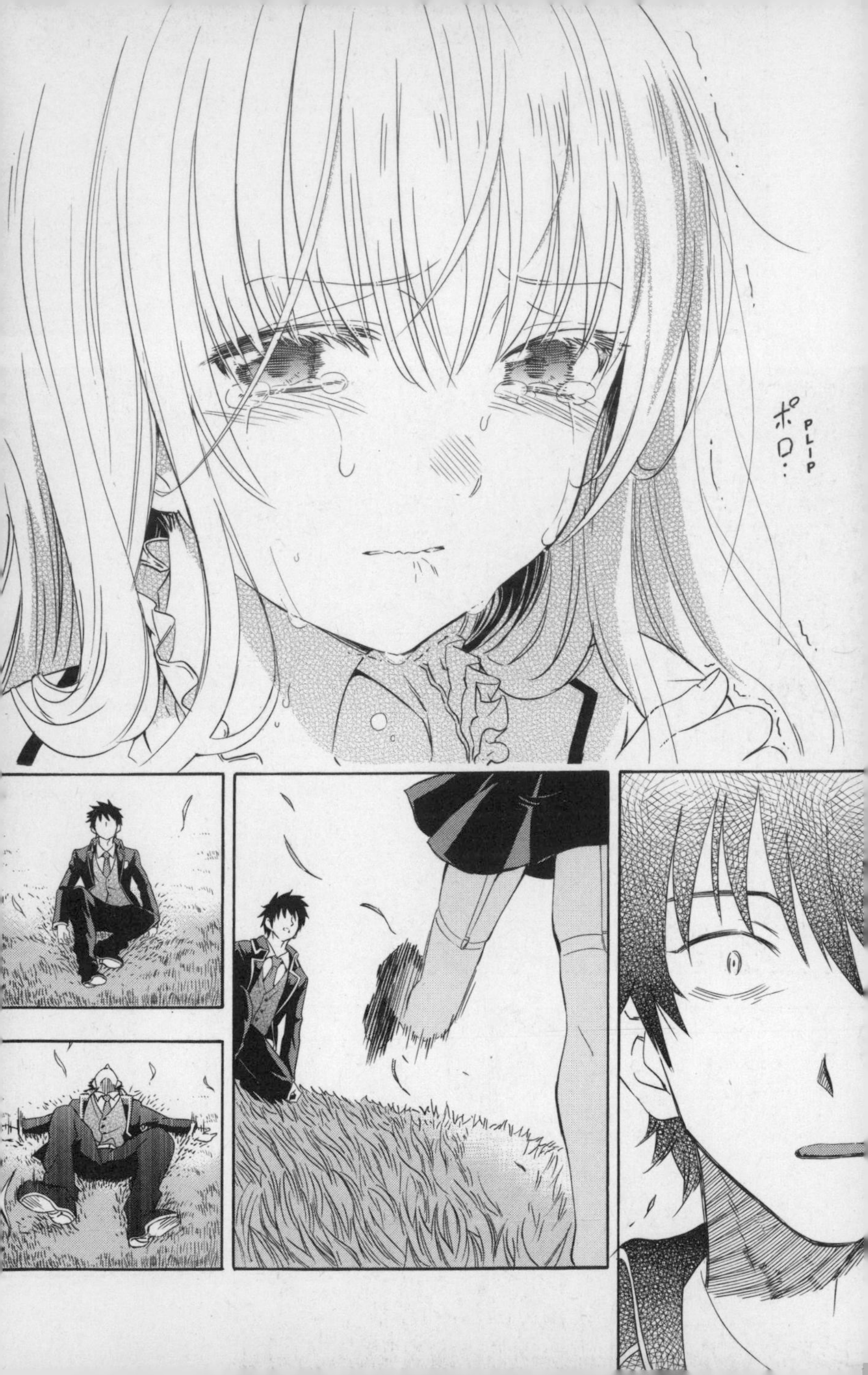
ポロ…
PLIP

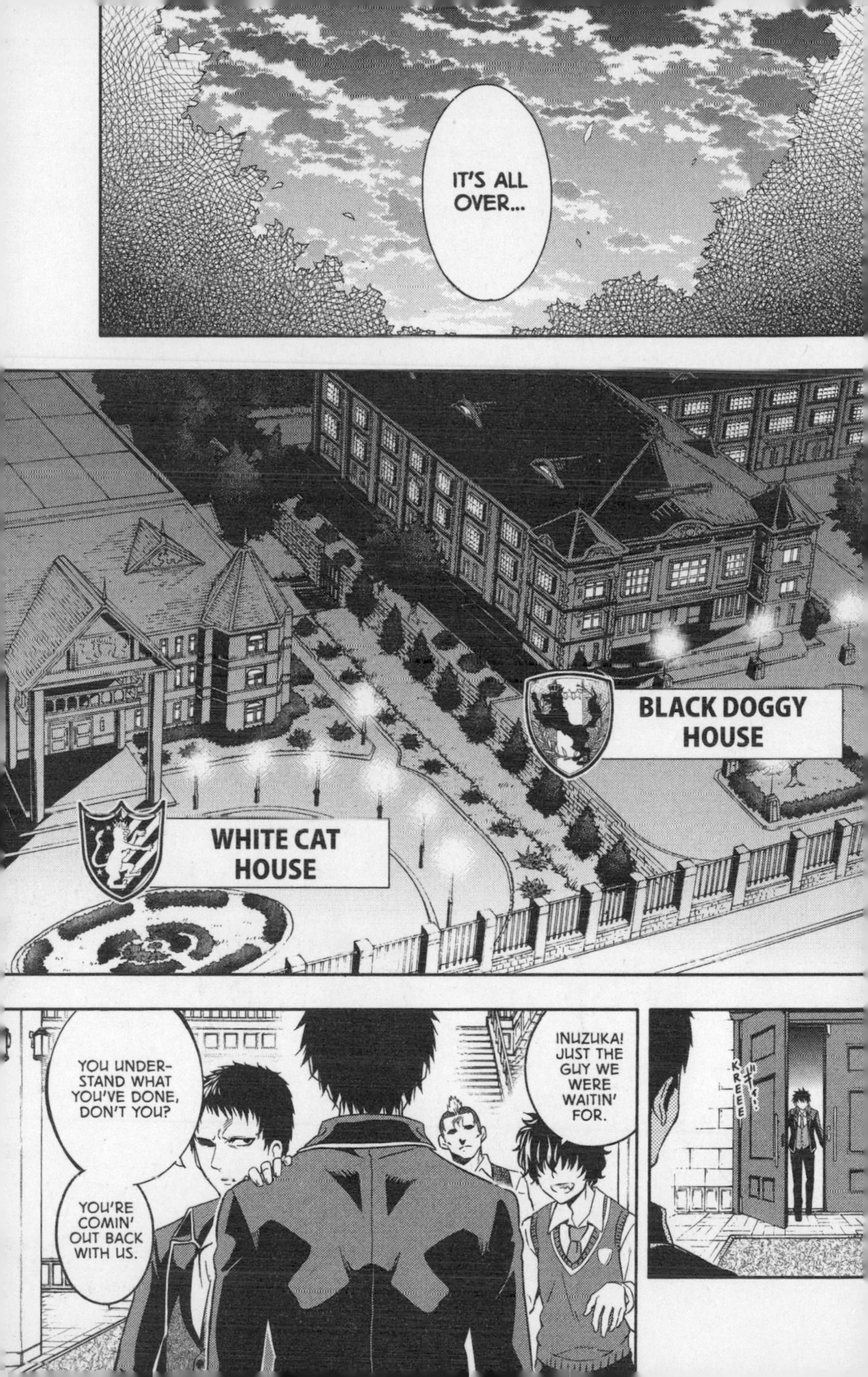
IT'S ALL OVER...
BLACK DOGGY HOUSE
WHITE CAT HOUSE
KREEE
INUZUKA! JUST THE GUY WE WERE WAITIN' FOR.
YOU UNDER-STAND WHAT YOU'VE DONE, DON'T YOU?
YOU'RE COMIN' OUT BACK WITH US.

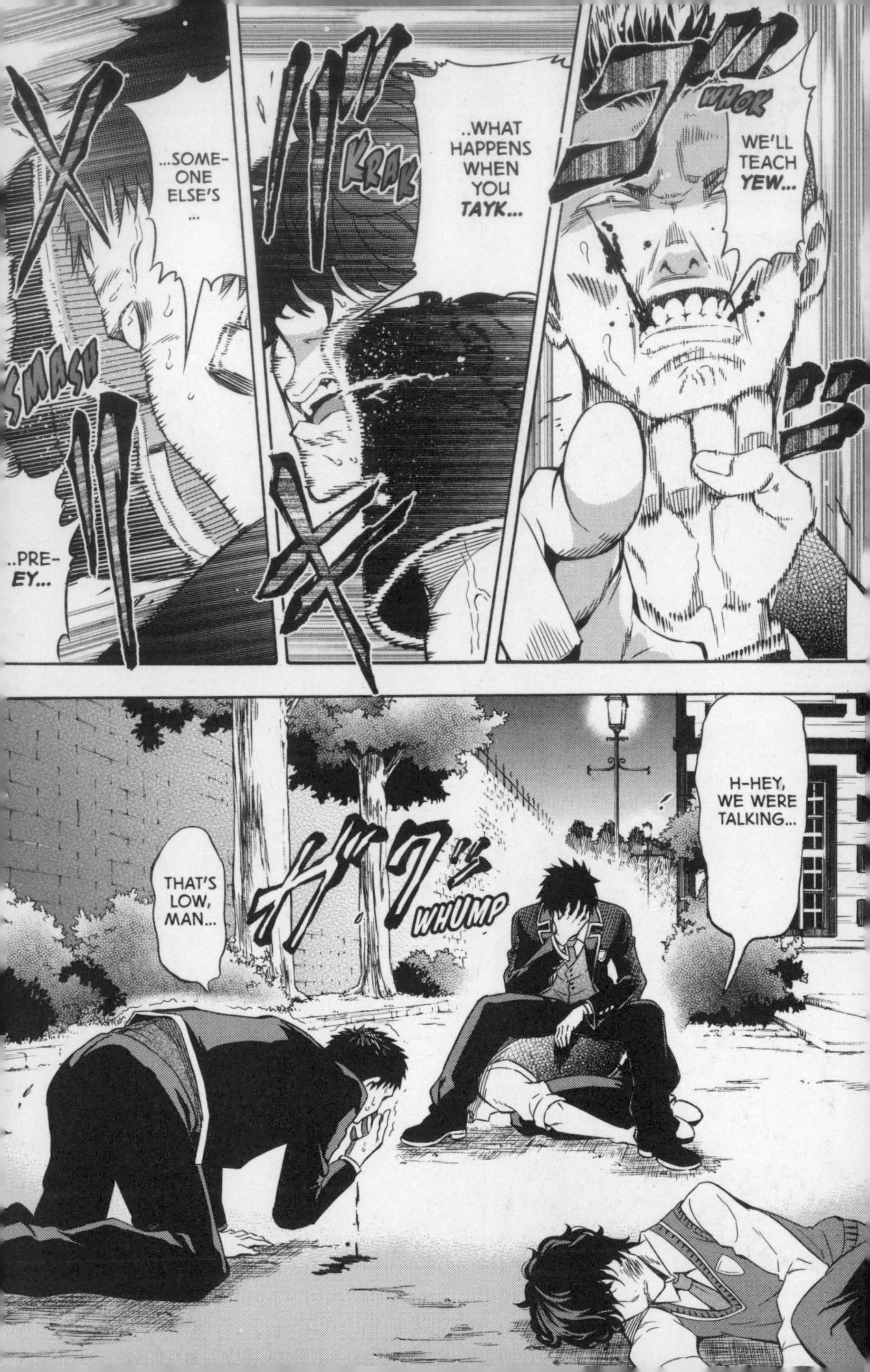
WHOK
WE'LL TEACH YEW...
..WHAT HAPPENS WHEN YOU TAYK...
KRAK
...SOME-ONE ELSE'S ...
SMASH
..PRE-EY...
H-HEY, WE WERE TALKING...
WHUMP
THAT'S LOW, MAN...

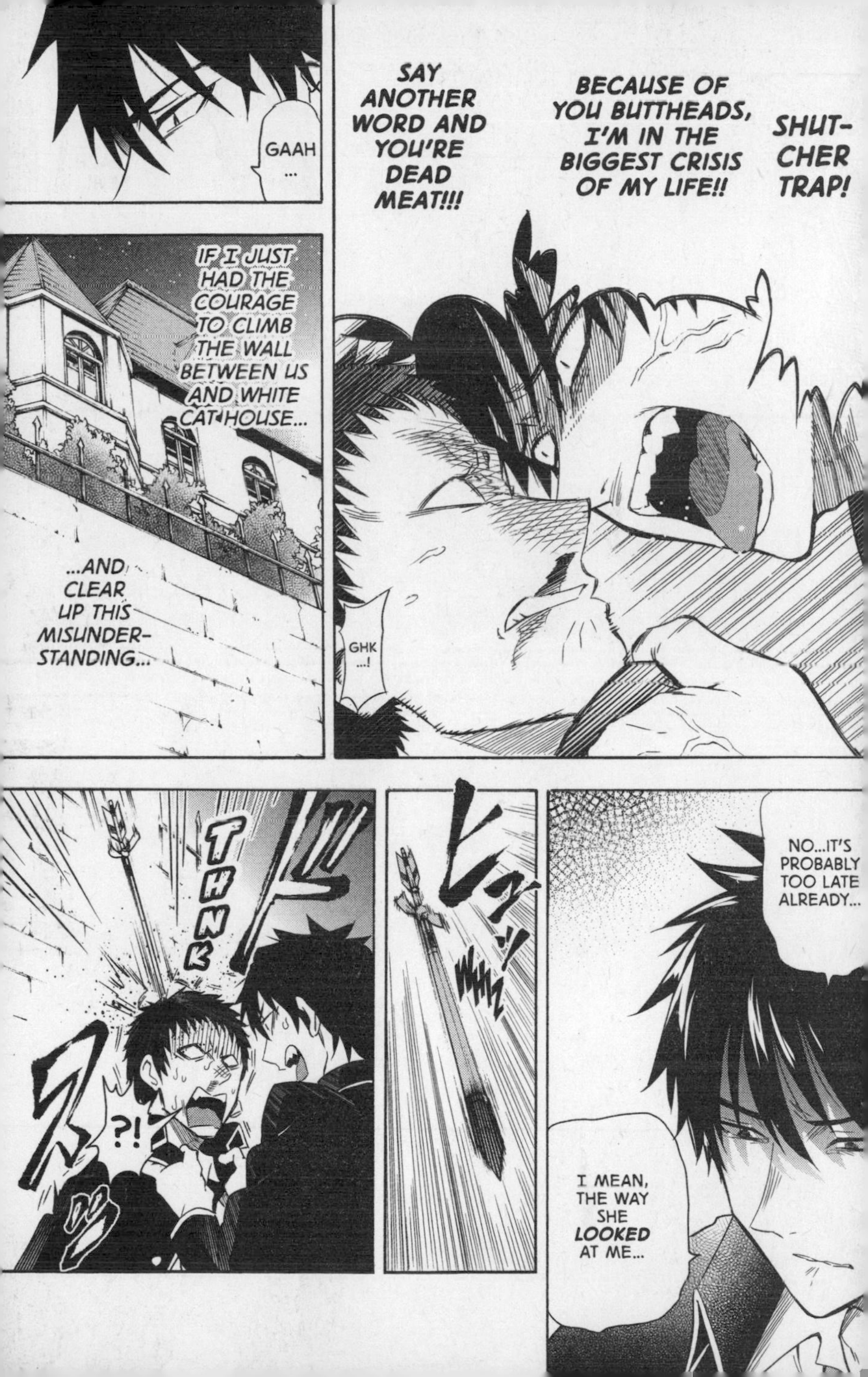
SHUT-CHER TRAP!
BECAUSE OF YOU BUTTHEADS, I'M IN THE BIGGEST CRISIS OF MY LIFE!!
SAY ANOTHER WORD AND YOU'RE DEAD MEAT!!!
GHK ...!
GAAH ...
IF I JUST HAD THE COURAGE TO CLIMB THE WALL BETWEEN US AND WHITE CAT HOUSE...
...AND CLEAR UP THIS MISUNDER-STANDING...
NO...IT'S PROBABLY TOO LATE ALREADY...
I MEAN, THE WAY SHE *LOOKED* AT ME...
WHIZ
THNK
?!

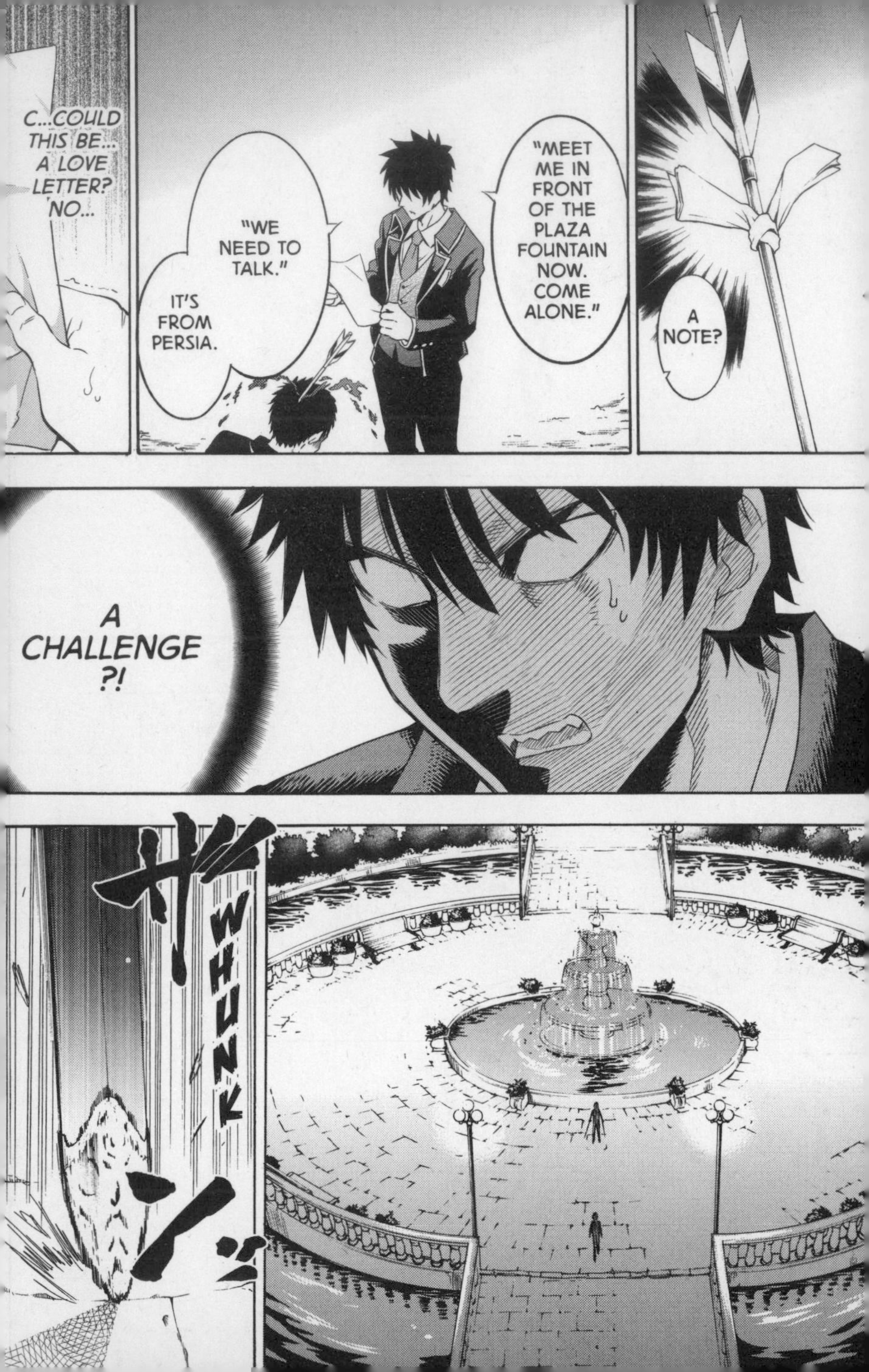
A NOTE?
"MEET ME IN FRONT OF THE PLAZA FOUNTAIN NOW. COME ALONE."
"WE NEED TO TALK."
IT'S FROM PERSIA.
C...COULD THIS BE... A LOVE LETTER? NO...
A CHALLENGE ?!
WHUNK

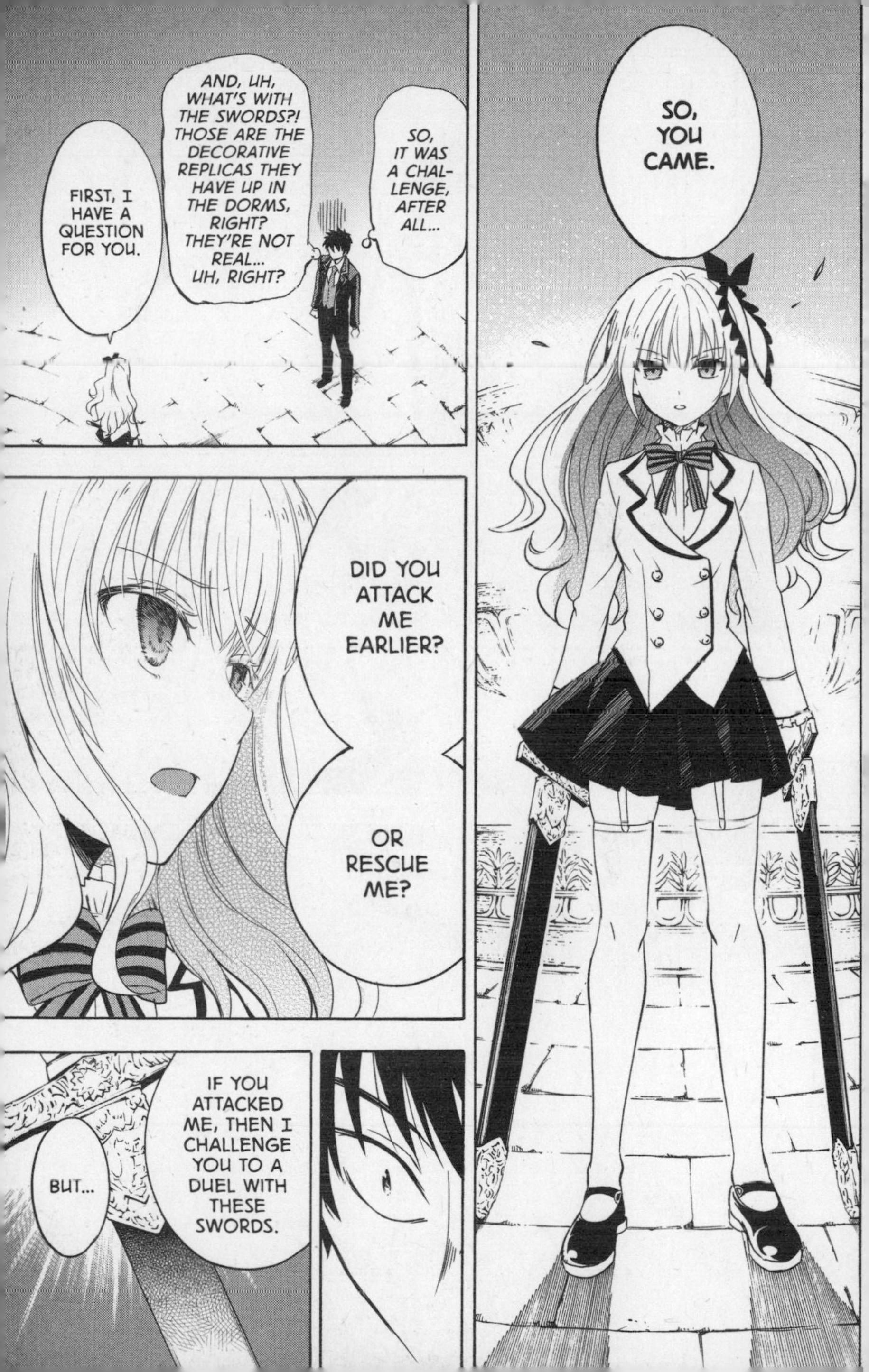
SO, YOU CAME.
SO, IT WAS A CHAL-LENGE, AFTER ALL...
AND, UH, WHAT'S WITH THE SWORDS?! THOSE ARE THE DECORATIVE REPLICAS THEY HAVE UP IN THE DORMS, RIGHT? THEY'RE NOT REAL... UH, RIGHT?
FIRST, I HAVE A QUESTION FOR YOU.
DID YOU ATTACK ME EARLIER?
OR RESCUE ME?
IF YOU ATTACKED ME, THEN I CHALLENGE YOU TO A DUEL WITH THESE SWORDS.
BUT...

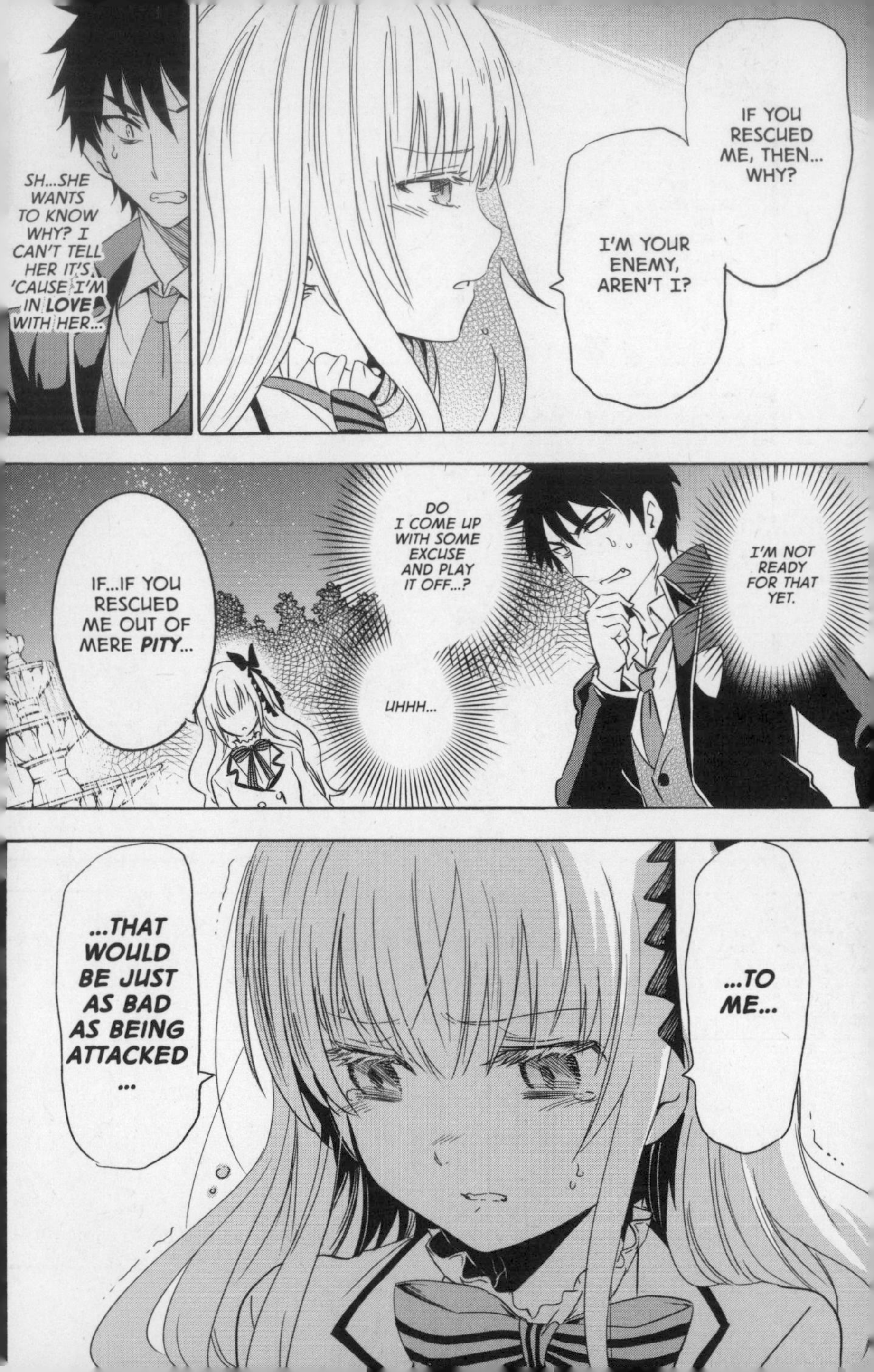
IF YOU RESCUED ME, THEN... WHY?
I'M YOUR ENEMY, AREN'T I?
SH...SHE WANTS TO KNOW WHY? I CAN'T TELL HER IT'S 'CAUSE I'M IN **LOVE** WITH HER...
I'M NOT READY FOR THAT YET.
DO I COME UP WITH SOME EXCUSE AND PLAY IT OFF...?
UHHH...
IF...IF YOU RESCUED ME OUT OF MERE **PITY**...
...TO ME...
...THAT WOULD BE JUST AS BAD AS BEING ATTACKED...

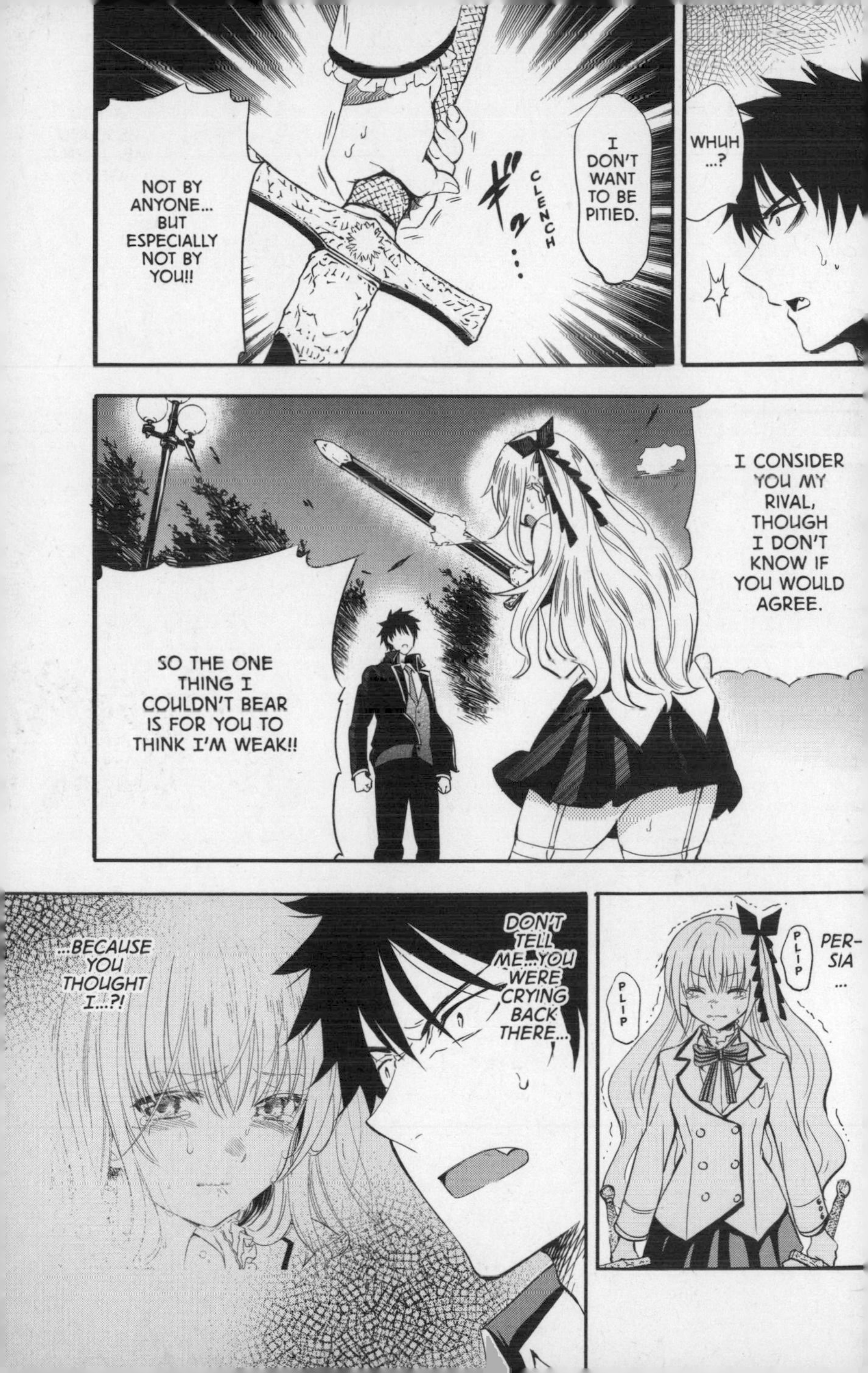
WHUH ...?
I DON'T WANT TO BE PITIED.
CLENCH
NOT BY ANYONE... BUT ESPECIALLY NOT BY YOU!!
I CONSIDER YOU MY RIVAL, THOUGH I DON'T KNOW IF YOU WOULD AGREE.
SO THE ONE THING I COULDN'T BEAR IS FOR YOU TO THINK I'M WEAK!!
PER-SIA ...
PLIP
PLIP
DON'T TELL ME... YOU WERE CRYING BACK THERE...
...BECAUSE YOU THOUGHT I...?!

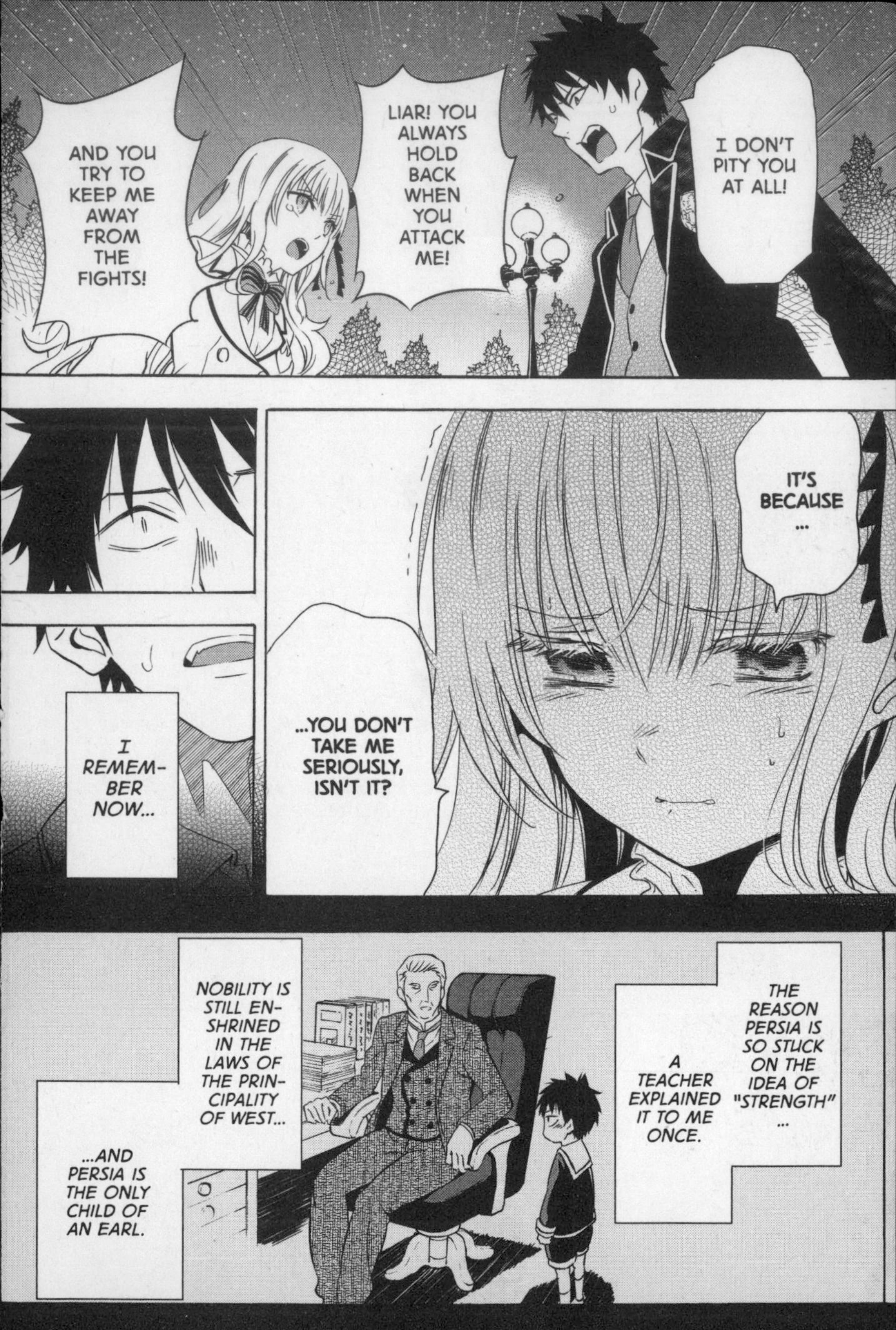
I DON'T PITY YOU AT ALL!
LIAR! YOU ALWAYS HOLD BACK WHEN YOU ATTACK ME!
AND YOU TRY TO KEEP ME AWAY FROM THE FIGHTS!
IT'S BECAUSE ...
...YOU DON'T TAKE ME SERIOUSLY, ISN'T IT?
I REMEMBER NOW...
THE REASON PERSIA IS SO STUCK ON THE IDEA OF "STRENGTH" ...
A TEACHER EXPLAINED IT TO ME ONCE.
NOBILITY IS STILL ENSHRINED IN THE LAWS OF THE PRINCIPALITY OF WEST...
...AND PERSIA IS THE ONLY CHILD OF AN EARL.

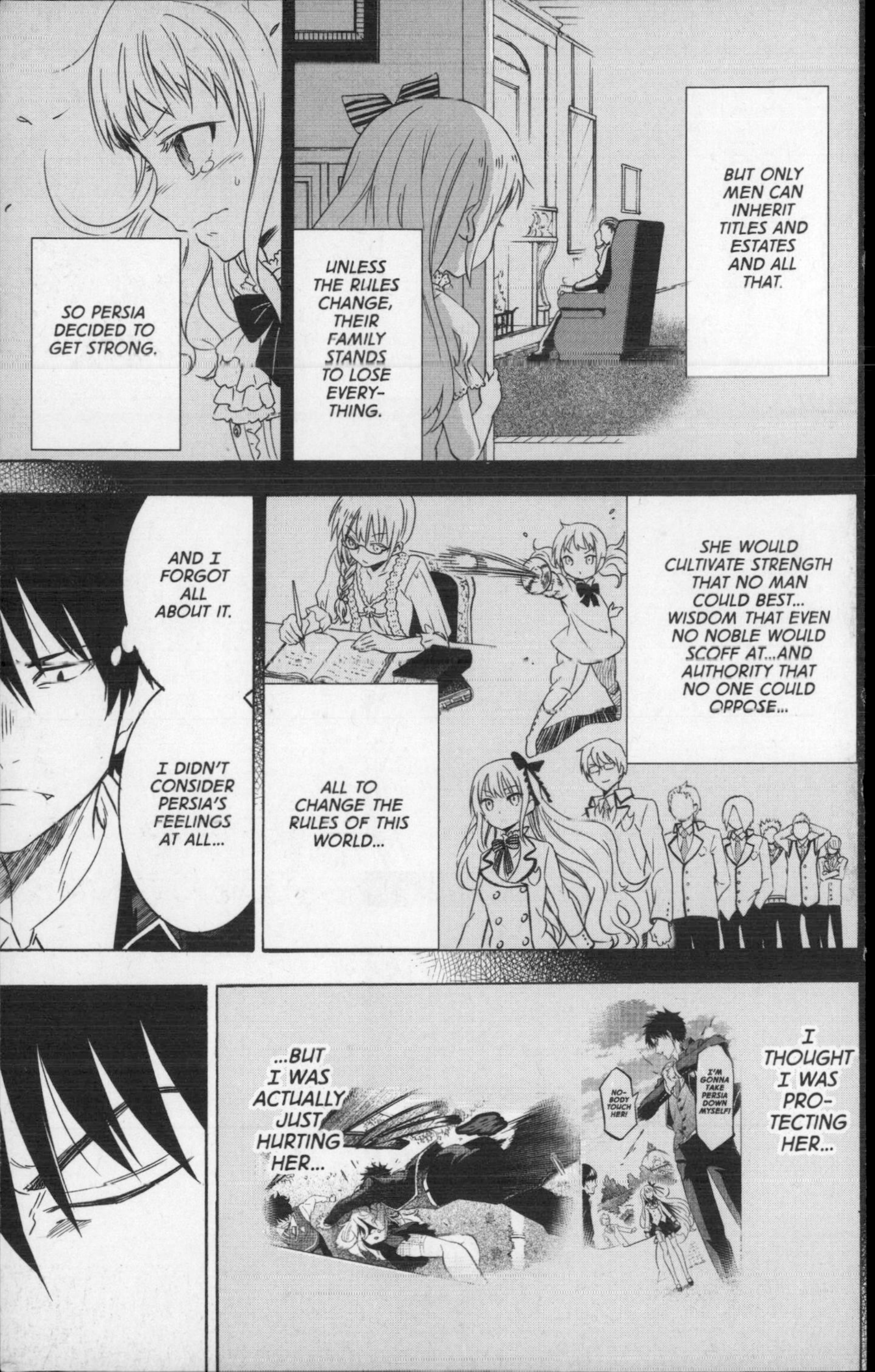
BUT ONLY MEN CAN INHERIT TITLES AND ESTATES AND ALL THAT.
UNLESS THE RULES CHANGE, THEIR FAMILY STANDS TO LOSE EVERY-THING.
SO PERSIA DECIDED TO GET STRONG.
SHE WOULD CULTIVATE STRENGTH THAT NO MAN COULD BEST... WISDOM THAT EVEN NO NOBLE WOULD SCOFF AT...AND AUTHORITY THAT NO ONE COULD OPPOSE...
ALL TO CHANGE THE RULES OF THIS WORLD...
AND I FORGOT ALL ABOUT IT.
I DIDN'T CONSIDER PERSIA'S FEELINGS AT ALL...
I THOUGHT I WAS PRO-TECTING HER...
I'M GONNA TAKE PERSIA DOWN MYSELF!
NO-BODY TOUCH HER!
...BUT I WAS ACTUALLY JUST HURTING HER...

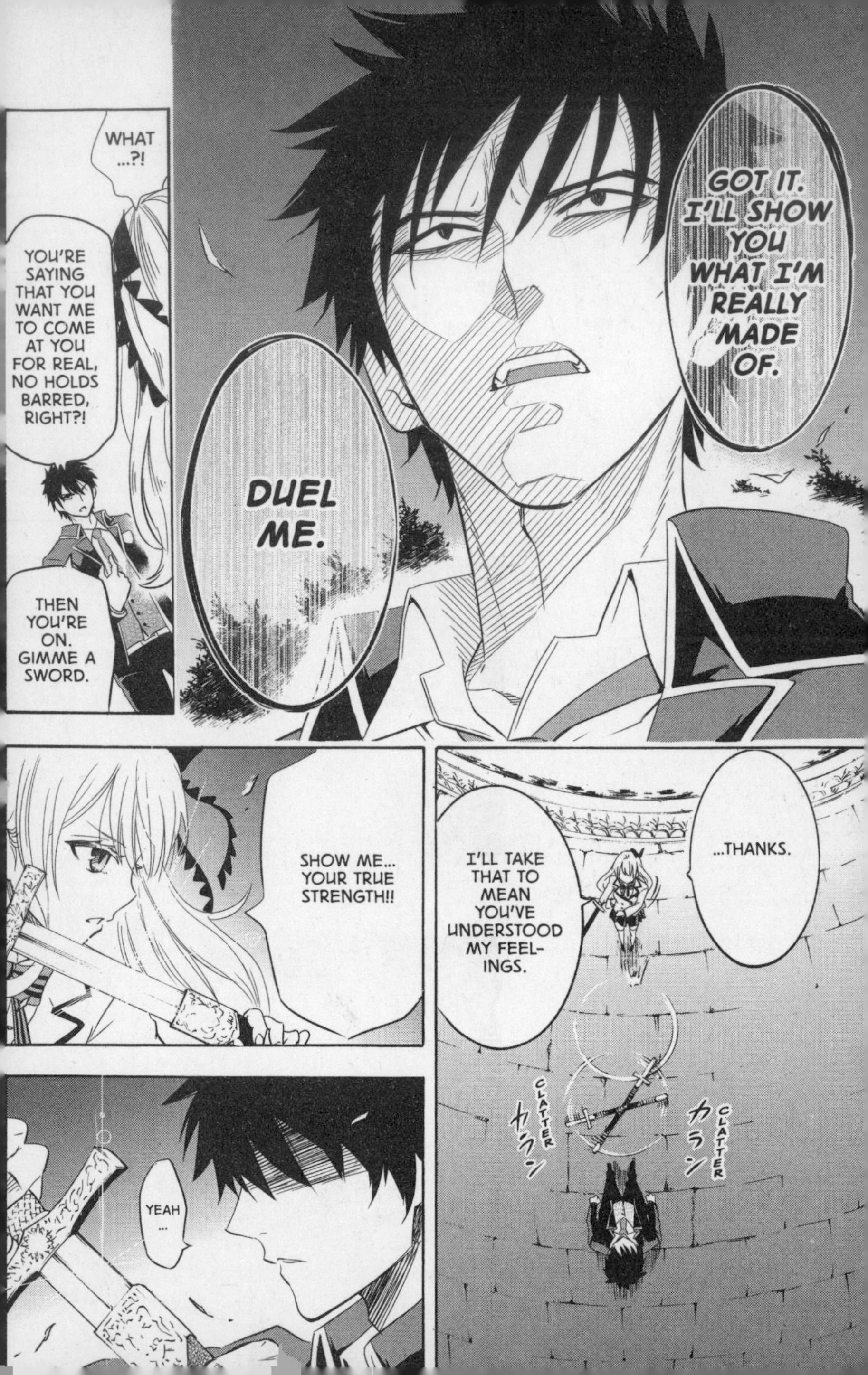
GOT IT. I'LL SHOW YOU WHAT I'M REALLY MADE OF.
DUEL ME.
WHAT ...?!
YOU'RE SAYING THAT YOU WANT ME TO COME AT YOU FOR REAL, NO HOLDS BARRED, RIGHT?!
THEN YOU'RE ON. GIMME A SWORD.
...THANKS.
I'LL TAKE THAT TO MEAN YOU'VE UNDERSTOOD MY FEEL-INGS.
カラン
CLATTER
カラン
CLATTER
SHOW ME... YOUR TRUE STRENGTH!!
YEAH ...

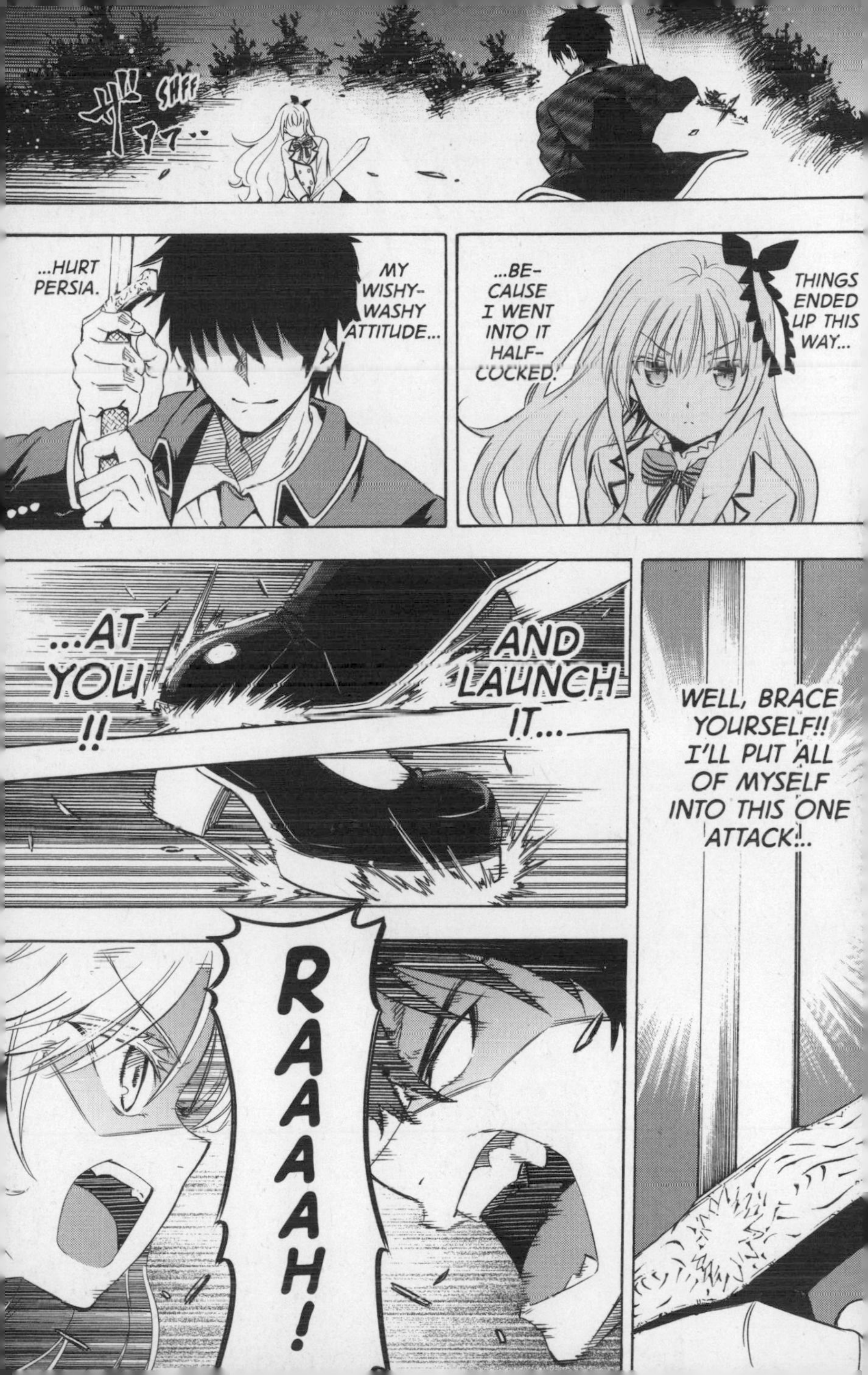
SHFF
THINGS ENDED UP THIS WAY...
...BE-CAUSE I WENT INTO IT HALF-COCKED.
MY WISHY-WASHY ATTITUDE...
...HURT PERSIA.
...
WELL, BRACE YOURSELF!! I'LL PUT ALL OF MYSELF INTO THIS ONE ATTACK!...
AND LAUNCH IT...
...AT YOU!!
RAAAAAH!

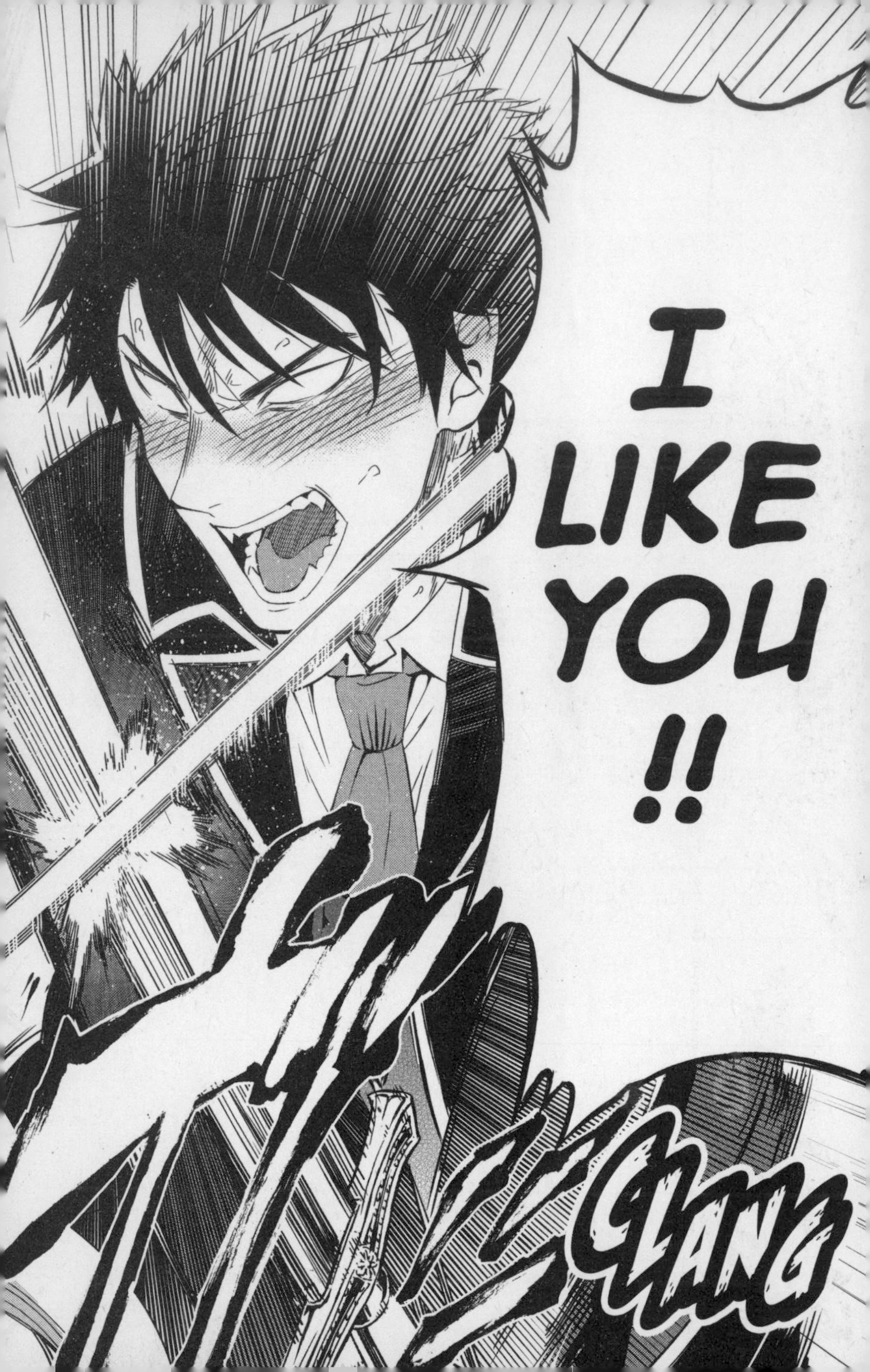
I LIKE YOU!!
CLANG

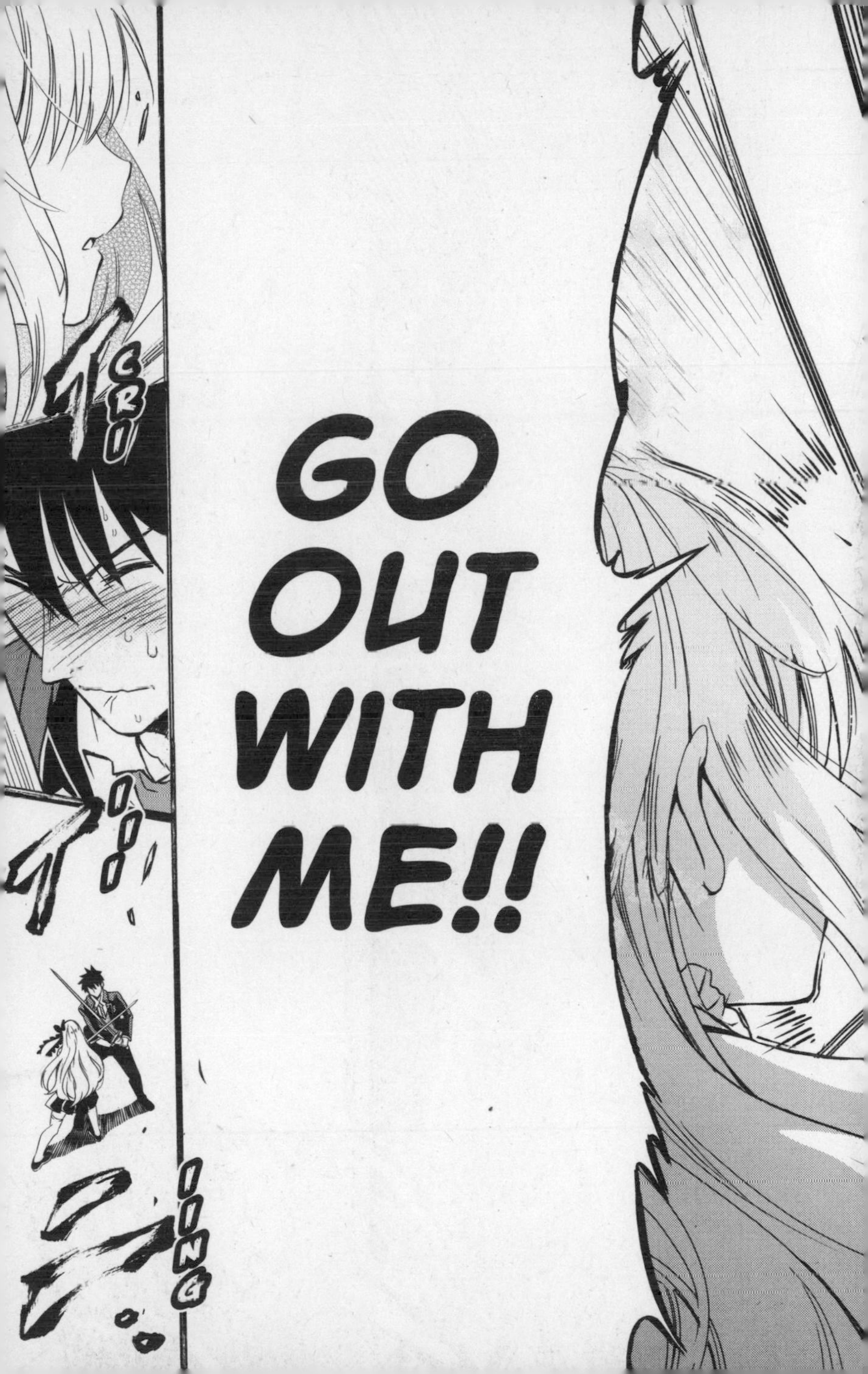
GO OUT WITH ME!!
CRI
IIING

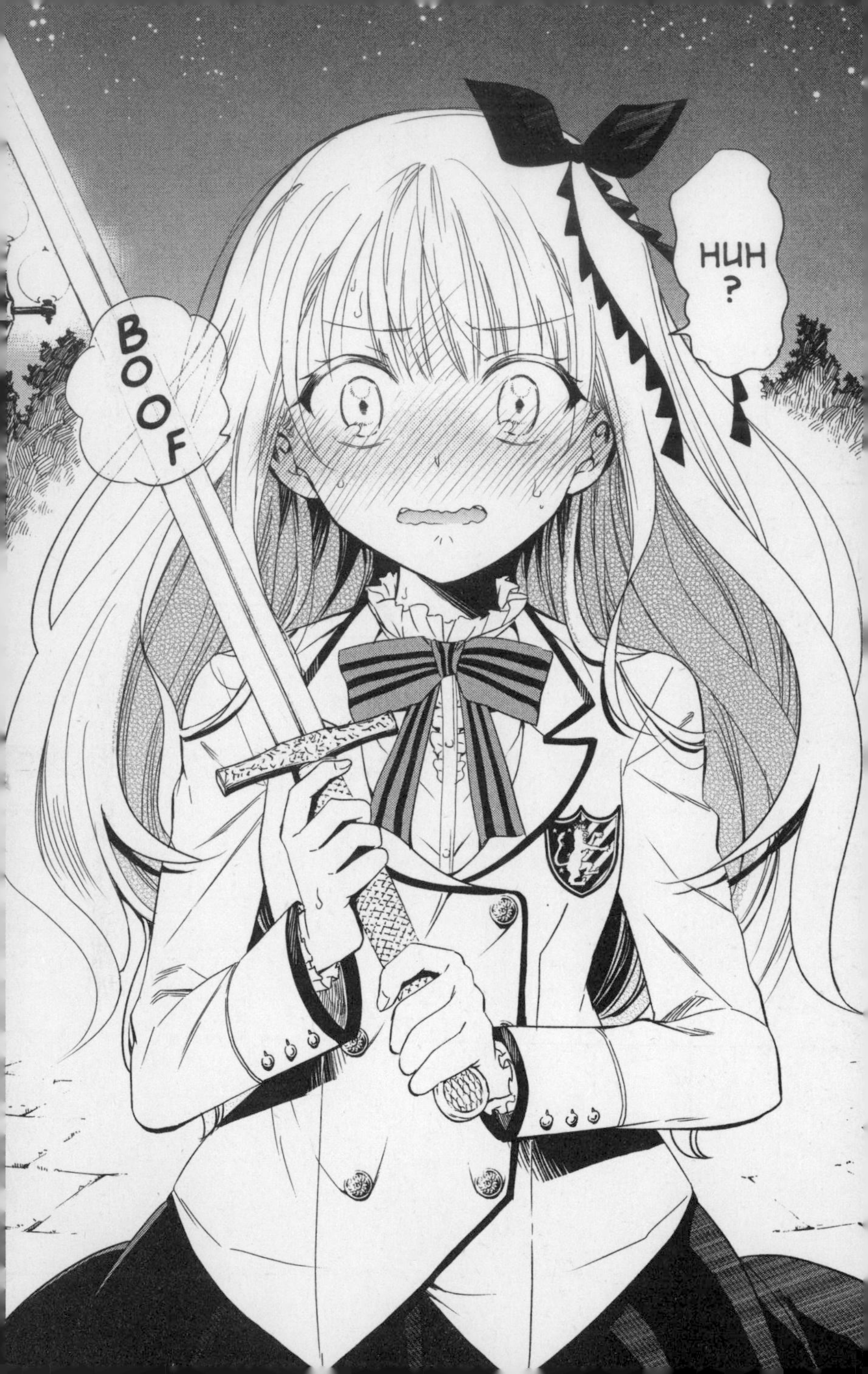
HUH
?
BOOF

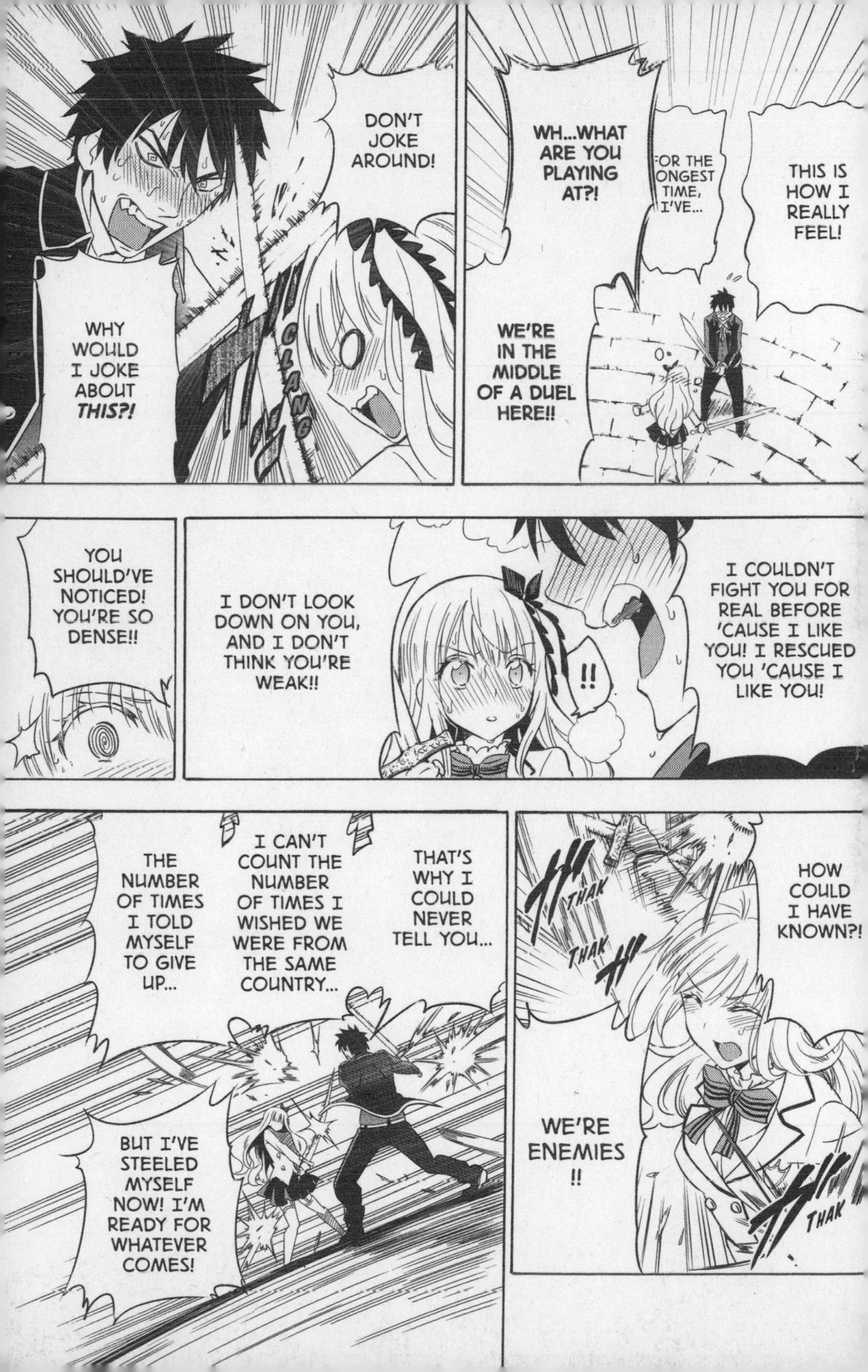
THIS IS HOW I REALLY FEEL!
FOR THE ONGEST TIME, I'VE...
WH...WHAT ARE YOU PLAYING AT?!
WE'RE IN THE MIDDLE OF A DUEL HERE!!
DON'T JOKE AROUND!
CLANG
WHY WOULD I JOKE ABOUT *THIS?!*
I COULDN'T FIGHT YOU FOR REAL BEFORE 'CAUSE I LIKE YOU! I RESCUED YOU 'CAUSE I LIKE YOU!
!!
I DON'T LOOK DOWN ON YOU, AND I DON'T THINK YOU'RE WEAK!!
YOU SHOULD'VE NOTICED! YOU'RE SO DENSE!!
HOW COULD I HAVE KNOWN?!
THAK
THAK
WE'RE ENEMIES !!
THAK
THAT'S WHY I COULD NEVER TELL YOU...
I CAN'T COUNT THE NUMBER OF TIMES I WISHED WE WERE FROM THE SAME COUNTRY...
THE NUMBER OF TIMES I TOLD MYSELF TO GIVE UP...
BUT I'VE STEELED MYSELF NOW! I'M READY FOR WHATEVER COMES!

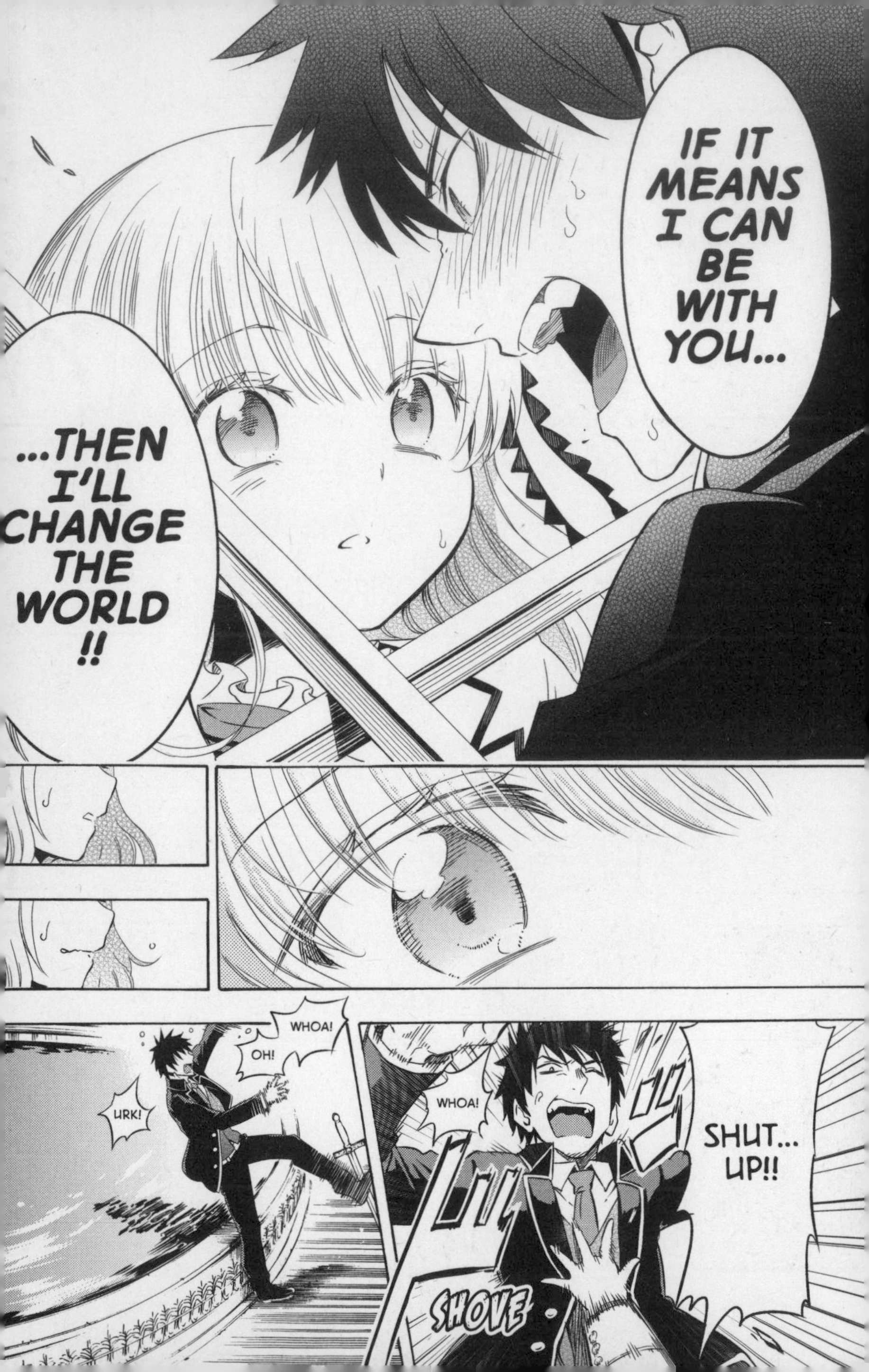
IF IT MEANS I CAN BE WITH YOU...
...THEN I'LL CHANGE THE WORLD !!
SHUT... UP!!
WHOA!
SHOVE
WHOA!
OH!
URK!

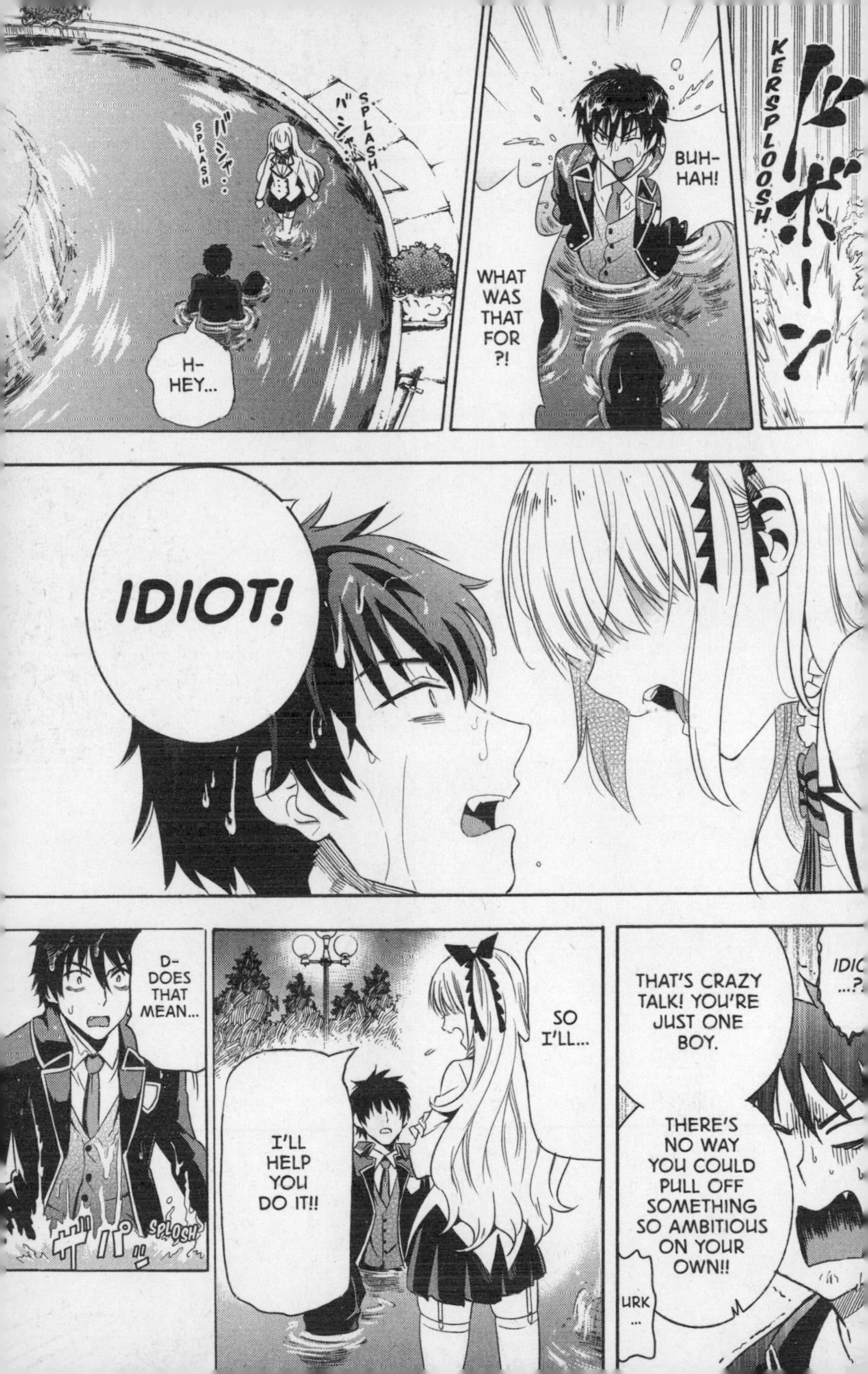
KERSPLOOSH
BUH-HAH!
WHAT WAS THAT FOR ?!
SPLASH
SPLASH
H-HEY...
IDIOT!
THAT'S CRAZY TALK! YOU'RE JUST ONE BOY.
THERE'S NO WAY YOU COULD PULL OFF SOMETHING SO AMBITIOUS ON YOUR OWN!!
URK ...
SO I'LL...
I'LL HELP YOU DO IT!!
D-DOES THAT MEAN...
SPLOSH

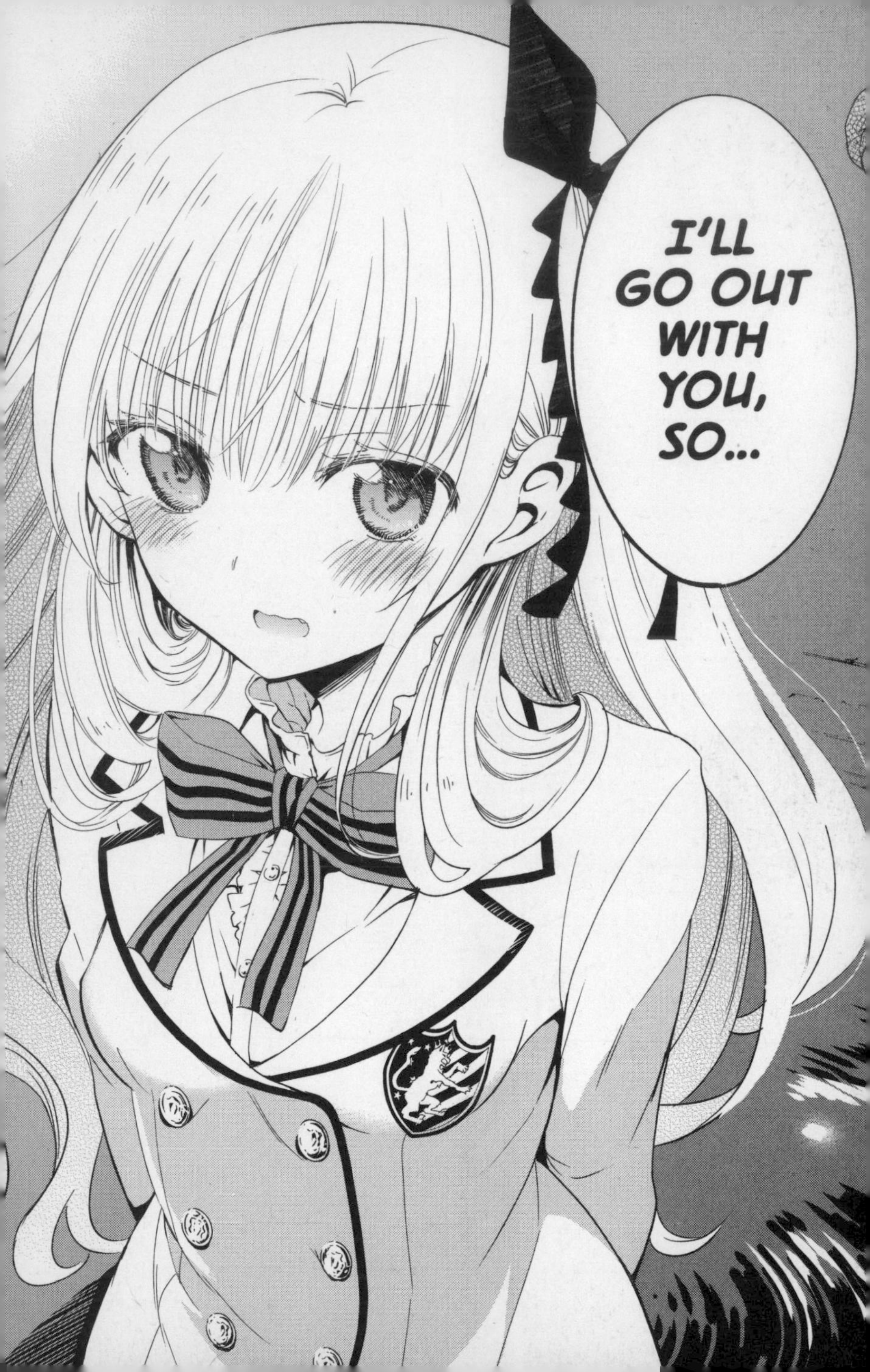
I'LL GO OUT WITH YOU, SO...

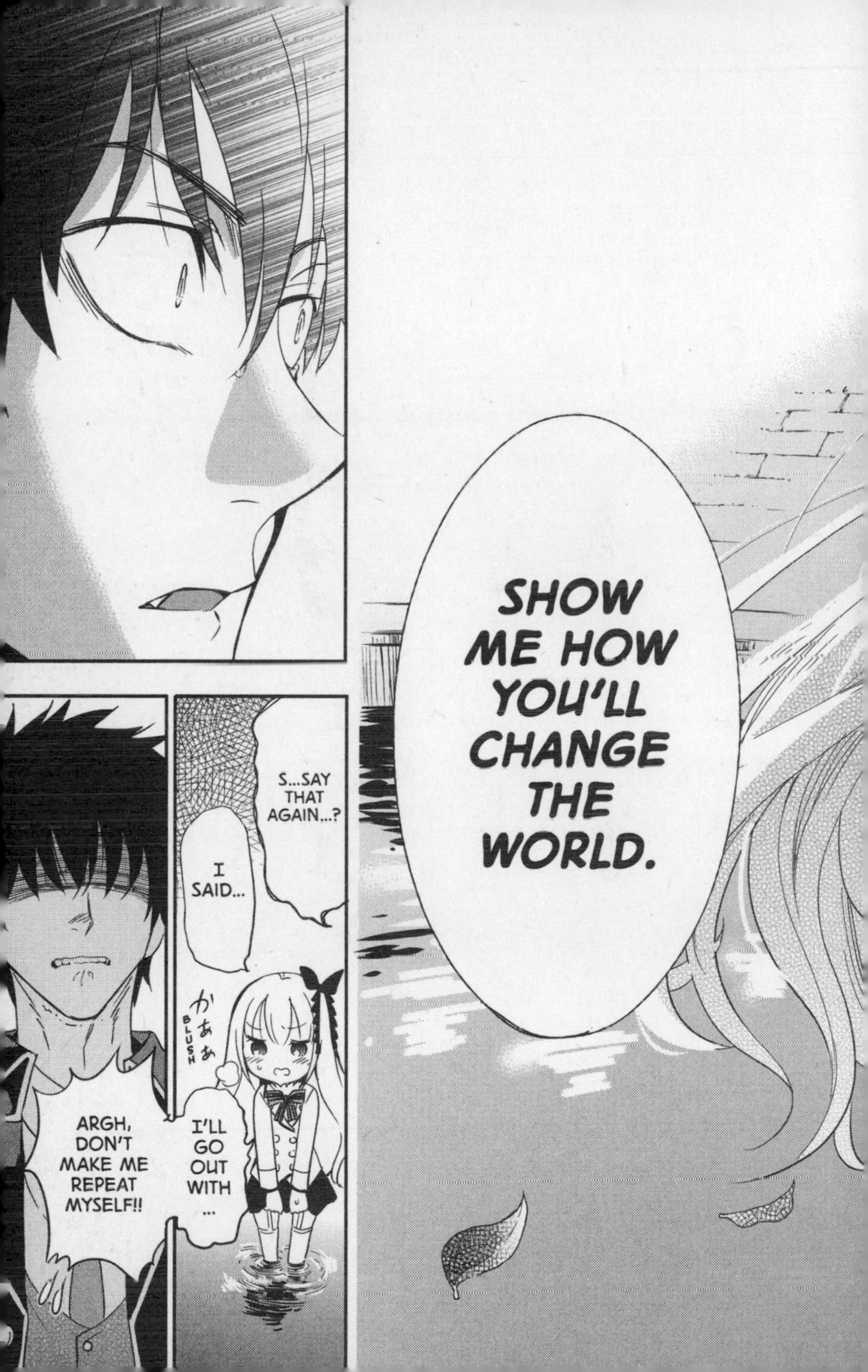
SHOW ME HOW YOU'LL CHANGE THE WORLD.
S...SAY THAT AGAIN...?
I SAID...
かぁぁ
BLUSH
I'LL GO OUT WITH ...
ARGH, DON'T MAKE ME REPEAT MYSELF!!

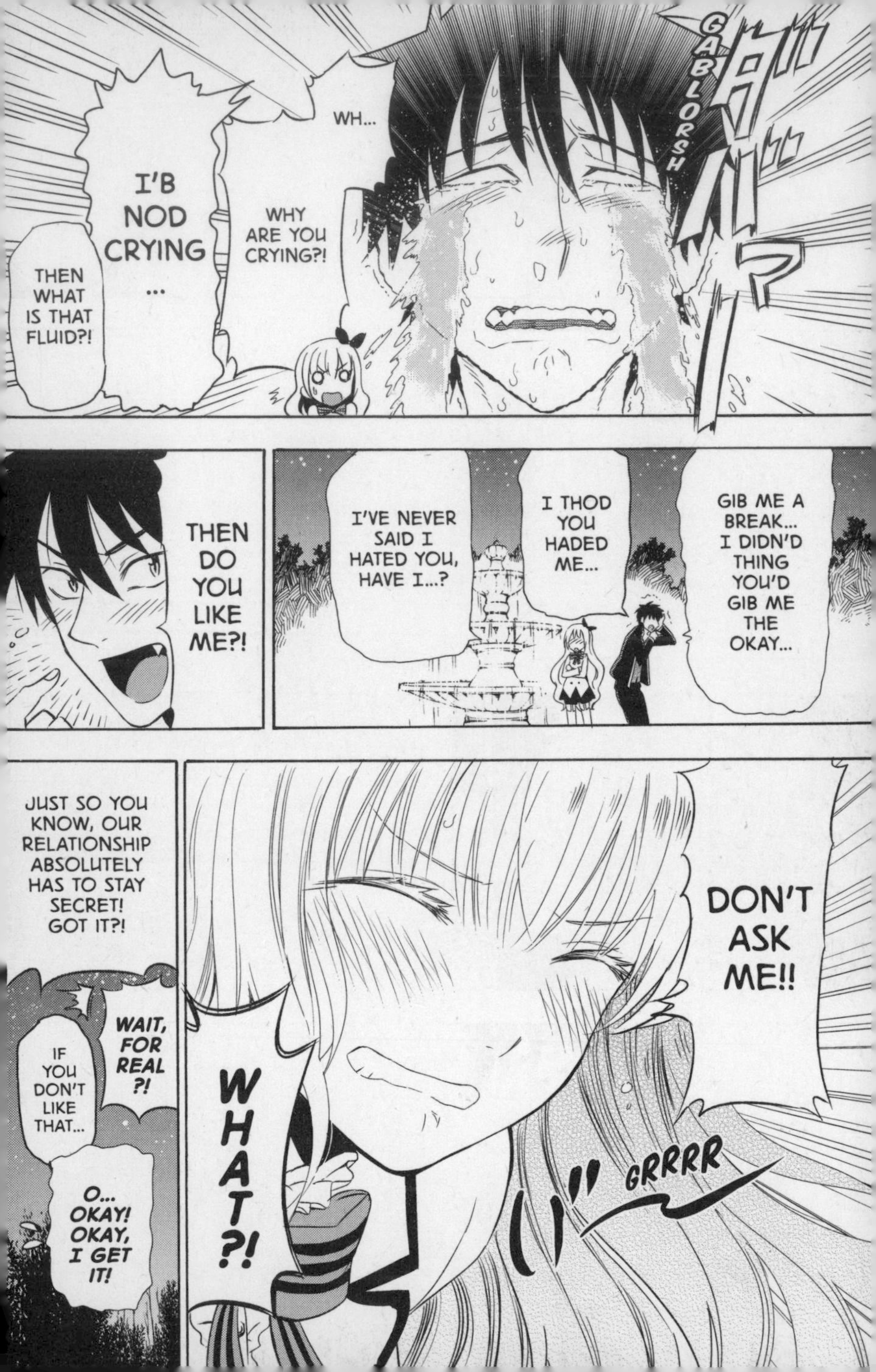
GABLORSH
WH...
WHY ARE YOU CRYING?!
I'B NOD CRYING ...
THEN WHAT IS THAT FLUID?!
GIB ME A BREAK... I DIDN'D THING YOU'D GIB ME THE OKAY...
I THOD YOU HADED ME...
I'VE NEVER SAID I HATED YOU, HAVE I...?
THEN DO YOU LIKE ME?!
DON'T ASK ME!!
WHAT?!
GRRRR
JUST SO YOU KNOW, OUR RELATIONSHIP ABSOLUTELY HAS TO STAY SECRET! GOT IT?!
WAIT, FOR REAL?!
IF YOU DON'T LIKE THAT...
O... OKAY! OKAY, I GET IT!

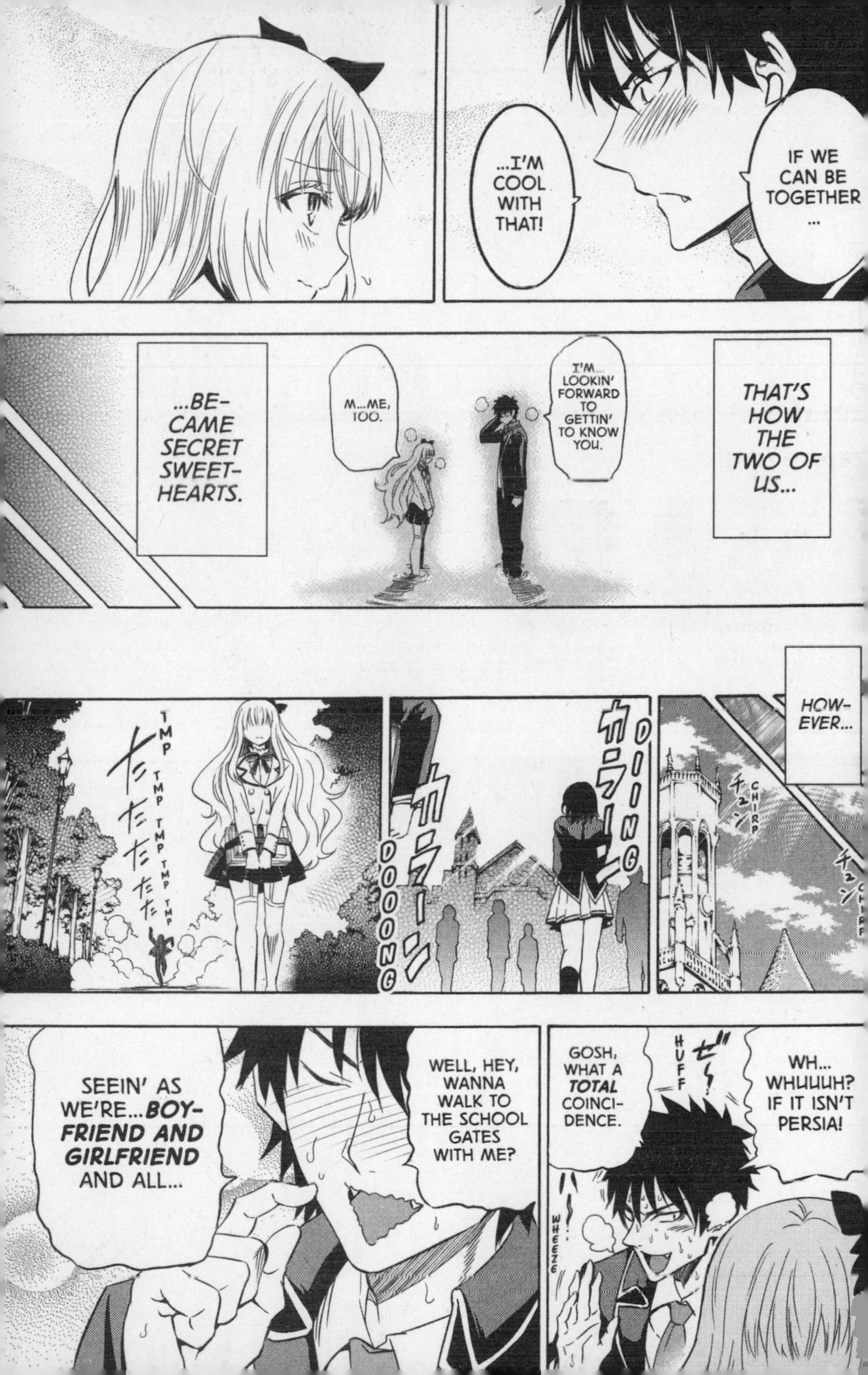
IF WE CAN BE TOGETHER ...
...I'M COOL WITH THAT!
THAT'S HOW THE TWO OF US...
I'M... LOOKIN' FORWARD TO GETTIN' TO KNOW YOU.
M...ME, TOO.
...BE-CAME SECRET SWEET-HEARTS.
HOW-EVER...
CHIRP
CHIRP
DIIING
DOOONG
TMP TMP TMP TMP TMP
WH... WHUUUH? IF IT ISN'T PERSIA!
HUFF
GOSH, WHAT A **TOTAL** COINCI-DENCE.
WHEEZE
WELL, HEY, WANNA WALK TO THE SCHOOL GATES WITH ME?
SEEIN' AS WE'RE... **BOY-FRIEND AND GIRLFRIEND** AND ALL...

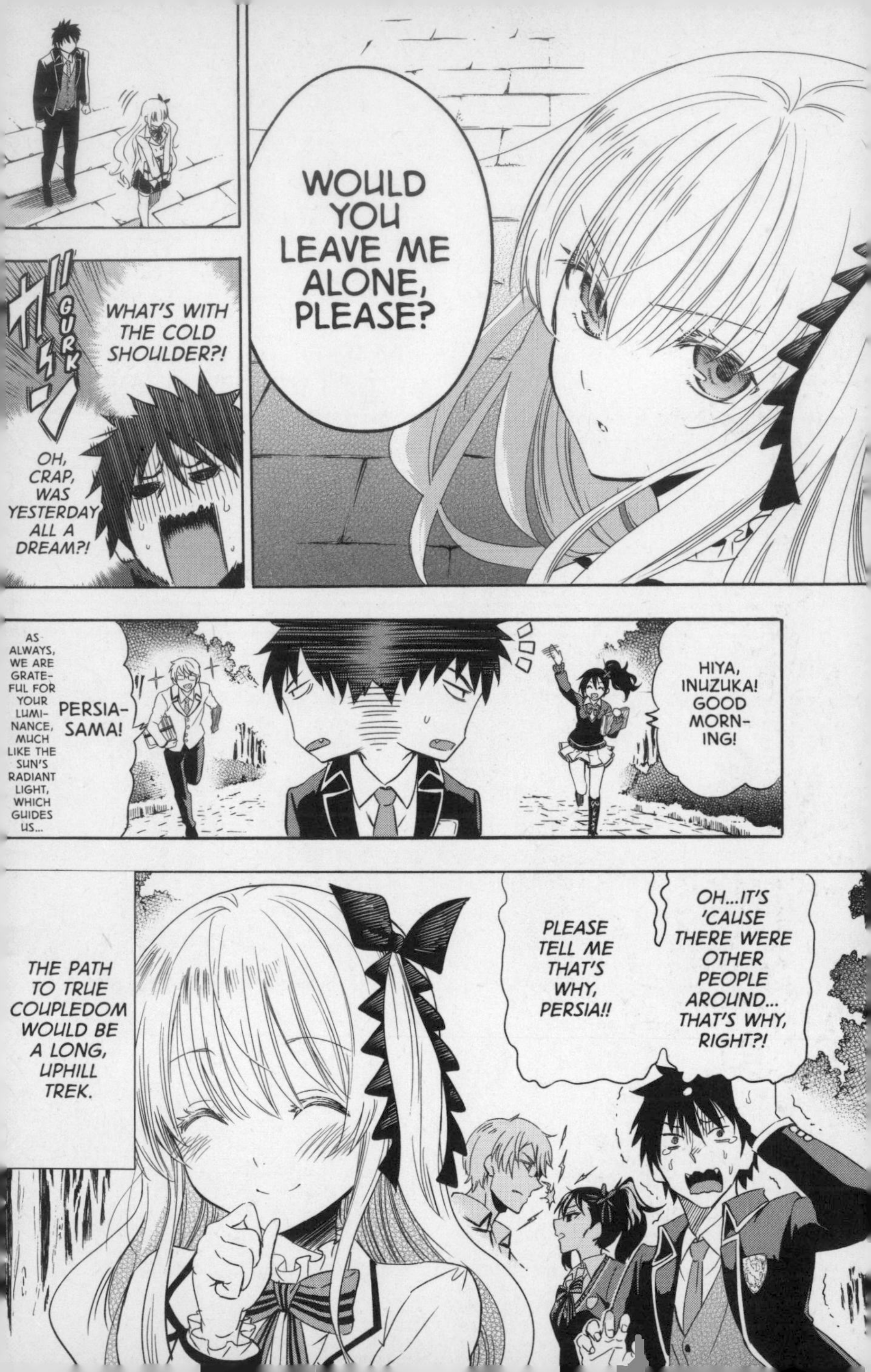
WOULD YOU LEAVE ME ALONE, PLEASE?
WHAT'S WITH THE COLD SHOULDER?!
GURK
OH, CRAP, WAS YESTERDAY ALL A DREAM?!
HIYA, INUZUKA! GOOD MORN-ING!
PERSIA-SAMA!
AS-ALWAYS, WE ARE GRATE-FUL FOR YOUR LUMI-NANCE, MUCH LIKE THE SUN'S RADIANT LIGHT, WHICH GUIDES US...
OH...IT'S 'CAUSE THERE WERE OTHER PEOPLE AROUND... THAT'S WHY, RIGHT?!
PLEASE TELL ME THAT'S WHY, PERSIA!!
THE PATH TO TRUE COUPLEDOM WOULD BE A LONG, UPHILL TREK.

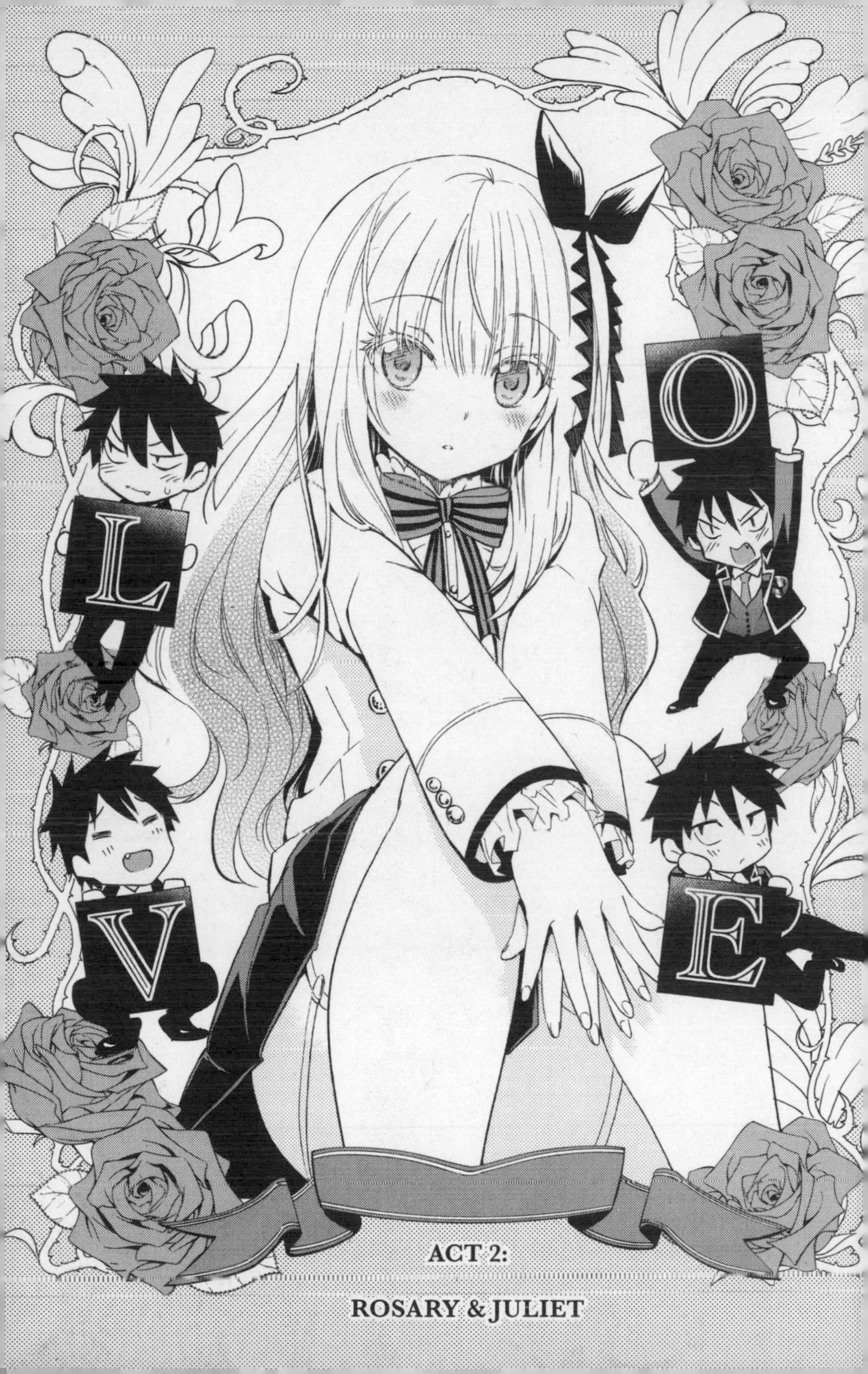
L
O
V
E

ACT 2:

ROSARY & JULIET

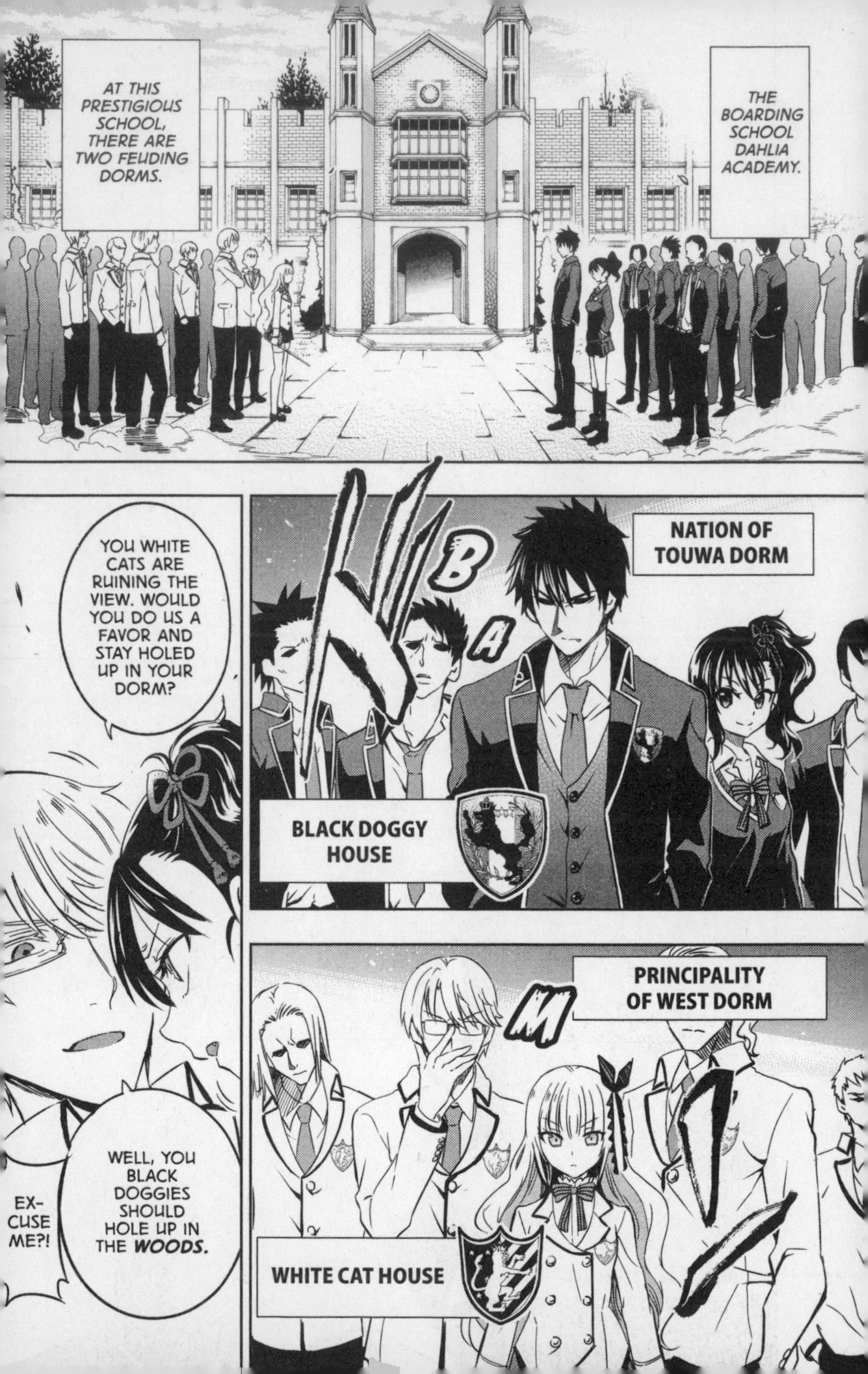
THE BOARDING SCHOOL DAHLIA ACADEMY.
AT THIS PRESTIGIOUS SCHOOL, THERE ARE TWO FEUDING DORMS.
NATION OF TOUWA DORM
BA
BLACK DOGGY HOUSE
PRINCIPALITY OF WEST DORM
M
WHITE CAT HOUSE
YOU WHITE CATS ARE RUINING THE VIEW. WOULD YOU DO US A FAVOR AND STAY HOLED UP IN YOUR DORM?
WELL, YOU BLACK DOGGIES SHOULD HOLE UP IN THE *WOODS.*
EX-CUSE ME?!

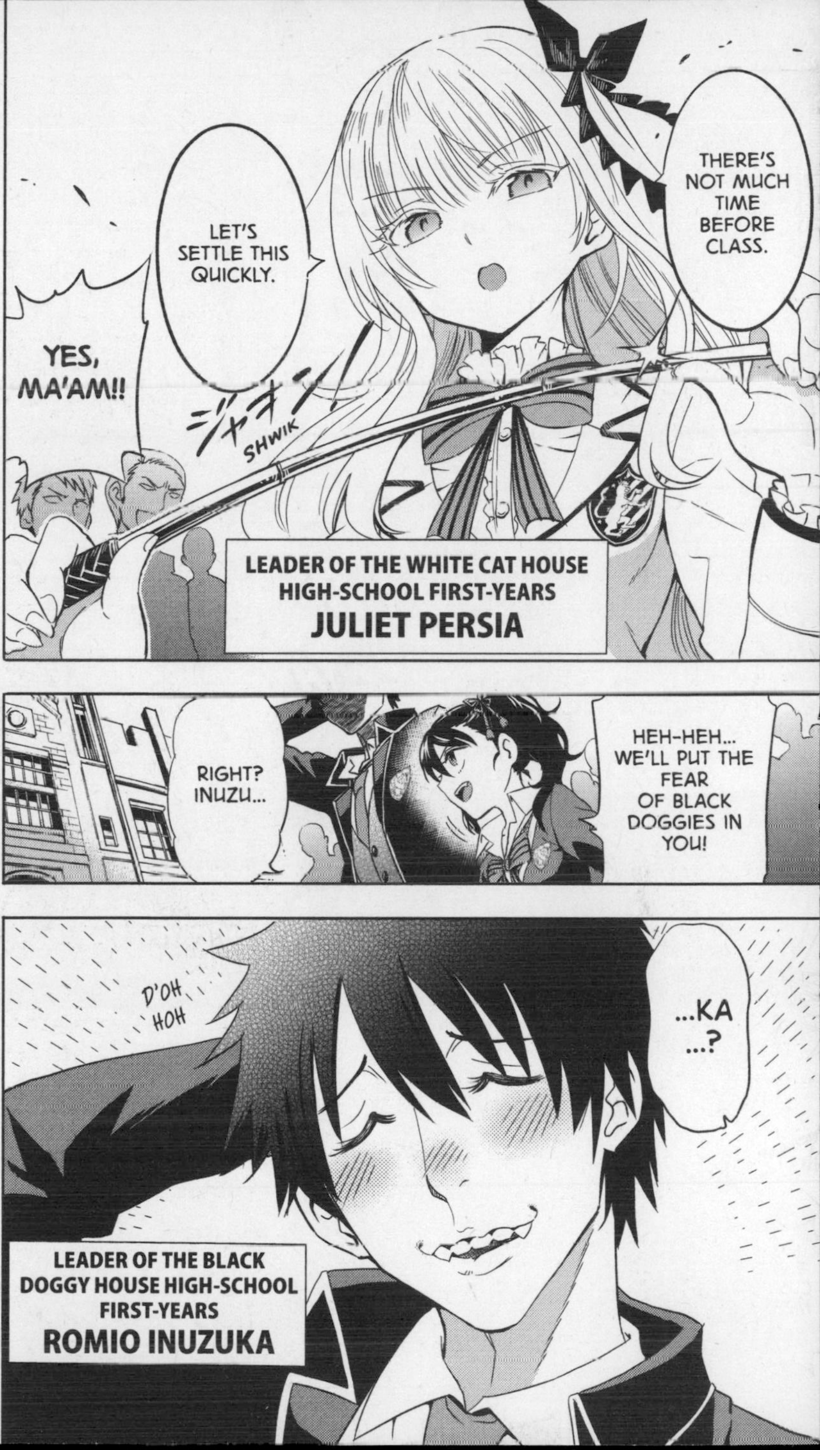
THERE'S NOT MUCH TIME BEFORE CLASS.
LET'S SETTLE THIS QUICKLY.
ジャキン
SHWIK
YES, MA'AM!!
LEADER OF THE WHITE CAT HOUSE HIGH-SCHOOL FIRST-YEARS JULIET PERSIA
HEH-HEH... WE'LL PUT THE FEAR OF BLACK DOGGIES IN YOU!
RIGHT? INUZU...
...KA ...?
D'OH HOH
LEADER OF THE BLACK DOGGY HOUSE HIGH-SCHOOL FIRST-YEARS ROMIO INUZUKA

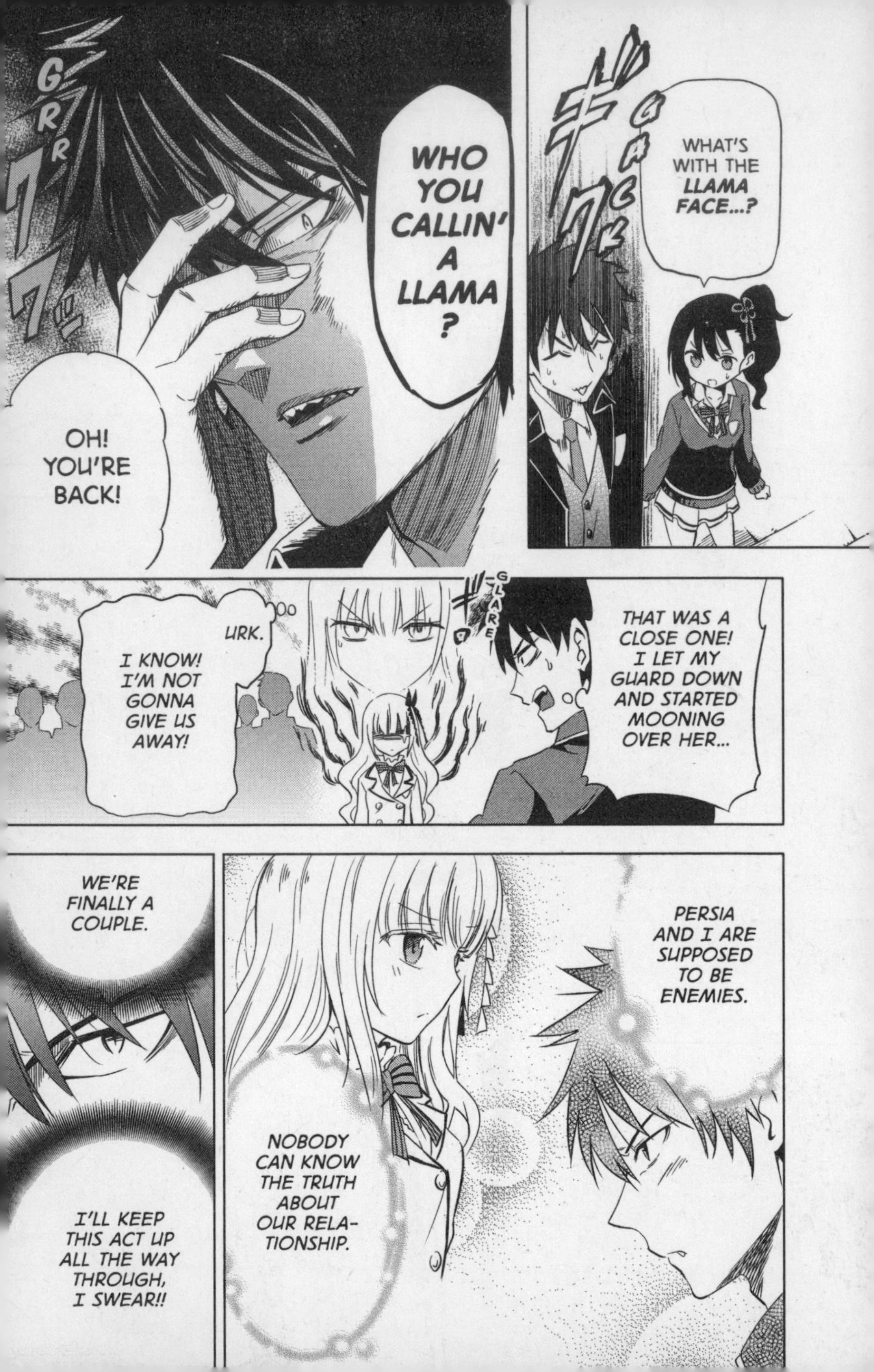
GACK
WHAT'S WITH THE LLAMA FACE...?
WHO YOU CALLIN' A LLAMA?
GRRR
OH! YOU'RE BACK!
THAT WAS A CLOSE ONE! I LET MY GUARD DOWN AND STARTED MOONING OVER HER...
GLARE
URK.
I KNOW! I'M NOT GONNA GIVE US AWAY!
PERSIA AND I ARE SUPPOSED TO BE ENEMIES.
NOBODY CAN KNOW THE TRUTH ABOUT OUR RELA-TIONSHIP.
WE'RE FINALLY A COUPLE.
I'LL KEEP THIS ACT UP ALL THE WAY THROUGH, I SWEAR!!

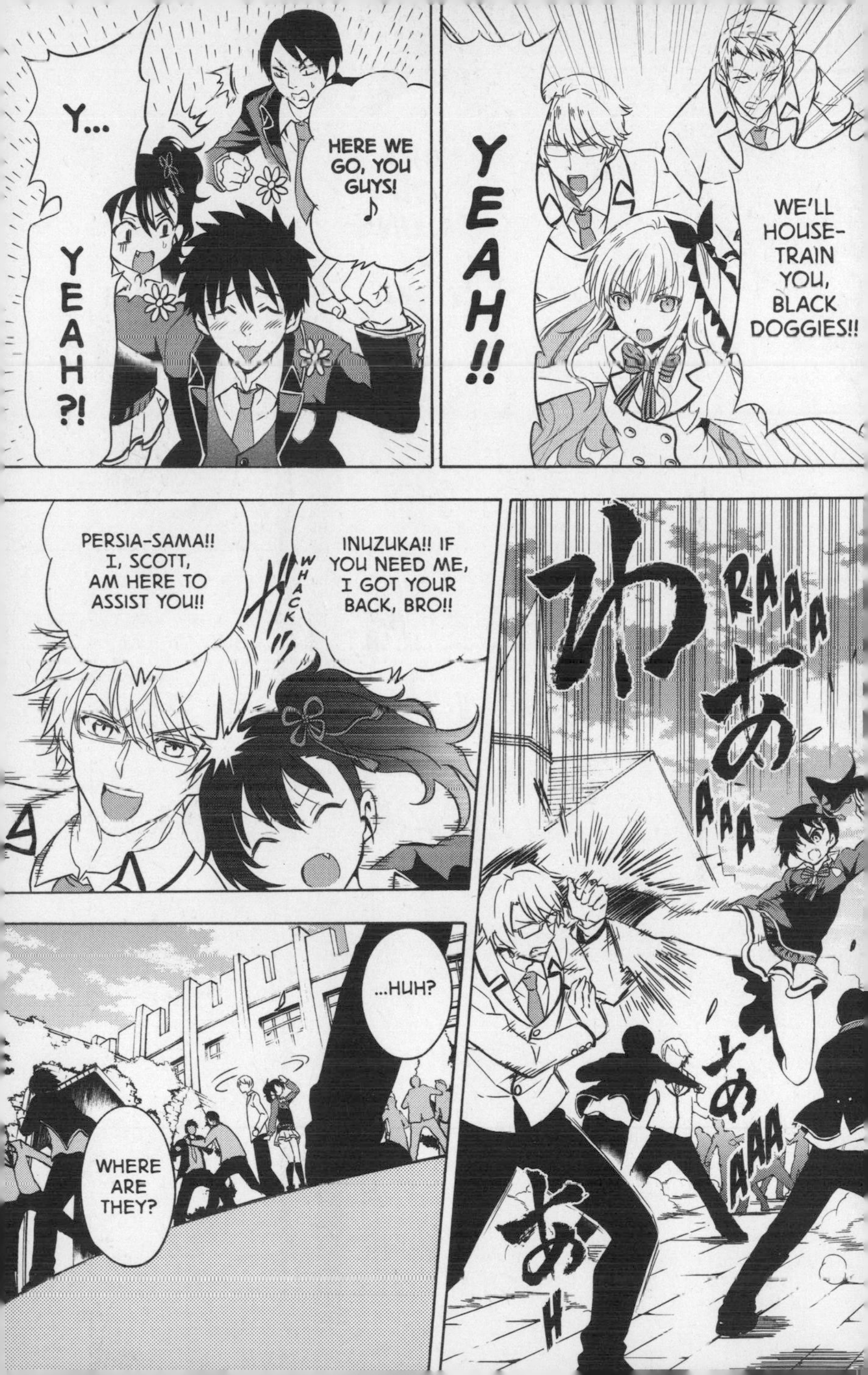
WE'LL HOUSE-TRAIN YOU, BLACK DOGGIES!!
YEAH!!
HERE WE GO, YOU GUYS! ♪
Y... YEAH?!
わあああ
RAAAAAAAAAAAH
INUZUKA!! IF YOU NEED ME, I GOT YOUR BACK, BRO!!
WHACK
PERSIA-SAMA!! I, SCOTT, AM HERE TO ASSIST YOU!!
...HUH?
WHERE ARE THEY?

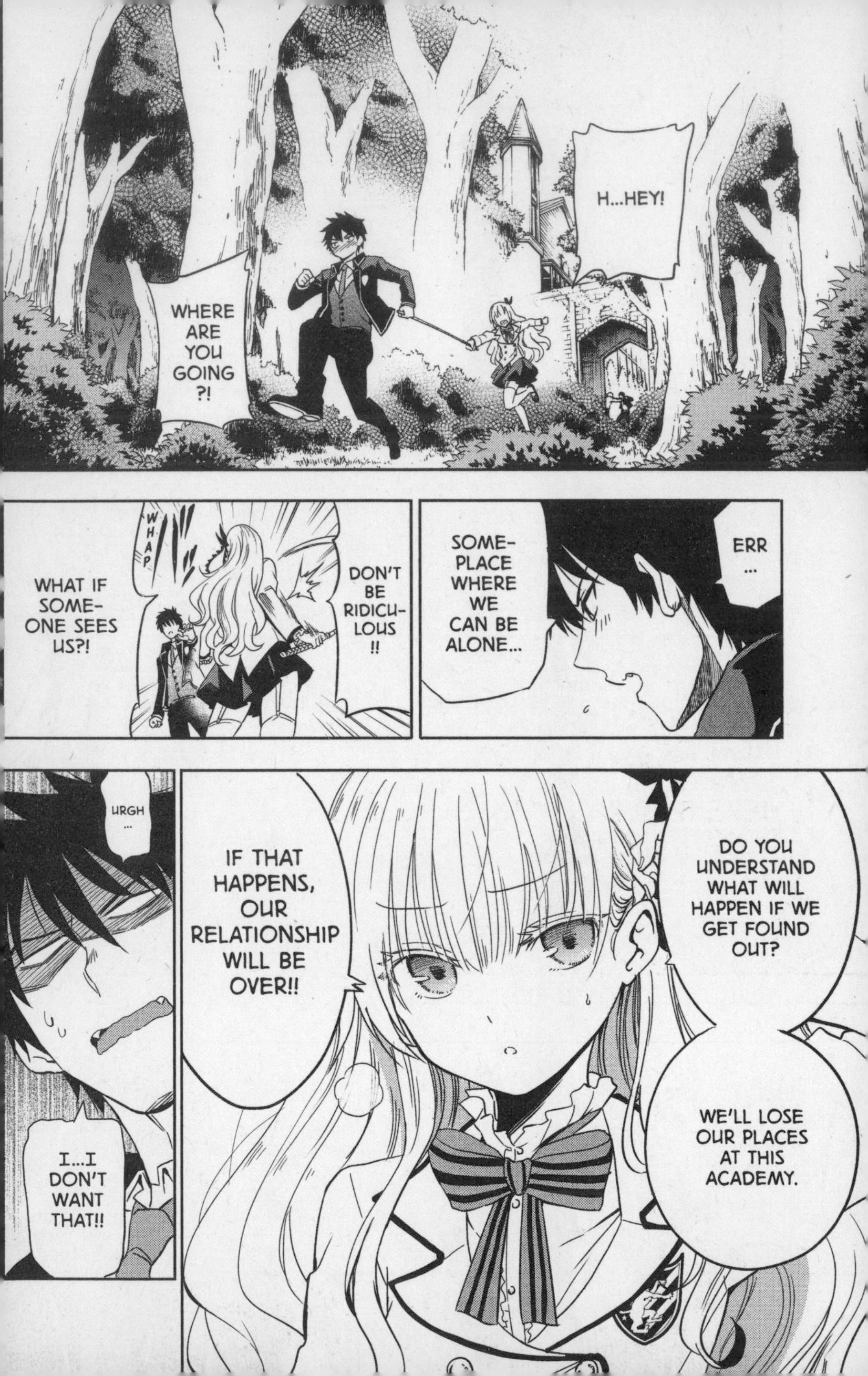
H...HEY!
WHERE ARE YOU GOING ?!
ERR ...
SOME-PLACE WHERE WE CAN BE ALONE...
DON'T BE RIDICU-LOUS !!
WHAP
WHAT IF SOME-ONE SEES US?!
DO YOU UNDERSTAND WHAT WILL HAPPEN IF WE GET FOUND OUT?
WE'LL LOSE OUR PLACES AT THIS ACADEMY.
IF THAT HAPPENS, OUR RELATIONSHIP WILL BE OVER!!
URGH ...
I...I DON'T WANT THAT!!

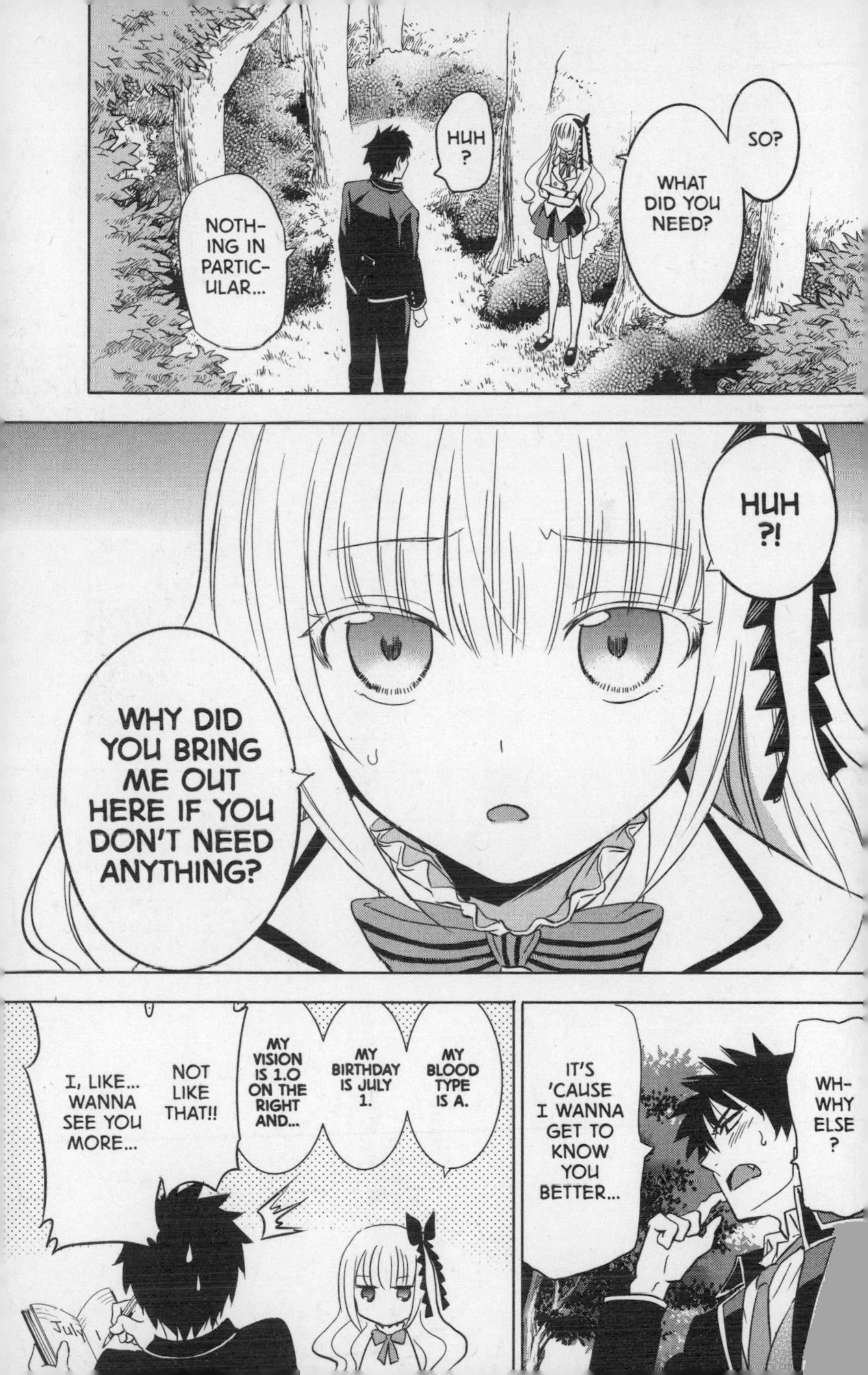
SO?
WHAT DID YOU NEED?
HUH ?
NOTHING IN PARTICULAR...
HUH ?!
WHY DID YOU BRING ME OUT HERE IF YOU DON'T NEED ANYTHING?
WH- WHY ELSE ?
IT'S 'CAUSE I WANNA GET TO KNOW YOU BETTER...
MY BLOOD TYPE IS A.
MY BIRTHDAY IS JULY 1.
MY VISION IS 1.0 ON THE RIGHT AND...
NOT LIKE THAT!!
I, LIKE... WANNA SEE YOU MORE...
July 1

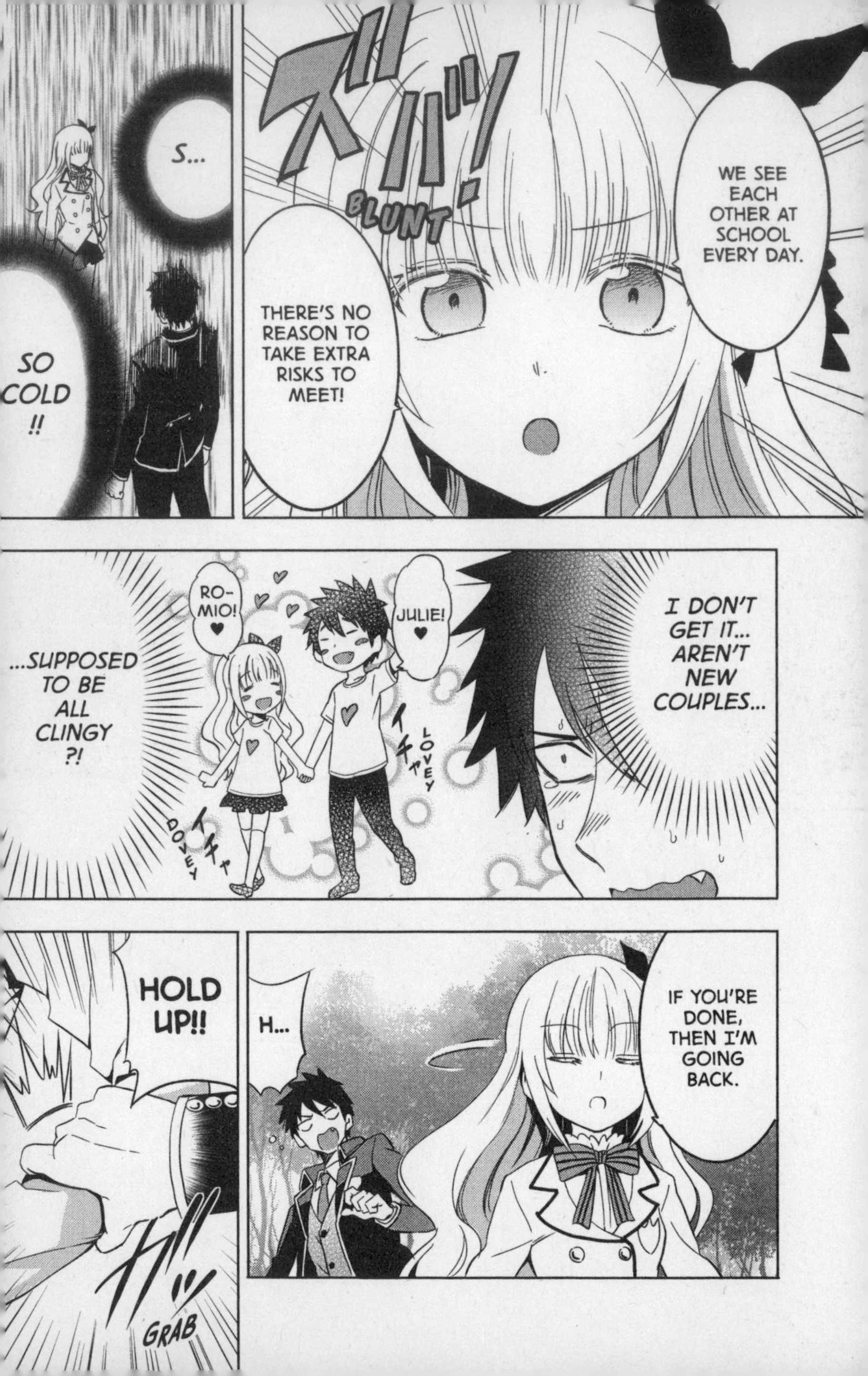
WE SEE EACH OTHER AT SCHOOL EVERY DAY.
ズバッ!
BLUNT
THERE'S NO REASON TO TAKE EXTRA RISKS TO MEET!
S...
SO COLD !!
I DON'T GET IT... AREN'T NEW COUPLES...
JULIE! ♥
RO-MIO! ♥
イチャ
LOVEY
イチャ
DOVEY
...SUPPOSED TO BE ALL CLINGY ?!
IF YOU'RE DONE, THEN I'M GOING BACK.
H...
HOLD UP!!
GRAB

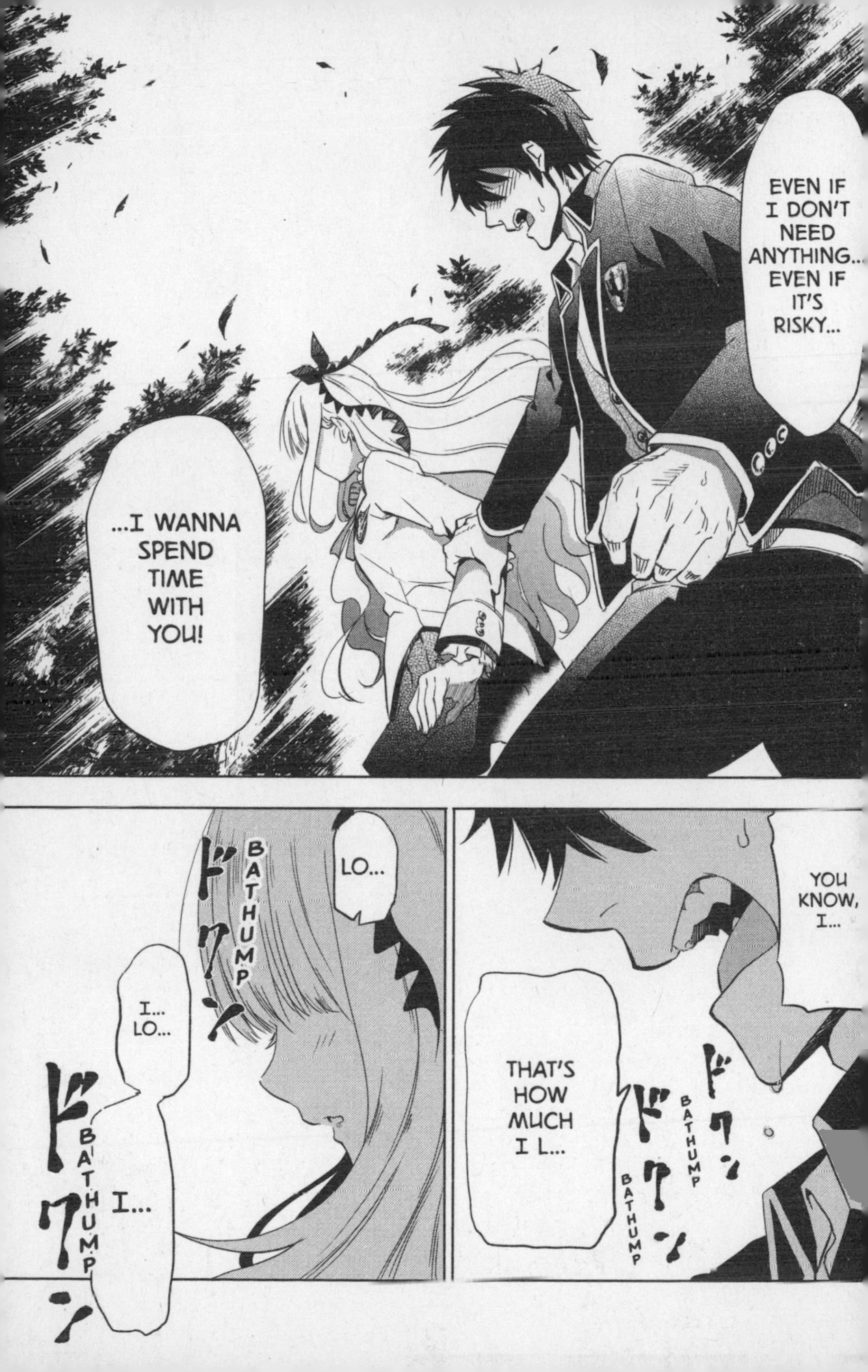
EVEN IF I DON'T NEED ANYTHING... EVEN IF IT'S RISKY...
...I WANNA SPEND TIME WITH YOU!
YOU KNOW, I...
THAT'S HOW MUCH I L...
BATHUMP
BATHUMP
LO...
BATHUMP
I... LO...
I...
BATHUMP

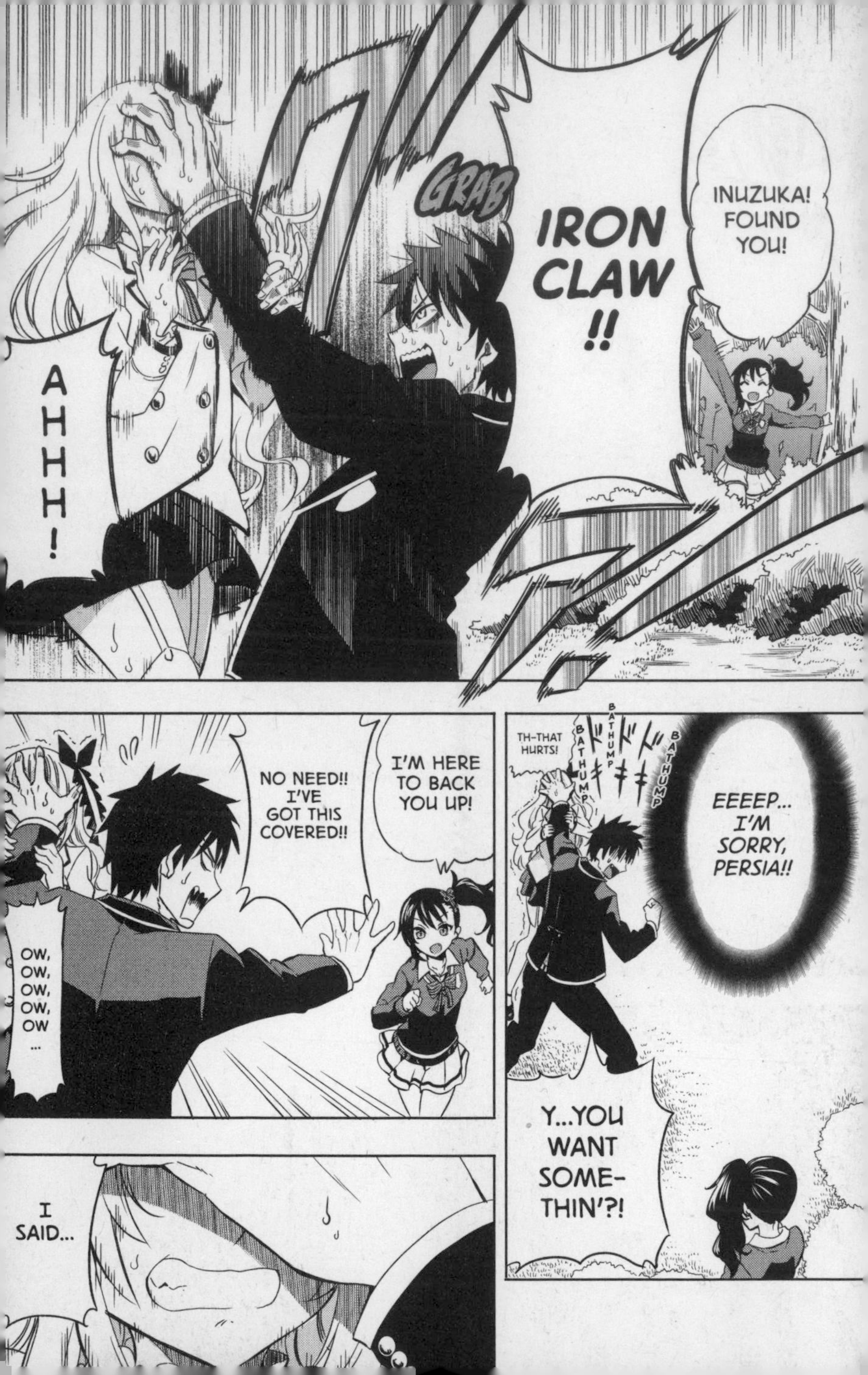
INUZUKA! FOUND YOU!
IRON CLAW !!
GRAB
AHHH!
TH-THAT HURTS!
BATHUMP
BATHUMP
BATHUMP
EEEEP... I'M SORRY, PERSIA!!
Y...YOU WANT SOME-THIN'?!
I'M HERE TO BACK YOU UP!
NO NEED!! I'VE GOT THIS COVERED!!
OW, OW, OW, OW, OW ...
I SAID...

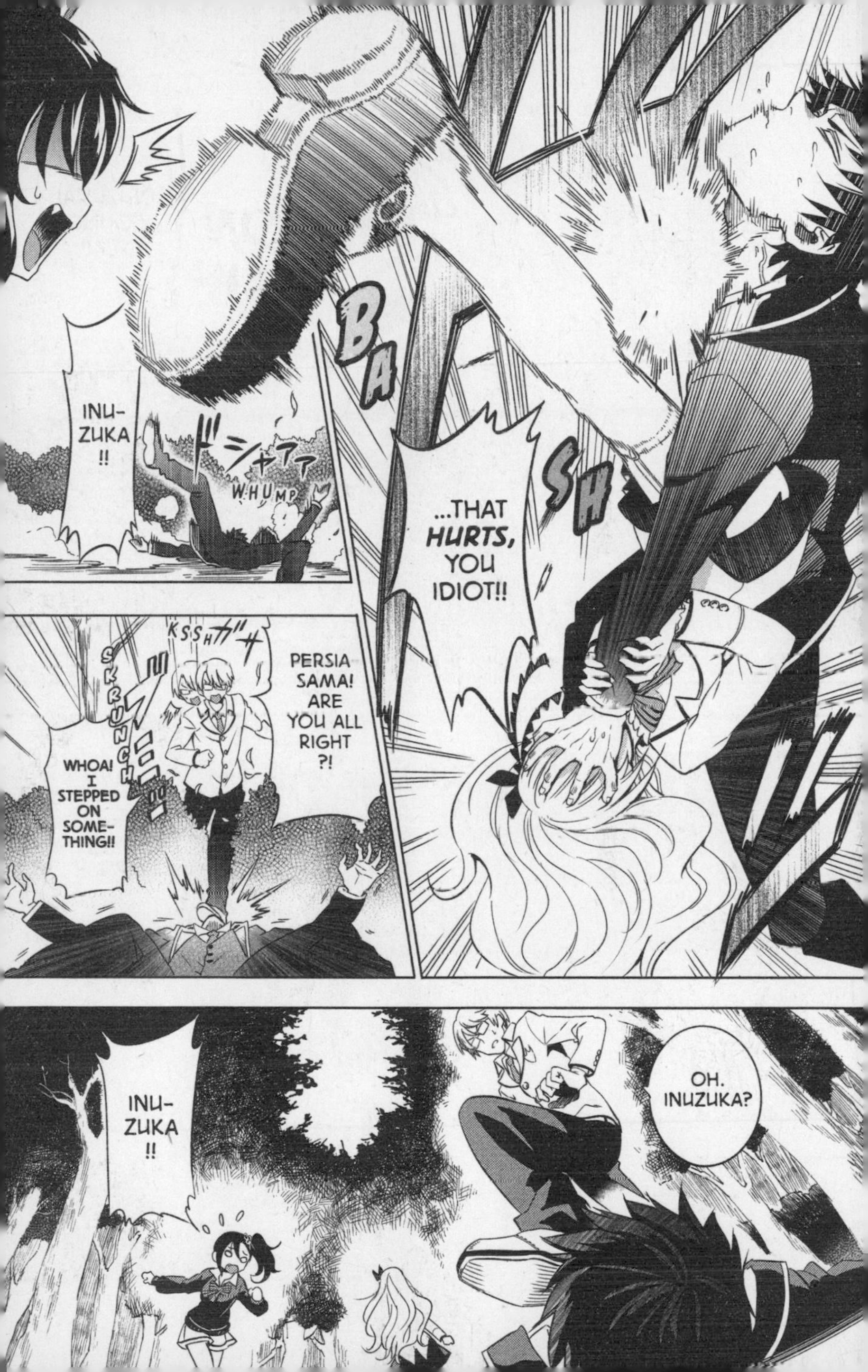
BA
SH
...THAT HURTS, YOU IDIOT!!
INU-ZUKA !!
WHUMP
PERSIA SAMA! ARE YOU ALL RIGHT ?!
KSSH
SKRUNCH
WHOA! I STEPPED ON SOME-THING!!
OH. INUZUKA?
INU-ZUKA !!

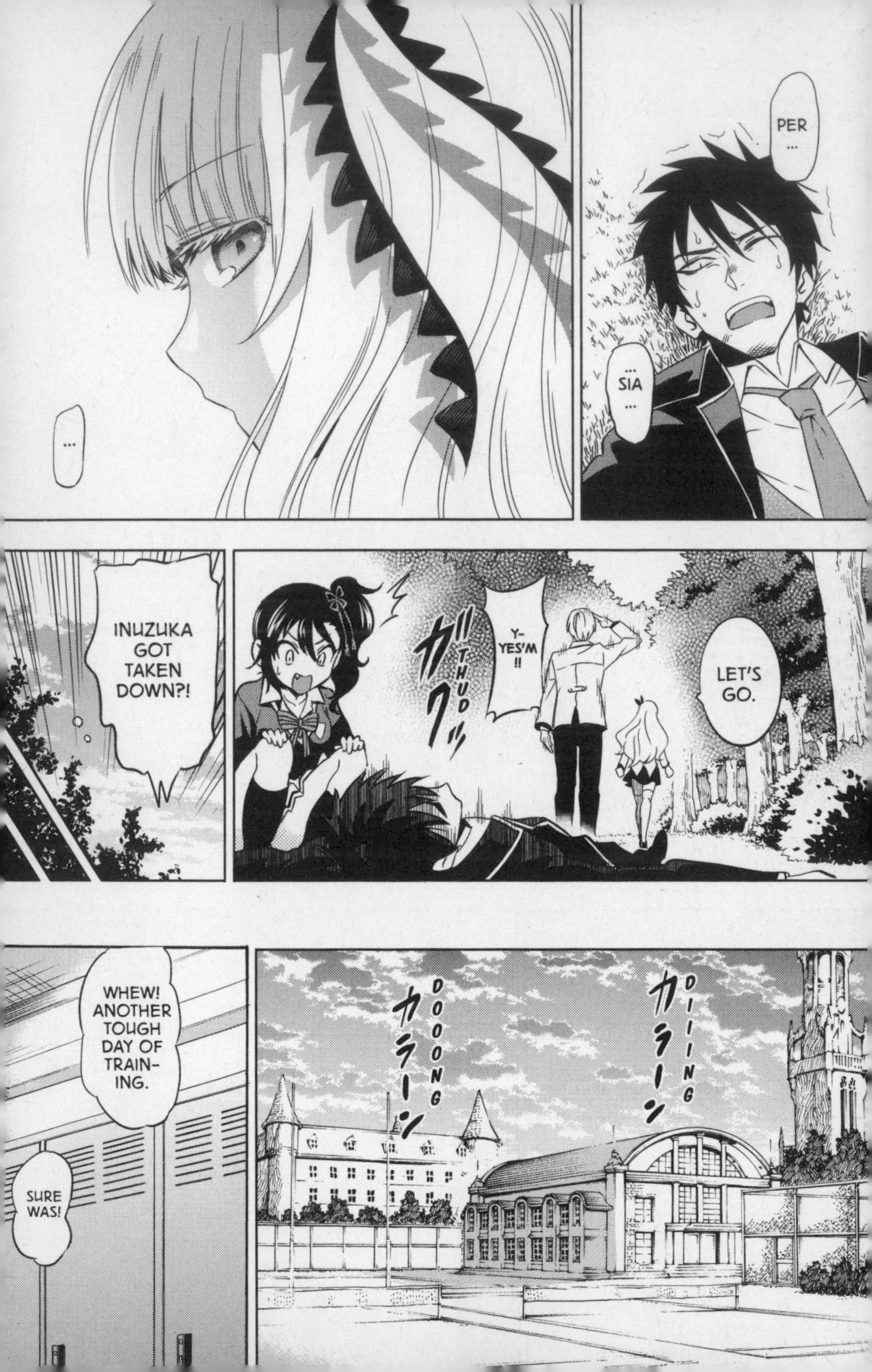
PER...
...SIA...
...
LET'S GO.
Y-YES'M!!
THUD
INUZUKA GOT TAKEN DOWN?!
DIIING
DOOONG
WHEW! ANOTHER TOUGH DAY OF TRAIN-ING.
SURE WAS!

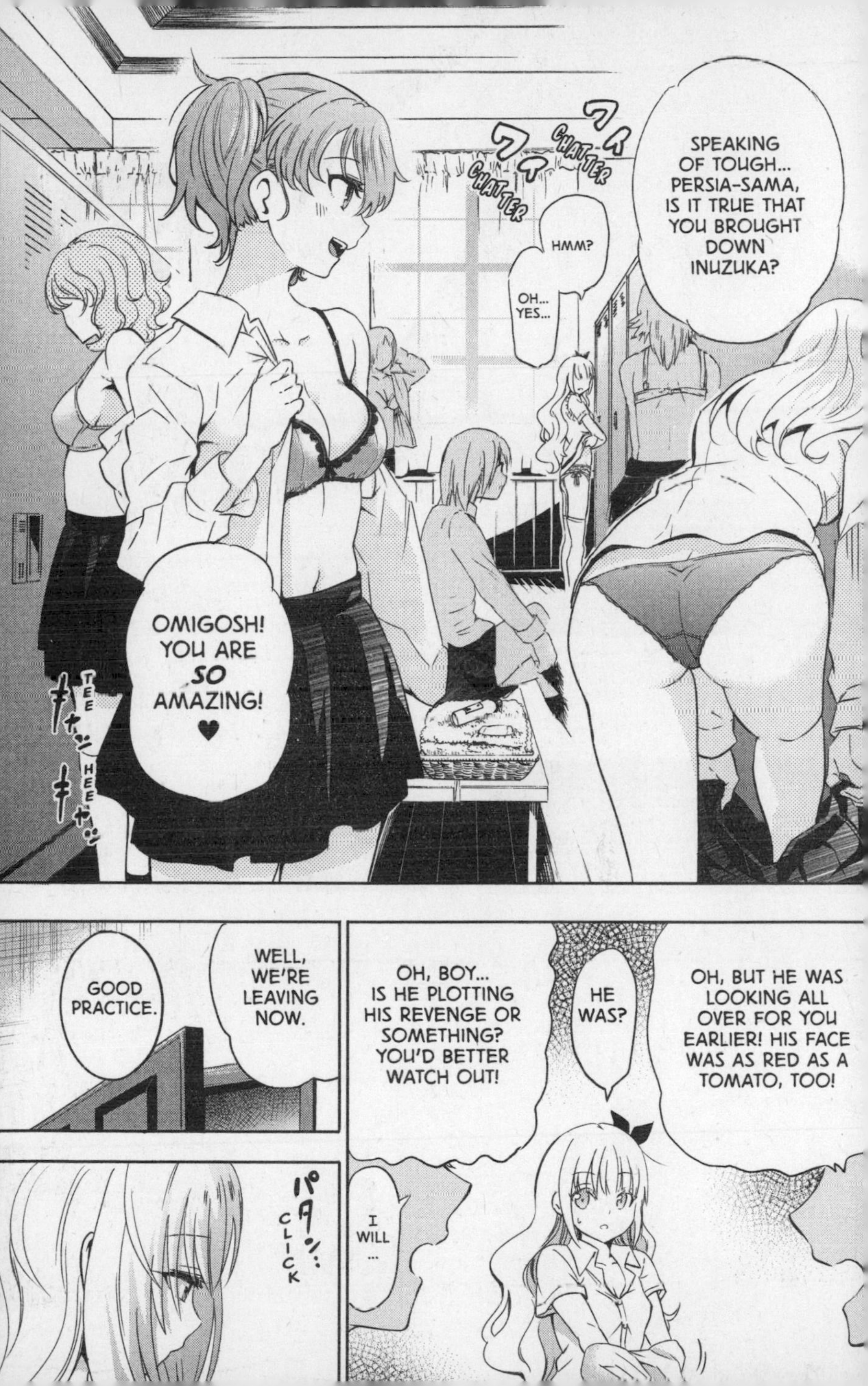
SPEAKING OF TOUGH... PERSIA-SAMA, IS IT TRUE THAT YOU BROUGHT DOWN INUZUKA?
CHATTER
CHATTER
HMM?
OH... YES...
OMIGOSH! YOU ARE SO AMAZING! ♥
TEE HEE
OH, BUT HE WAS LOOKING ALL OVER FOR YOU EARLIER! HIS FACE WAS AS RED AS A TOMATO, TOO!
HE WAS?
OH, BOY... IS HE PLOTTING HIS REVENGE OR SOMETHING? YOU'D BETTER WATCH OUT!
WELL, WE'RE LEAVING NOW.
GOOD PRACTICE.
I WILL ...
CLICK

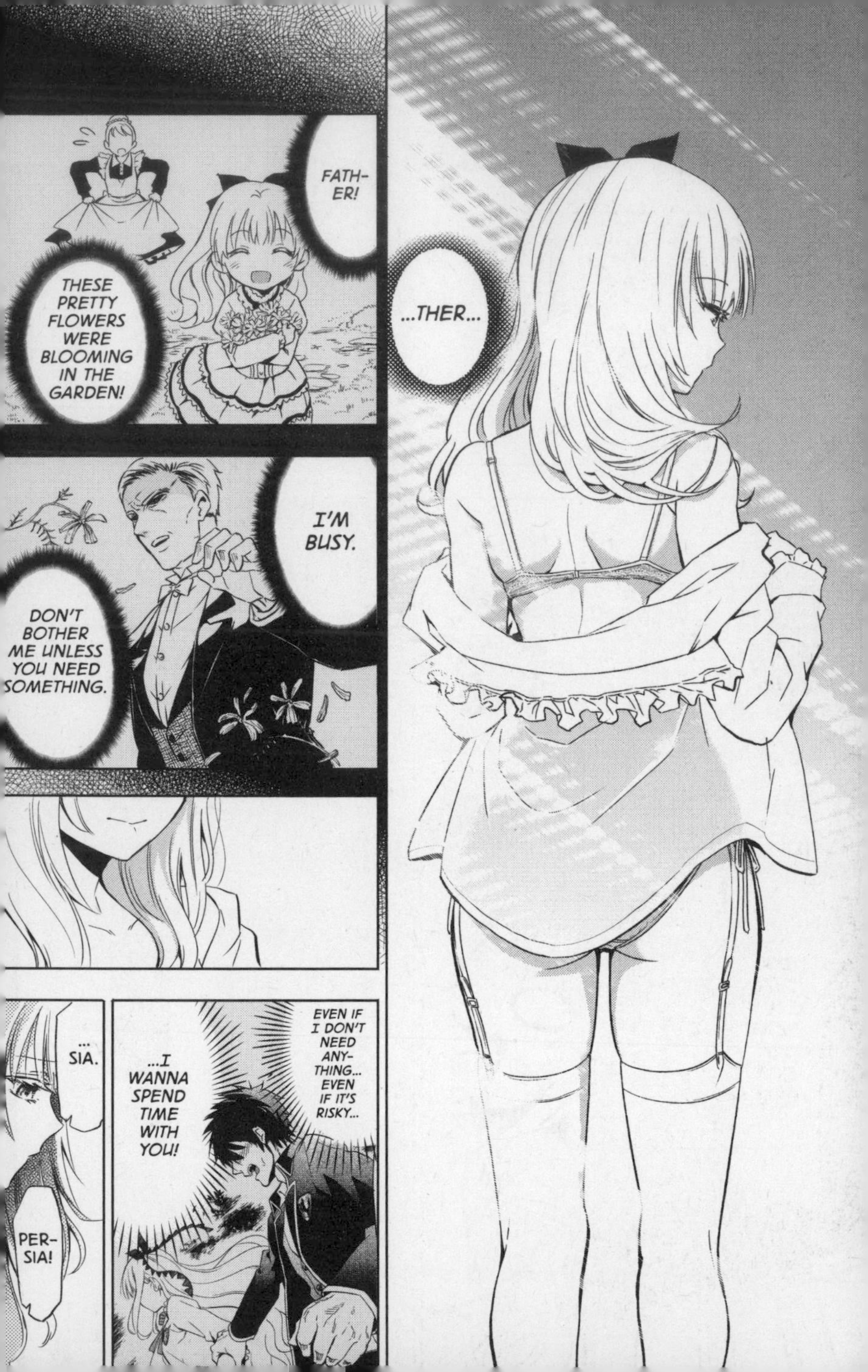
...THER...
FATHER-ER!
THESE PRETTY FLOWERS WERE BLOOMING IN THE GARDEN!
I'M BUSY.
DON'T BOTHER ME UNLESS YOU NEED SOMETHING.
EVEN IF I DON'T NEED ANYTHING... EVEN IF IT'S RISKY...
...I WANNA SPEND TIME WITH YOU!
...SIA.
PER-SIA!

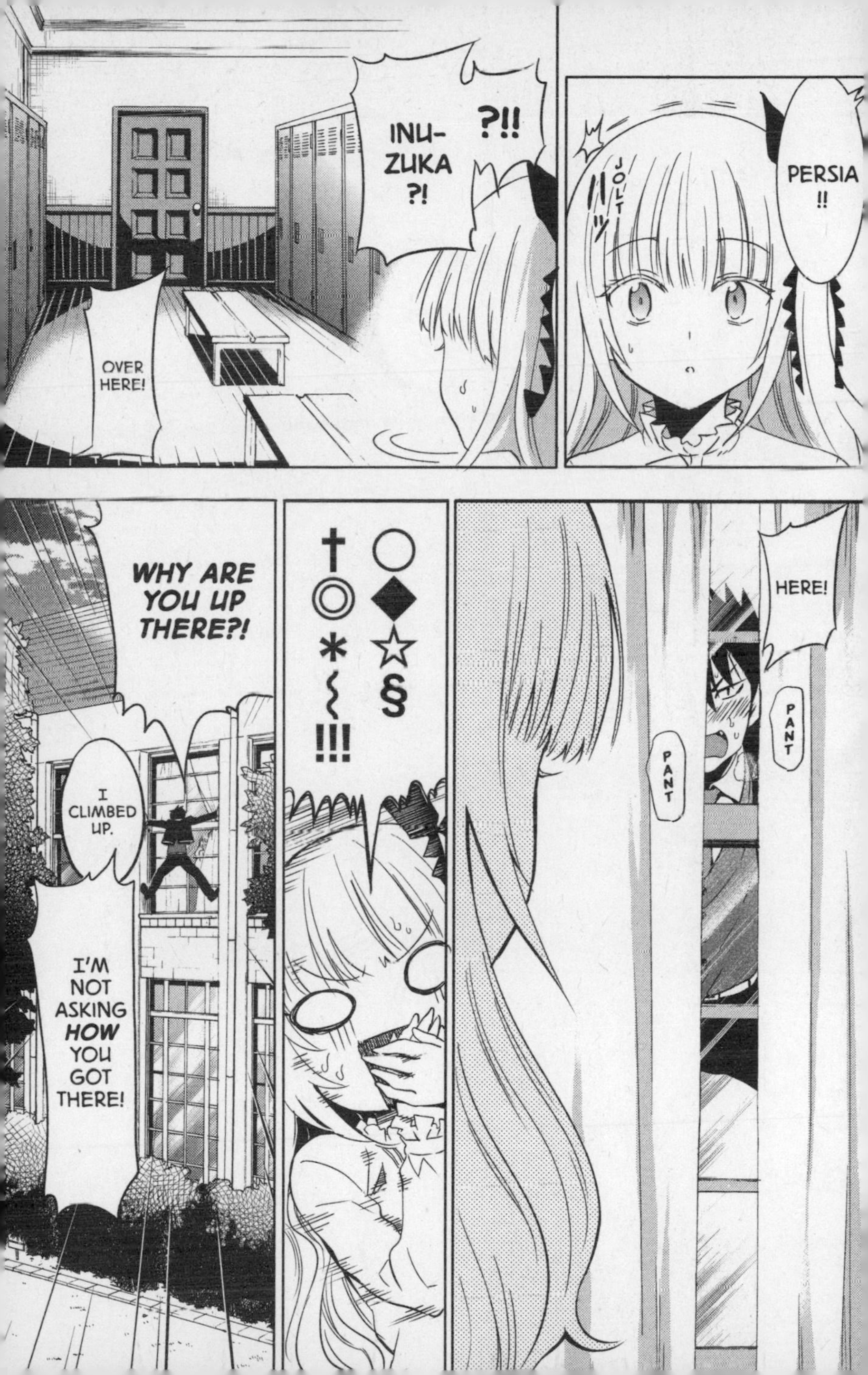
PERSIA !!
JOLT
?!!
INU-ZUKA ?!
OVER HERE!
HERE!
PANT
PANT
○◆☆§
†◎*~!!!
WHY ARE YOU UP THERE?!
I CLIMBED UP.
I'M NOT ASKING *HOW* YOU GOT THERE!

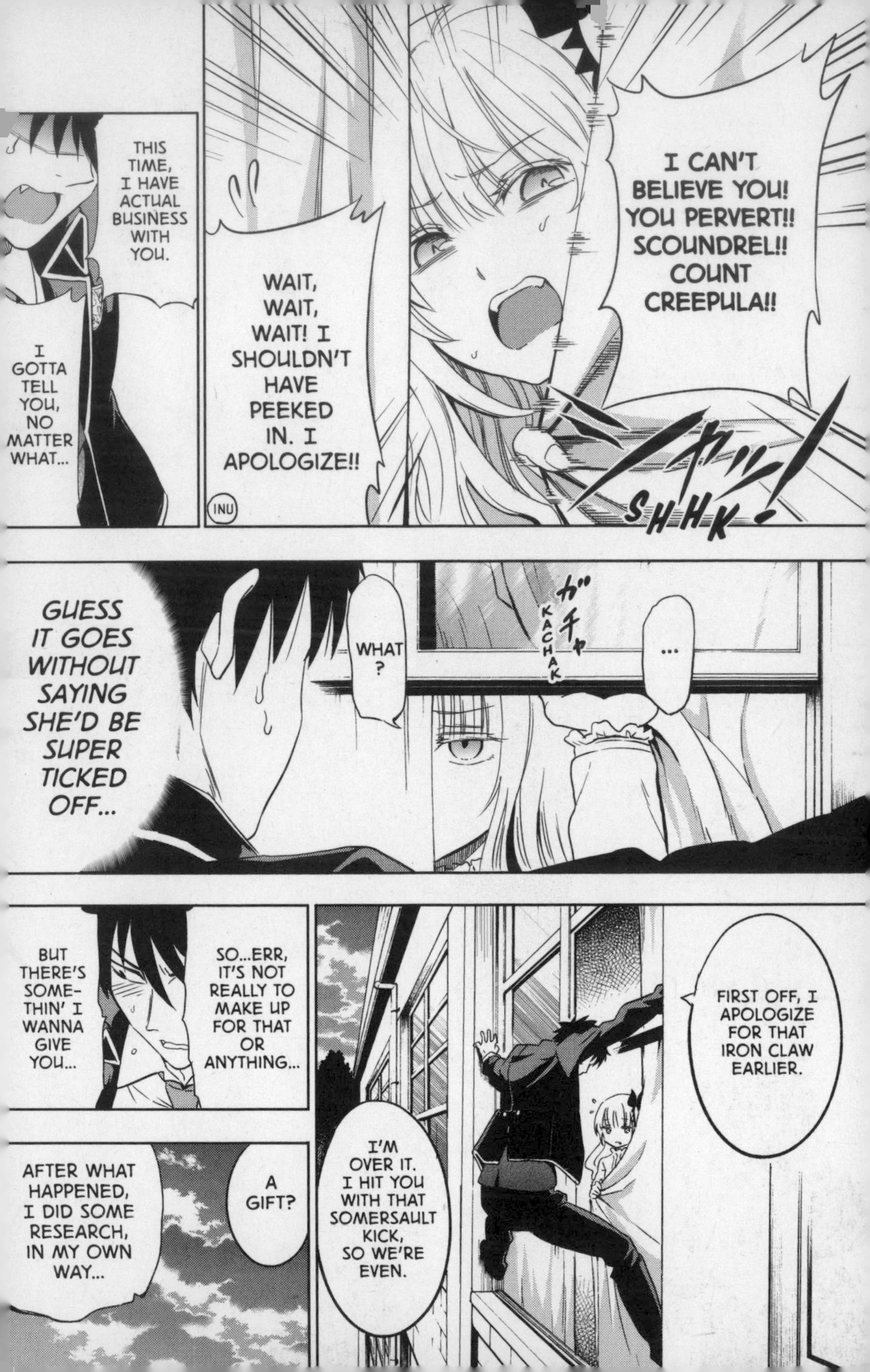
I CAN'T BELIEVE YOU! YOU PERVERT!! SCOUNDREL!! COUNT CREEPULA!!
SHHK!
WAIT, WAIT, WAIT! I SHOULDN'T HAVE PEEKED IN. I APOLOGIZE!!
INU
THIS TIME, I HAVE ACTUAL BUSINESS WITH YOU.
I GOTTA TELL YOU, NO MATTER WHAT...
...
ガチャ KACHAK
WHAT?
GUESS IT GOES WITHOUT SAYING SHE'D BE SUPER TICKED OFF...
FIRST OFF, I APOLOGIZE FOR THAT IRON CLAW EARLIER.
I'M OVER IT. I HIT YOU WITH THAT SOMERSAULT KICK, SO WE'RE EVEN.
SO...ERR, IT'S NOT REALLY TO MAKE UP FOR THAT OR ANYTHING...
BUT THERE'S SOMETHIN' I WANNA GIVE YOU...
A GIFT?
AFTER WHAT HAPPENED, I DID SOME RESEARCH, IN MY OWN WAY...

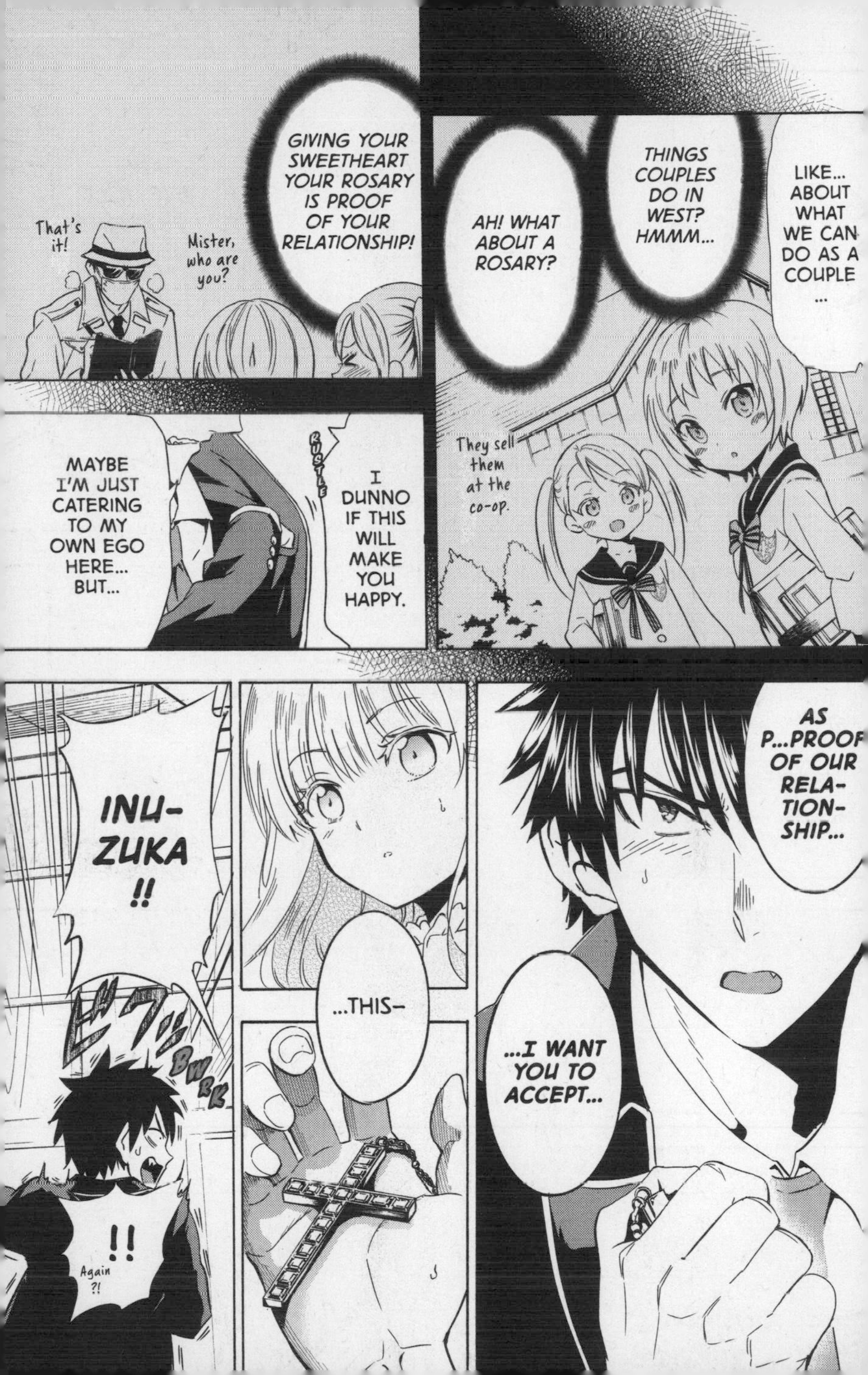
LIKE... ABOUT WHAT WE CAN DO AS A COUPLE ...
THINGS COUPLES DO IN WEST? HMMM...
AH! WHAT ABOUT A ROSARY?
They sell them at the co-op.
GIVING YOUR SWEETHEART YOUR ROSARY IS PROOF OF YOUR RELATIONSHIP!
Mister, who are you?
That's it!
RUSTLE
I DUNNO IF THIS WILL MAKE YOU HAPPY.
MAYBE I'M JUST CATERING TO MY OWN EGO HERE... BUT...
AS P...PROOF OF OUR RELATIONSHIP...
...I WANT YOU TO ACCEPT...
...THIS-
INU-ZUKA !!
BWRK
!!
Again ?!

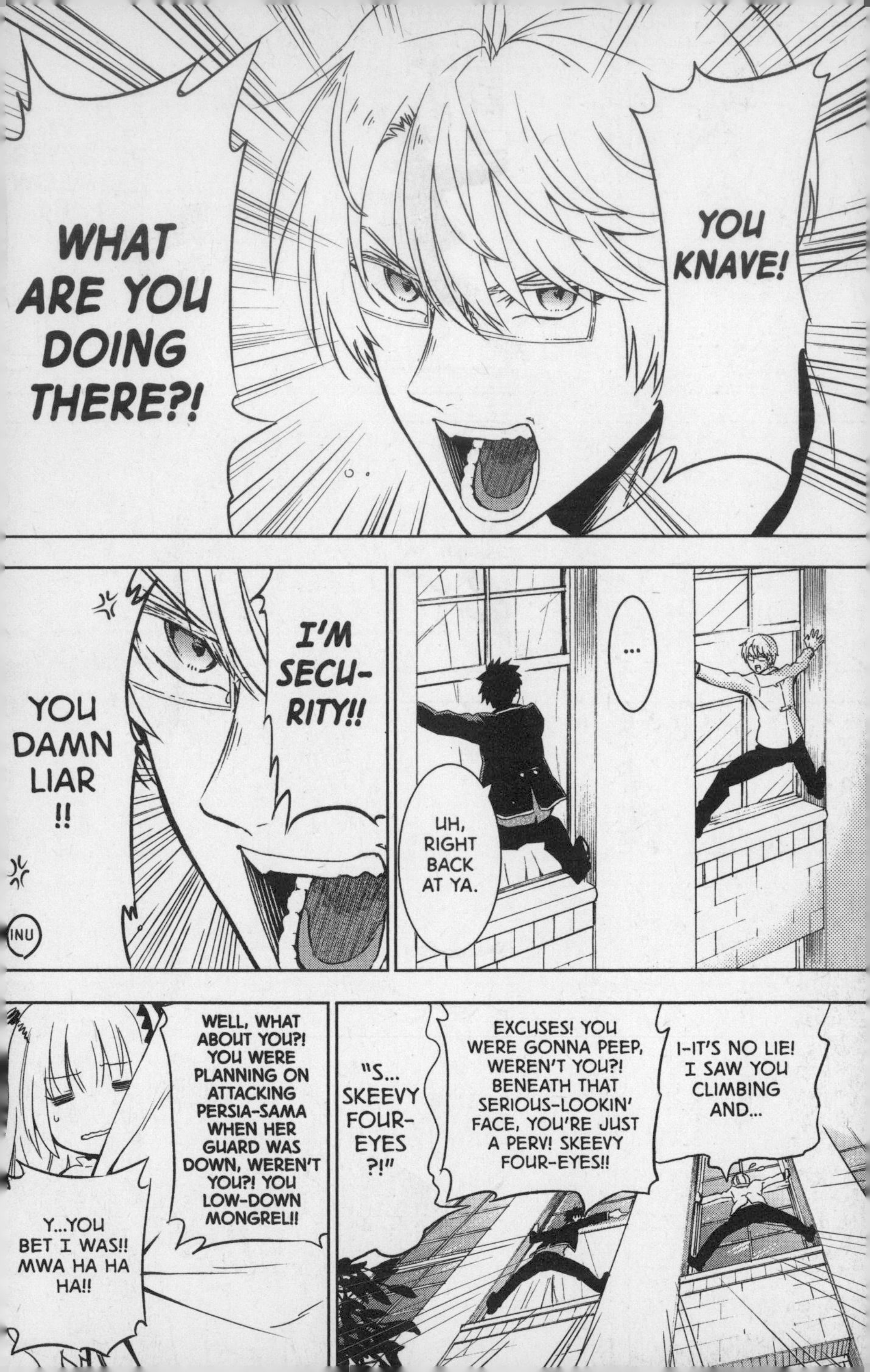
YOU KNAVE!
WHAT ARE YOU DOING THERE?!
...
UH, RIGHT BACK AT YA.
I'M SECU-RITY!!
YOU DAMN LIAR !!
INU
I-IT'S NO LIE! I SAW YOU CLIMBING AND...
EXCUSES! YOU WERE GONNA PEEP, WEREN'T YOU?! BENEATH THAT SERIOUS-LOOKIN' FACE, YOU'RE JUST A PERV! SKEEVY FOUR-EYES!!
"S... SKEEVY FOUR-EYES ?!"
WELL, WHAT ABOUT YOU?! YOU WERE PLANNING ON ATTACKING PERSIA-SAMA WHEN HER GUARD WAS DOWN, WEREN'T YOU?! YOU LOW-DOWN MONGREL!!
Y...YOU BET I WAS!! MWA HA HA HA!!

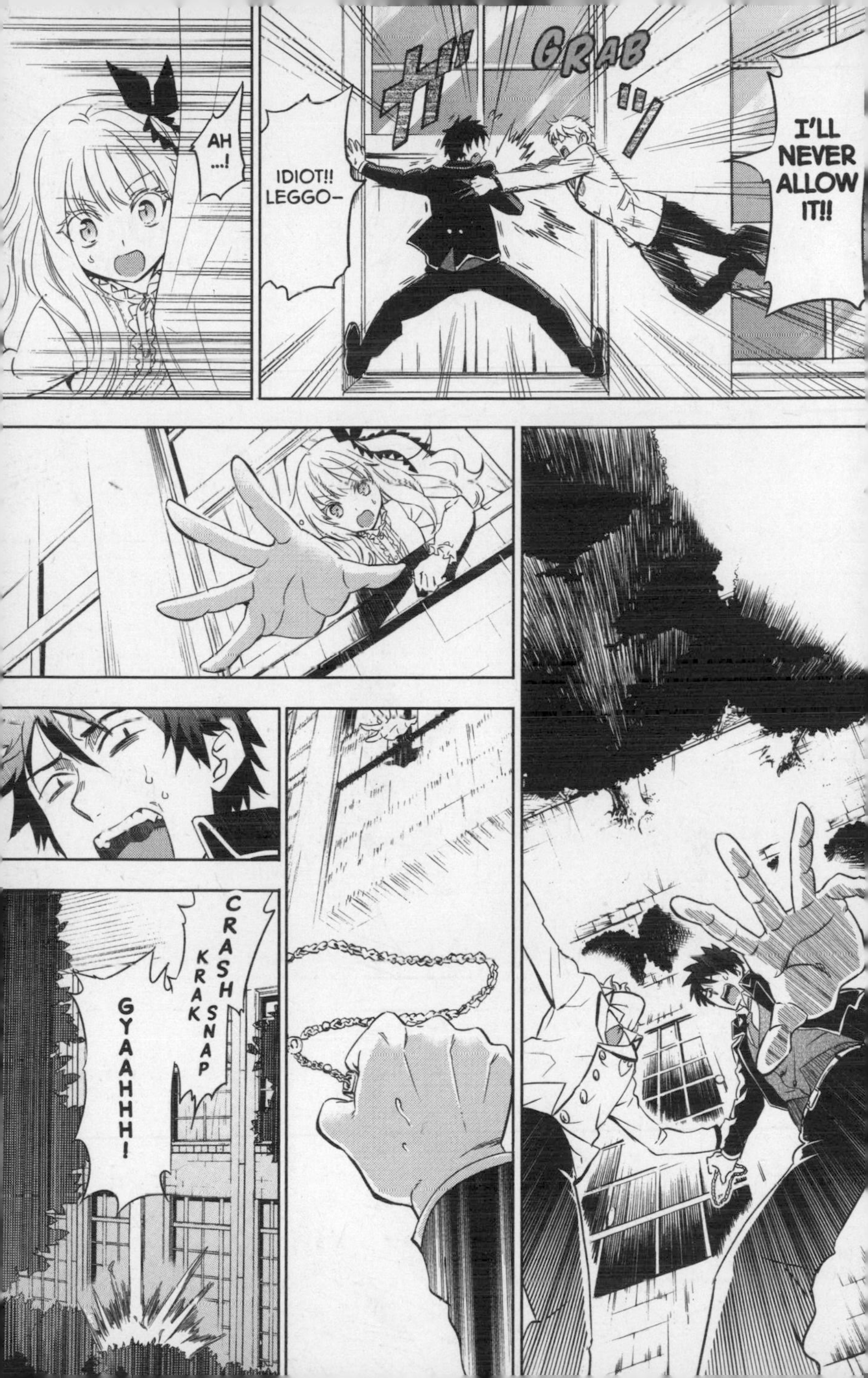
GRAB
I'LL NEVER ALLOW IT!!
IDIOT!! LEGGO–
AH ...!
CRASH
SNAP
KRAK
GYAAHHH!

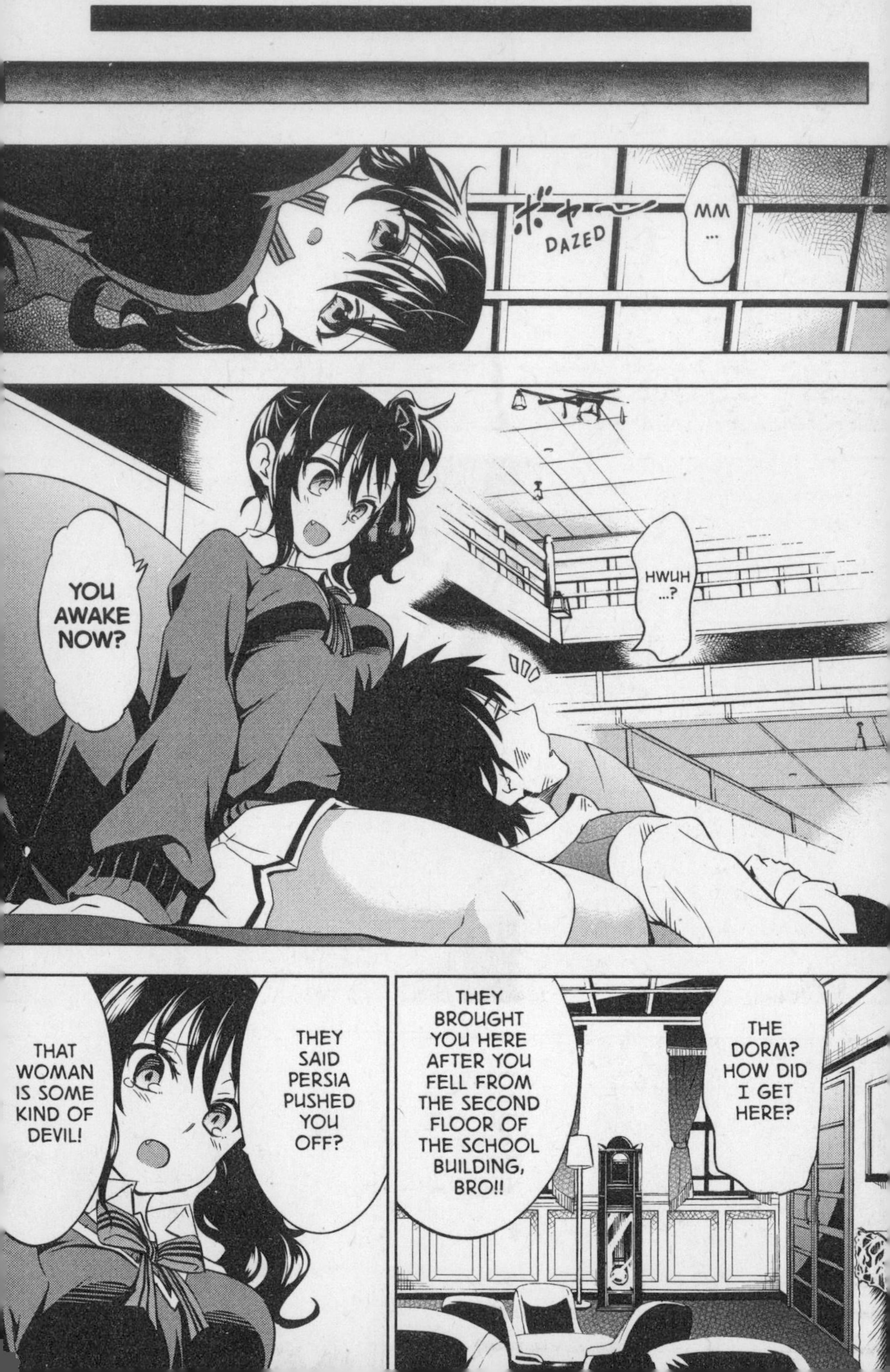
MM ...
ボヤ～
DAZED
HWUH ...?
YOU AWAKE NOW?
THE DORM? HOW DID I GET HERE?
THEY BROUGHT YOU HERE AFTER YOU FELL FROM THE SECOND FLOOR OF THE SCHOOL BUILDING, BRO!!
THEY SAID PERSIA PUSHED YOU OFF?
THAT WOMAN IS SOME KIND OF DEVIL!

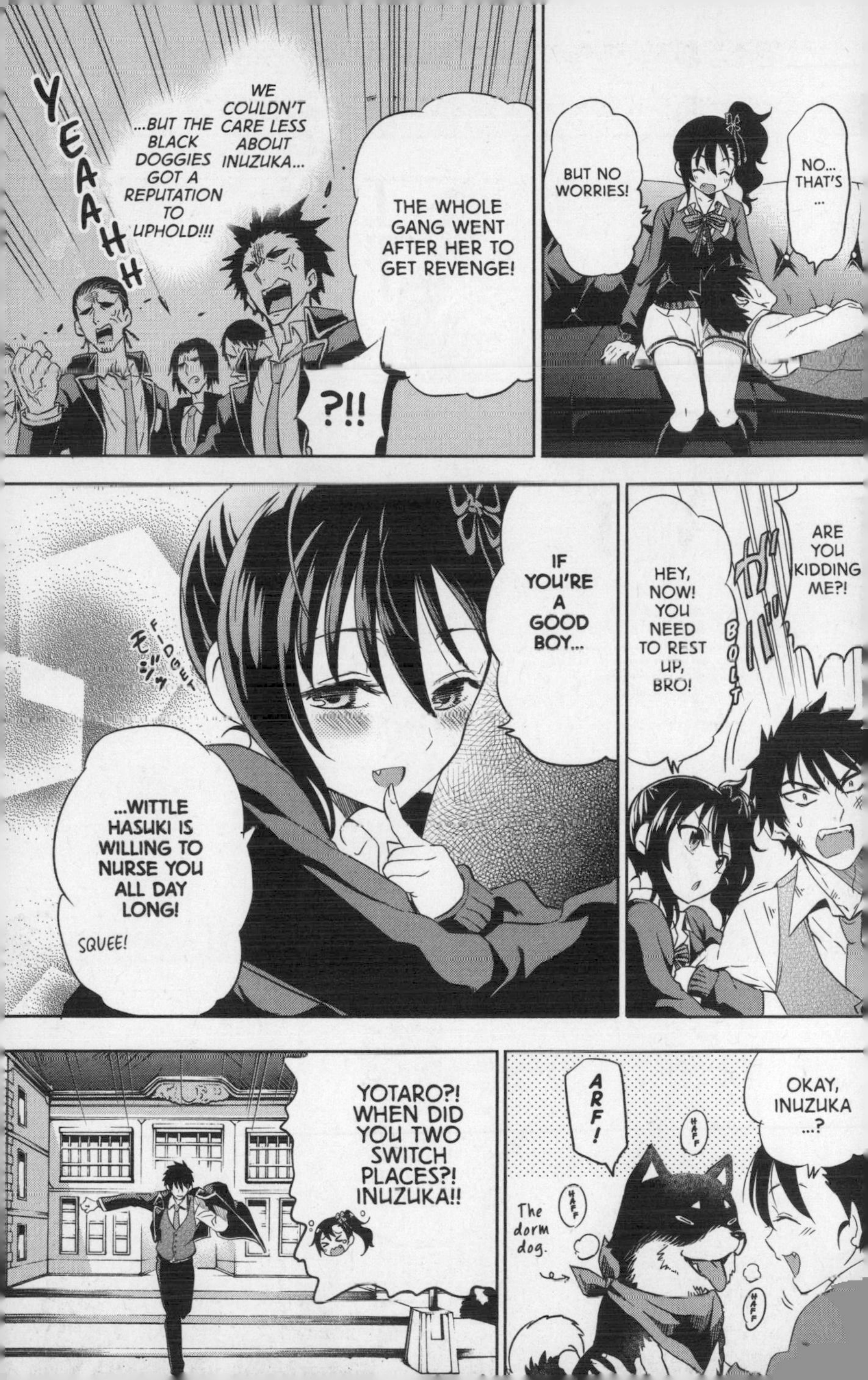
NO... THAT'S ...
BUT NO WORRIES!
THE WHOLE GANG WENT AFTER HER TO GET REVENGE!
WE COULDN'T CARE LESS ABOUT INUZUKA...
...BUT THE BLACK DOGGIES GOT A REPUTATION TO UPHOLD!!!
YEAAHHH
?!!
ARE YOU KIDDING ME?!
BOLT
HEY, NOW! YOU NEED TO REST UP, BRO!
IF YOU'RE A GOOD BOY...
FIDGET
...WITTLE HASUKI IS WILLING TO NURSE YOU ALL DAY LONG!
SQUEE!
OKAY, INUZUKA ...?
ARF!
HAFF
HAFF
HAFF
The dorm dog.
YOTARO?! WHEN DID YOU TWO SWITCH PLACES?! INUZUKA!!

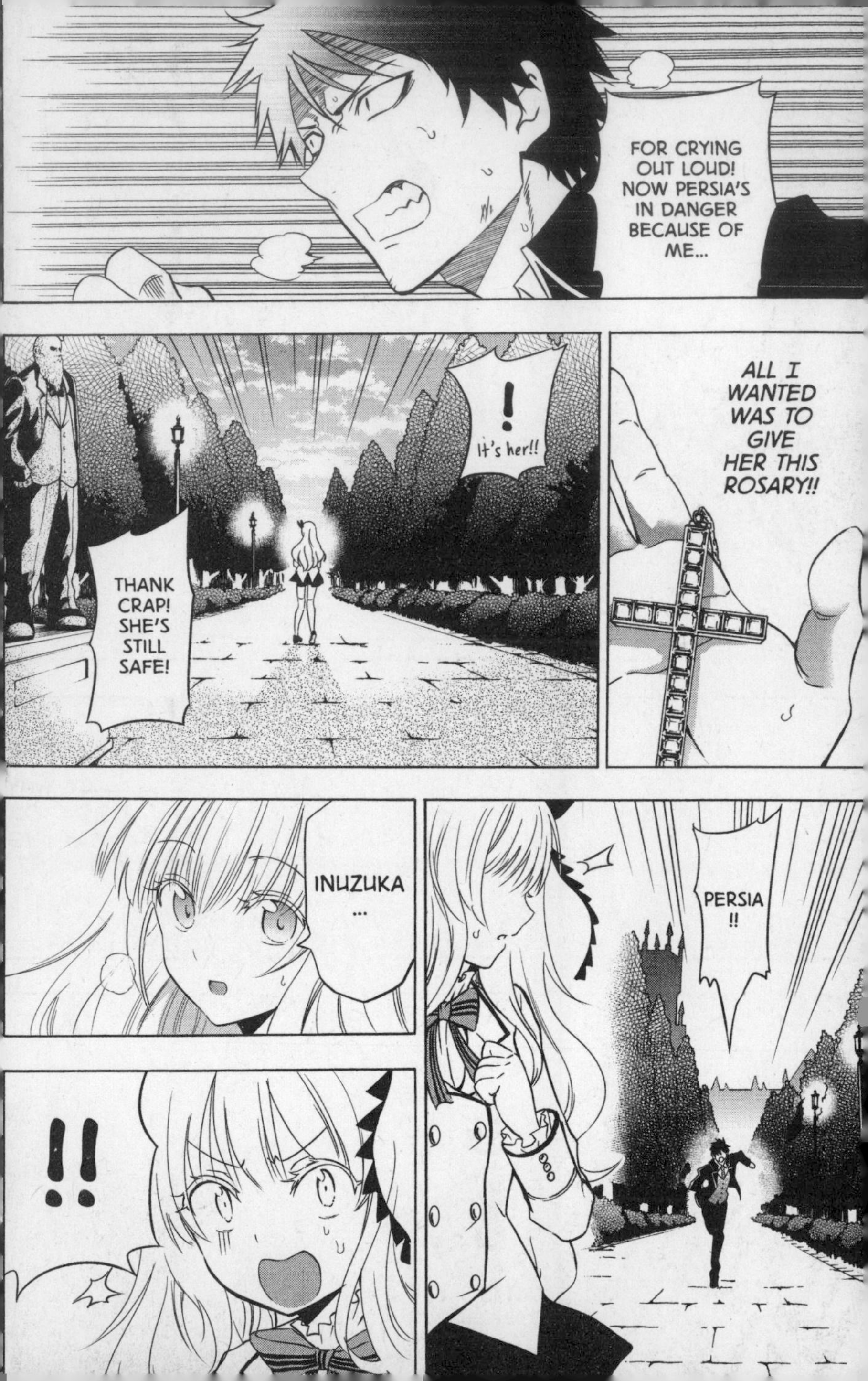
FOR CRYING OUT LOUD! NOW PERSIA'S IN DANGER BECAUSE OF ME...
ALL I WANTED WAS TO GIVE HER THIS ROSARY!!
!
It's her!!
THANK CRAP! SHE'S STILL SAFE!
PERSIA !!
INUZUKA ...
!!

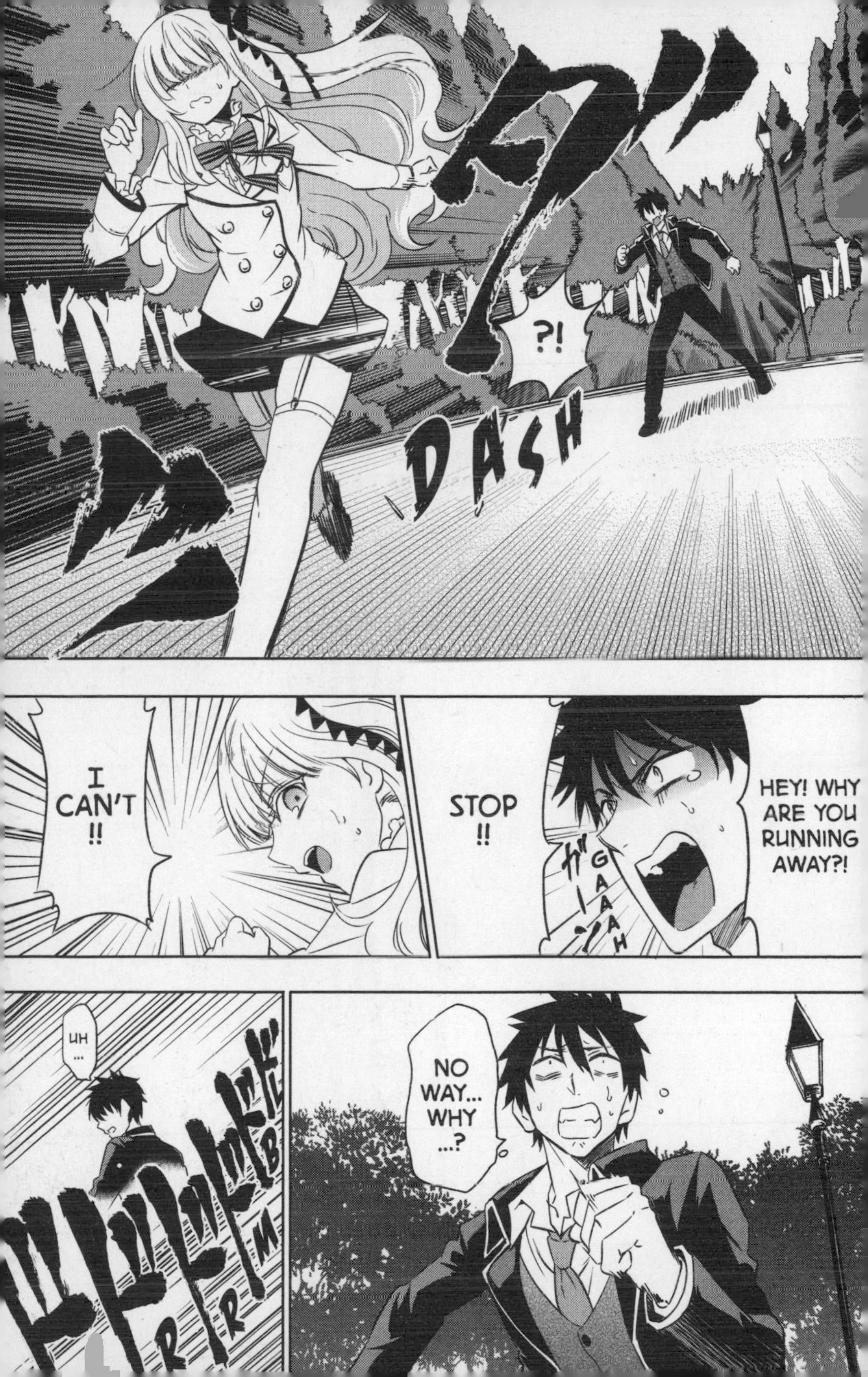

ダッ
?!
DASH
HEY! WHY ARE YOU RUNNING AWAY?!
GAAAH
STOP !!
I CAN'T !!
NO WAY... WHY ...?
UH ...
BRRRRM

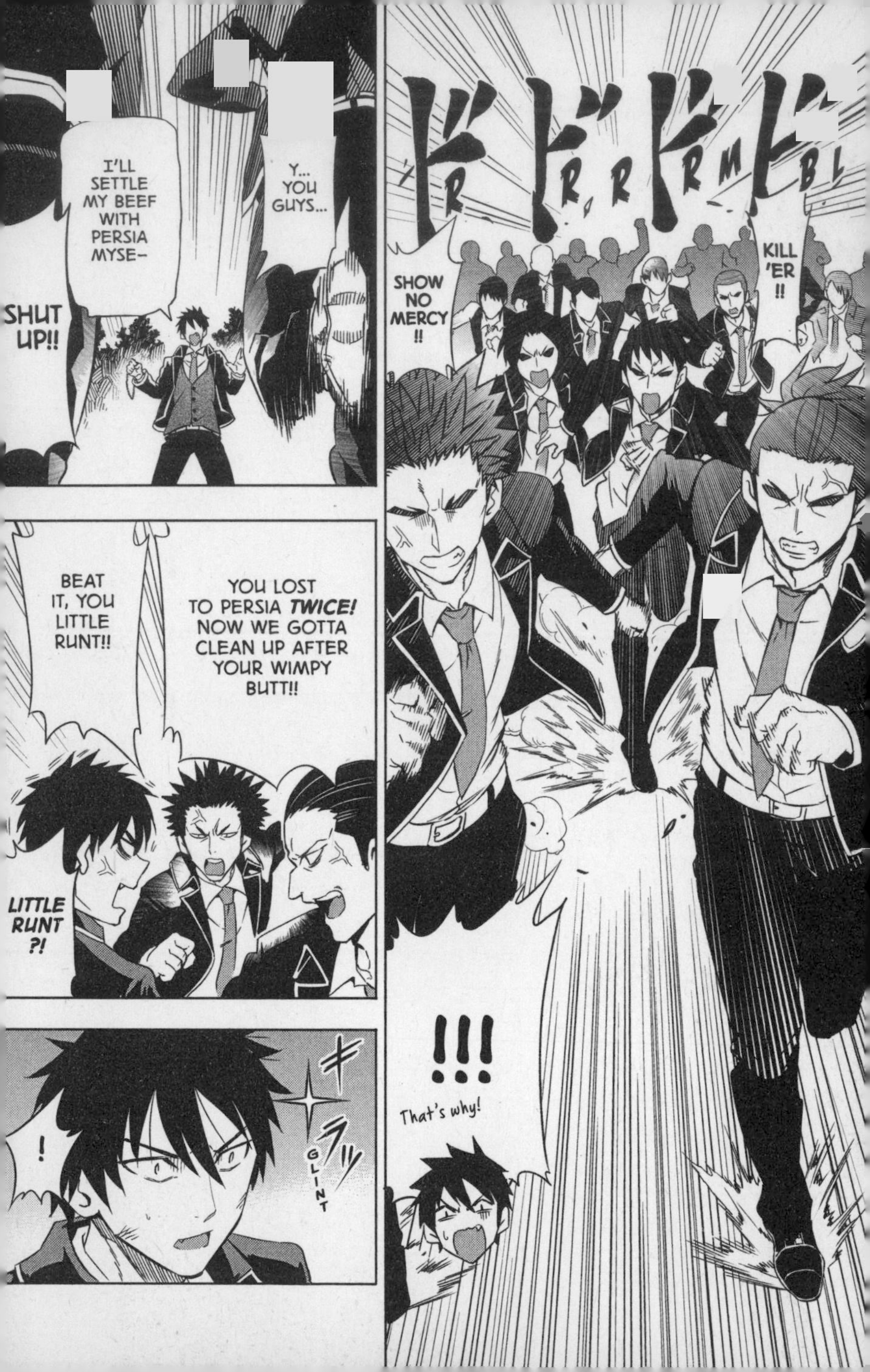
R R R R M B L
KILL 'ER!!
SHOW NO MERCY!!
!!!
That's why!
Y... YOU GUYS...
I'LL SETTLE MY BEEF WITH PERSIA MYSE–
SHUT UP!!
YOU LOST TO PERSIA TWICE! NOW WE GOTTA CLEAN UP AFTER YOUR WIMPY BUTT!!
BEAT IT, YOU LITTLE RUNT!!
LITTLE RUNT?!
!
GLINT

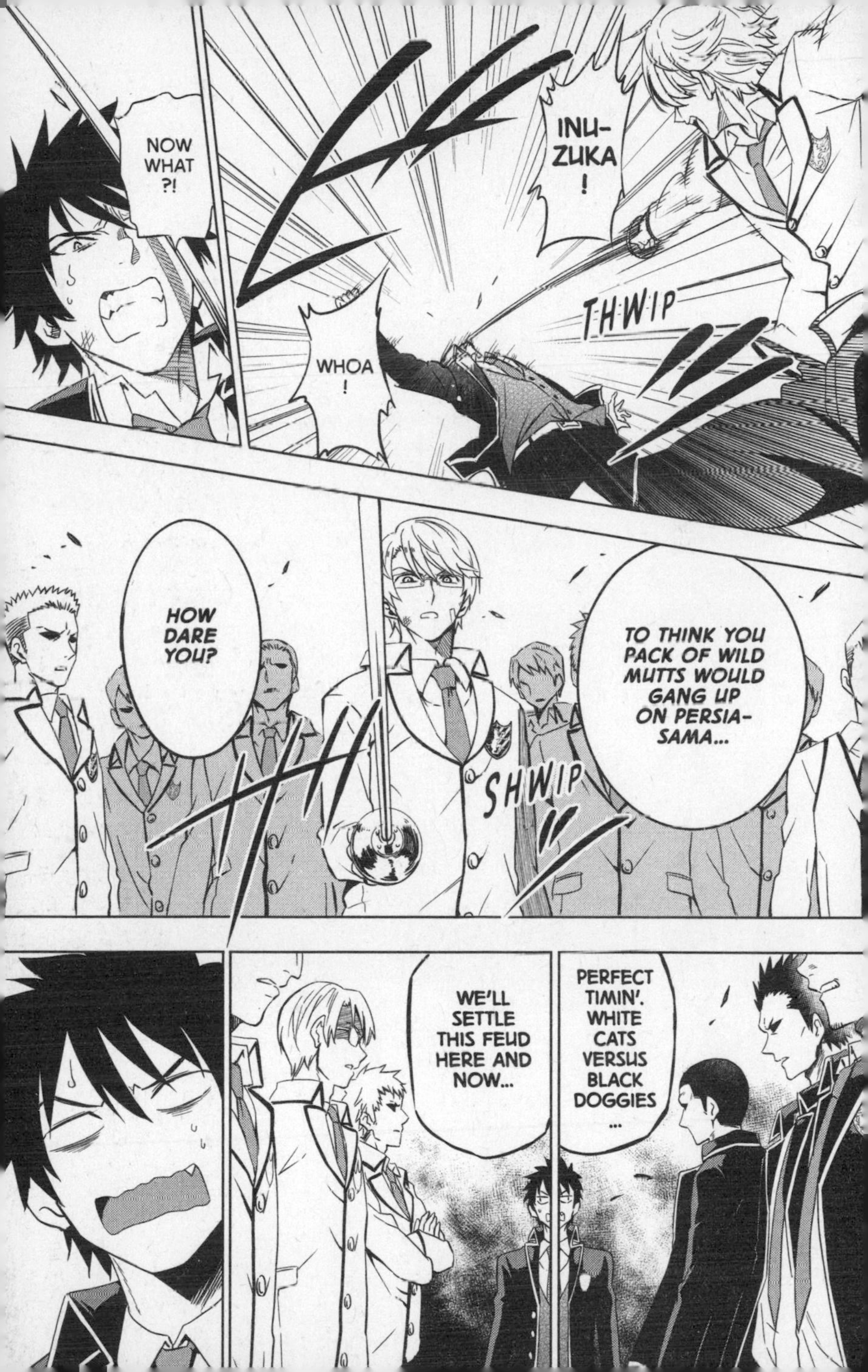
INUZUKA!
WHOA!
THWIP
NOW WHAT?!
TO THINK YOU PACK OF WILD MUTTS WOULD GANG UP ON PERSIA-SAMA...
SHWIP
HOW DARE YOU?
PERFECT TIMIN'. WHITE CATS VERSUS BLACK DOGGIES...
WE'LL SETTLE THIS FEUD HERE AND NOW...

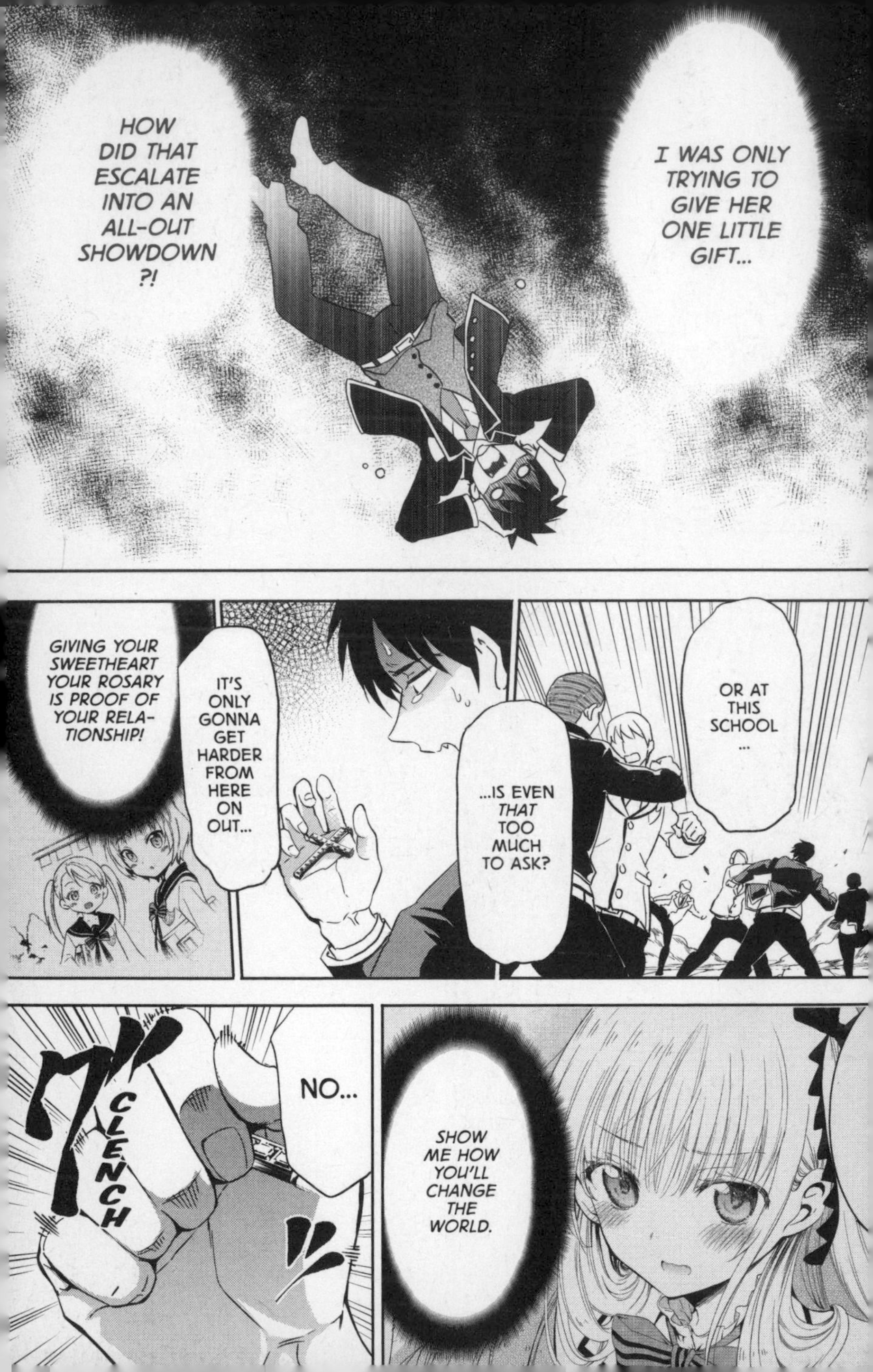
I WAS ONLY TRYING TO GIVE HER ONE LITTLE GIFT...
HOW DID THAT ESCALATE INTO AN ALL-OUT SHOWDOWN ?!
OR AT THIS SCHOOL ...
...IS EVEN THAT TOO MUCH TO ASK?
IT'S ONLY GONNA GET HARDER FROM HERE ON OUT...
GIVING YOUR SWEETHEART YOUR ROSARY IS PROOF OF YOUR RELA- TIONSHIP!
SHOW ME HOW YOU'LL CHANGE THE WORLD.
NO...
CLENCH

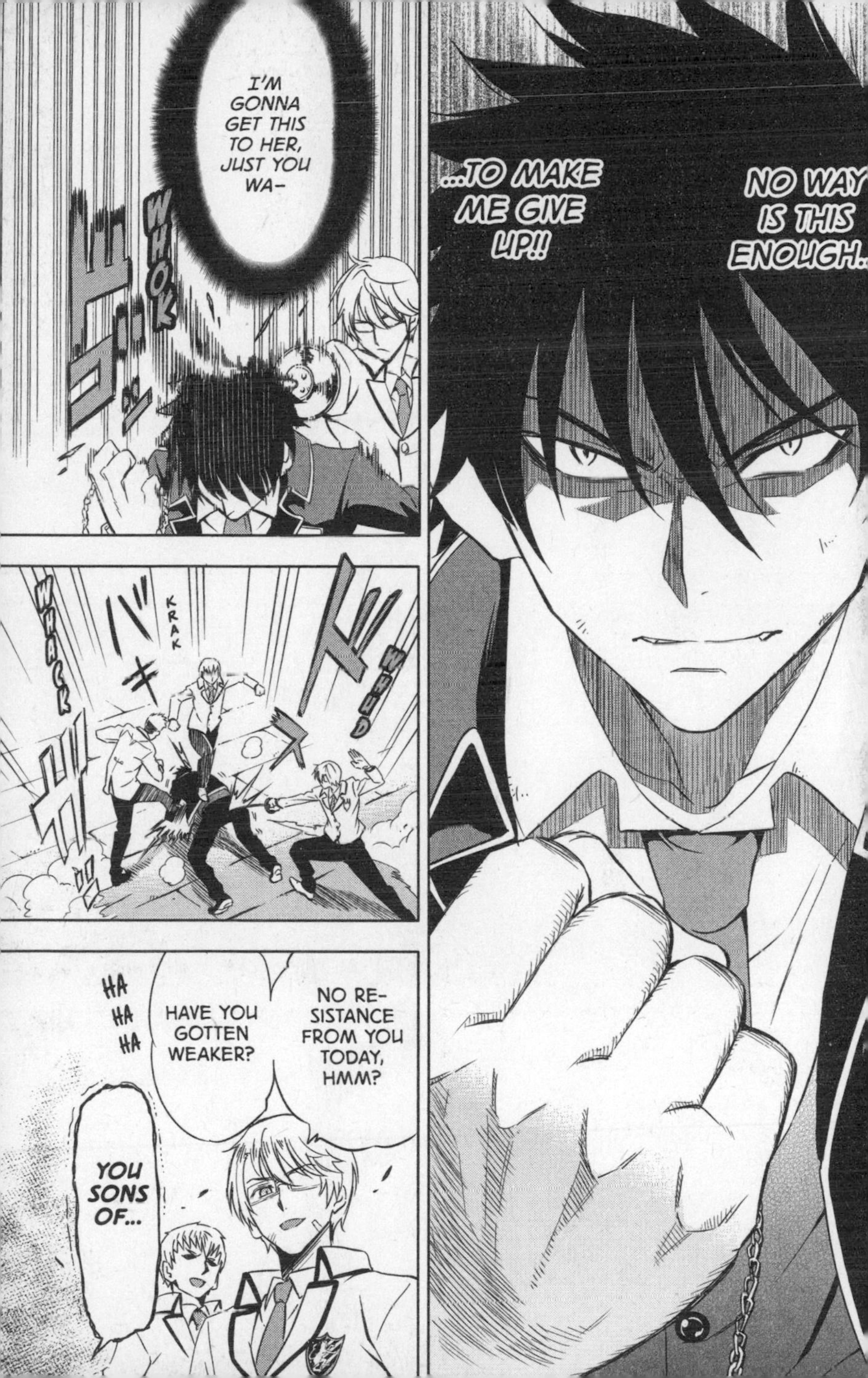
NO WAY IS THIS ENOUGH...
...TO MAKE ME GIVE UP!!
I'M GONNA GET THIS TO HER, JUST YOU WA–
WHOK
WHUD
KRAK
WHACK
NO RE-SISTANCE FROM YOU TODAY, HMM?
HAVE YOU GOTTEN WEAKER?
HA HA HA
YOU SONS OF...

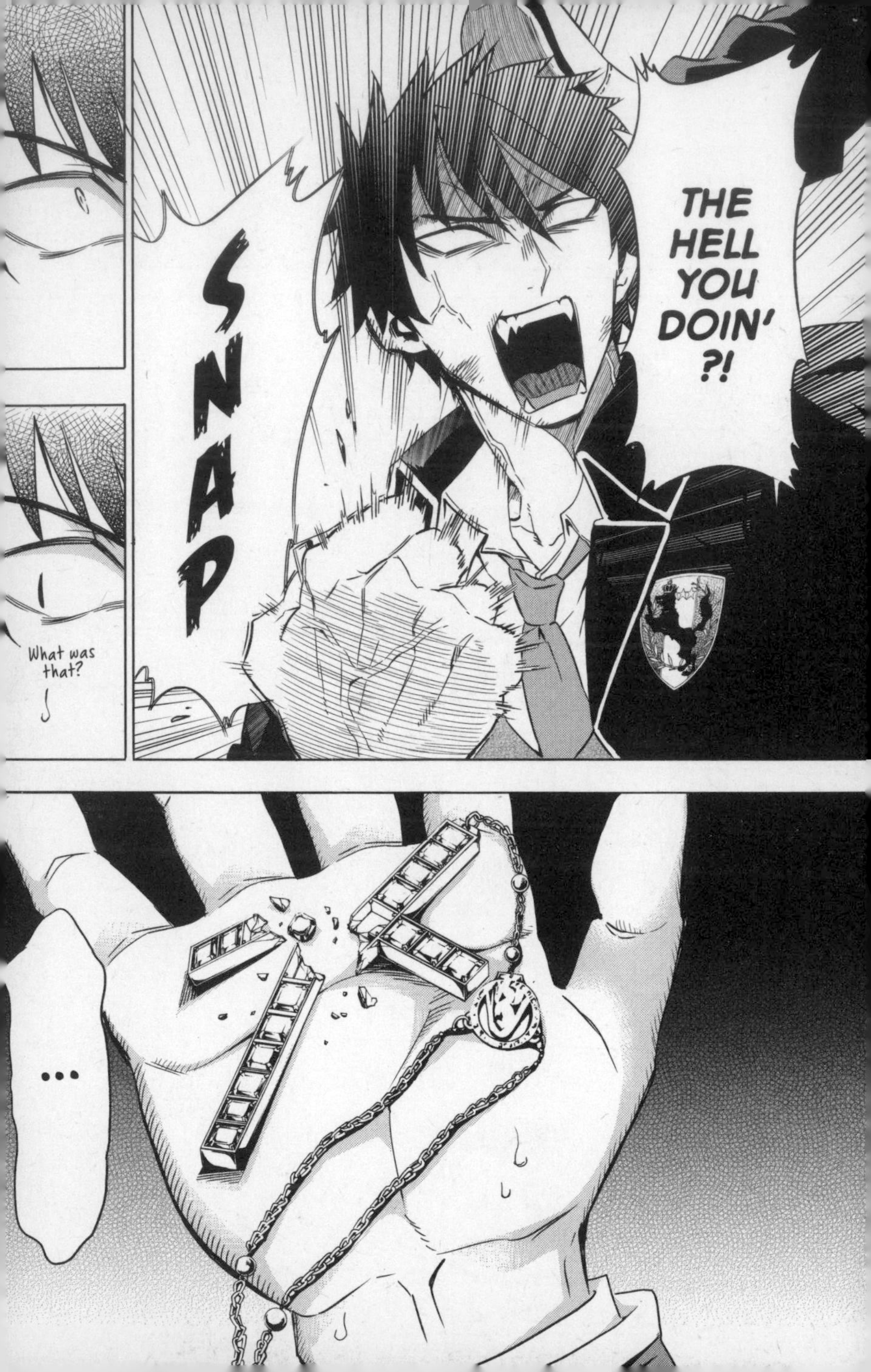
THE HELL YOU DOIN' ?!
SNAP
What was that?
...

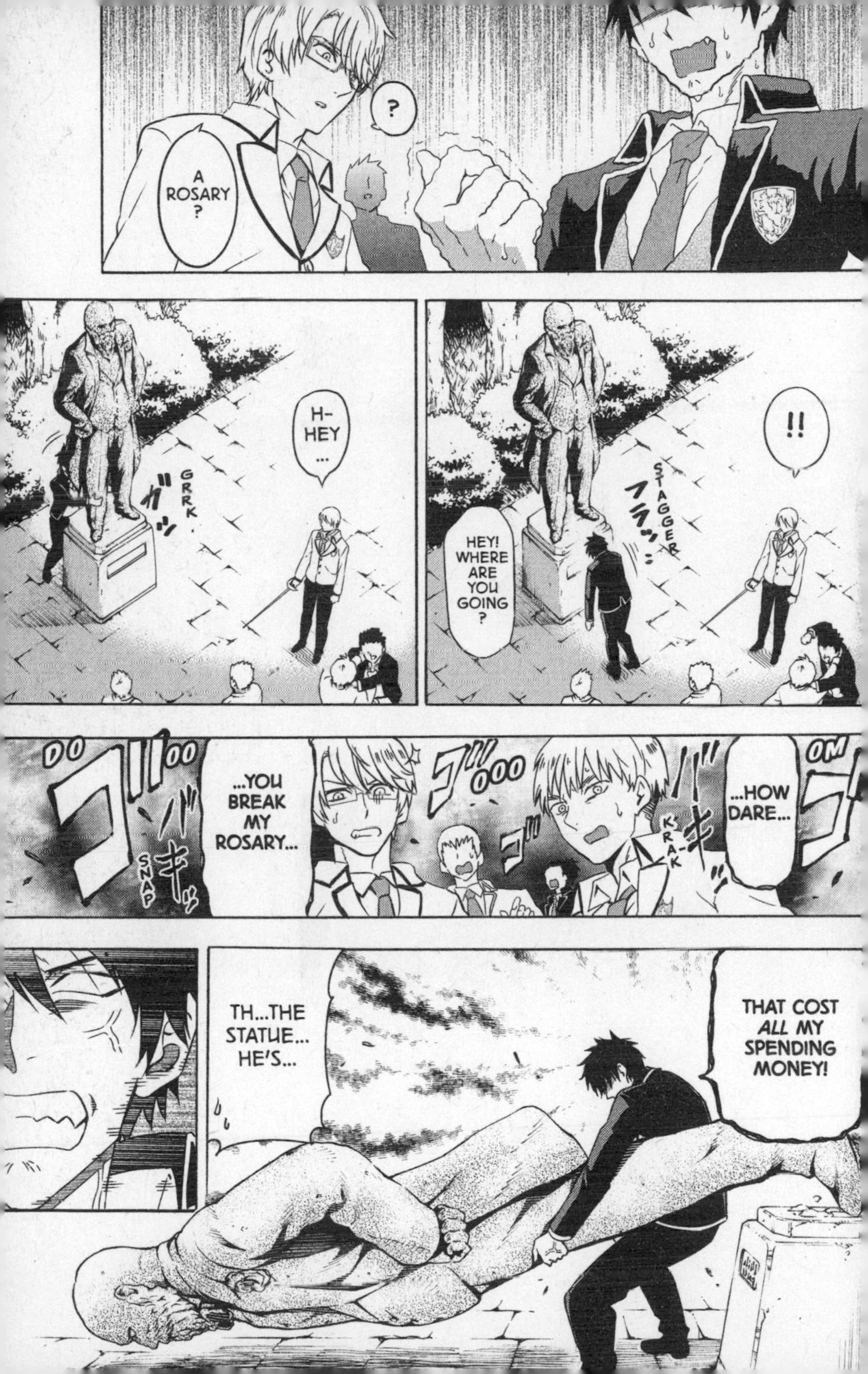
?
A ROSARY ?
!!
STAGGER
HEY! WHERE ARE YOU GOING ?
H-HEY ...
GRRK
OM
...HOW DARE...
KRAK
OOO
...YOU BREAK MY ROSARY...
DO
OO
SNAP
THAT COST *ALL* MY SPENDING MONEY!
TH...THE STATUE... HE'S...

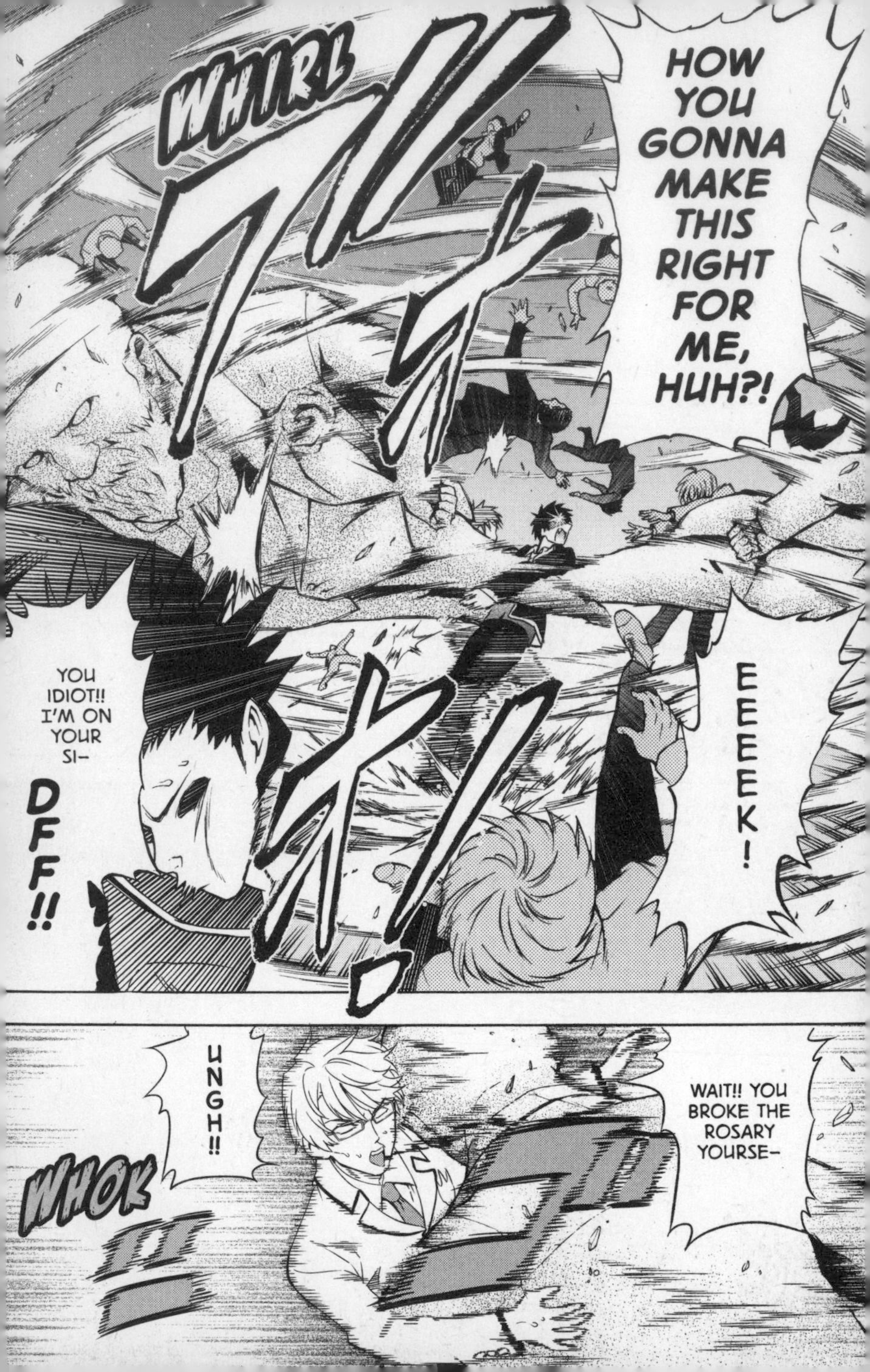
HOW YOU GONNA MAKE THIS RIGHT FOR ME, HUH?!
WHIRL
EEEEEK!
YOU IDIOT!! I'M ON YOUR SI—
DFF!!
WAIT!! YOU BROKE THE ROSARY YOURSE—
UNGH!!
WHOK

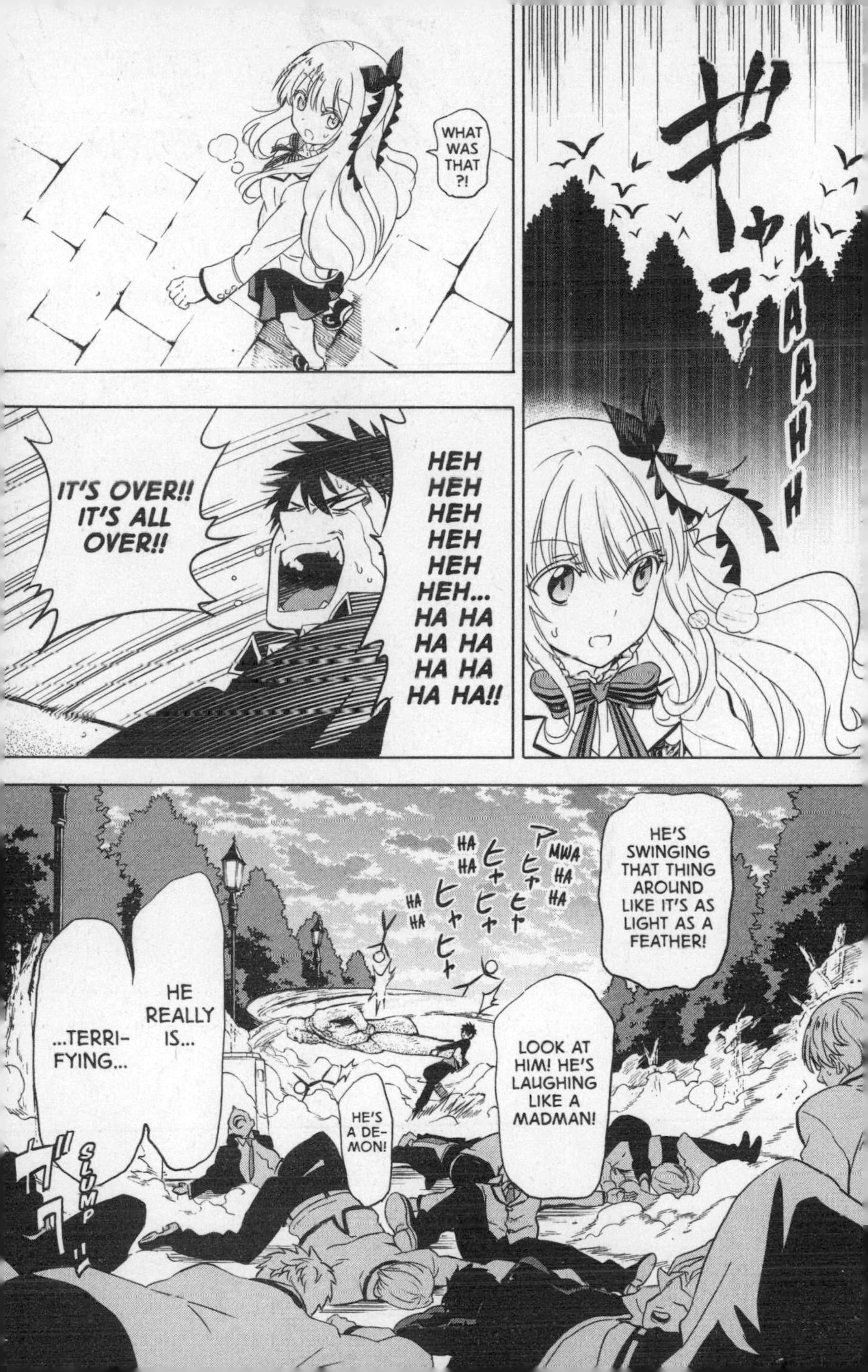
ギャァ
AAAHH
WHAT WAS THAT?!
HEH HEH HEH HEH HEH HEH... HA HA HA HA HA HA HA HA!!
IT'S OVER!! IT'S ALL OVER!!
HE'S SWINGING THAT THING AROUND LIKE IT'S AS LIGHT AS A FEATHER!
MWA HA HA
HA HA
HA HA
LOOK AT HIM! HE'S LAUGHING LIKE A MADMAN!
HE'S A DE-MON!
HE REALLY IS...
...TERRI-FYING...
SLUMP

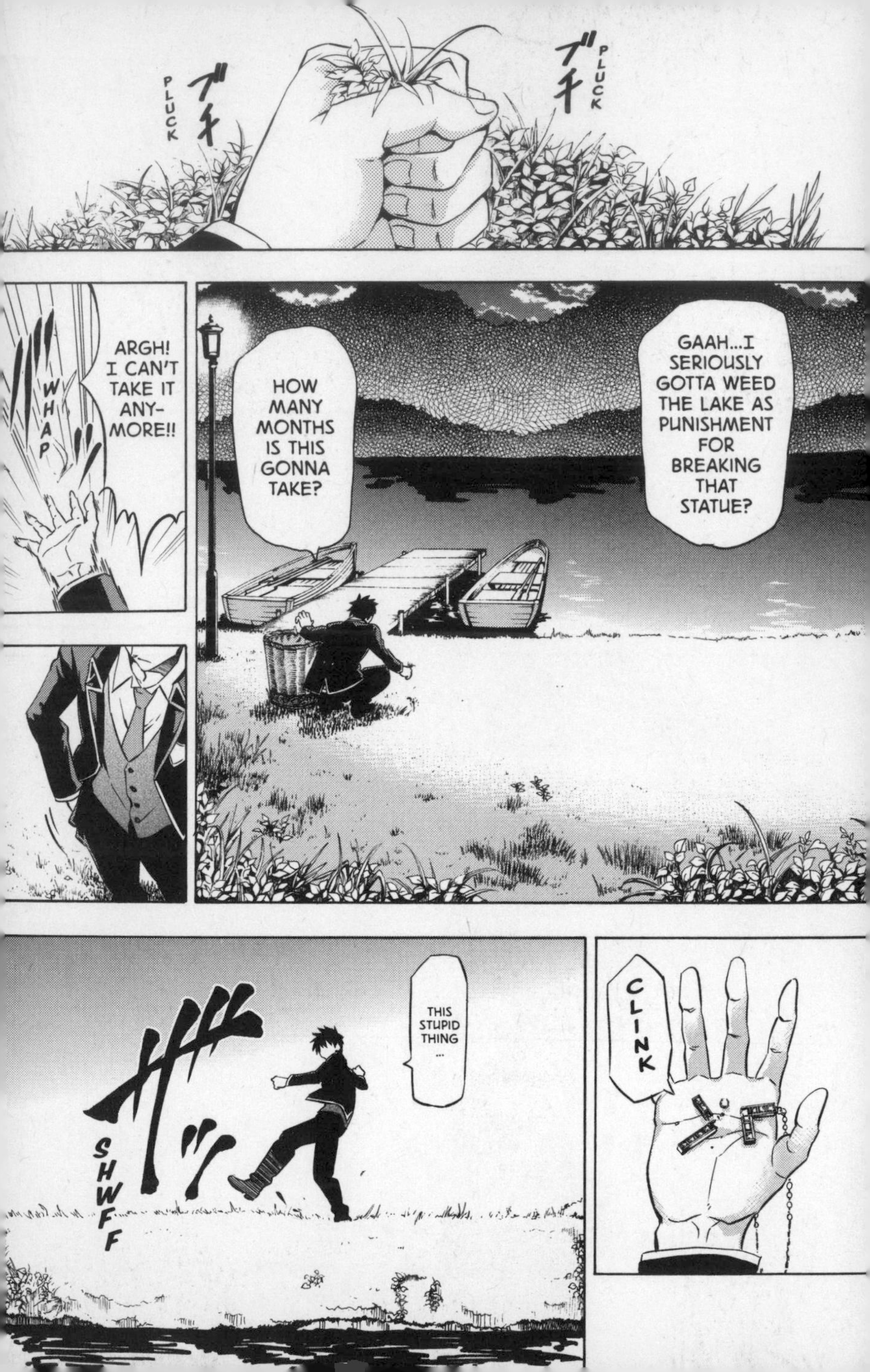
ブチ PLUCK
ブチ PLUCK
GAAH...I SERIOUSLY GOTTA WEED THE LAKE AS PUNISHMENT FOR BREAKING THAT STATUE?
HOW MANY MONTHS IS THIS GONNA TAKE?
ARGH! I CAN'T TAKE IT ANY-MORE!!
WHAP
CLINK
THIS STUPID THING ...
SHWFF

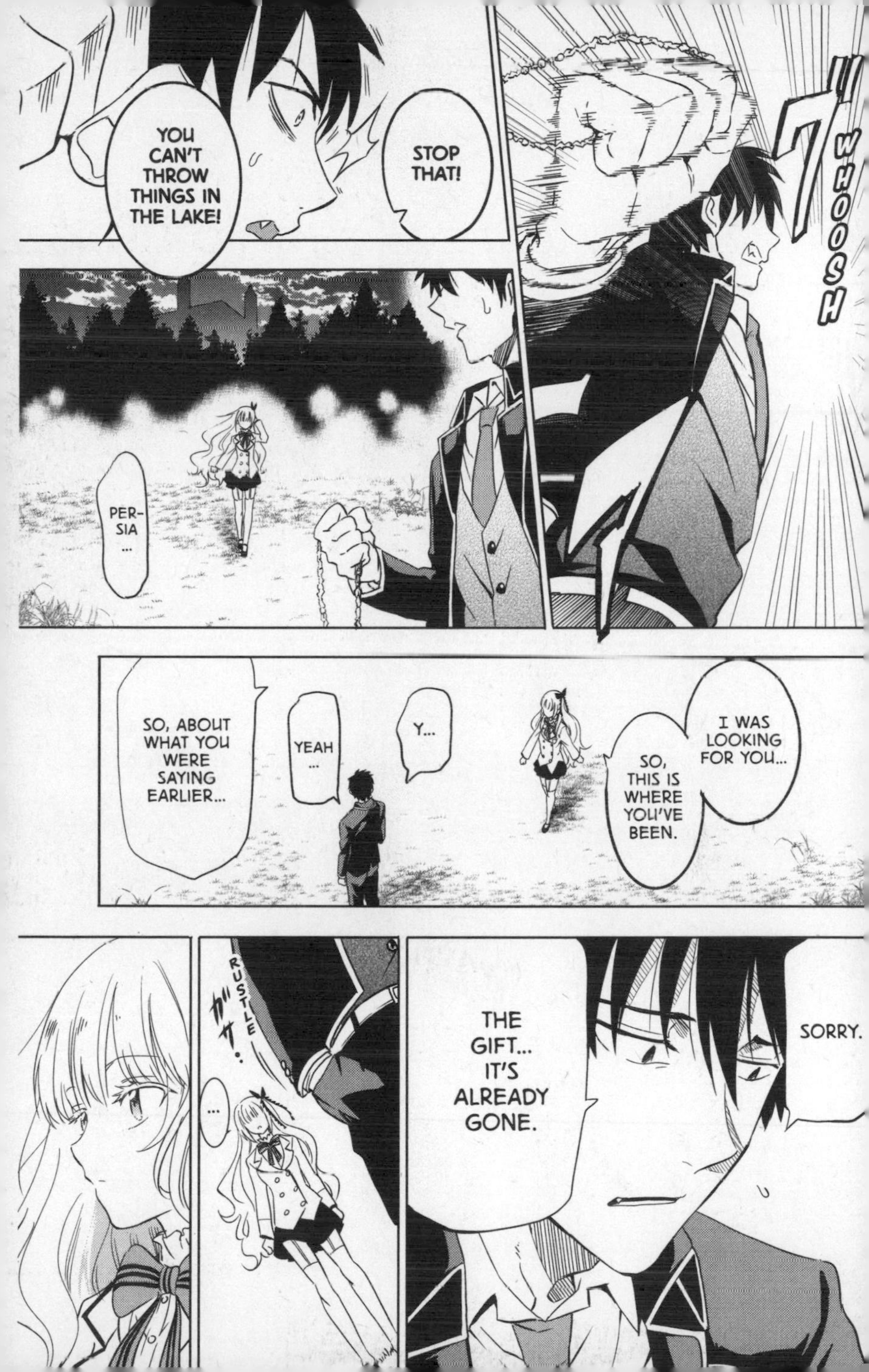
WHOOSH
STOP THAT!
YOU CAN'T THROW THINGS IN THE LAKE!
PER-SIA ...
I WAS LOOKING FOR YOU...
SO, THIS IS WHERE YOU'VE BEEN.
Y...
YEAH ...
SO, ABOUT WHAT YOU WERE SAYING EARLIER...
SORRY.
THE GIFT... IT'S ALREADY GONE.
RUSTLE
...

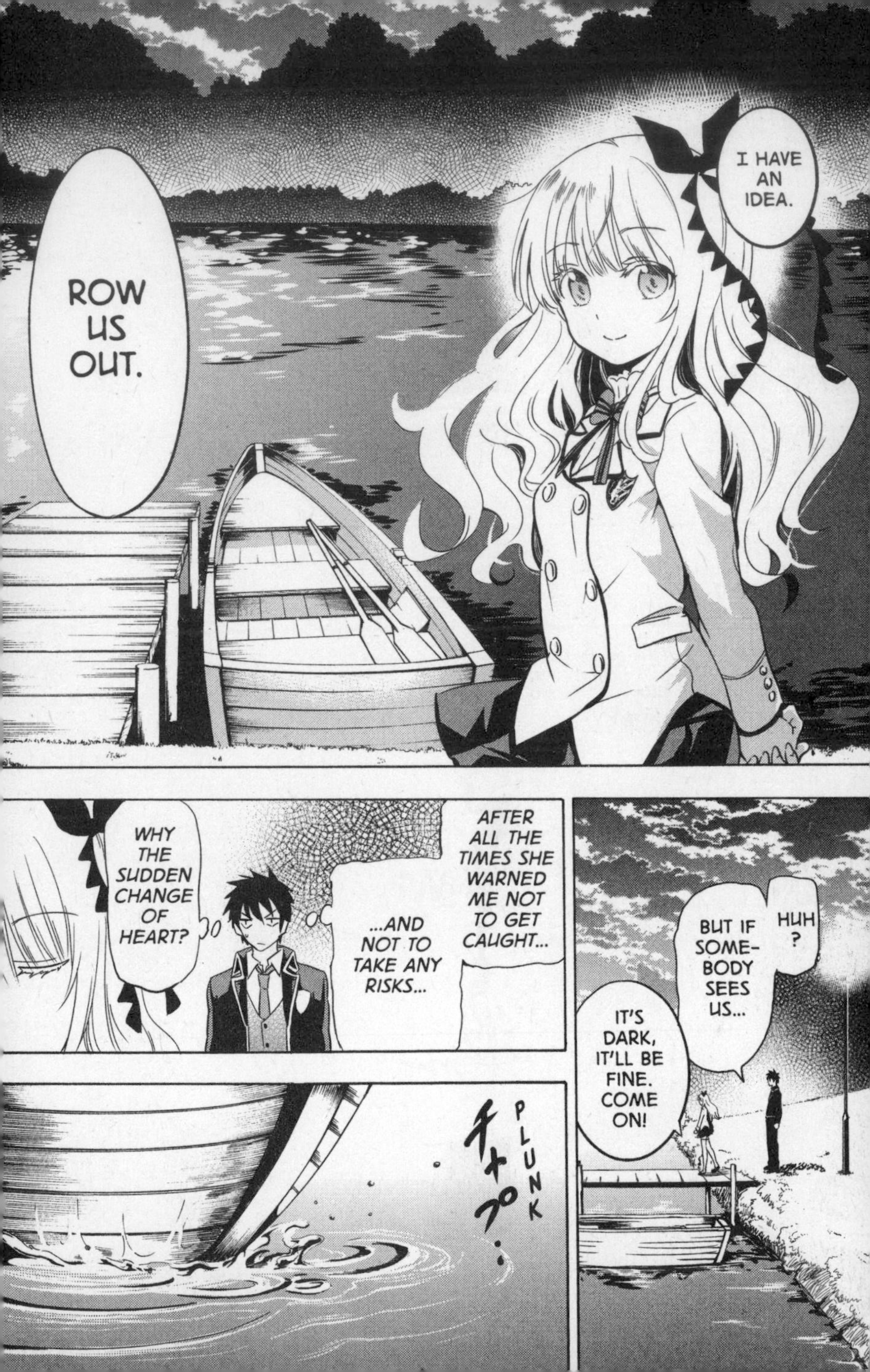
I HAVE AN IDEA.
ROW US OUT.
HUH?
BUT IF SOMEBODY SEES US...
IT'S DARK, IT'LL BE FINE. COME ON!
AFTER ALL THE TIMES SHE WARNED ME NOT TO GET CAUGHT...
...AND NOT TO TAKE ANY RISKS...
WHY THE SUDDEN CHANGE OF HEART?
チャプ
PLUNK

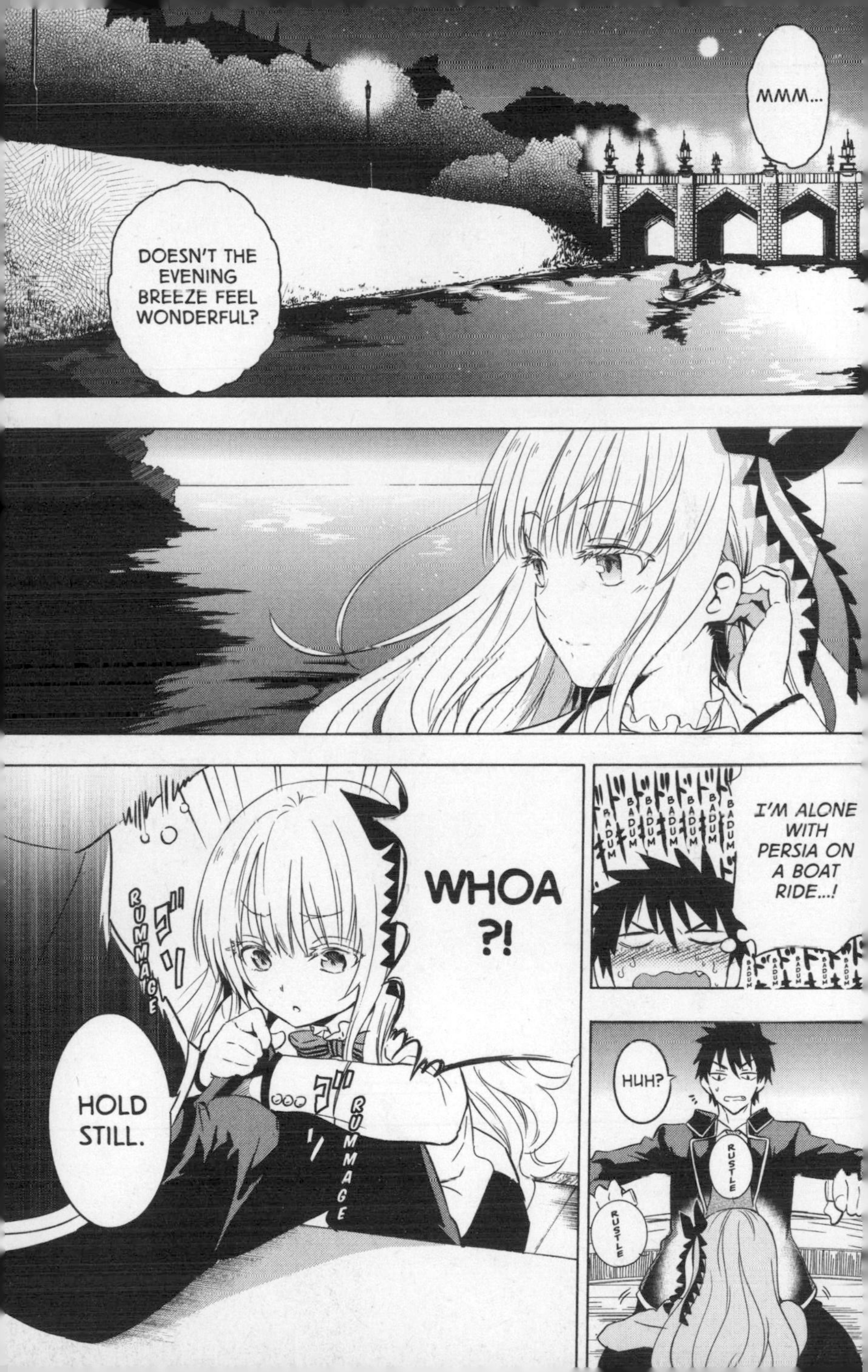
MMM...
DOESN'T THE EVENING BREEZE FEEL WONDERFUL?
BADUM BADUM BADUM BADUM BADUM BADUM BADUM
I'M ALONE WITH PERSIA ON A BOAT RIDE...!
BADUM BADUM BADUM BADUM
HUH?
RUSTLE
RUSTLE
WHOA ?!
RUMMAGE
RUMMAGE
HOLD STILL.

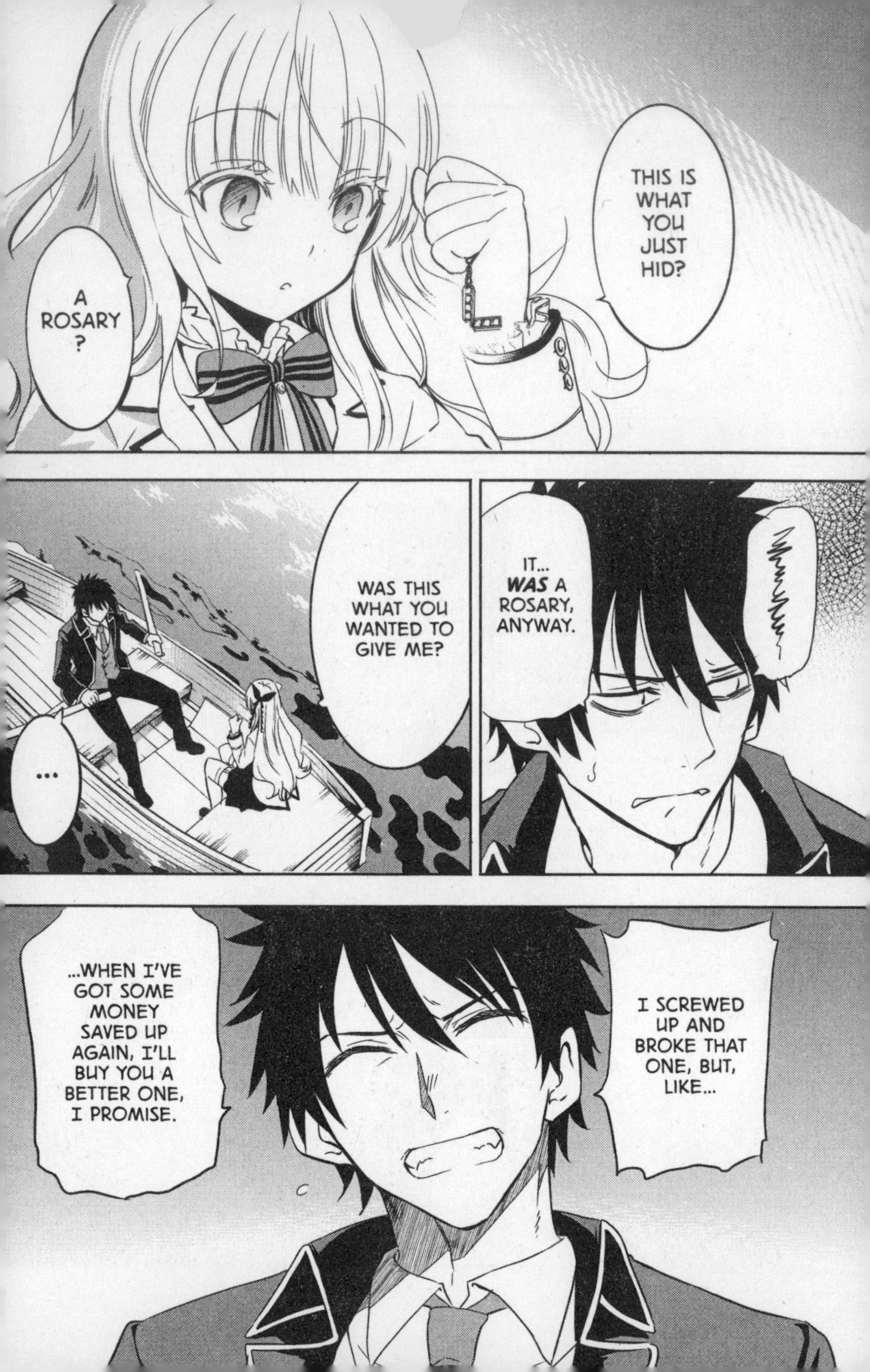
THIS IS WHAT YOU JUST HID?
A ROSARY?
IT... *WAS* A ROSARY, ANYWAY.
WAS THIS WHAT YOU WANTED TO GIVE ME?
...
I SCREWED UP AND BROKE THAT ONE, BUT, LIKE...
...WHEN I'VE GOT SOME MONEY SAVED UP AGAIN, I'LL BUY YOU A BETTER ONE, I PROMISE.

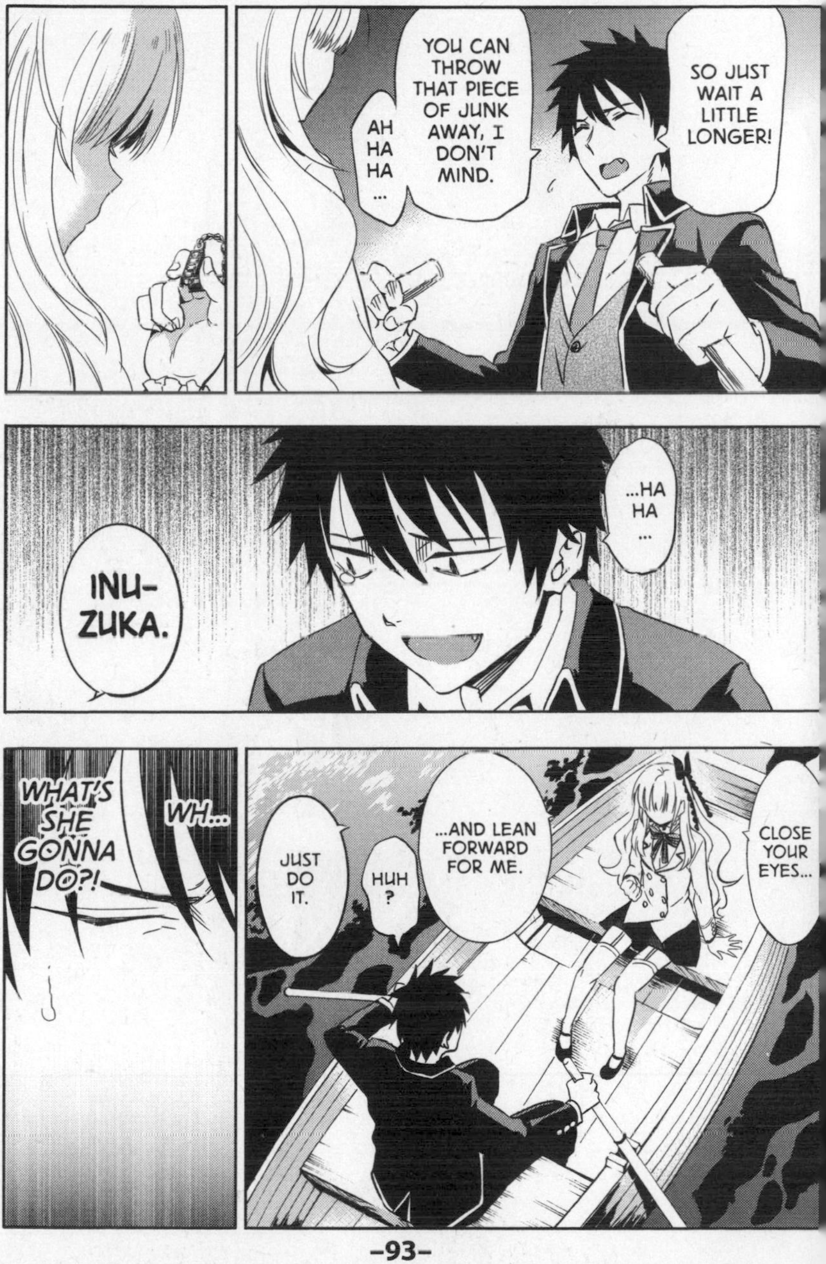
SO JUST WAIT A LITTLE LONGER!
YOU CAN THROW THAT PIECE OF JUNK AWAY, I DON'T MIND.
AH HA HA ...
...HA HA ...
INU-ZUKA.
CLOSE YOUR EYES...
...AND LEAN FORWARD FOR ME.
HUH ?
JUST DO IT.
WH...
WHAT'S SHE GONNA DO?!

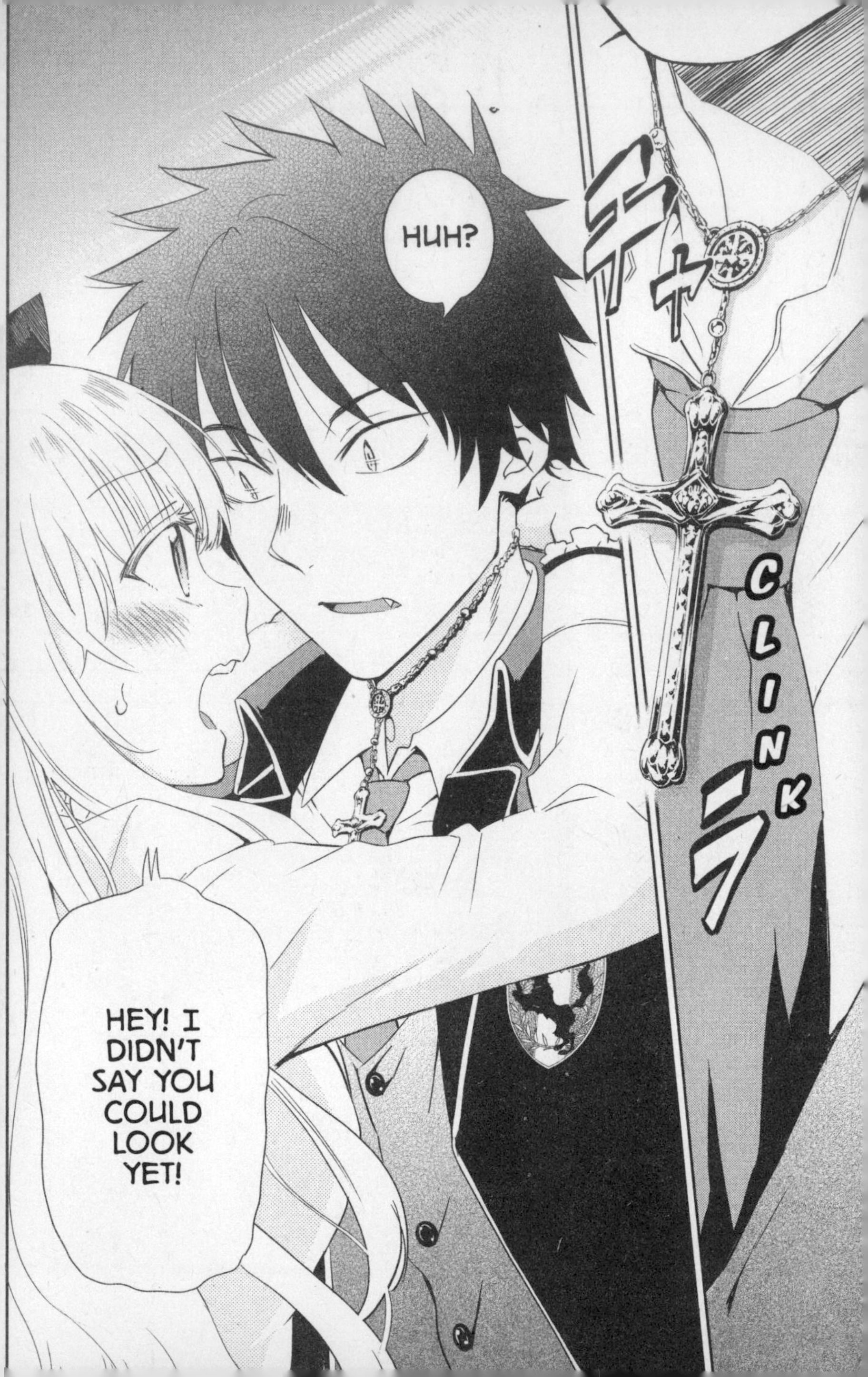
HUH?
CLINK
HEY! I DIDN'T SAY YOU COULD LOOK YET!

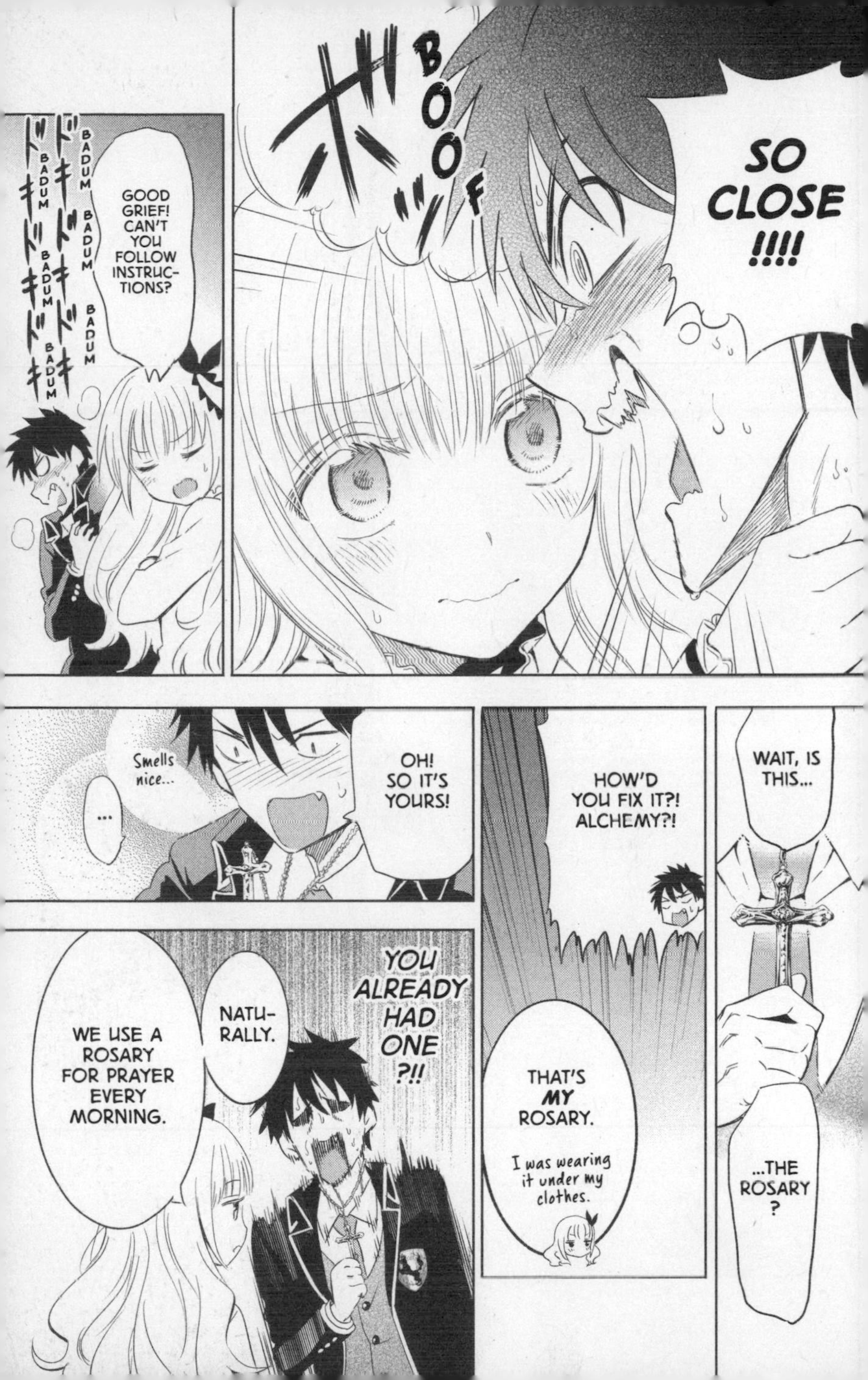
BOOF
SO CLOSE !!!!
BADUM BADUM BADUM BADUM BADUM BADUM
GOOD GRIEF! CAN'T YOU FOLLOW INSTRUC-TIONS?
WAIT, IS THIS...
...THE ROSARY?
HOW'D YOU FIX IT?! ALCHEMY?!
THAT'S MY ROSARY.
I was wearing it under my clothes.
OH! SO IT'S YOURS!
Smells nice...
...
YOU ALREADY HAD ONE ?!!
NATU-RALLY.
WE USE A ROSARY FOR PRAYER EVERY MORNING.

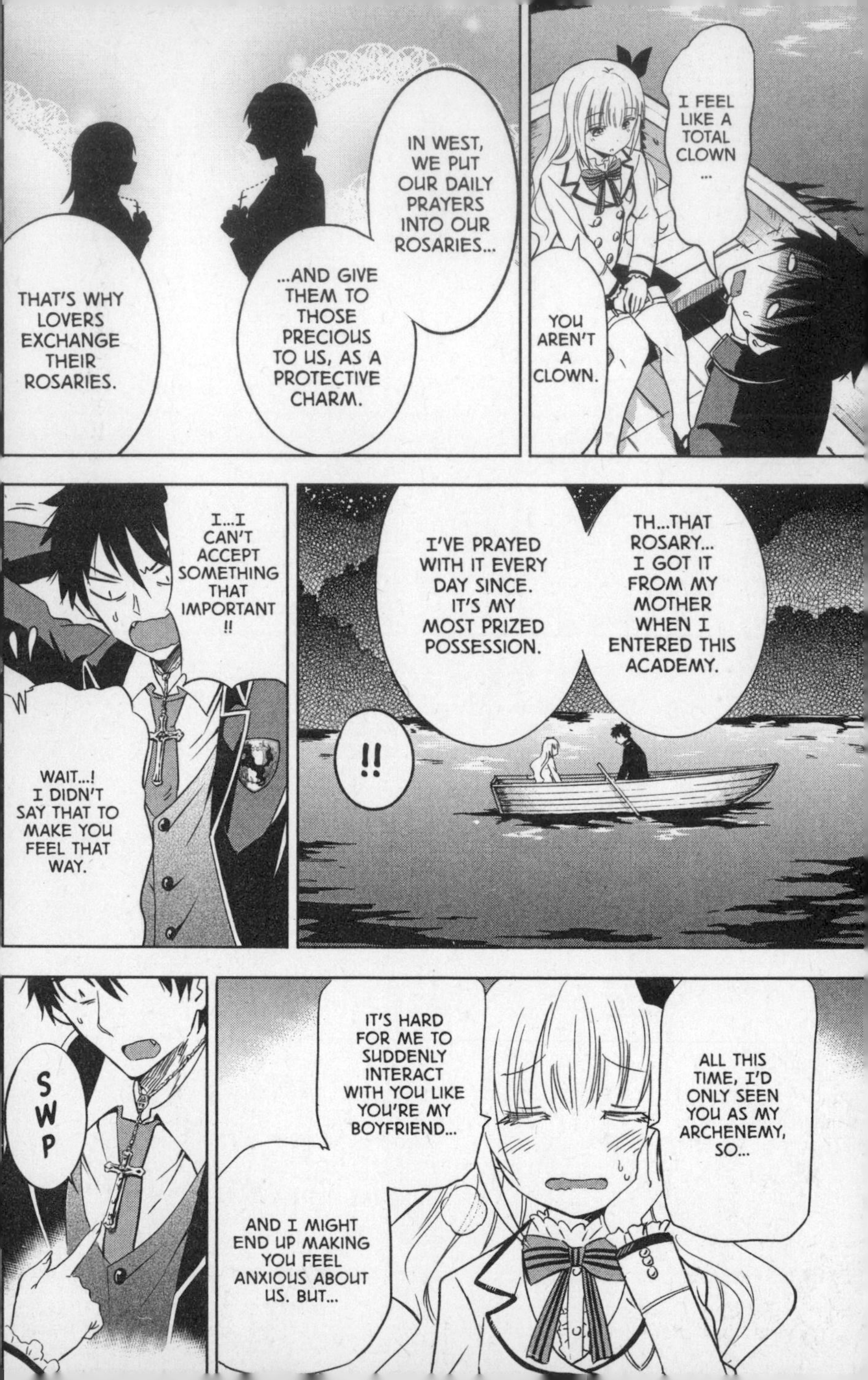
I FEEL LIKE A TOTAL CLOWN ...
YOU AREN'T A CLOWN.
IN WEST, WE PUT OUR DAILY PRAYERS INTO OUR ROSARIES...
...AND GIVE THEM TO THOSE PRECIOUS TO US, AS A PROTECTIVE CHARM.
THAT'S WHY LOVERS EXCHANGE THEIR ROSARIES.
TH...THAT ROSARY... I GOT IT FROM MY MOTHER WHEN I ENTERED THIS ACADEMY.
I'VE PRAYED WITH IT EVERY DAY SINCE. IT'S MY MOST PRIZED POSSESSION.
!!
I...I CAN'T ACCEPT SOMETHING THAT IMPORTANT !!
WAIT...! I DIDN'T SAY THAT TO MAKE YOU FEEL THAT WAY.
ALL THIS TIME, I'D ONLY SEEN YOU AS MY ARCHENEMY, SO...
IT'S HARD FOR ME TO SUDDENLY INTERACT WITH YOU LIKE YOU'RE MY BOYFRIEND...
AND I MIGHT END UP MAKING YOU FEEL ANXIOUS ABOUT US. BUT...
SWP

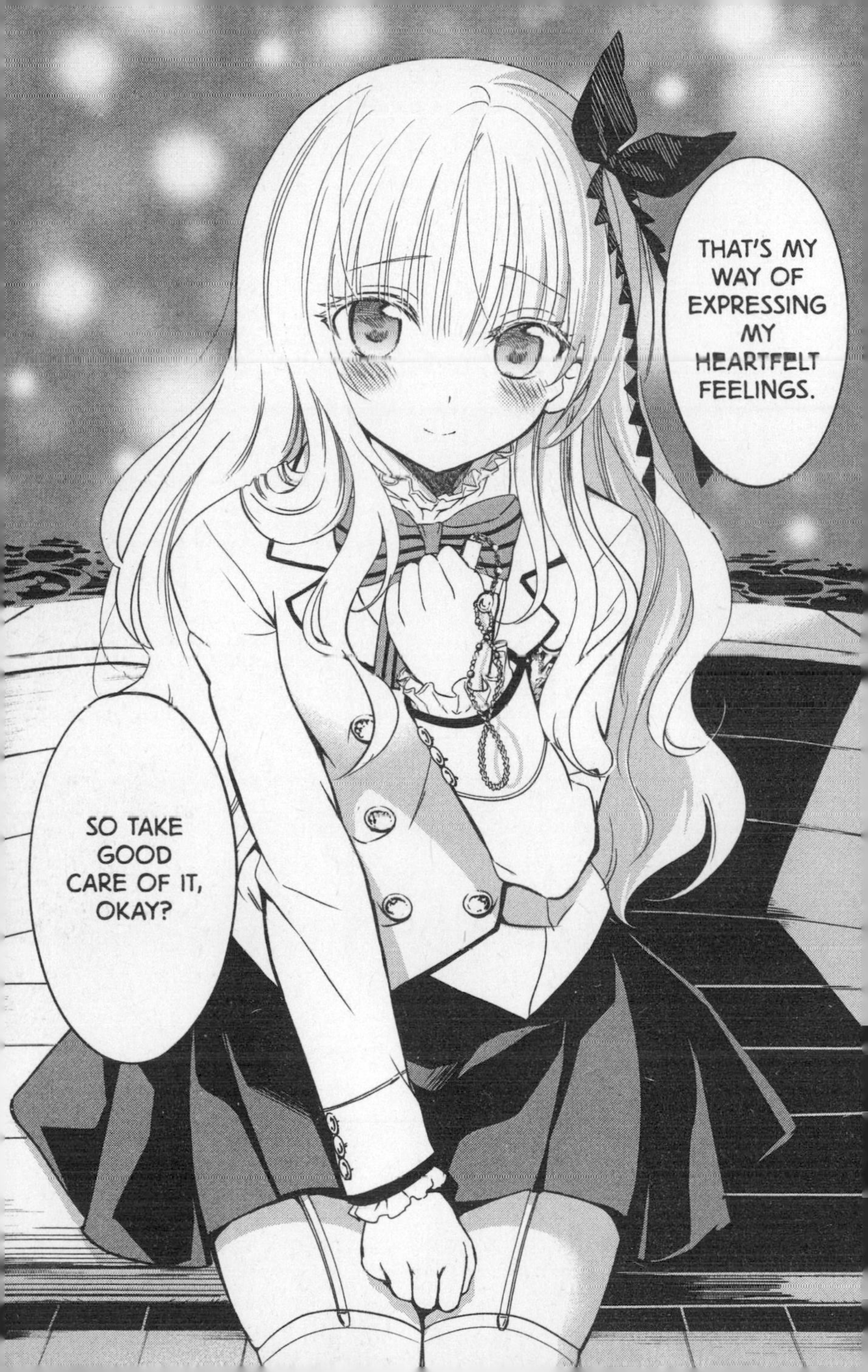
THAT'S MY WAY OF EXPRESSING MY HEARTFELT FEELINGS.
SO TAKE GOOD CARE OF IT, OKAY?

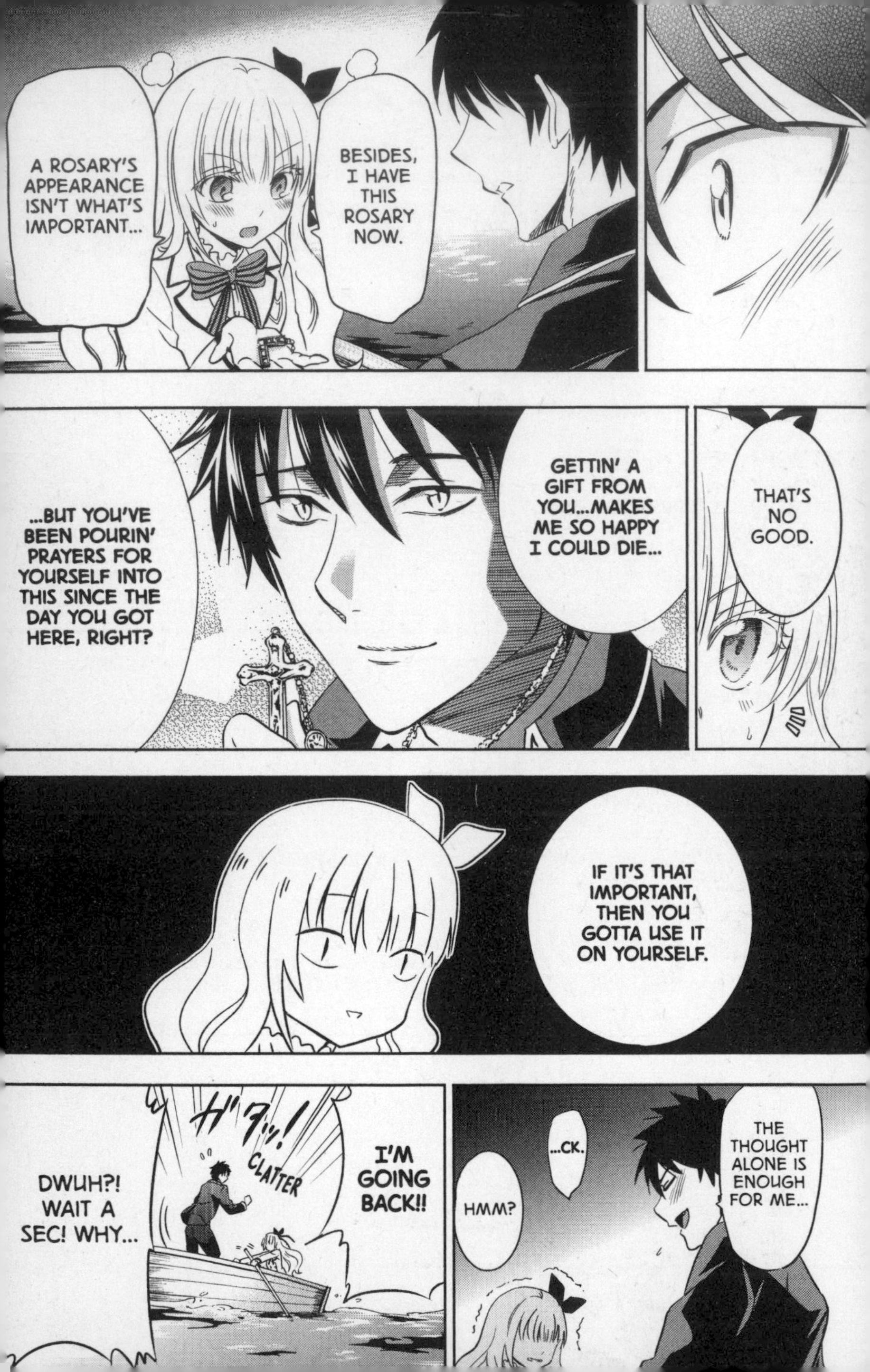
BESIDES, I HAVE THIS ROSARY NOW.
A ROSARY'S APPEARANCE ISN'T WHAT'S IMPORTANT...
THAT'S NO GOOD.
GETTIN' A GIFT FROM YOU...MAKES ME SO HAPPY I COULD DIE...
...BUT YOU'VE BEEN POURIN' PRAYERS FOR YOURSELF INTO THIS SINCE THE DAY YOU GOT HERE, RIGHT?
IF IT'S THAT IMPORTANT, THEN YOU GOTTA USE IT ON YOURSELF.
THE THOUGHT ALONE IS ENOUGH FOR ME...
...CK.
HMM?
I'M GOING BACK!!
ガタッ!
CLATTER
DWUH?! WAIT A SEC! WHY...

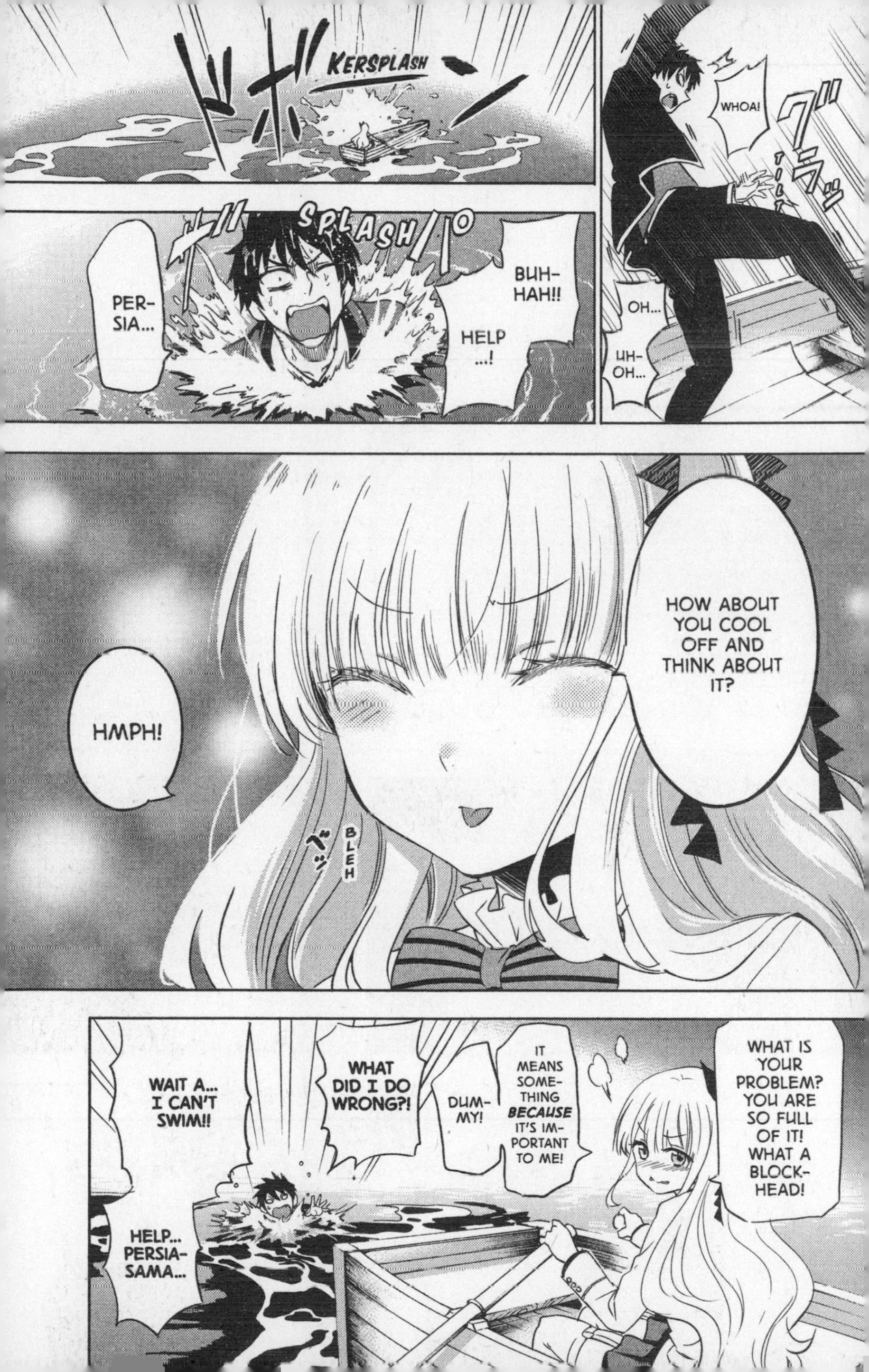
WHOA!
TILT
OH...
UH-OH...
KERSPLASH
BUH-HAH!!
HELP ...!
SPLASH
PER-SIA...
HOW ABOUT YOU COOL OFF AND THINK ABOUT IT?
BLEH
HMPH!
WHAT IS YOUR PROBLEM? YOU ARE SO FULL OF IT! WHAT A BLOCK-HEAD!
IT MEANS SOME-THING *BECAUSE* IT'S IM-PORTANT TO ME!
DUM-MY!
WHAT DID I DO WRONG?!
WAIT A... I CAN'T SWIM!!
HELP... PERSIA-SAMA...

Boarding
School *Juliet*

ACT 3:
DATE & JULIET

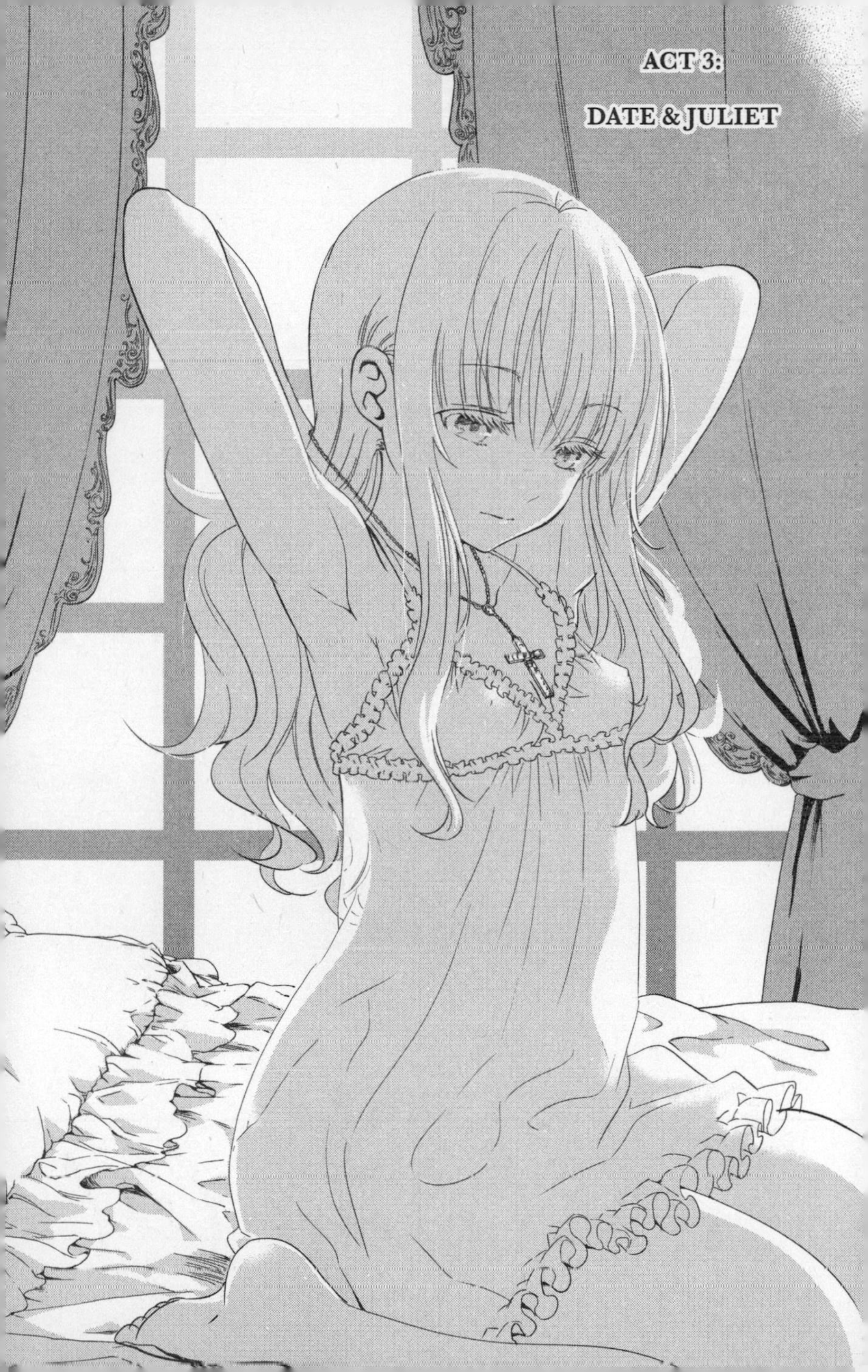

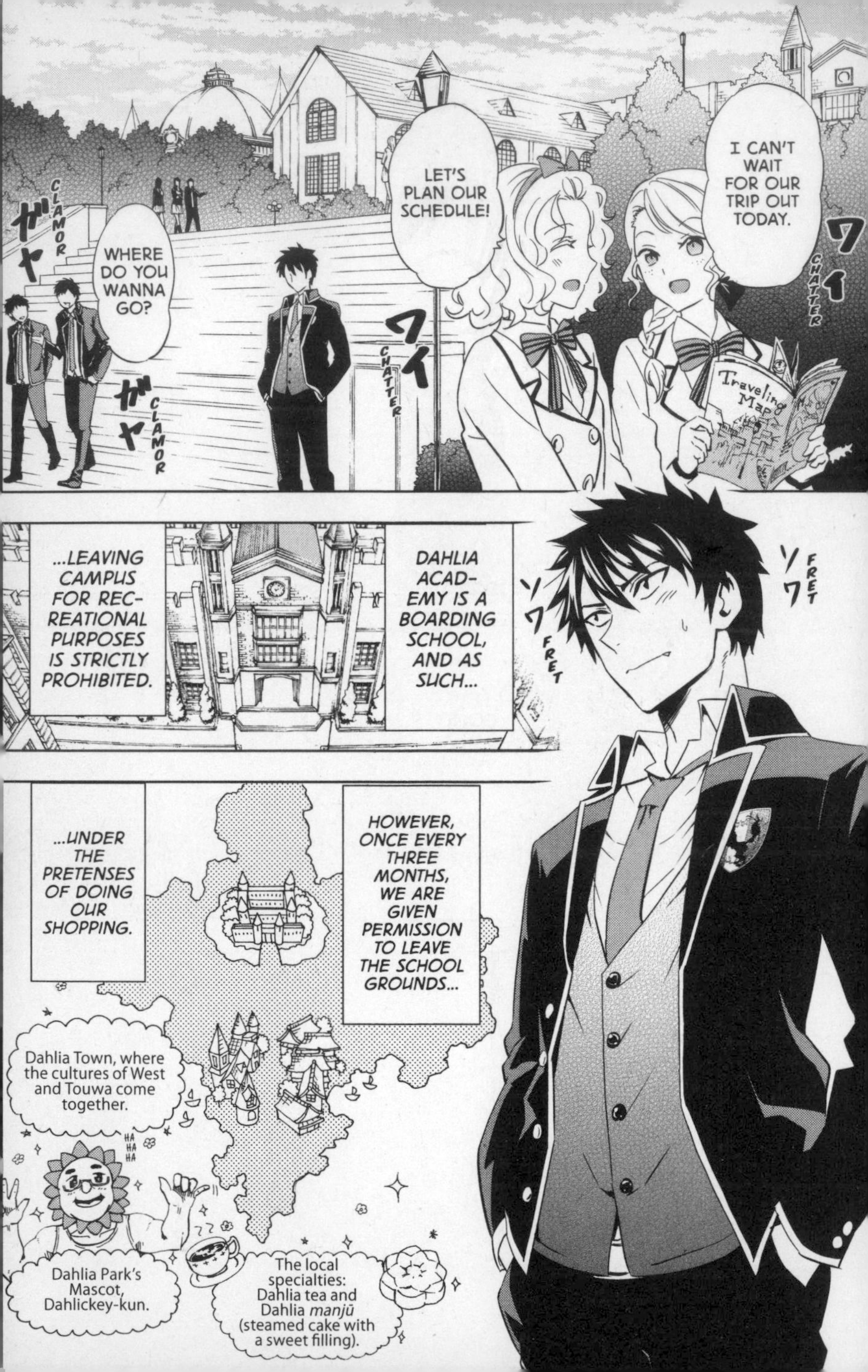
ワイ CHATTER
I CAN'T WAIT FOR OUR TRIP OUT TODAY.
Traveling Map
LET'S PLAN OUR SCHEDULE!
ワイ CHATTER
WHERE DO YOU WANNA GO?
ガヤ CLAMOR
ガヤ CLAMOR
ソワ FRET
ソワ FRET
DAHLIA ACAD-EMY IS A BOARDING SCHOOL, AND AS SUCH...
...LEAVING CAMPUS FOR REC-REATIONAL PURPOSES IS STRICTLY PROHIBITED.
HOWEVER, ONCE EVERY THREE MONTHS, WE ARE GIVEN PERMISSION TO LEAVE THE SCHOOL GROUNDS...
...UNDER THE PRETENSES OF DOING OUR SHOPPING.
Dahlia Town, where the cultures of West and Touwa come together.
HA HA HA
Dahlia Park's Mascot, Dahlickey-kun.
The local specialties: Dahlia tea and Dahlia *manjū* (steamed cake with a sweet filling).

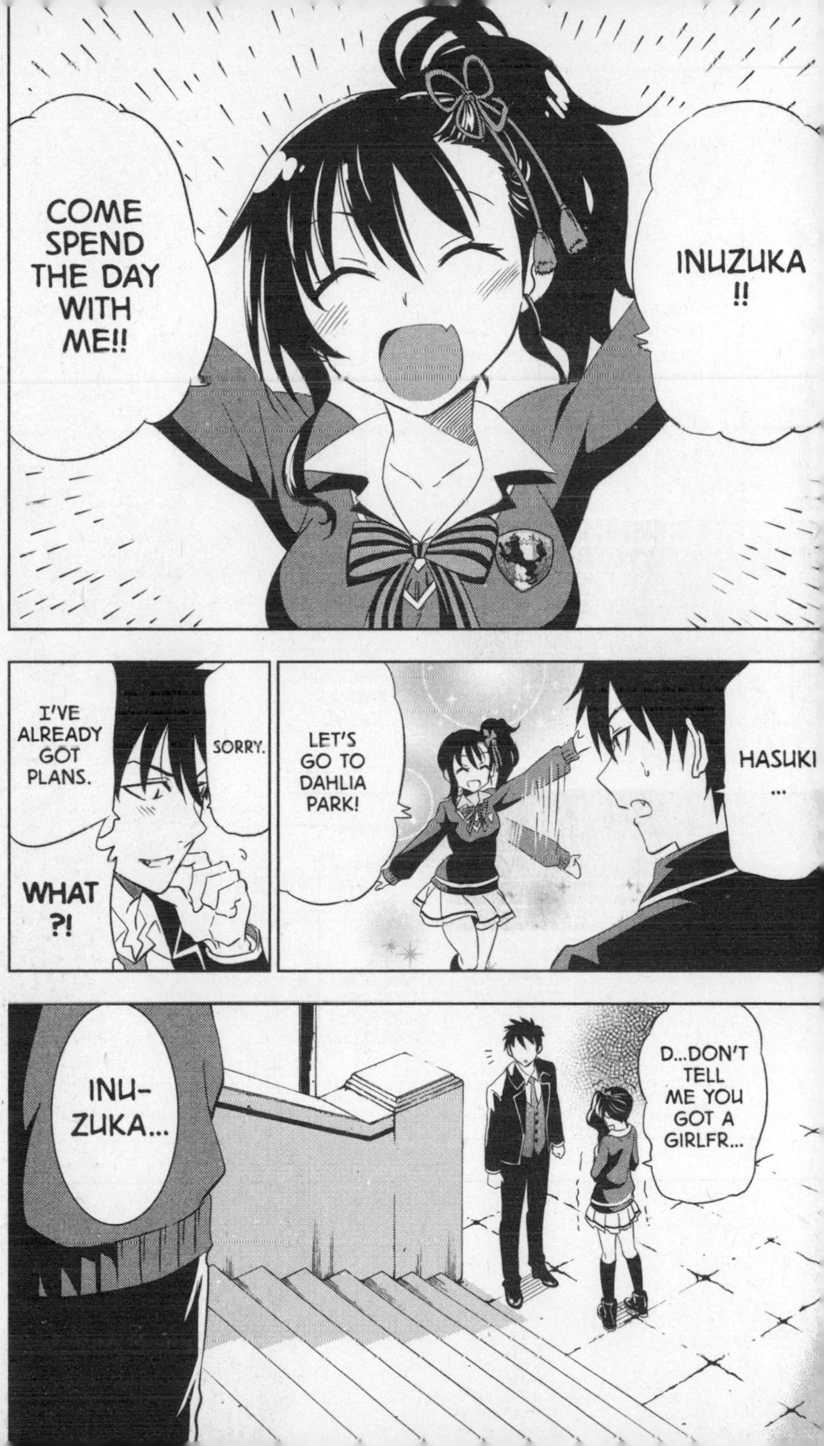
INUZUKA !!
COME SPEND THE DAY WITH ME!!
HASUKI ...
LET'S GO TO DAHLIA PARK!
SORRY.
I'VE ALREADY GOT PLANS.
WHAT ?!
D...DON'T TELL ME YOU GOT A GIRLFR...
INU-ZUKA...

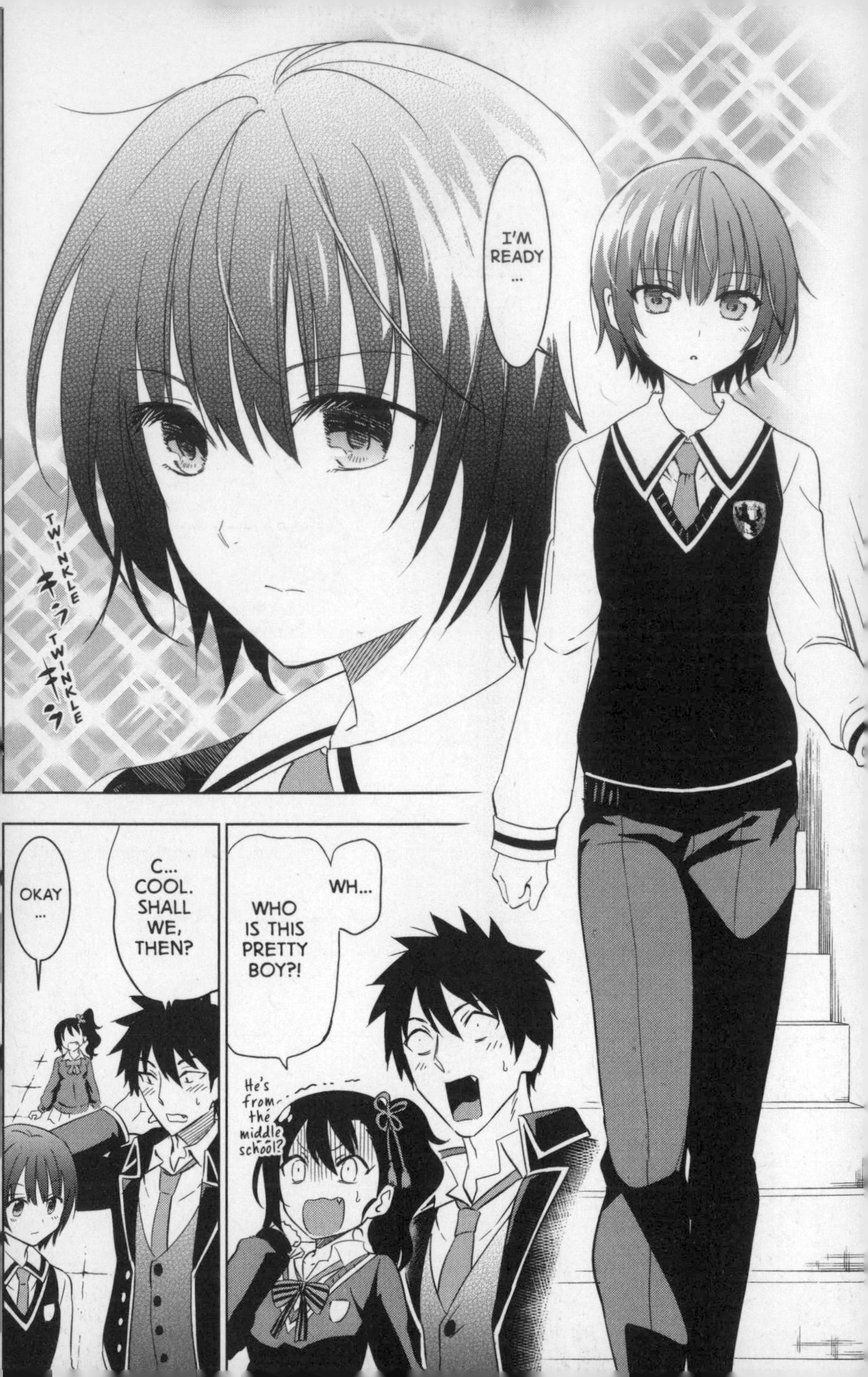
I'M READY ...
TWINKLE
TWINKLE
WH...
WHO IS THIS PRETTY BOY?!
He's from the middle school?
C... COOL. SHALL WE, THEN?
OKAY ...

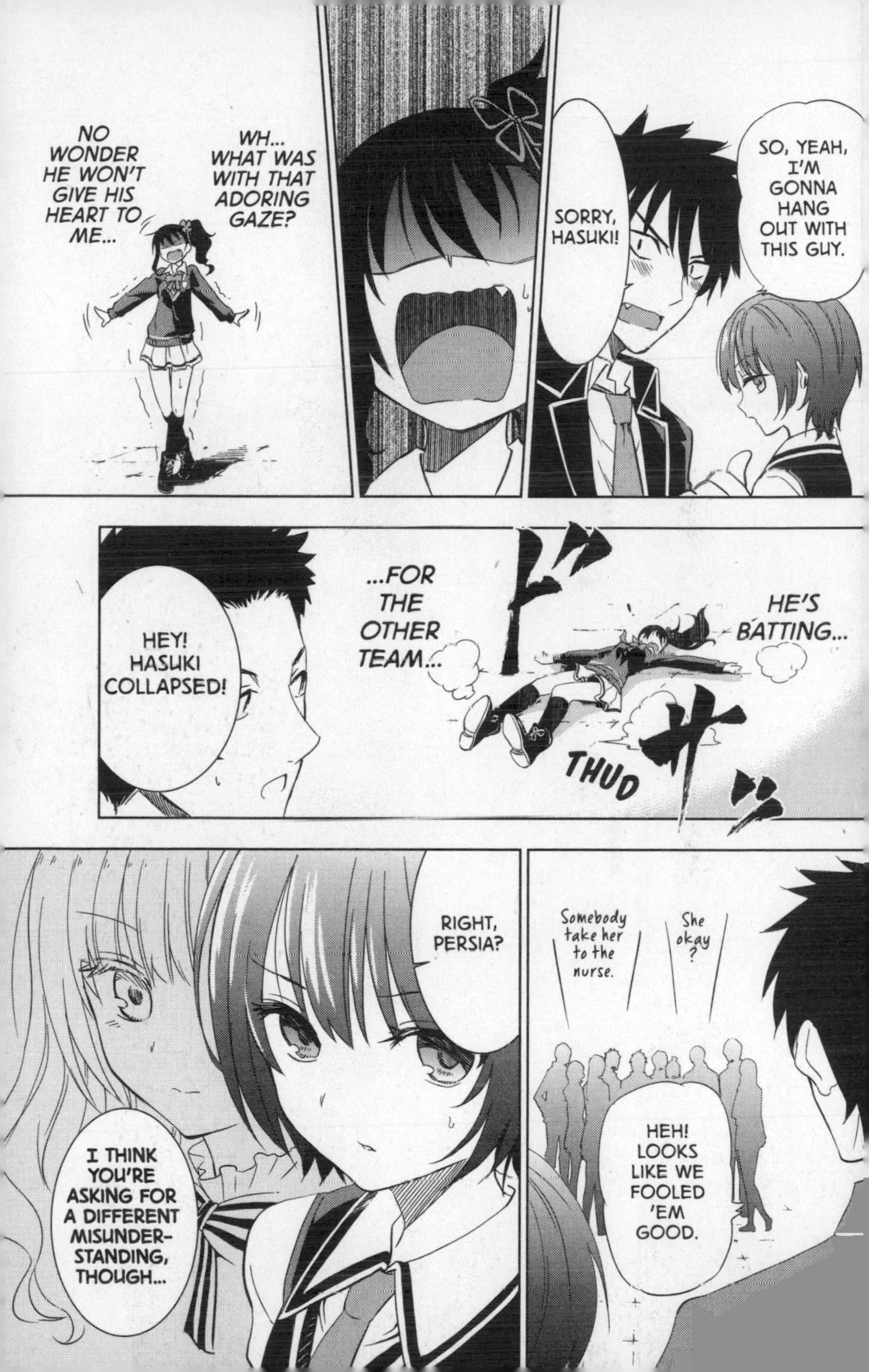
SO, YEAH, I'M GONNA HANG OUT WITH THIS GUY.
SORRY, HASUKI!
WH... WHAT WAS WITH THAT ADORING GAZE?
NO WONDER HE WON'T GIVE HIS HEART TO ME...
HE'S BATTING...
ドサッ
THUD
...FOR THE OTHER TEAM...
HEY! HASUKI COLLAPSED!
She okay?
Somebody take her to the nurse.
HEH! LOOKS LIKE WE FOOLED 'EM GOOD.
RIGHT, PERSIA?
I THINK YOU'RE ASKING FOR A DIFFERENT MISUNDER-STANDING, THOUGH...

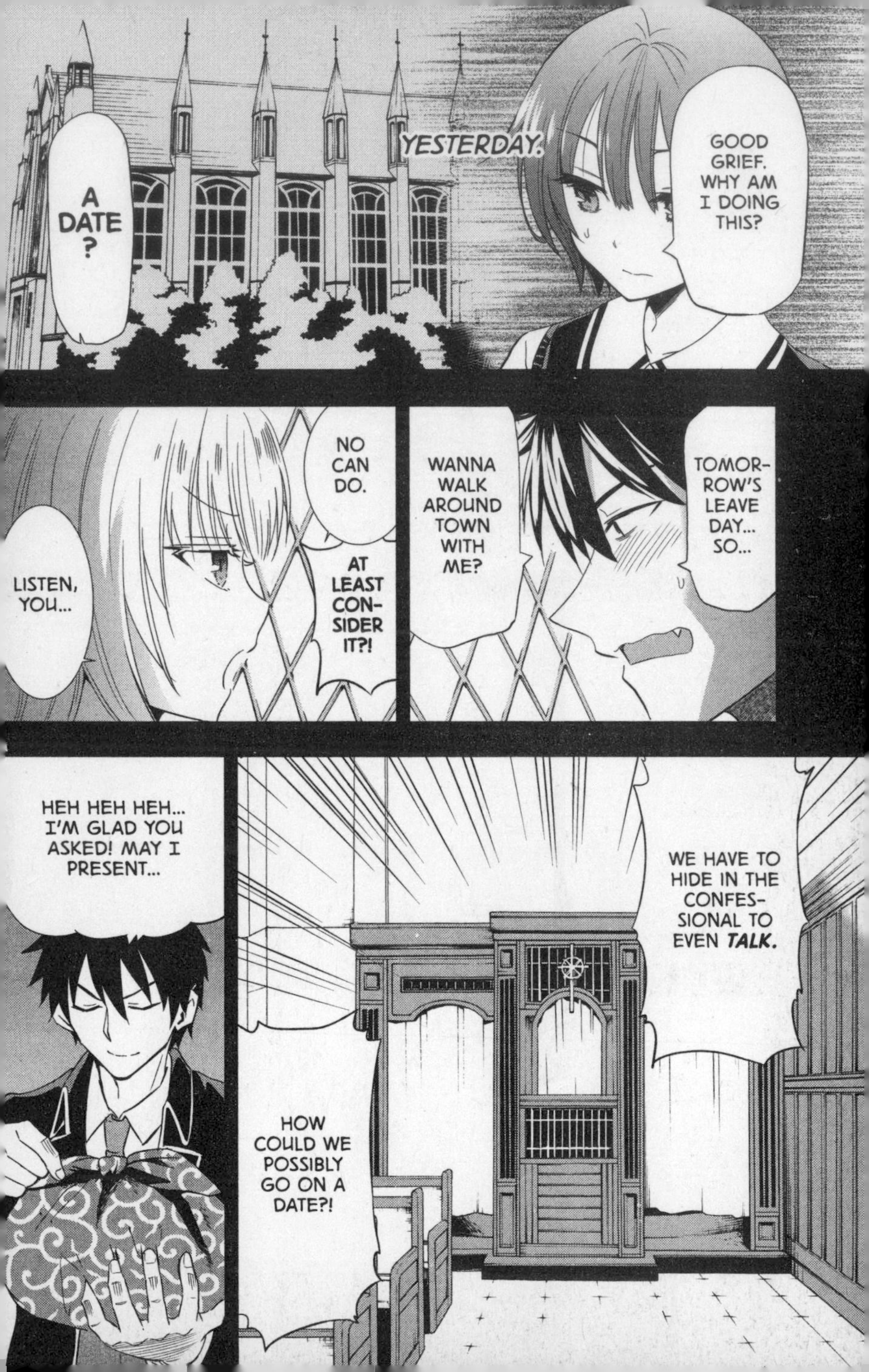
YESTERDAY.
GOOD GRIEF. WHY AM I DOING THIS?
A DATE ?
TOMORROW'S LEAVE DAY... SO...
WANNA WALK AROUND TOWN WITH ME?
NO CAN DO.
AT LEAST CONSIDER IT?!
LISTEN, YOU...
WE HAVE TO HIDE IN THE CONFESSIONAL TO EVEN *TALK.*
HOW COULD WE POSSIBLY GO ON A DATE?!
HEH HEH HEH... I'M GLAD YOU ASKED! MAY I PRESENT...

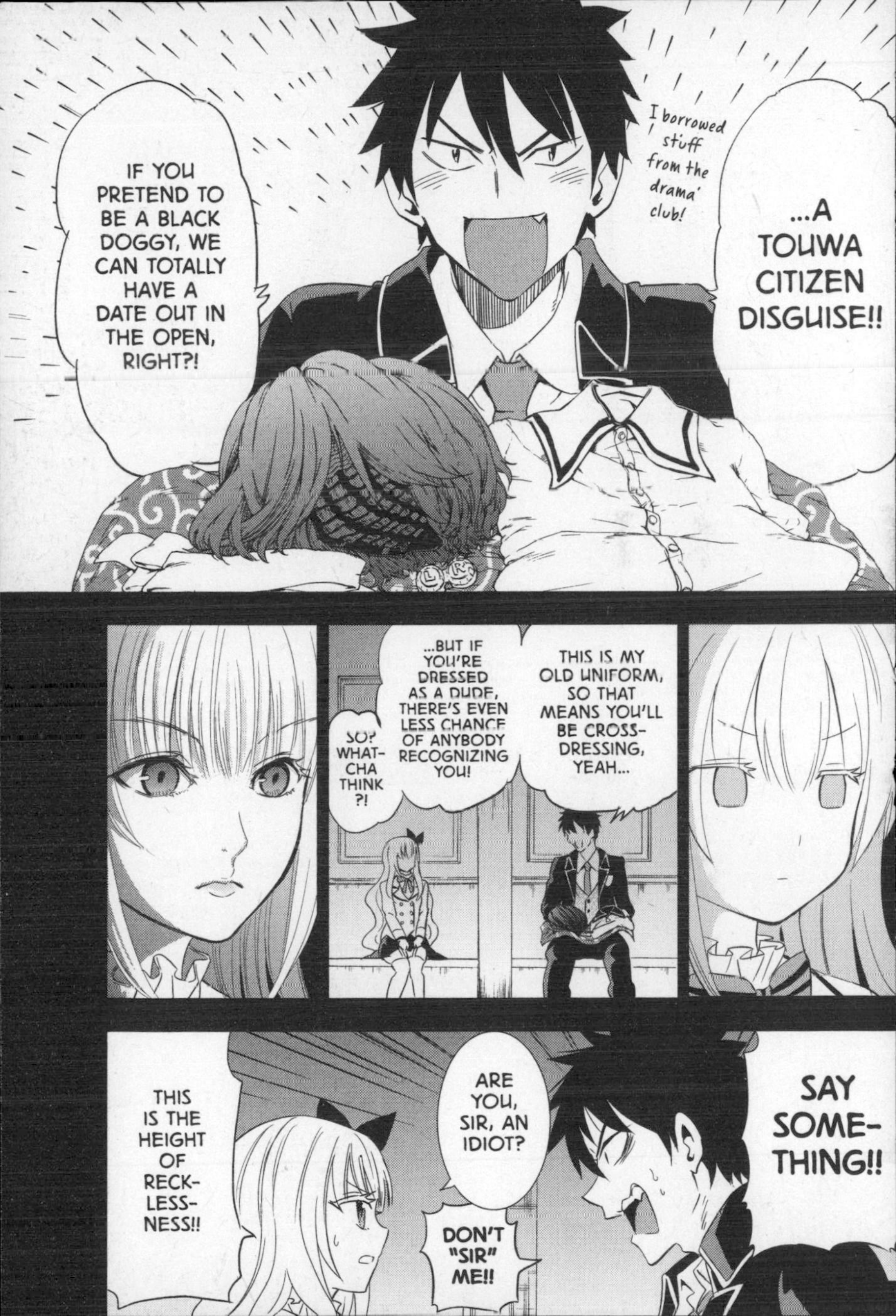
...A TOUWA CITIZEN DISGUISE!!
I borrowed stuff from the drama club!
IF YOU PRETEND TO BE A BLACK DOGGY, WE CAN TOTALLY HAVE A DATE OUT IN THE OPEN, RIGHT?!
THIS IS MY OLD UNIFORM, SO THAT MEANS YOU'LL BE CROSS-DRESSING, YEAH...
...BUT IF YOU'RE DRESSED AS A DUDE, THERE'S EVEN LESS CHANCE OF ANYBODY RECOGNIZING YOU!
SO? WHATCHA THINK?!
SAY SOMETHING!!
ARE YOU, SIR, AN IDIOT?
DON'T "SIR" ME!!
THIS IS THE HEIGHT OF RECKLESSNESS!!

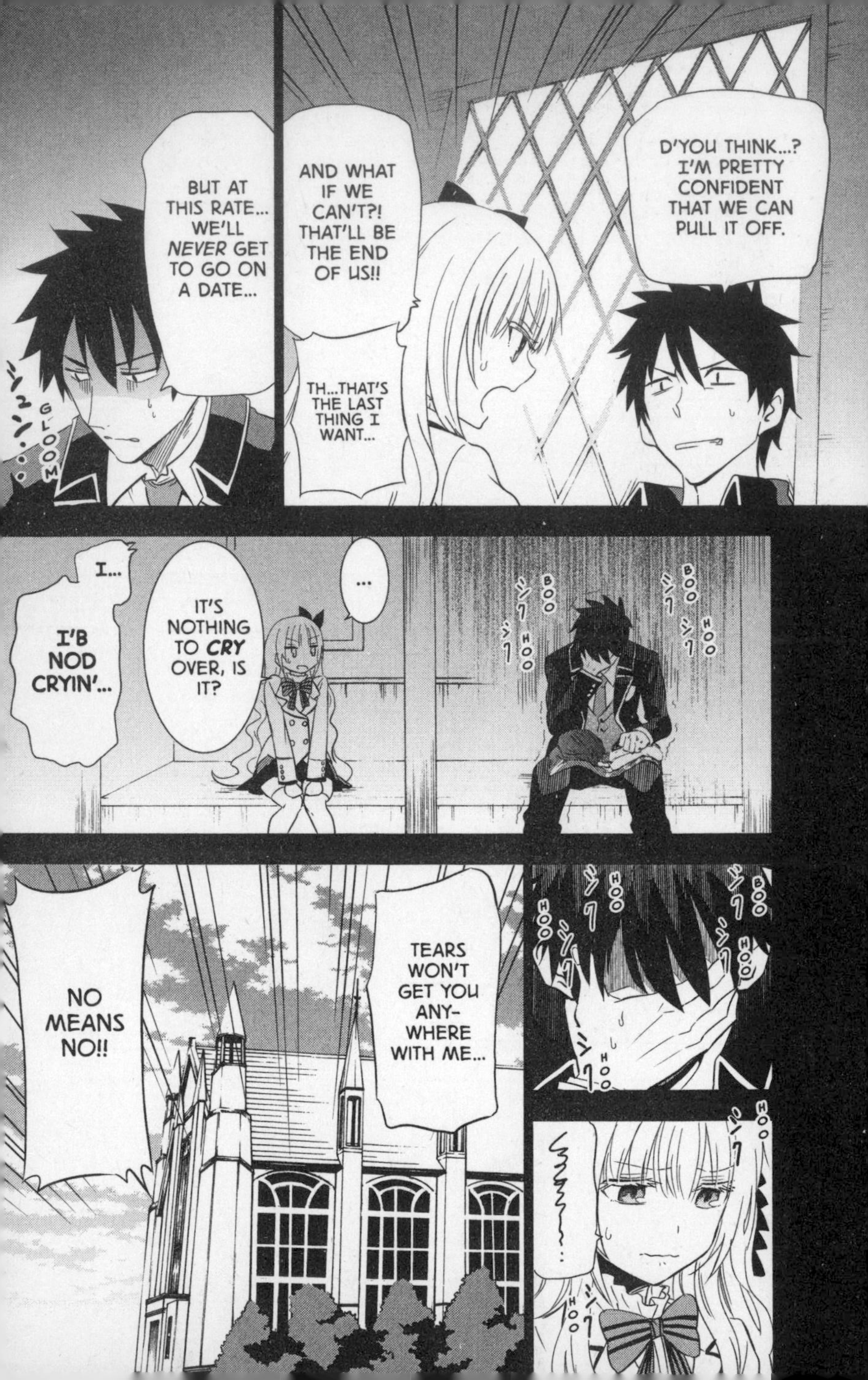
D'YOU THINK...? I'M PRETTY CONFIDENT THAT WE CAN PULL IT OFF.
AND WHAT IF WE CAN'T?! THAT'LL BE THE END OF US!!
TH...THAT'S THE LAST THING I WANT...
BUT AT THIS RATE... WE'LL *NEVER* GET TO GO ON A DATE...
GLOOM
BOO HOO
HOO
...
IT'S NOTHING TO **CRY** OVER, IS IT?
I...
I'B NOD CRYIN'...
BOO HOO
HOO
HOO
HOO
TEARS WON'T GET YOU ANY-WHERE WITH ME...
NO MEANS NO!!
HOO
HOO

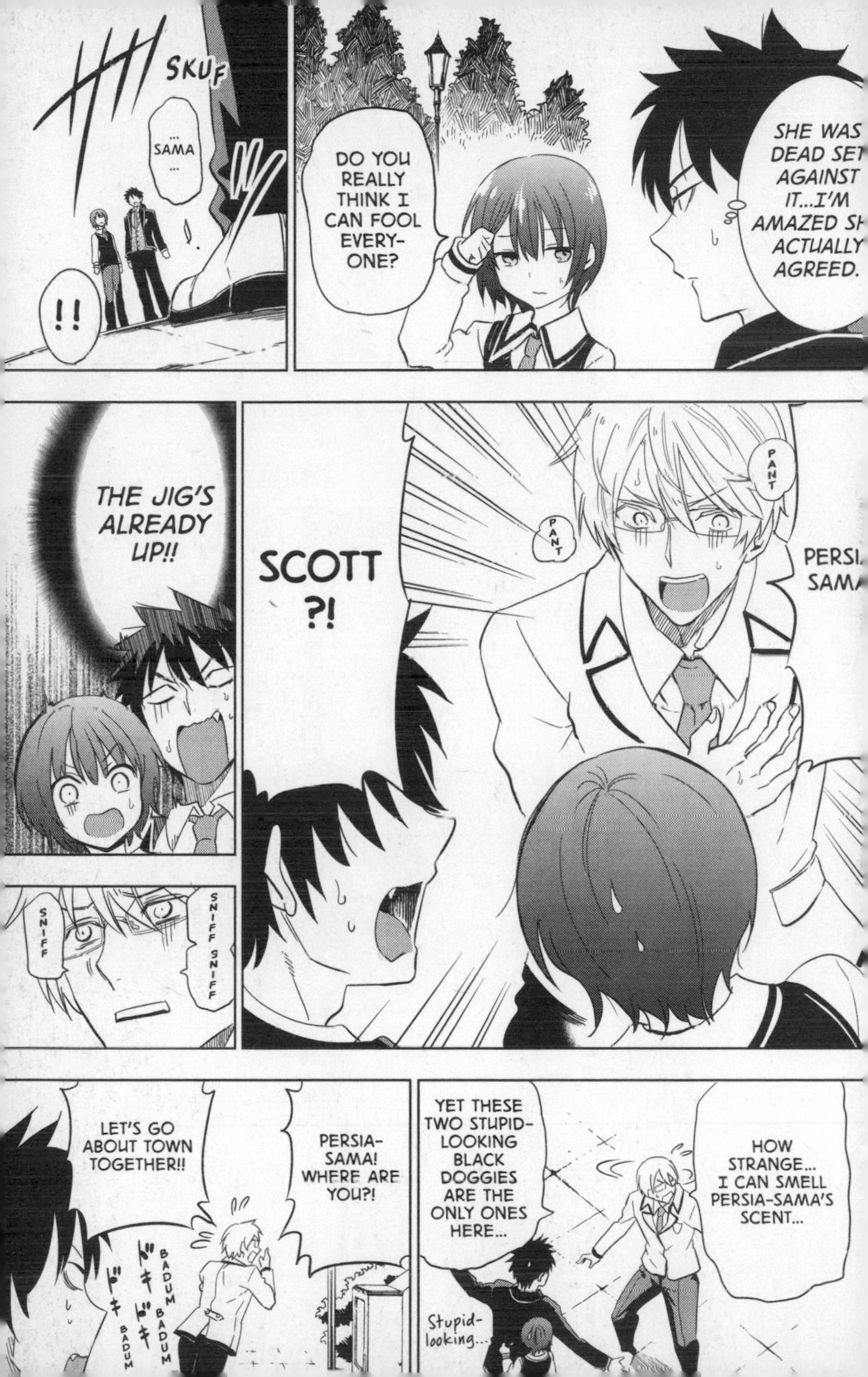
SHE WAS DEAD SET AGAINST IT...I'M AMAZED SH ACTUALLY AGREED.
DO YOU REALLY THINK I CAN FOOL EVERY-ONE?
SKUF
... SAMA ...
!!
PANT
PANT
PERSIA SAMA
SCOTT ?!
THE JIG'S ALREADY UP!!
SNIFF
SNIFF SNIFF
HOW STRANGE... I CAN SMELL PERSIA-SAMA'S SCENT...
YET THESE TWO STUPID-LOOKING BLACK DOGGIES ARE THE ONLY ONES HERE...
Stupid-looking...
PERSIA-SAMA! WHERE ARE YOU?!
LET'S GO ABOUT TOWN TOGETHER!!
ドキ ドキ
BADUM BADUM BADUM

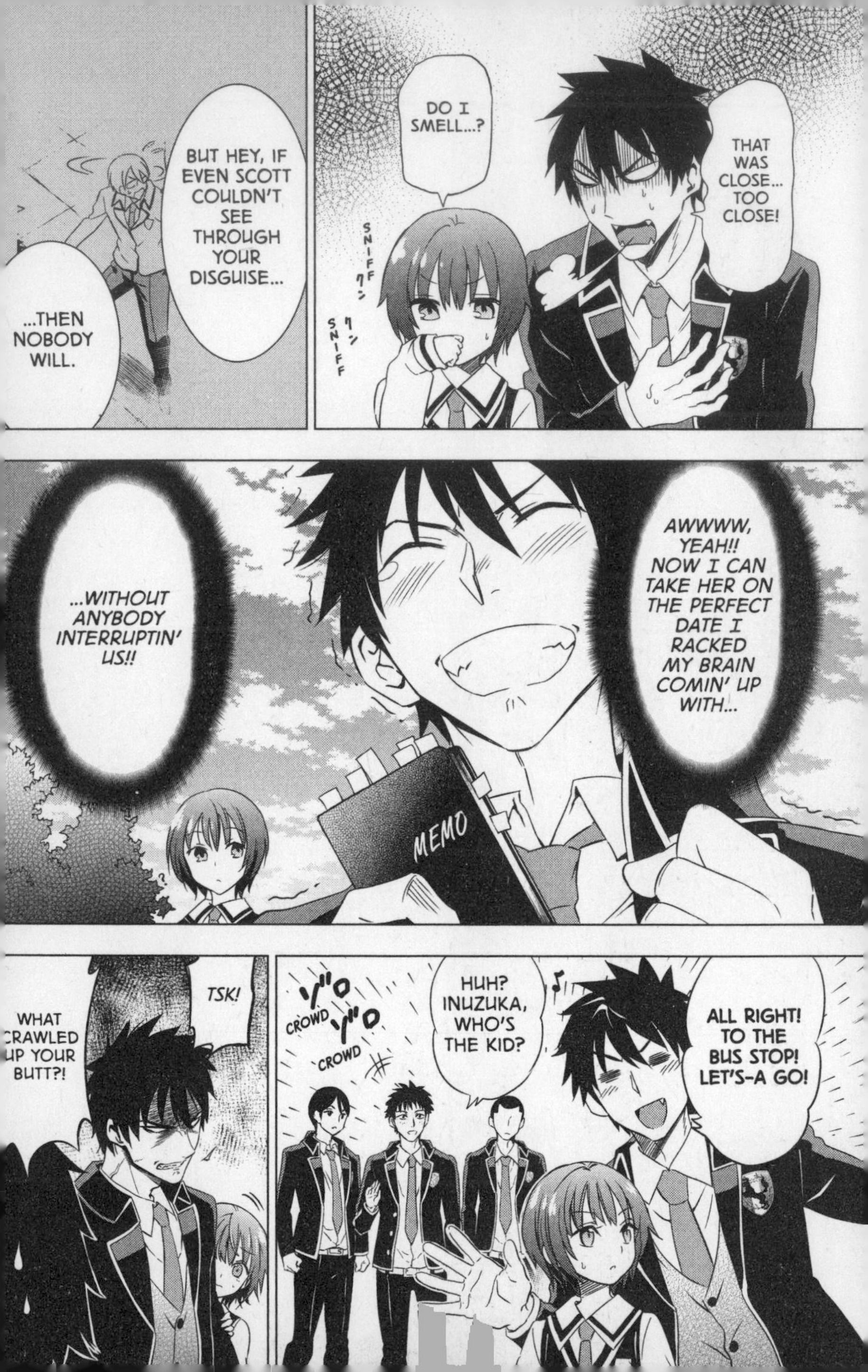
THAT WAS CLOSE... TOO CLOSE!
DO I SMELL...?
SNIFF
SNIFF
BUT HEY, IF EVEN SCOTT COULDN'T SEE THROUGH YOUR DISGUISE...
...THEN NOBODY WILL.
AWWWW, YEAH!! NOW I CAN TAKE HER ON THE PERFECT DATE I RACKED MY BRAIN COMIN' UP WITH...
...WITHOUT ANYBODY INTERRUPTIN' US!!
MEMO
ALL RIGHT! TO THE BUS STOP! LET'S-A GO!
HUH? INUZUKA, WHO'S THE KID?
CROWD
CROWD
TSK!
WHAT CRAWLED UP YOUR BUTT?!

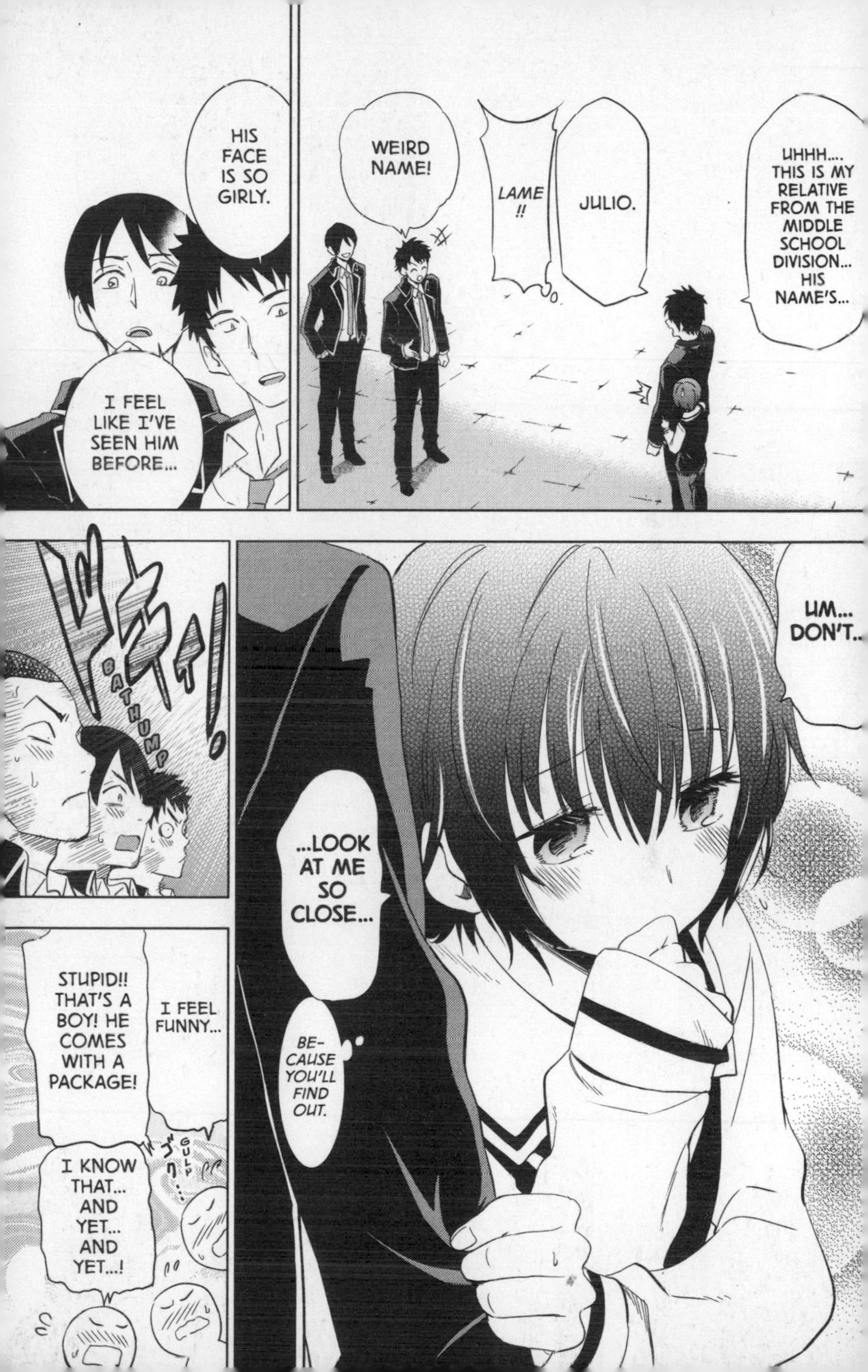
UHHH.... THIS IS MY RELATIVE FROM THE MIDDLE SCHOOL DIVISION... HIS NAME'S...
JULIO.
LAME !!
WEIRD NAME!
HIS FACE IS SO GIRLY.
I FEEL LIKE I'VE SEEN HIM BEFORE...
UM... DON'T..
...LOOK AT ME SO CLOSE...
BE-CAUSE YOU'LL FIND OUT.
BATHUMP
STUPID!! THAT'S A BOY! HE COMES WITH A PACKAGE!
I FEEL FUNNY...
GULP
I KNOW THAT... AND YET... AND YET...!

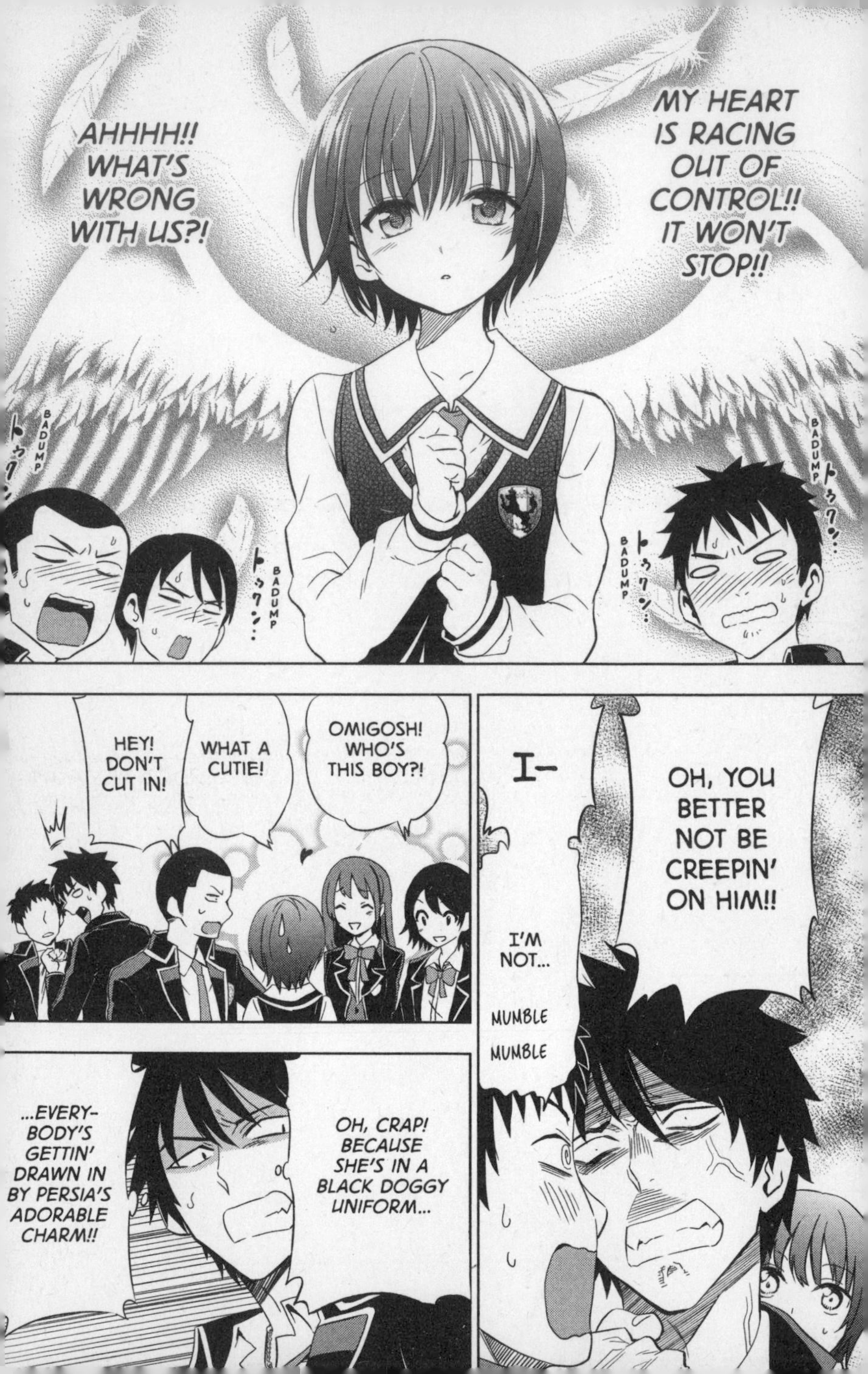
MY HEART IS RACING OUT OF CONTROL!! IT WON'T STOP!!
BADUMP
BADUMP
AHHHH!! WHAT'S WRONG WITH US?!
BADUMP
BADUMP
OH, YOU BETTER NOT BE CREEPIN' ON HIM!!
I—
I'M NOT...
MUMBLE
MUMBLE
OMIGOSH! WHO'S THIS BOY?!
WHAT A CUTIE!
HEY! DON'T CUT IN!
OH, CRAP! BECAUSE SHE'S IN A BLACK DOGGY UNIFORM...
...EVERY-BODY'S GETTIN' DRAWN IN BY PERSIA'S ADORABLE CHARM!!

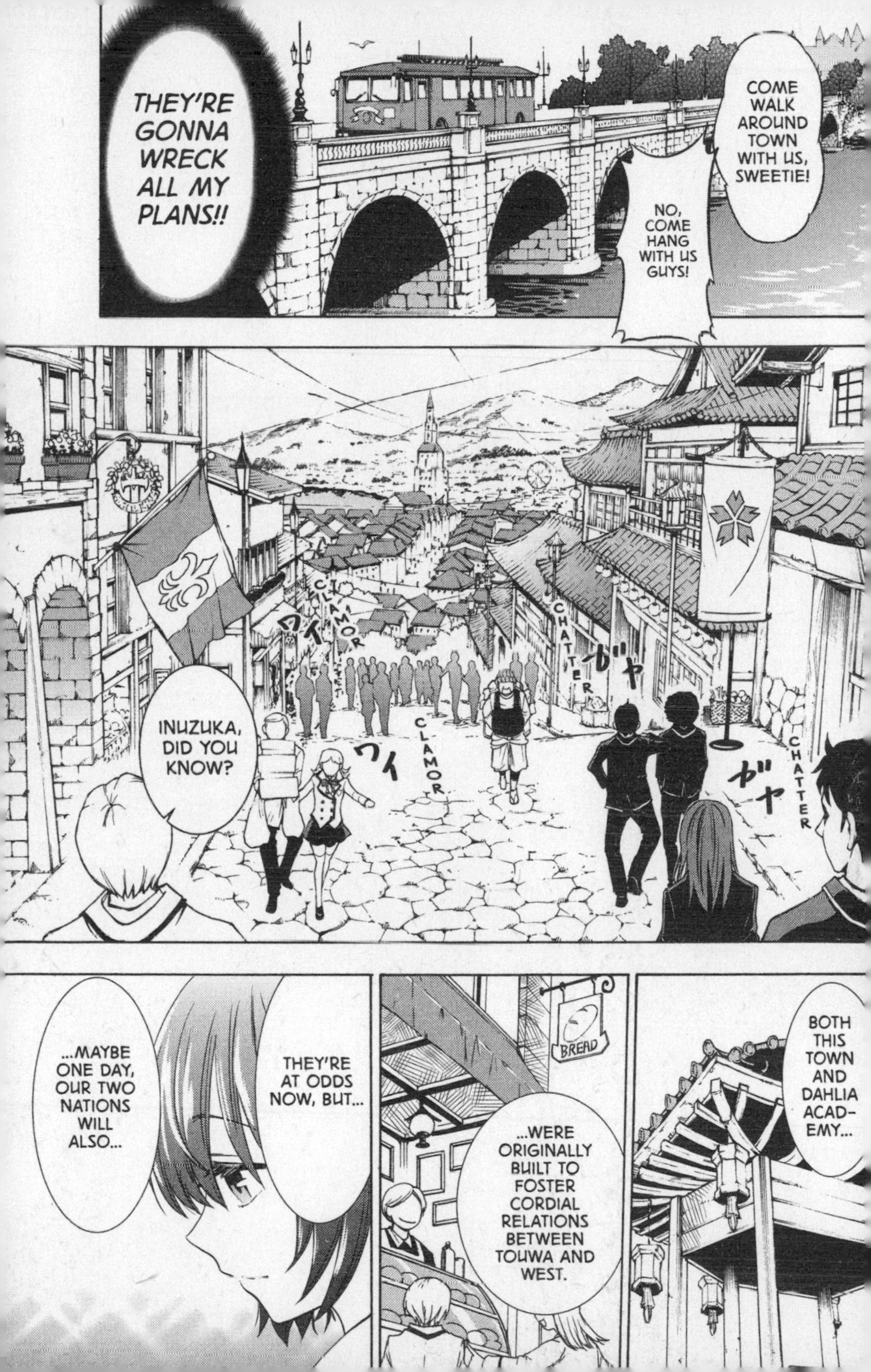
COME WALK AROUND TOWN WITH US, SWEETIE!
NO, COME HANG WITH US GUYS!
THEY'RE GONNA WRECK ALL MY PLANS!!
ガヤ CHATTER
ガヤ CHATTER
ワイ CLAMOR
ワイ CLAMOR
INUZUKA, DID YOU KNOW?
BOTH THIS TOWN AND DAHLIA ACAD-EMY...
BREAD
...WERE ORIGINALLY BUILT TO FOSTER CORDIAL RELATIONS BETWEEN TOUWA AND WEST.
THEY'RE AT ODDS NOW, BUT...
...MAYBE ONE DAY, OUR TWO NATIONS WILL ALSO...

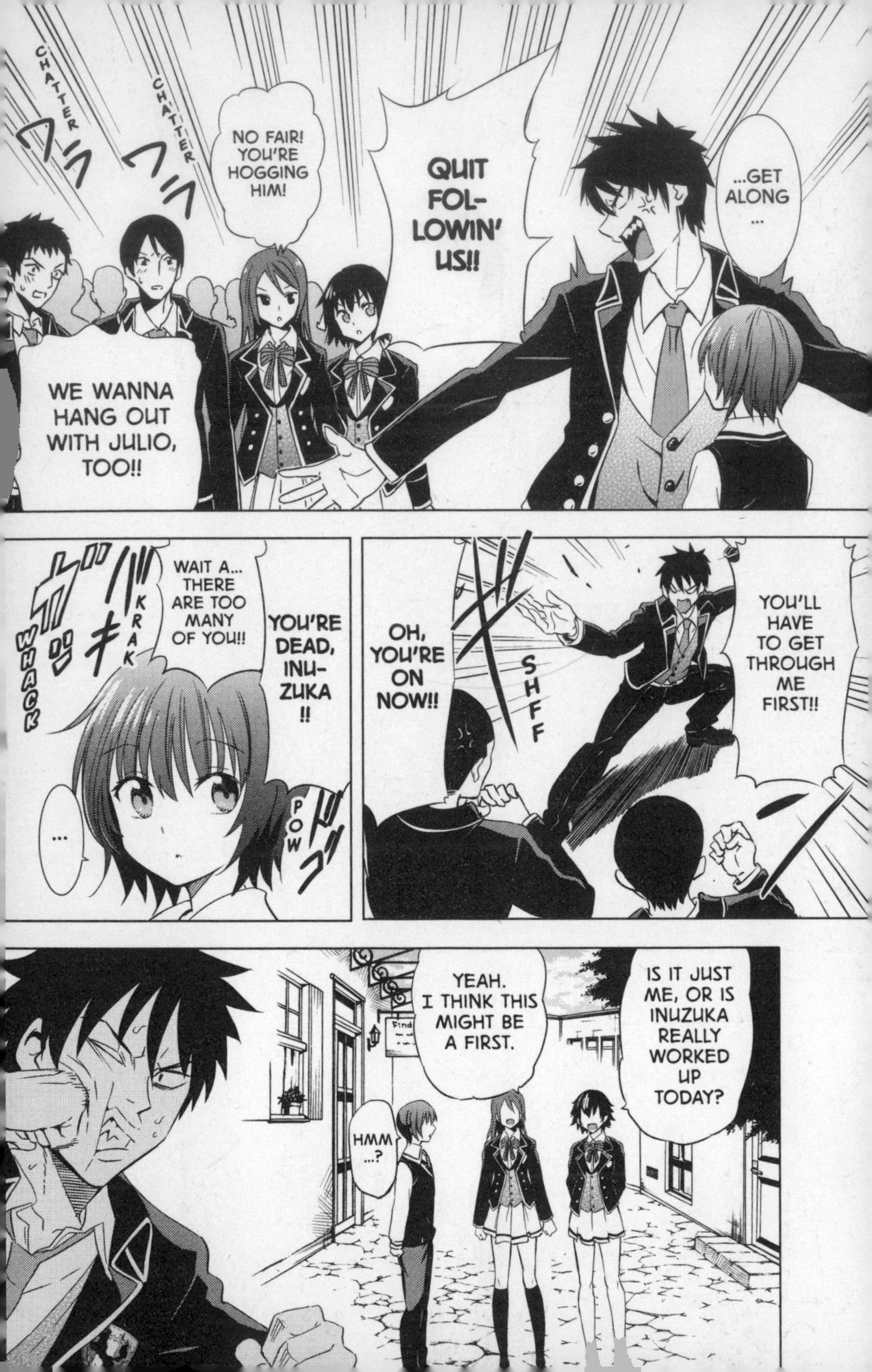
...GET ALONG ...
QUIT FOL- LOWIN' US!!
NO FAIR! YOU'RE HOGGING HIM!
CHATTER
CHATTER
WE WANNA HANG OUT WITH JULIO, TOO!!
YOU'LL HAVE TO GET THROUGH ME FIRST!!
SHFF
OH, YOU'RE ON NOW!!
YOU'RE DEAD, INU- ZUKA !!
WAIT A... THERE ARE TOO MANY OF YOU!!
KRAK
WHACK
POW
...
IS IT JUST ME, OR IS INUZUKA REALLY WORKED UP TODAY?
YEAH. I THINK THIS MIGHT BE A FIRST.
HMM ...?

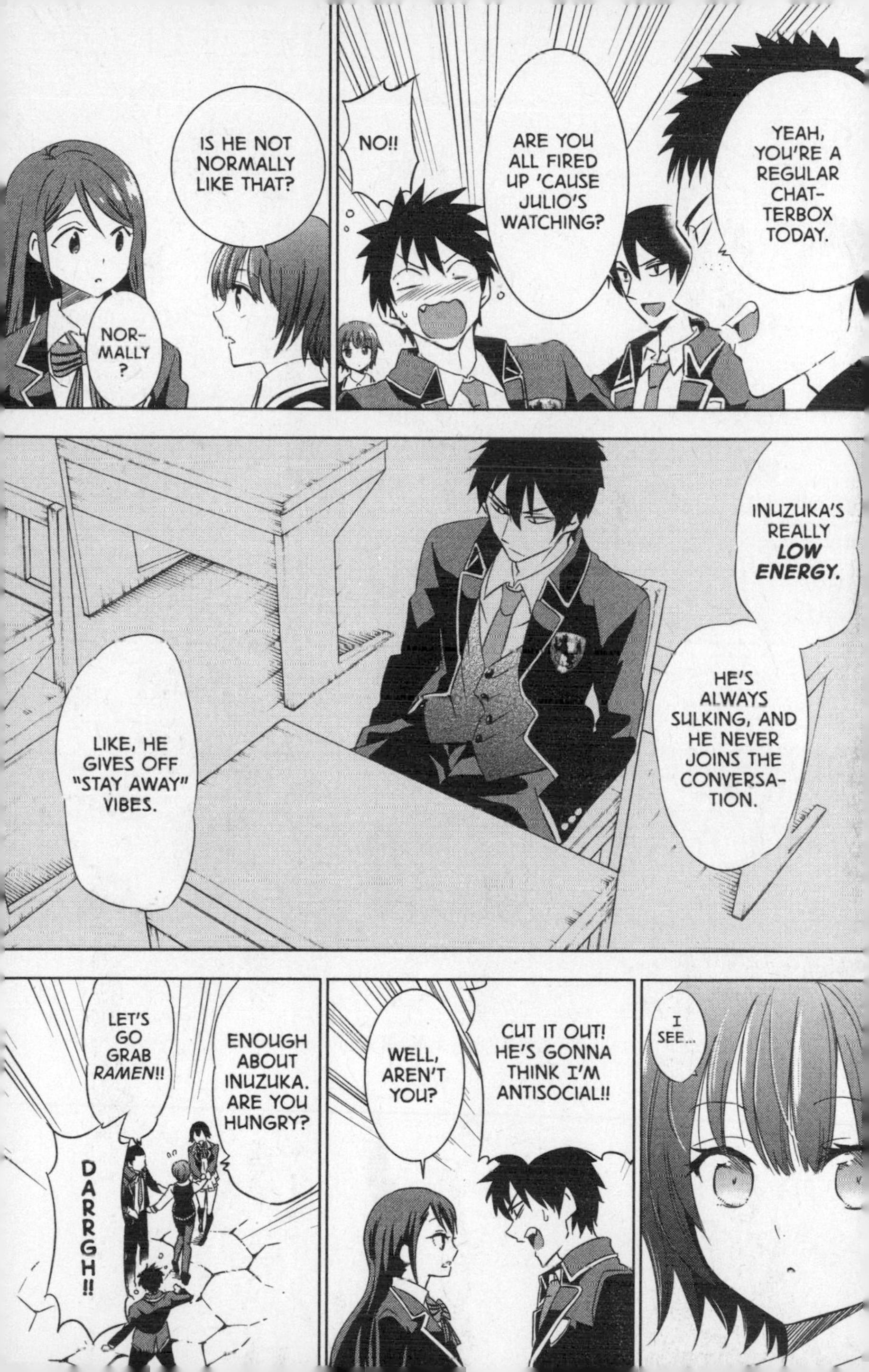
YEAH, YOU'RE A REGULAR CHAT-TERBOX TODAY.
ARE YOU ALL FIRED UP 'CAUSE JULIO'S WATCHING?
NO!!
IS HE NOT NORMALLY LIKE THAT?
NOR-MALLY?
INUZUKA'S REALLY *LOW ENERGY.*
HE'S ALWAYS SULKING, AND HE NEVER JOINS THE CONVERSA-TION.
LIKE, HE GIVES OFF "STAY AWAY" VIBES.
I SEE...
CUT IT OUT! HE'S GONNA THINK I'M ANTISOCIAL!!
WELL, AREN'T YOU?
ENOUGH ABOUT INUZUKA. ARE YOU HUNGRY?
LET'S GO GRAB *RAMEN*!!
DARRGH!!

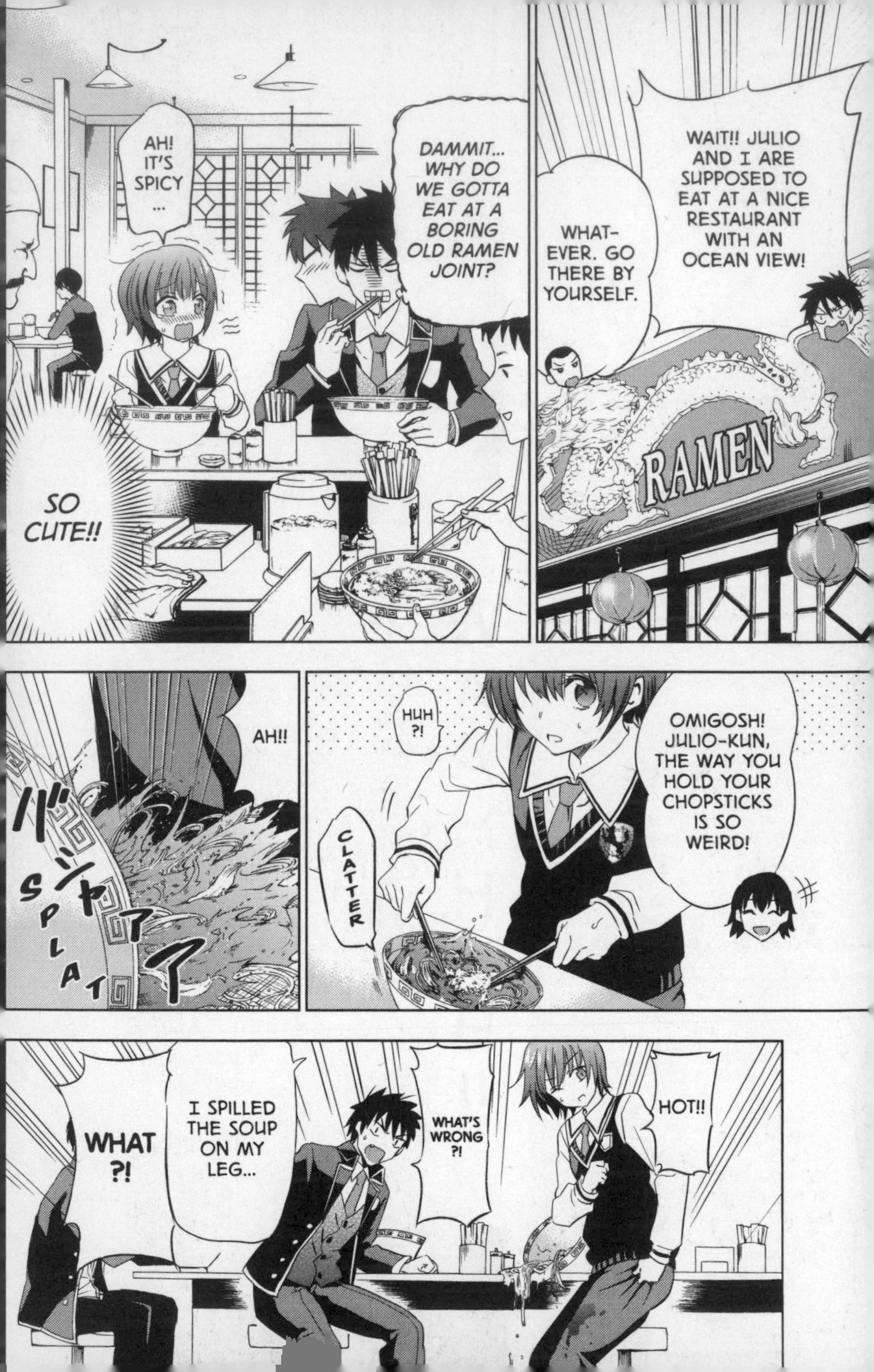
WAIT!! JULIO AND I ARE SUPPOSED TO EAT AT A NICE RESTAURANT WITH AN OCEAN VIEW!
WHAT-EVER. GO THERE BY YOURSELF.
RAMEN
DAMMIT... WHY DO WE GOTTA EAT AT A BORING OLD RAMEN JOINT?
AH! IT'S SPICY ...
SO CUTE!!
OMIGOSH! JULIO-KUN, THE WAY YOU HOLD YOUR CHOPSTICKS IS SO WEIRD!
HUH ?!
CLATTER
AH!!
SPLAT
HOT!!
WHAT'S WRONG ?!
I SPILLED THE SOUP ON MY LEG...
WHAT ?!

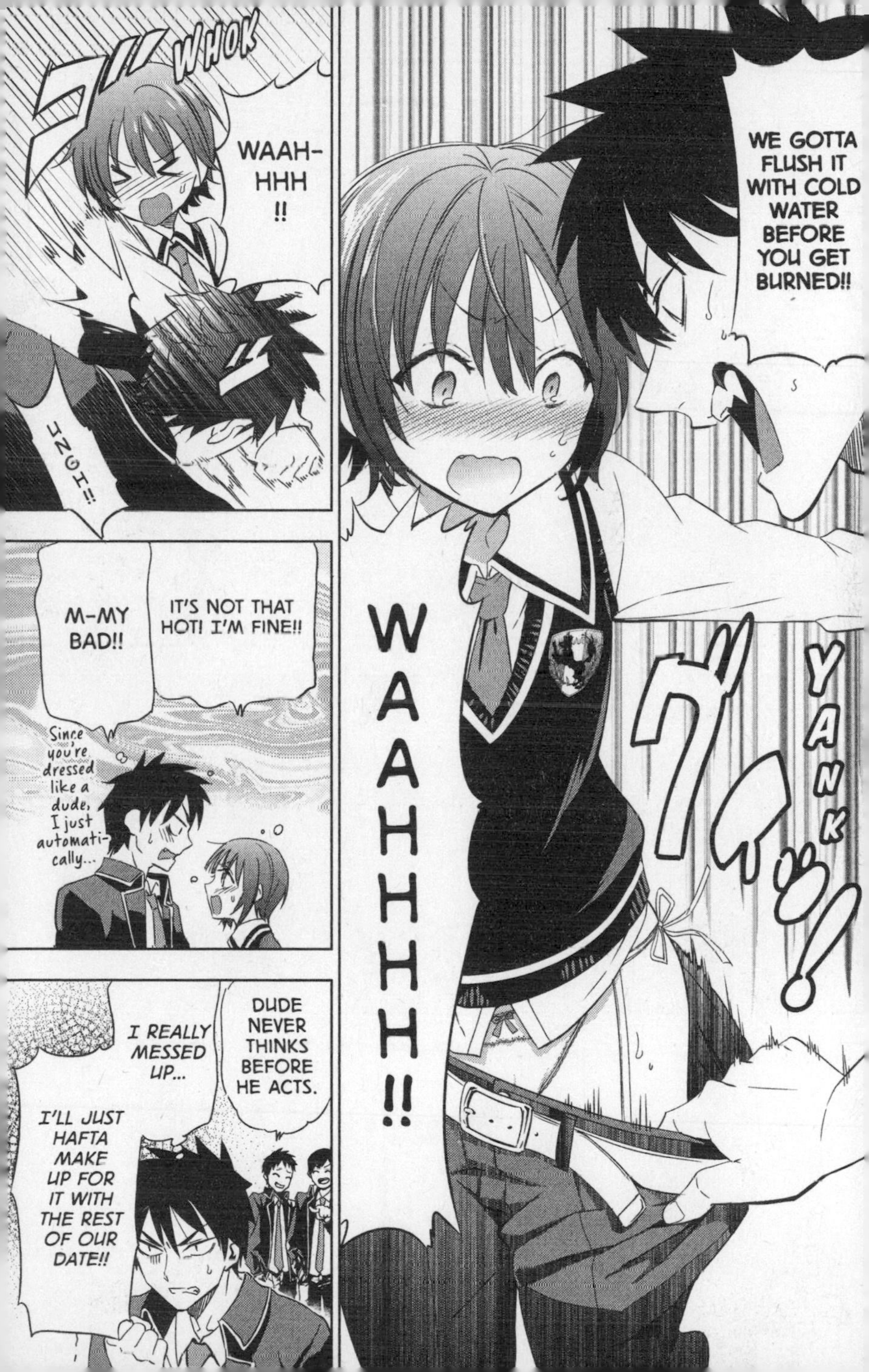
WE GOTTA FLUSH IT WITH COLD WATER BEFORE YOU GET BURNED!!
YANK
WAAHHHH!!
WHOK
WAAH-HHH !!
UNGH!!
IT'S NOT THAT HOT! I'M FINE!!
M-MY BAD!!
Since you're dressed like a dude, I just automatically...
DUDE NEVER THINKS BEFORE HE ACTS.
I REALLY MESSED UP...
I'LL JUST HAFTA MAKE UP FOR IT WITH THE REST OF OUR DATE!!

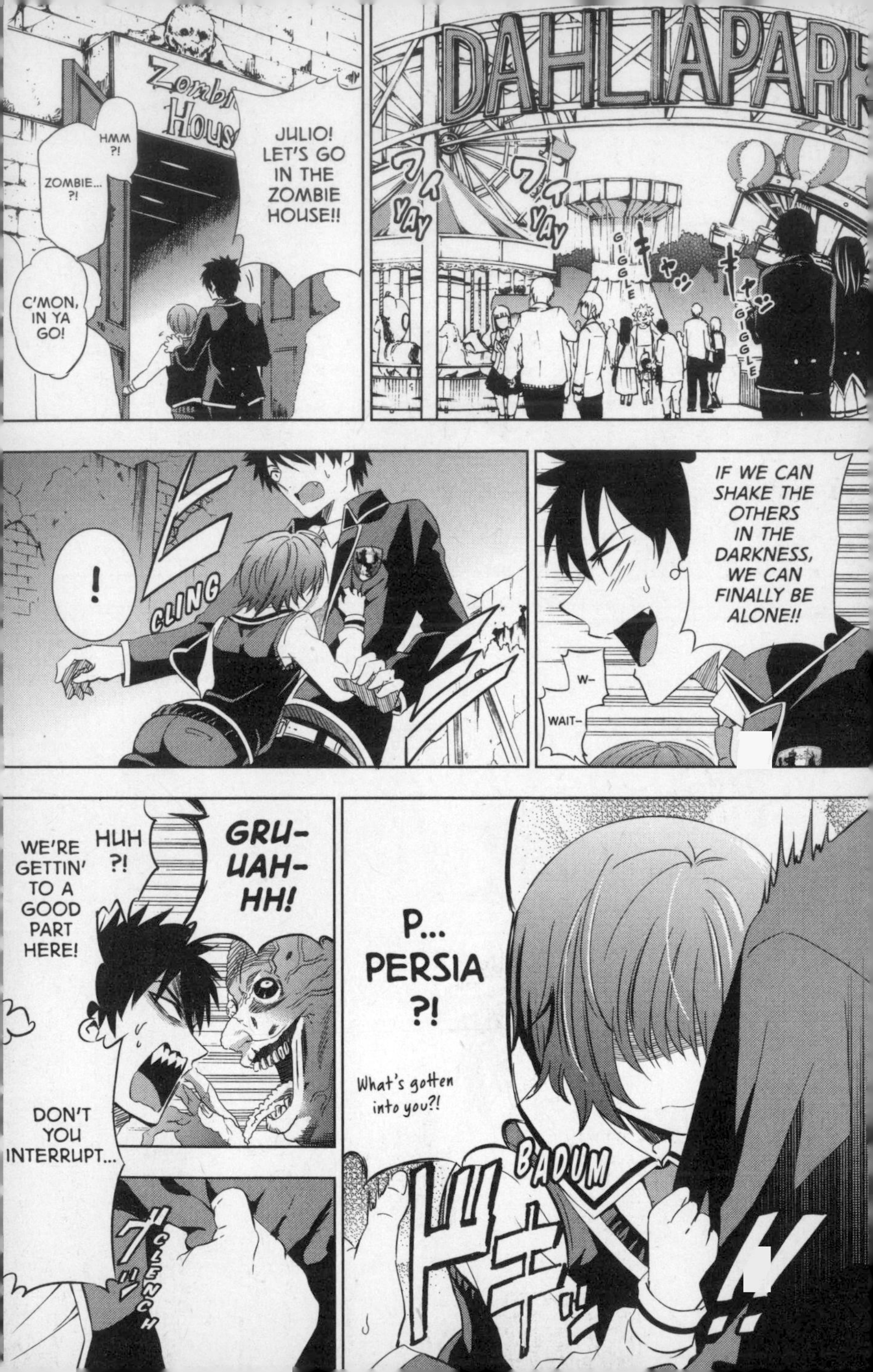
DAHLIAPAR
ワイ
YAY
ワイ
YAY
キャッ
GIGGLE
キャッ
GIGGLE
JULIO! LET'S GO IN THE ZOMBIE HOUSE!!
Zombie House
HMM ?!
ZOMBIE... ?!
C'MON, IN YA GO!
IF WE CAN SHAKE THE OTHERS IN THE DARKNESS, WE CAN FINALLY BE ALONE!!
W—
WAIT—
!
CLING
P... PERSIA ?!
What's gotten into you?!
BADUM
ドキッ
GRU-UAH-HH!
HUH ?!
WE'RE GETTIN' TO A GOOD PART HERE!
DON'T YOU INTERRUPT...
グッ
CLENCH

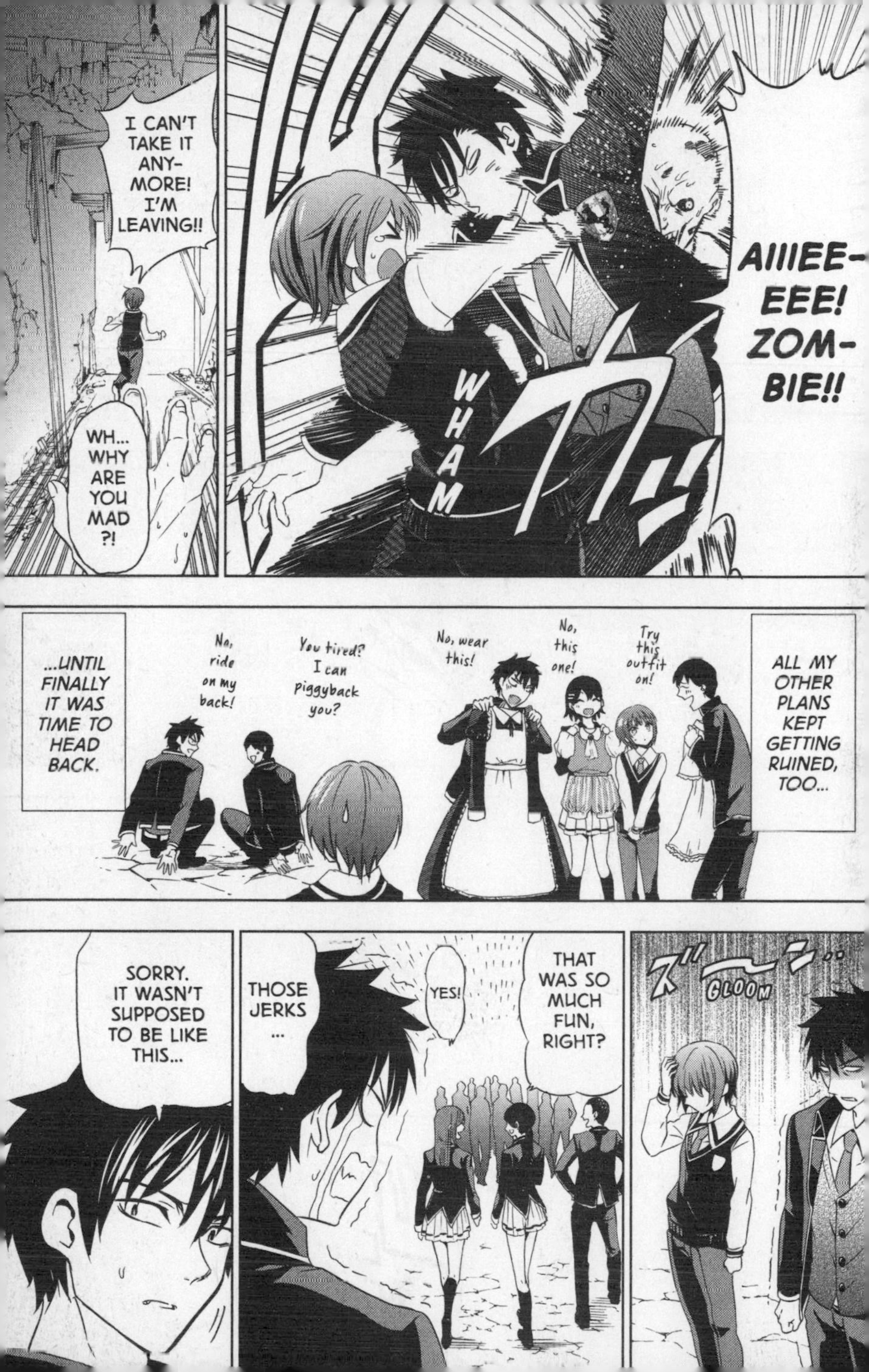
AIIIEE-EEE! ZOMBIE!!
WHAM
I CAN'T TAKE IT ANY-MORE! I'M LEAVING!!
WH... WHY ARE YOU MAD ?!
ALL MY OTHER PLANS KEPT GETTING RUINED, TOO...
Try this outfit on!
No, this one!
No, wear this!
You tired? I can piggyback you?
No, ride on my back!
...UNTIL FINALLY IT WAS TIME TO HEAD BACK.
GLOOM
THAT WAS SO MUCH FUN, RIGHT?
YES!
THOSE JERKS ...
SORRY. IT WASN'T SUPPOSED TO BE LIKE THIS...

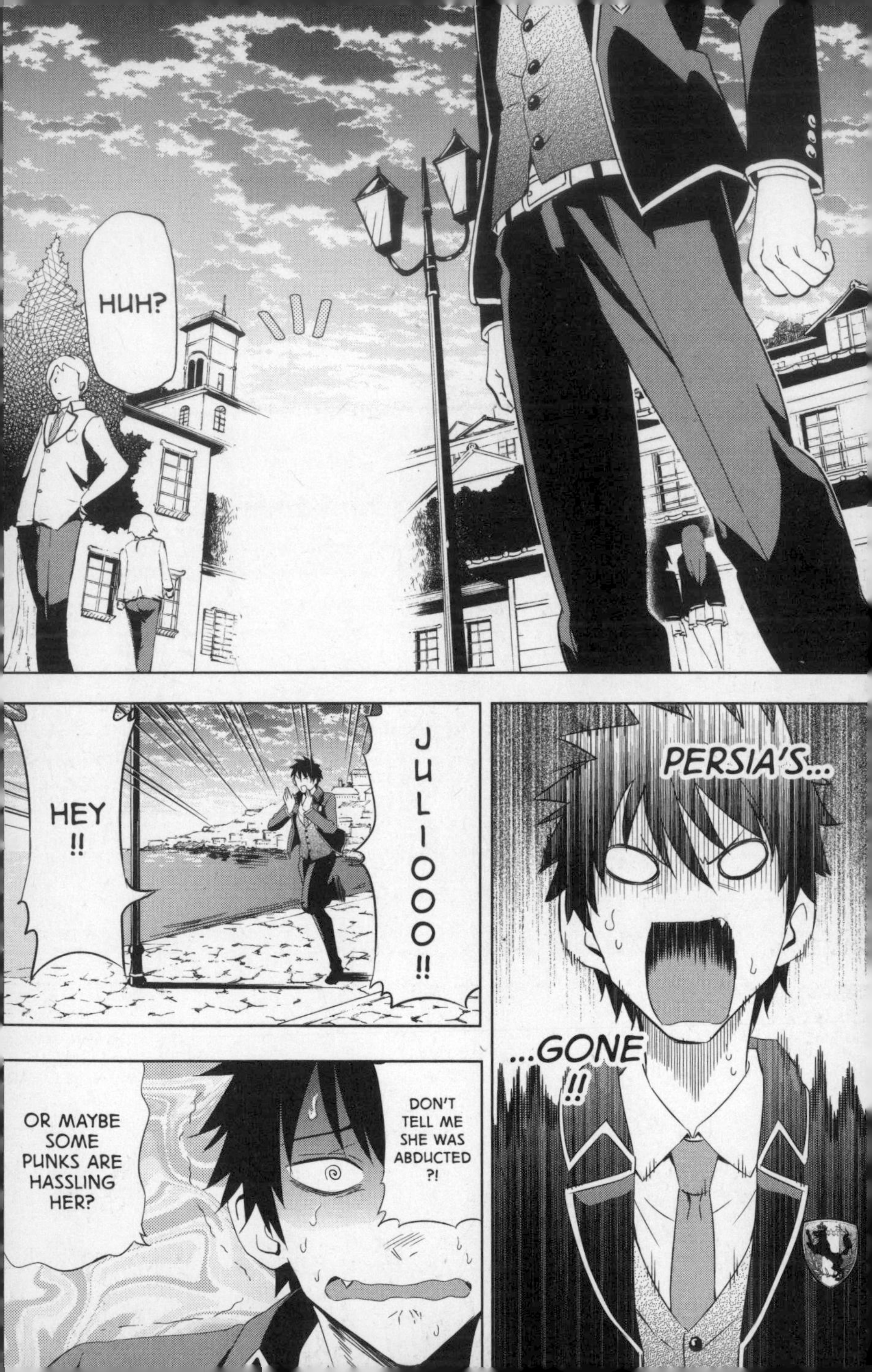
HUH?
PERSIA'S...
...GONE!!
JULIOOO!!
HEY!!
DON'T TELL ME SHE WAS ABDUCTED?!
OR MAYBE SOME PUNKS ARE HASSLING HER?

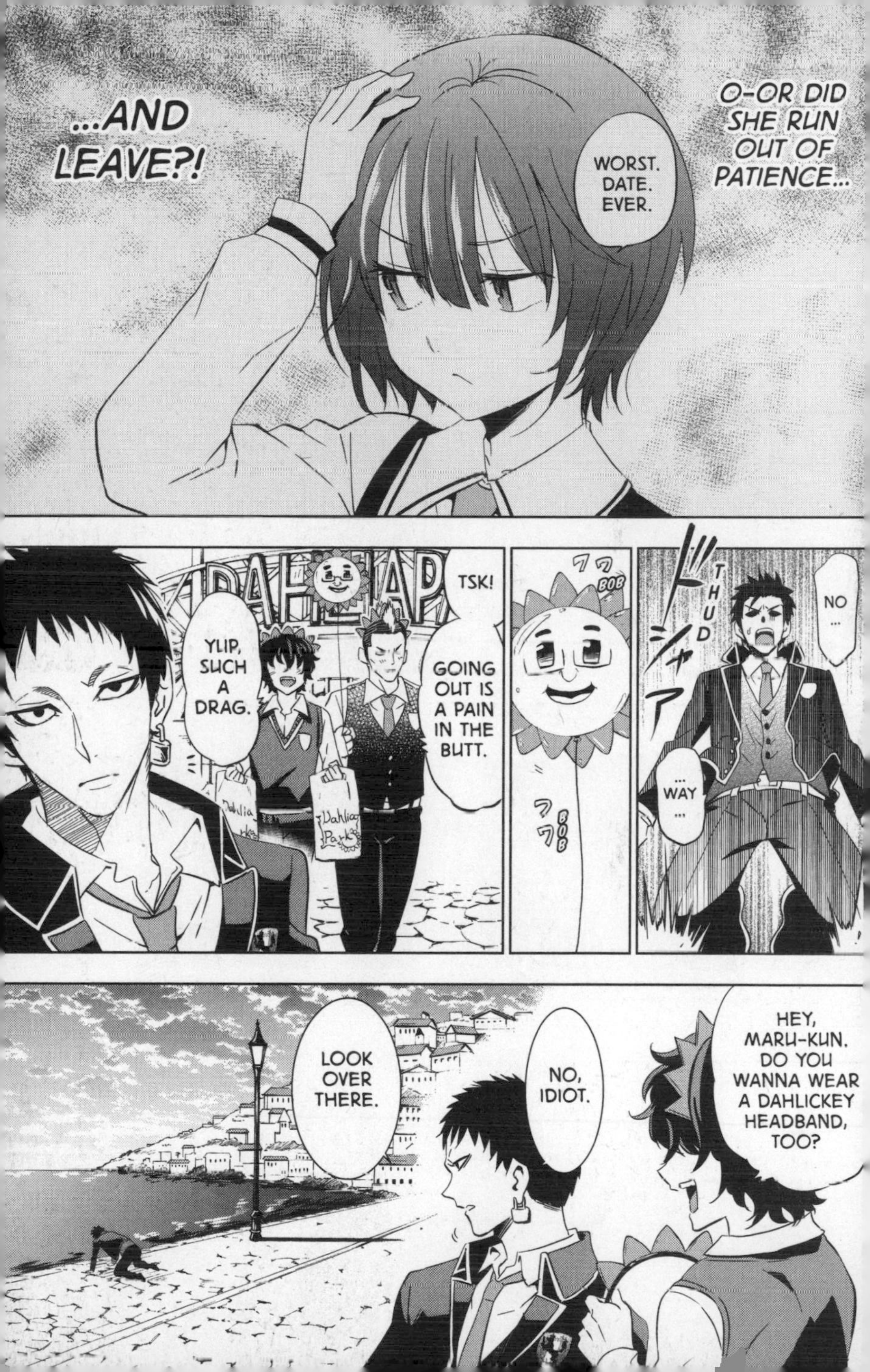
O-OR DID SHE RUN OUT OF PATIENCE...
WORST. DATE. EVER.
...AND LEAVE?!
THUD
NO ...
... WAY ...
BOB
BOB
TSK!
GOING OUT IS A PAIN IN THE BUTT.
YUP, SUCH A DRAG.
Dahlia Park
HEY, MARU-KUN. DO YOU WANNA WEAR A DAHLICKEY HEADBAND, TOO?
NO, IDIOT.
LOOK OVER THERE.

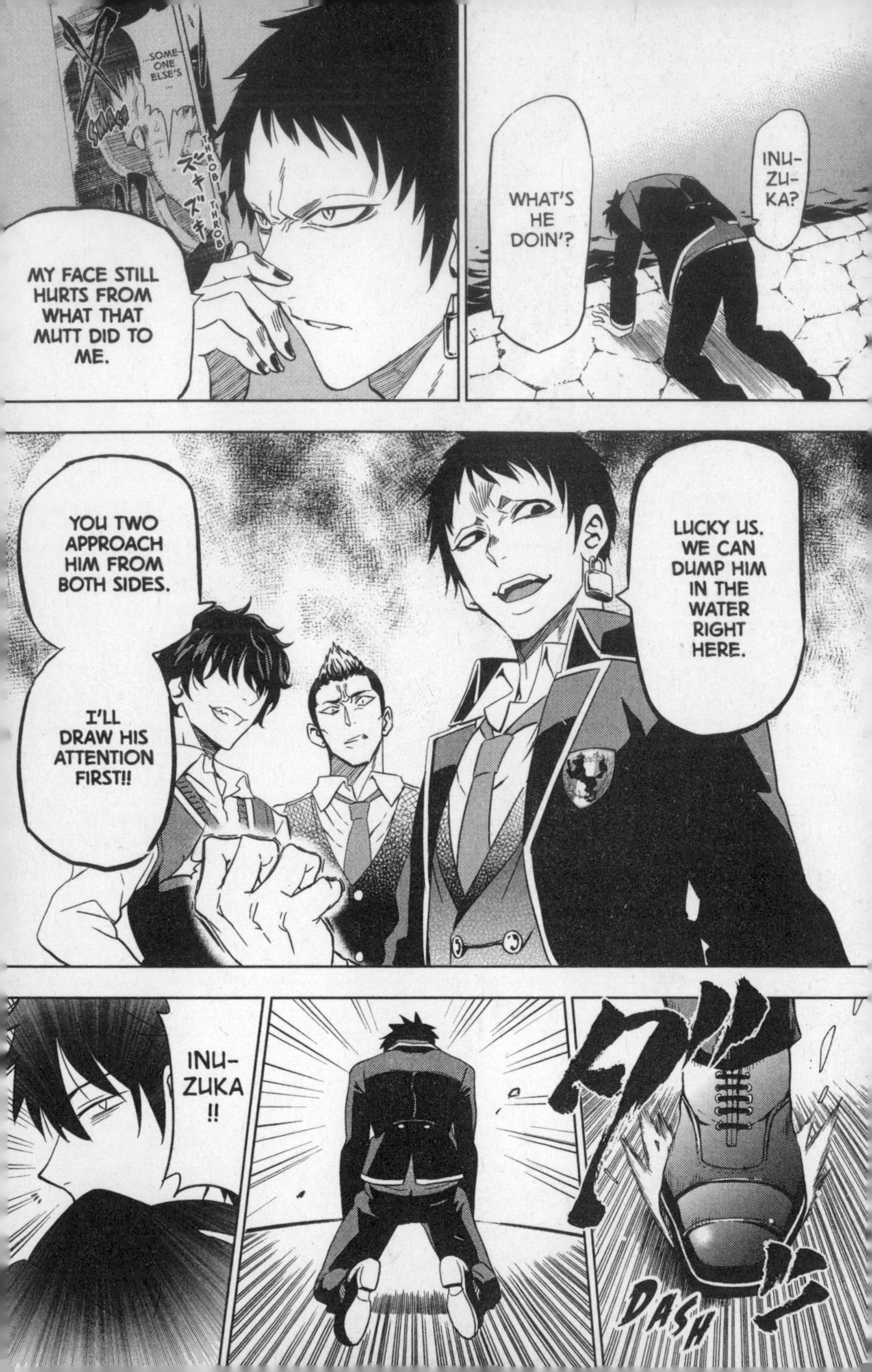
INU-ZUKA?
WHAT'S HE DOIN'?
...SOME-ONE ELSE'S ...
SMASH
THROB THROB
MY FACE STILL HURTS FROM WHAT THAT MUTT DID TO ME.
LUCKY US. WE CAN DUMP HIM IN THE WATER RIGHT HERE.
YOU TWO APPROACH HIM FROM BOTH SIDES.
I'LL DRAW HIS ATTENTION FIRST!!
DASH
INU-ZUKA !!

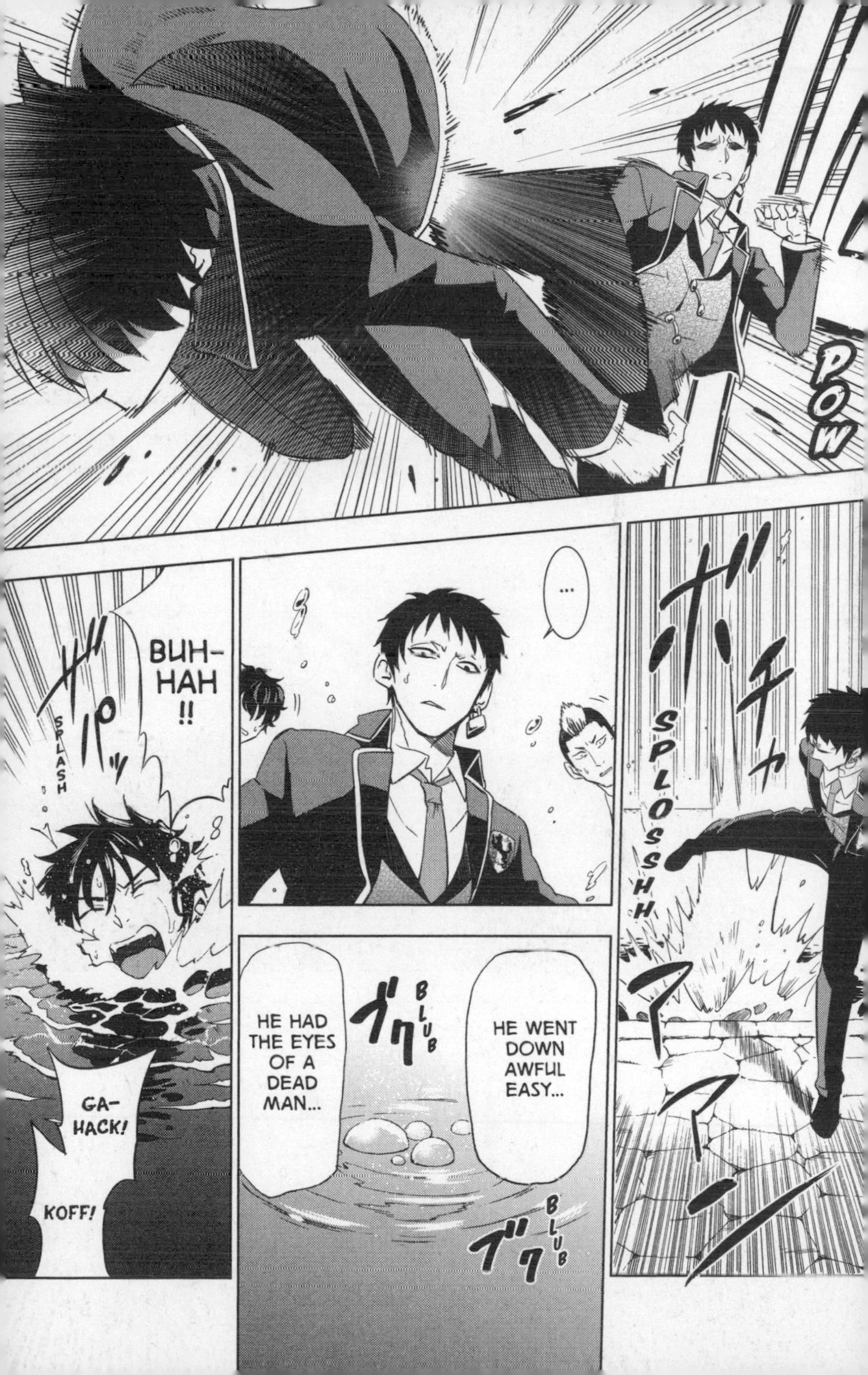
POW
SPLOSSHH
...
HE WENT DOWN AWFUL EASY...
BLUB
HE HAD THE EYES OF A DEAD MAN...
BLUB
BUH-HAH!!
SPLASH
GA-HACK!
KOFF!

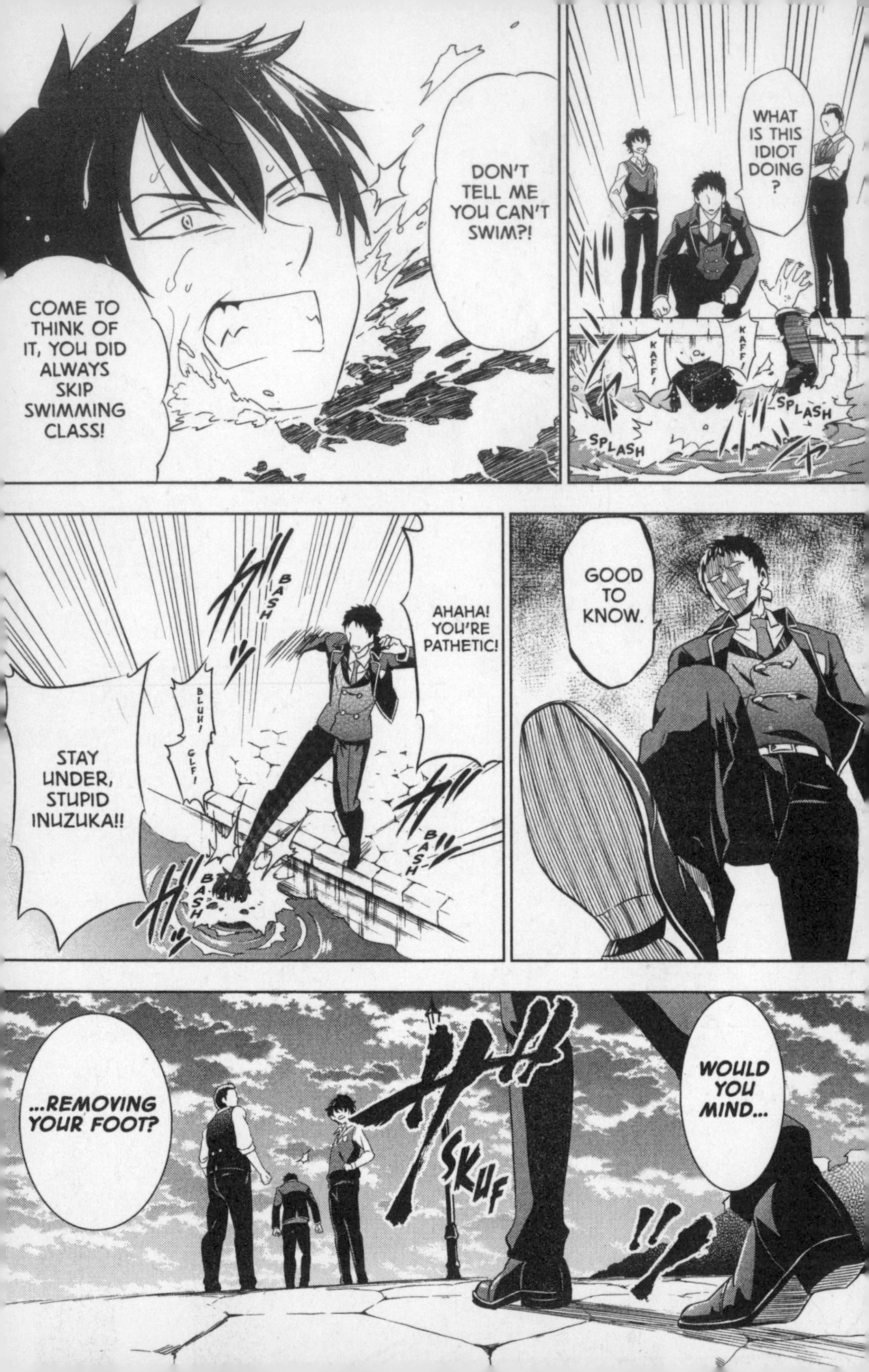
WHAT IS THIS IDIOT DOING?
KAFF!
KAFF!
SPLASH
SPLASH
DON'T TELL ME YOU CAN'T SWIM?!
COME TO THINK OF IT, YOU DID ALWAYS SKIP SWIMMING CLASS!
GOOD TO KNOW.
AHAHA! YOU'RE PATHETIC!
BASH
BLUH! GLF!
STAY UNDER, STUPID INUZUKA!!
BASH
BASH
WOULD YOU MIND...
SKUF
!!
...REMOVING YOUR FOOT?

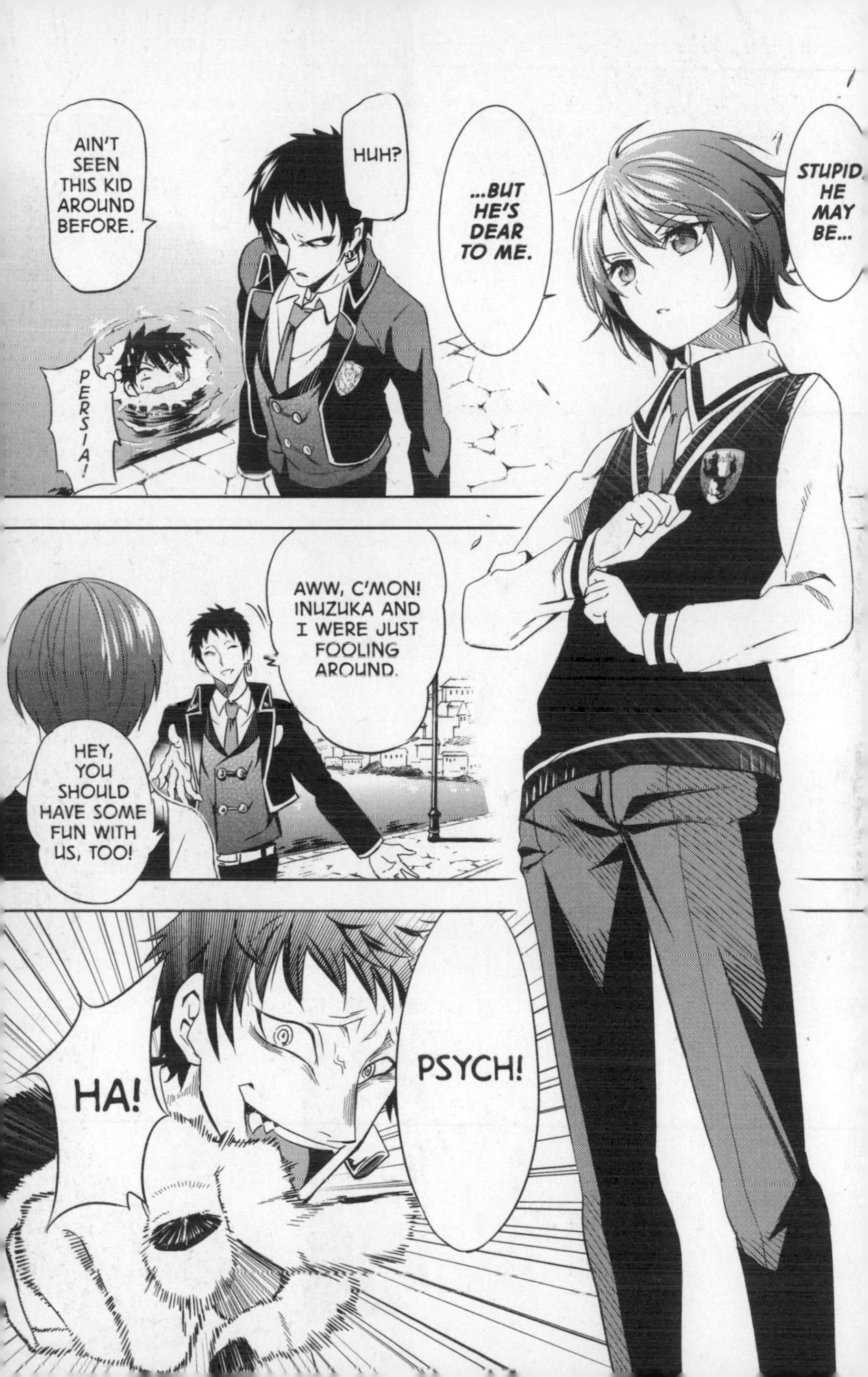
STUPID, HE MAY BE...
...BUT HE'S DEAR TO ME.
HUH?
AIN'T SEEN THIS KID AROUND BEFORE.
PERSIA!
AWW, C'MON! INUZUKA AND I WERE JUST FOOLING AROUND.
HEY, YOU SHOULD HAVE SOME FUN WITH US, TOO!
PSYCH!
HA!

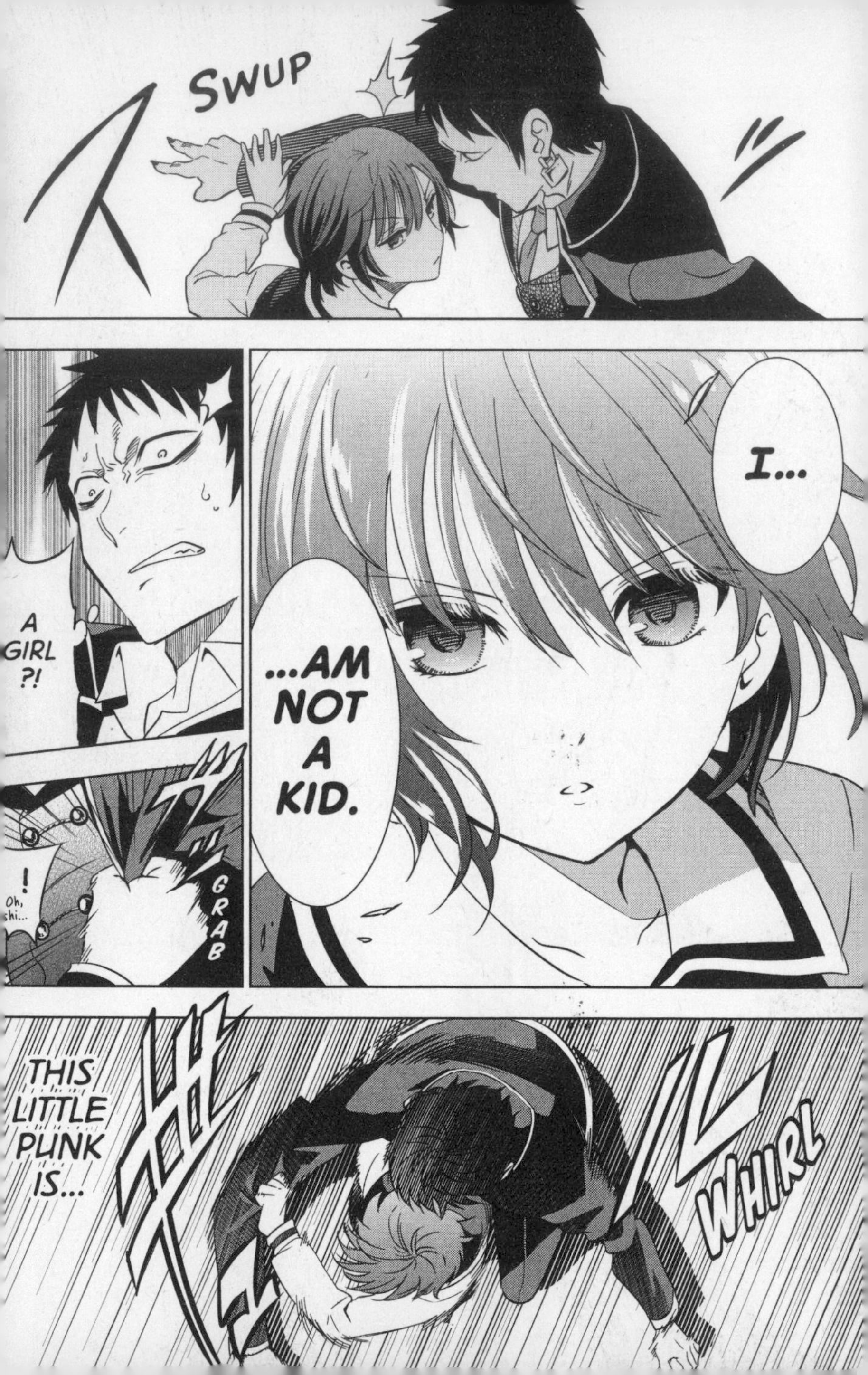
SWUP
I...
...AM NOT A KID.
A GIRL ?!
!
Oh, shi...
GRAB
WHIRL
THIS LITTLE PUNK IS...

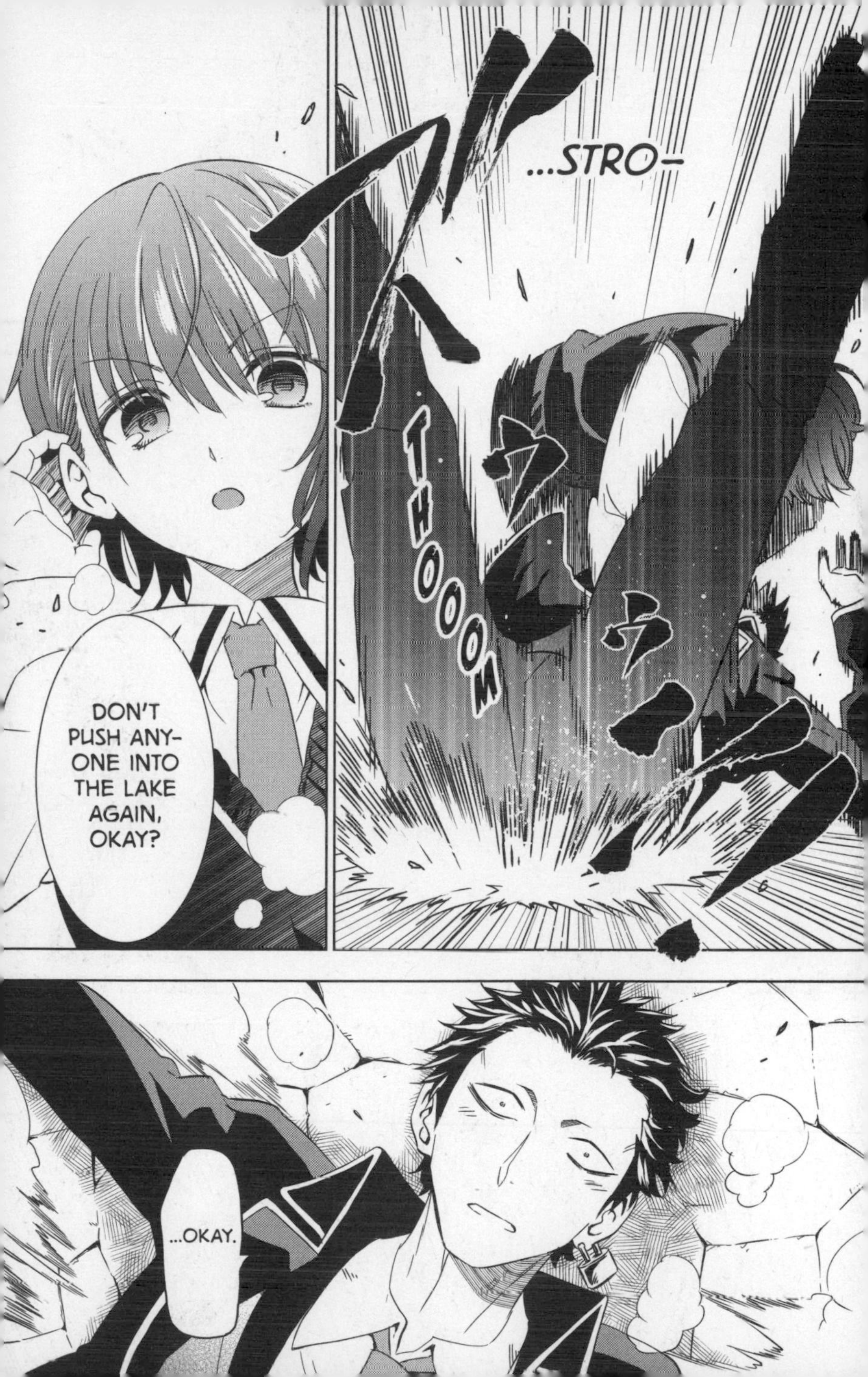
...STRO-
THOOOM
DON'T PUSH ANY-ONE INTO THE LAKE AGAIN, OKAY?
...OKAY.

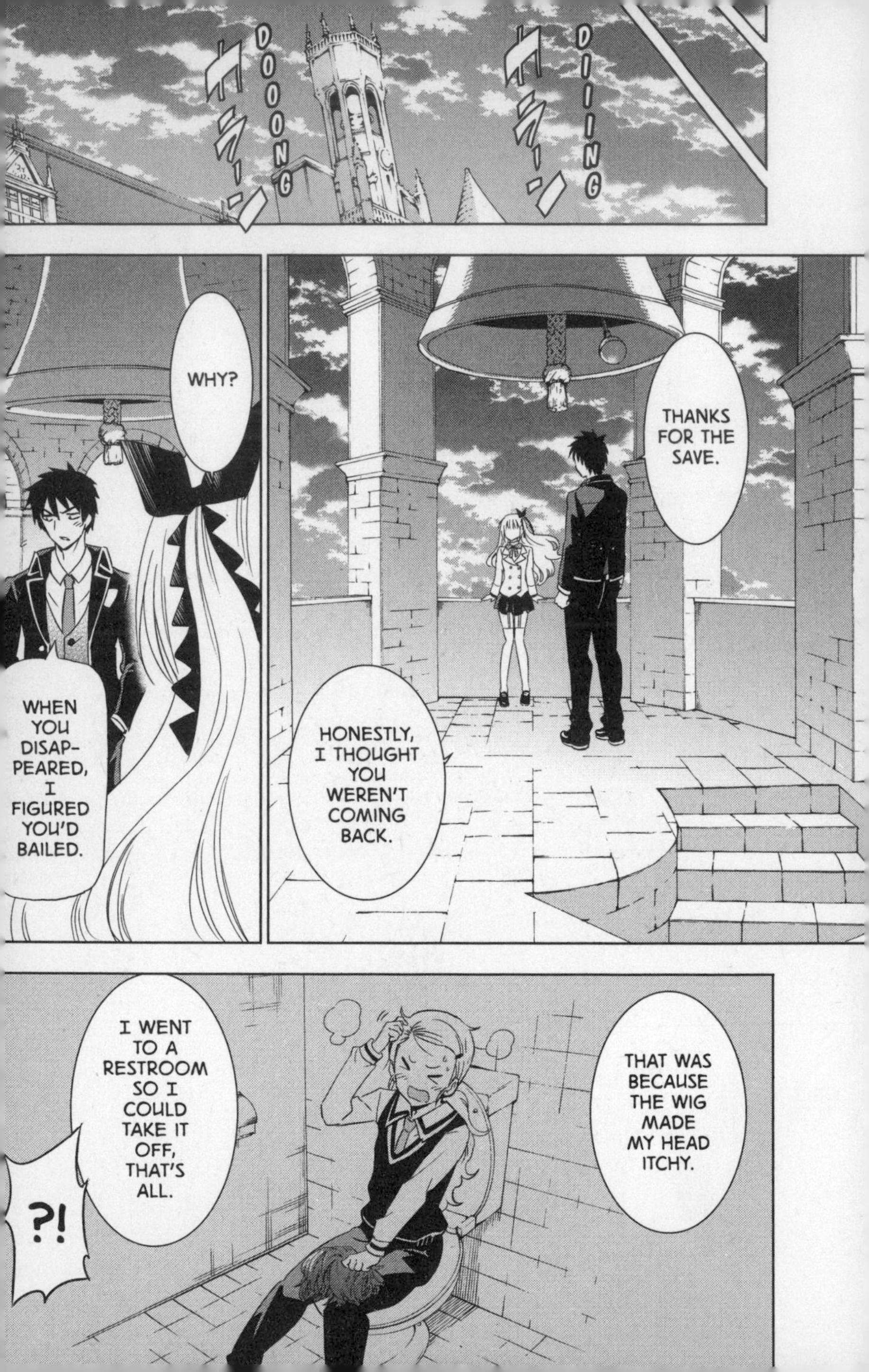
DIIING
DOOONG
THANKS FOR THE SAVE.
HONESTLY, I THOUGHT YOU WEREN'T COMING BACK.
WHY?
WHEN YOU DISAP-PEARED, I FIGURED YOU'D BAILED.
THAT WAS BECAUSE THE WIG MADE MY HEAD ITCHY.
I WENT TO A RESTROOM SO I COULD TAKE IT OFF, THAT'S ALL.
?!

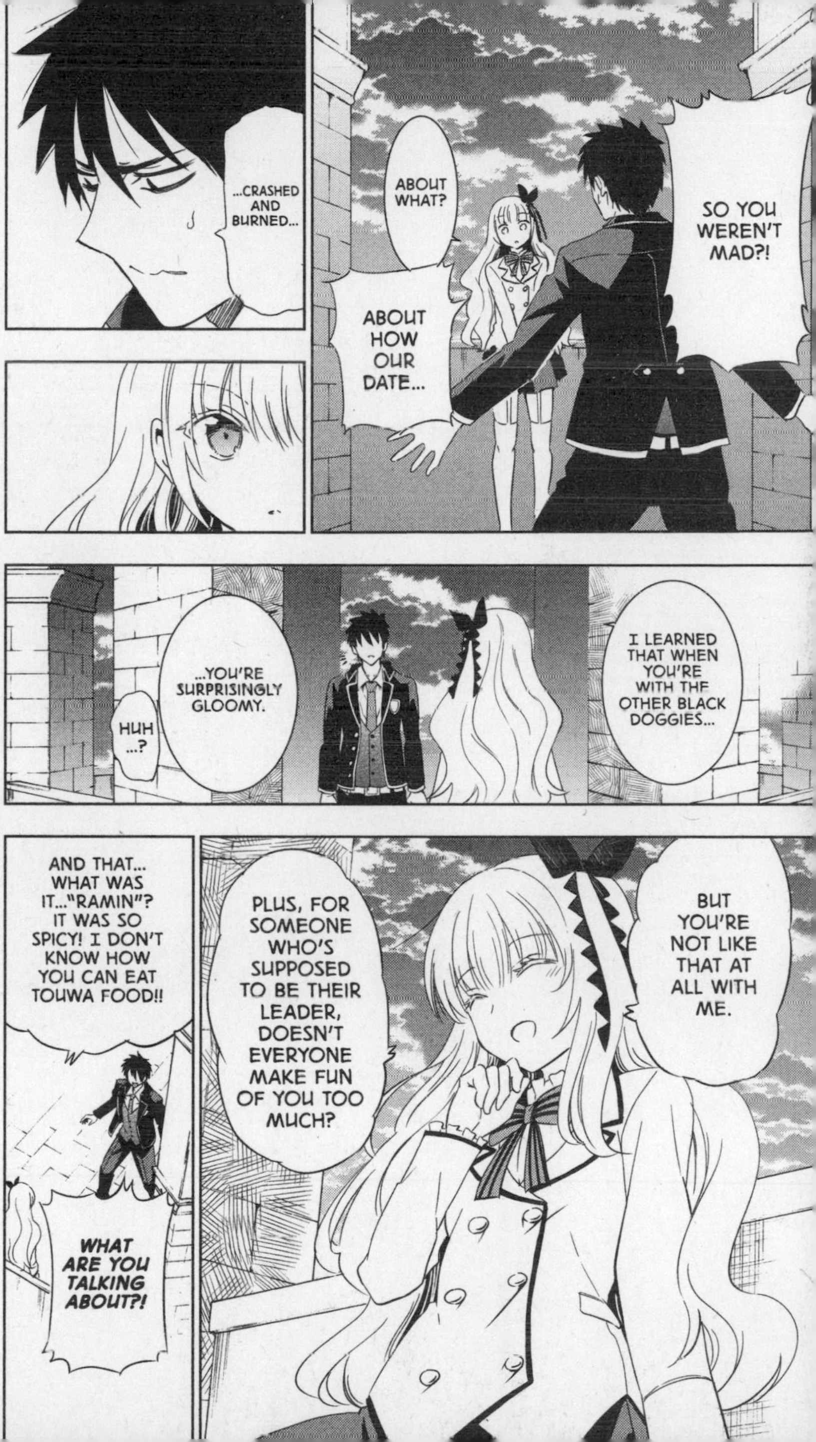
SO YOU WEREN'T MAD?!
ABOUT WHAT?
ABOUT HOW OUR DATE...
...CRASHED AND BURNED...
I LEARNED THAT WHEN YOU'RE WITH THE OTHER BLACK DOGGIES...
...YOU'RE SURPRISINGLY GLOOMY.
HUH ...?
BUT YOU'RE NOT LIKE THAT AT ALL WITH ME.
PLUS, FOR SOMEONE WHO'S SUPPOSED TO BE THEIR LEADER, DOESN'T EVERYONE MAKE FUN OF YOU TOO MUCH?
AND THAT... WHAT WAS IT..."RAMIN"? IT WAS SO SPICY! I DON'T KNOW HOW YOU CAN EAT TOUWA FOOD!!
WHAT ARE YOU TALKING ABOUT?!

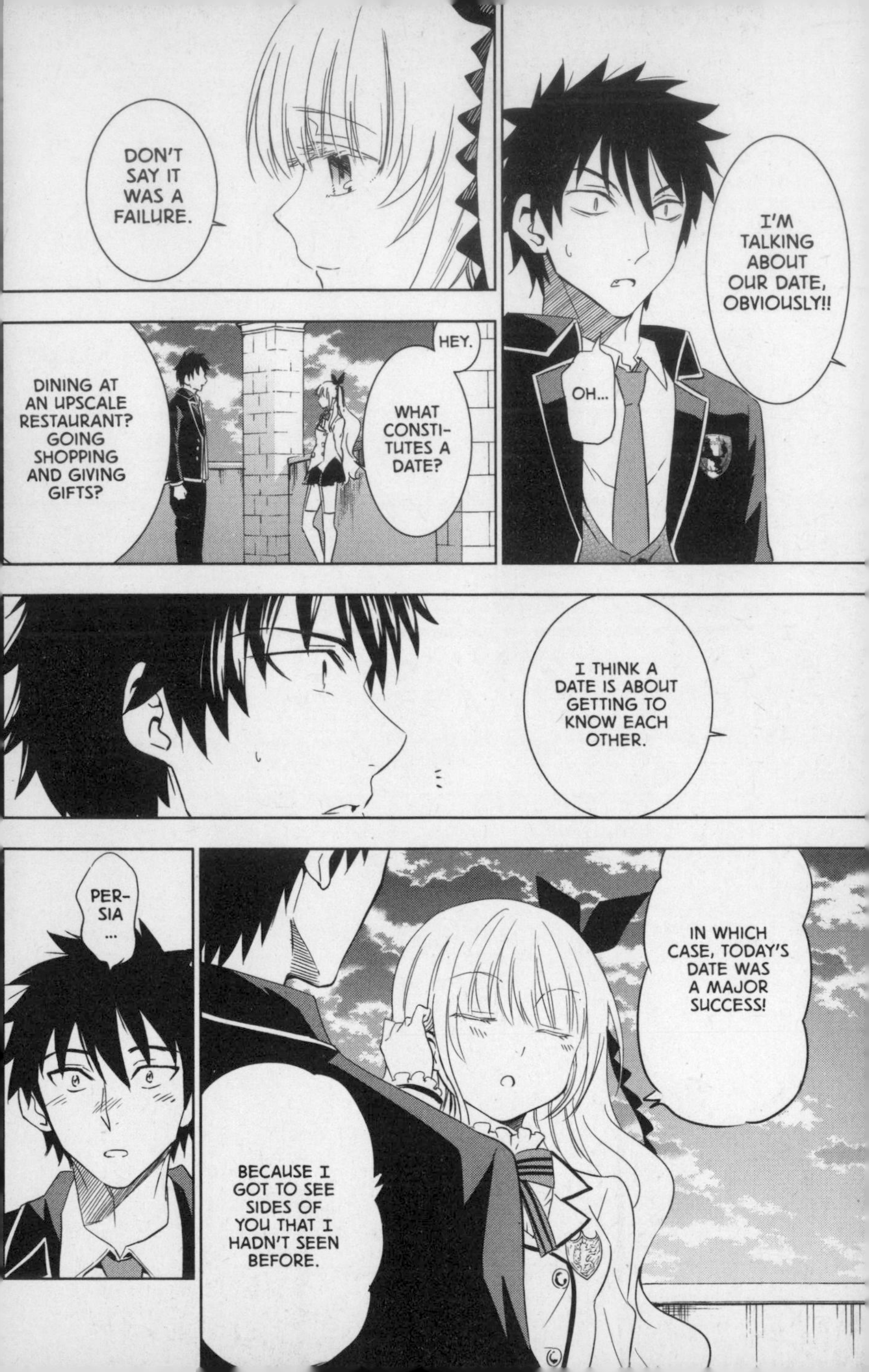
I'M TALKING ABOUT OUR DATE, OBVIOUSLY!!
OH...
DON'T SAY IT WAS A FAILURE.
HEY.
WHAT CONSTI- TUTES A DATE?
DINING AT AN UPSCALE RESTAURANT? GOING SHOPPING AND GIVING GIFTS?
I THINK A DATE IS ABOUT GETTING TO KNOW EACH OTHER.
IN WHICH CASE, TODAY'S DATE WAS A MAJOR SUCCESS!
BECAUSE I GOT TO SEE SIDES OF YOU THAT I HADN'T SEEN BEFORE.
PER- SIA ...

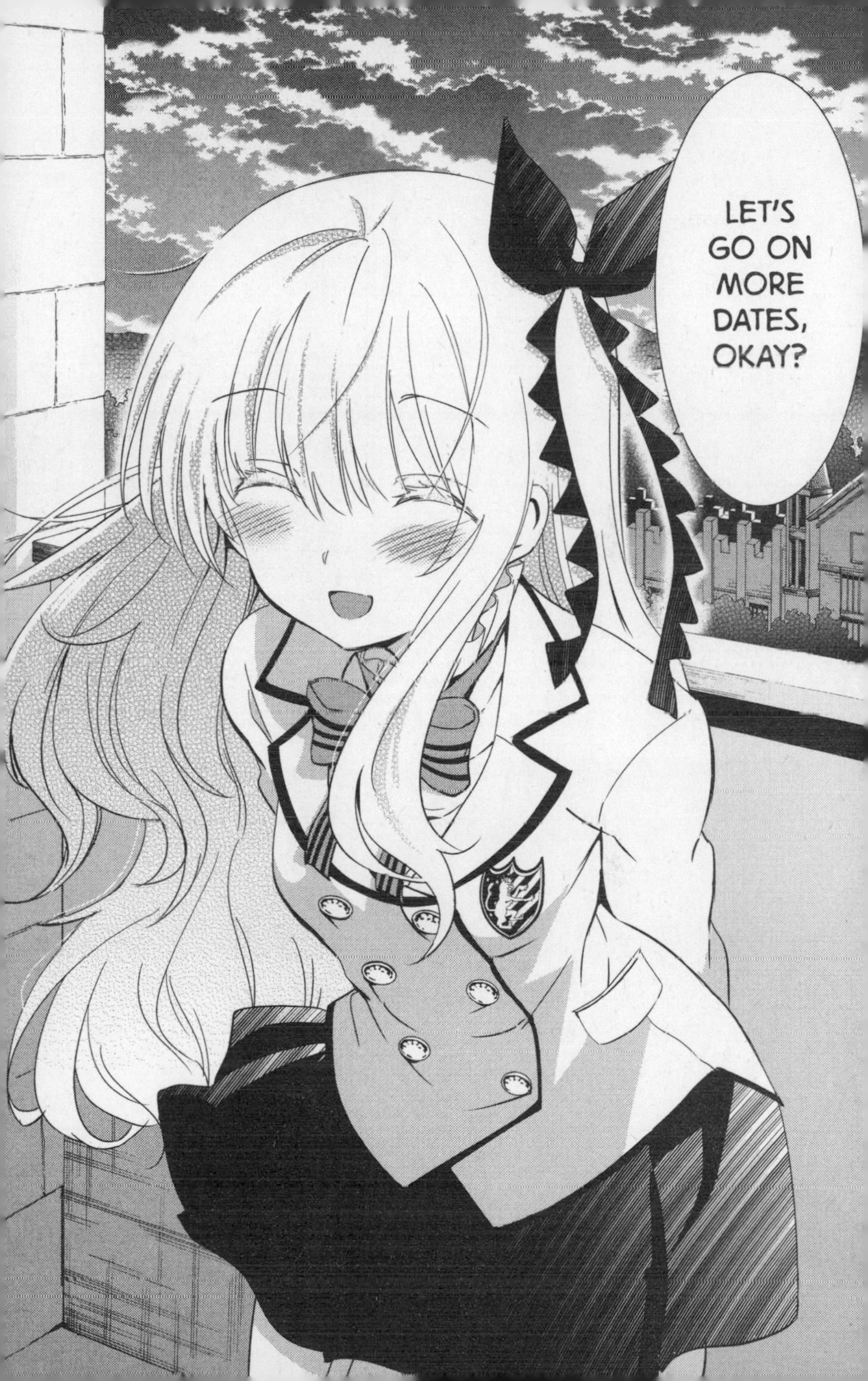
LET'S GO ON MORE DATES, OKAY?

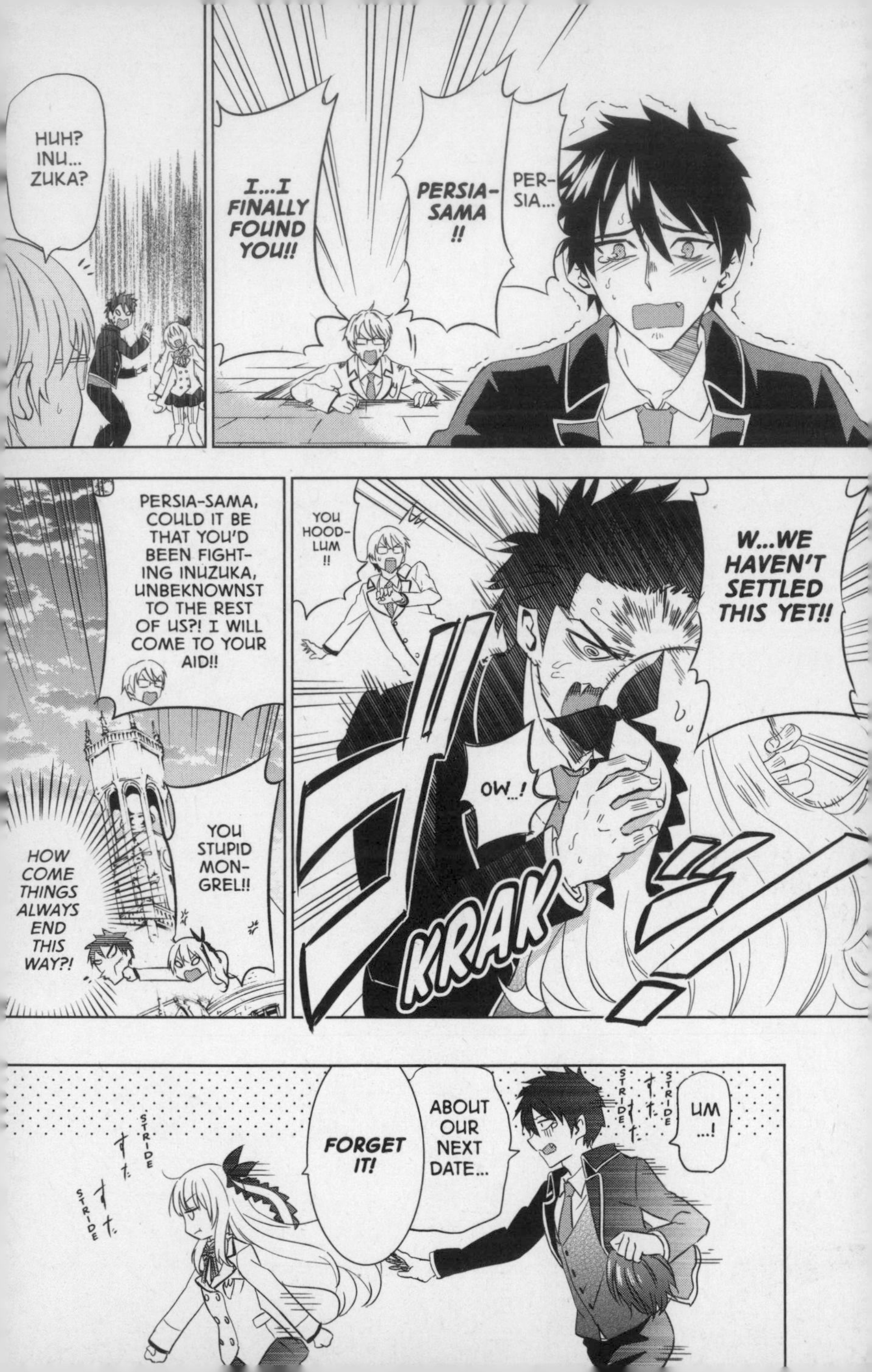
PER-SIA...
PERSIA-SAMA!!
I...I FINALLY FOUND YOU!!
HUH? INU...ZUKA?
W...WE HAVEN'T SETTLED THIS YET!!
YOU HOODLUM!!
OW..!
KRAK
PERSIA-SAMA, COULD IT BE THAT YOU'D BEEN FIGHTING INUZUKA, UNBEKNOWNST TO THE REST OF US?! I WILL COME TO YOUR AID!!
YOU STUPID MONGREL!!
HOW COME THINGS ALWAYS END THIS WAY?!
UM...!
STRIDE すた
STRIDE すた
ABOUT OUR NEXT DATE...
FORGET IT!
STRIDE すた
STRIDE すた

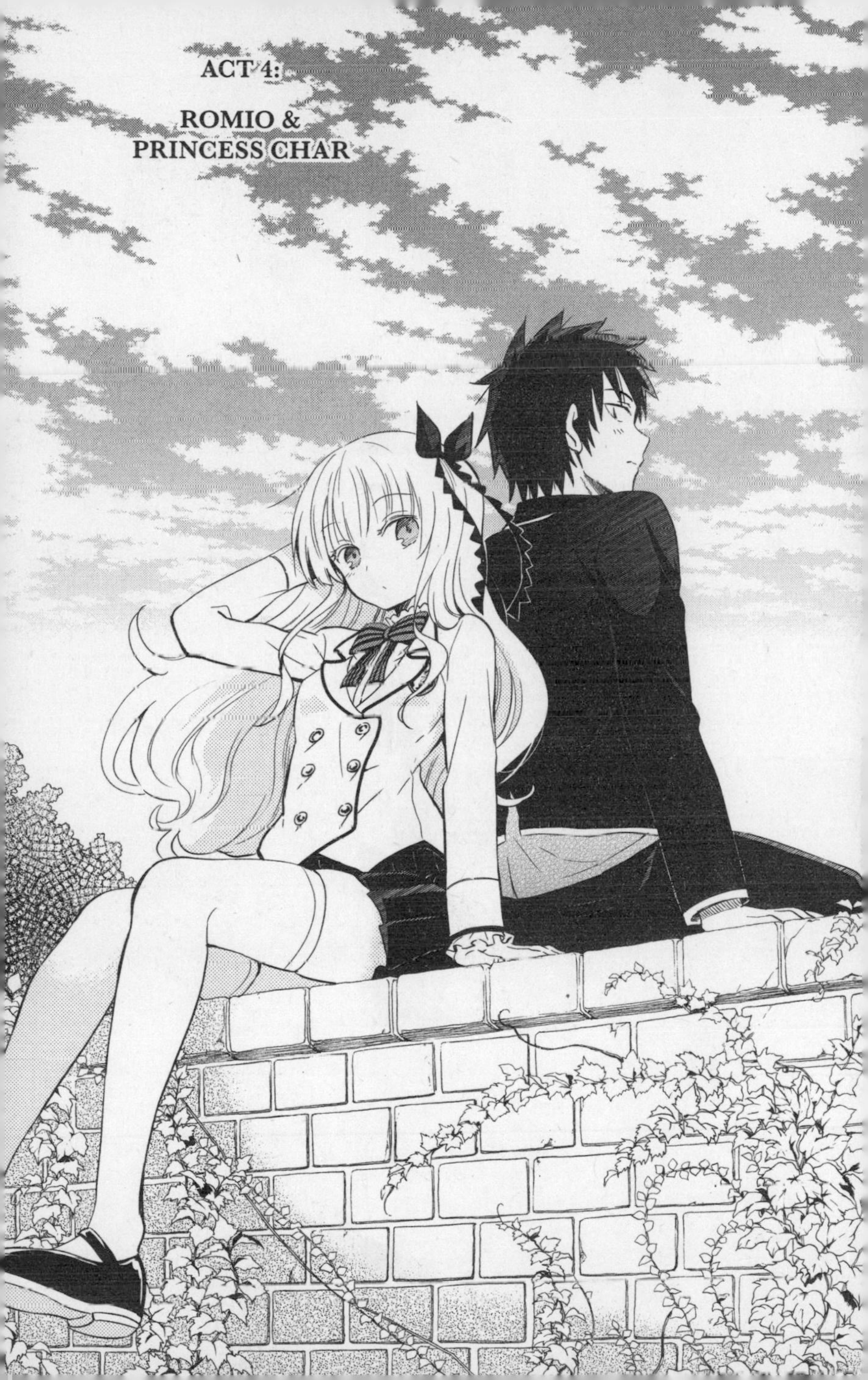
ACT 4:
ROMIO &
PRINCESS CHAR

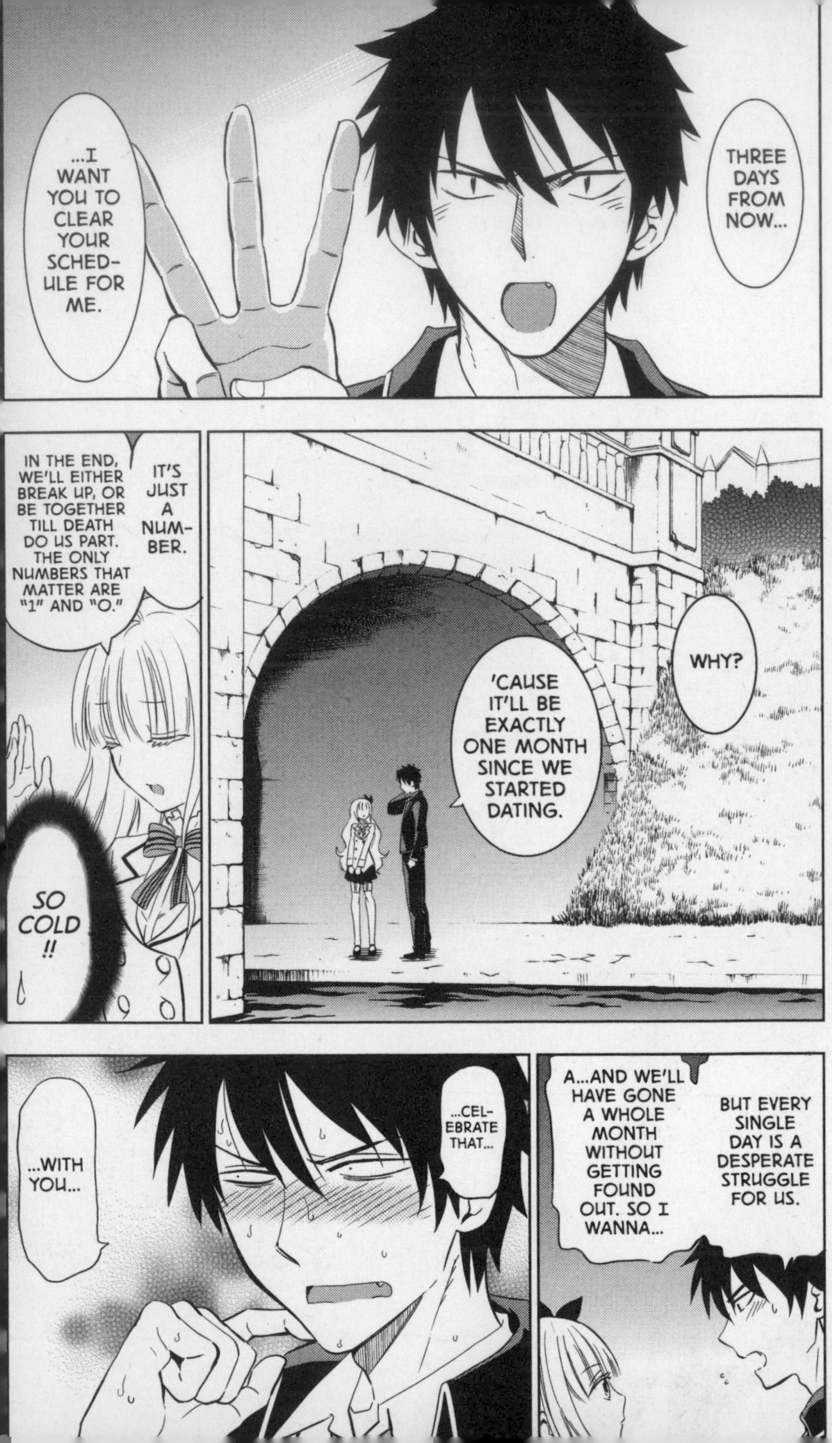
THREE DAYS FROM NOW...
...I WANT YOU TO CLEAR YOUR SCHED-ULE FOR ME.
WHY?
'CAUSE IT'LL BE EXACTLY ONE MONTH SINCE WE STARTED DATING.
IT'S JUST A NUM-BER.
IN THE END, WE'LL EITHER BREAK UP, OR BE TOGETHER TILL DEATH DO US PART. THE ONLY NUMBERS THAT MATTER ARE "1" AND "O."
SO COLD!!
BUT EVERY SINGLE DAY IS A DESPERATE STRUGGLE FOR US.
A...AND WE'LL HAVE GONE A WHOLE MONTH WITHOUT GETTING FOUND OUT. SO I WANNA...
...CEL-EBRATE THAT...
...WITH YOU...

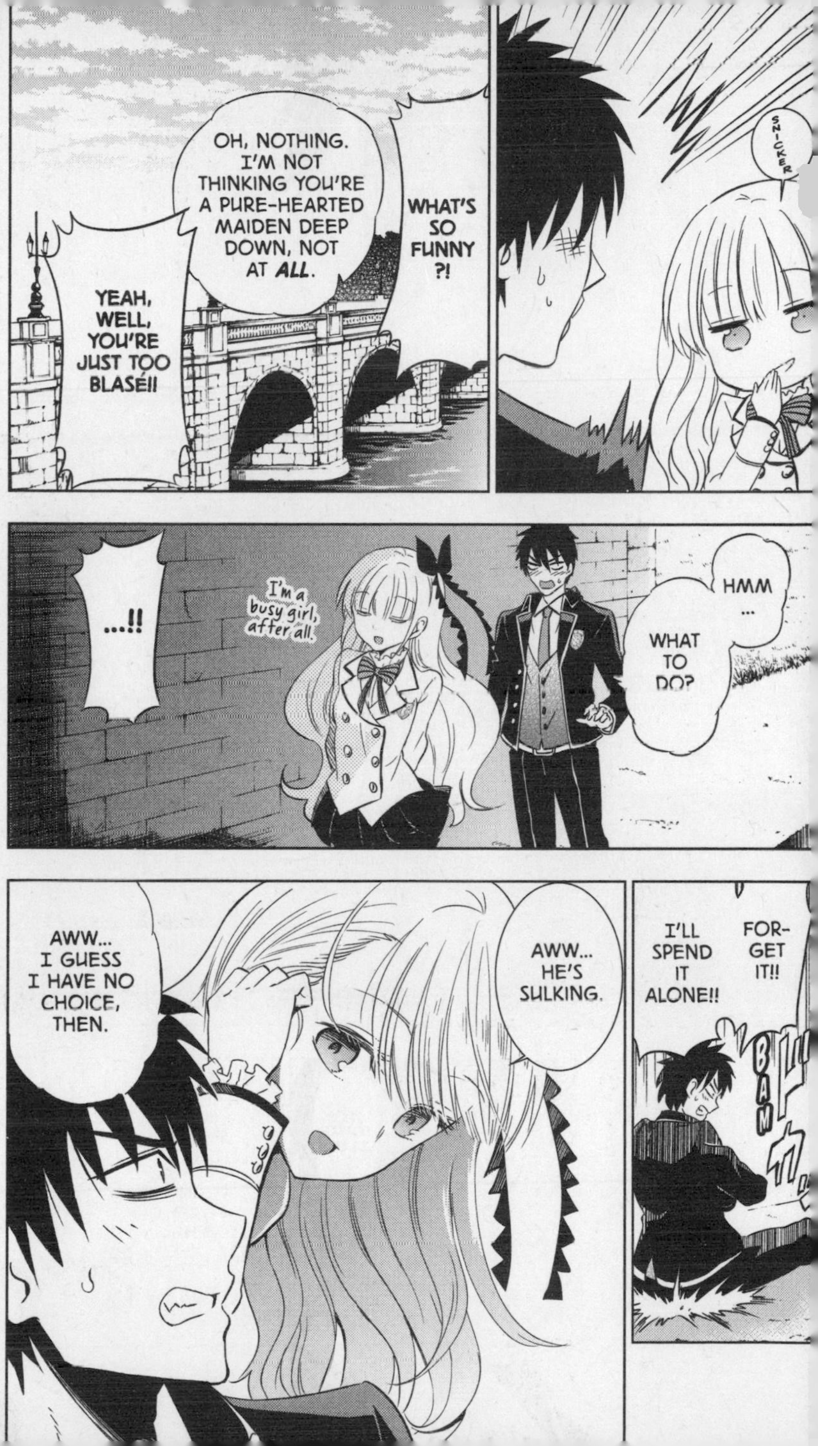
SNICKER
WHAT'S SO FUNNY?!
OH, NOTHING. I'M NOT THINKING YOU'RE A PURE-HEARTED MAIDEN DEEP DOWN, NOT AT ALL.
YEAH, WELL, YOU'RE JUST TOO BLASÉ!!
HMM... WHAT TO DO?
I'm a busy girl, after all.
...!!
FOR-GET IT!!
I'LL SPEND IT ALONE!!
BAM
AWW... HE'S SULKING.
AWW... I GUESS I HAVE NO CHOICE, THEN.

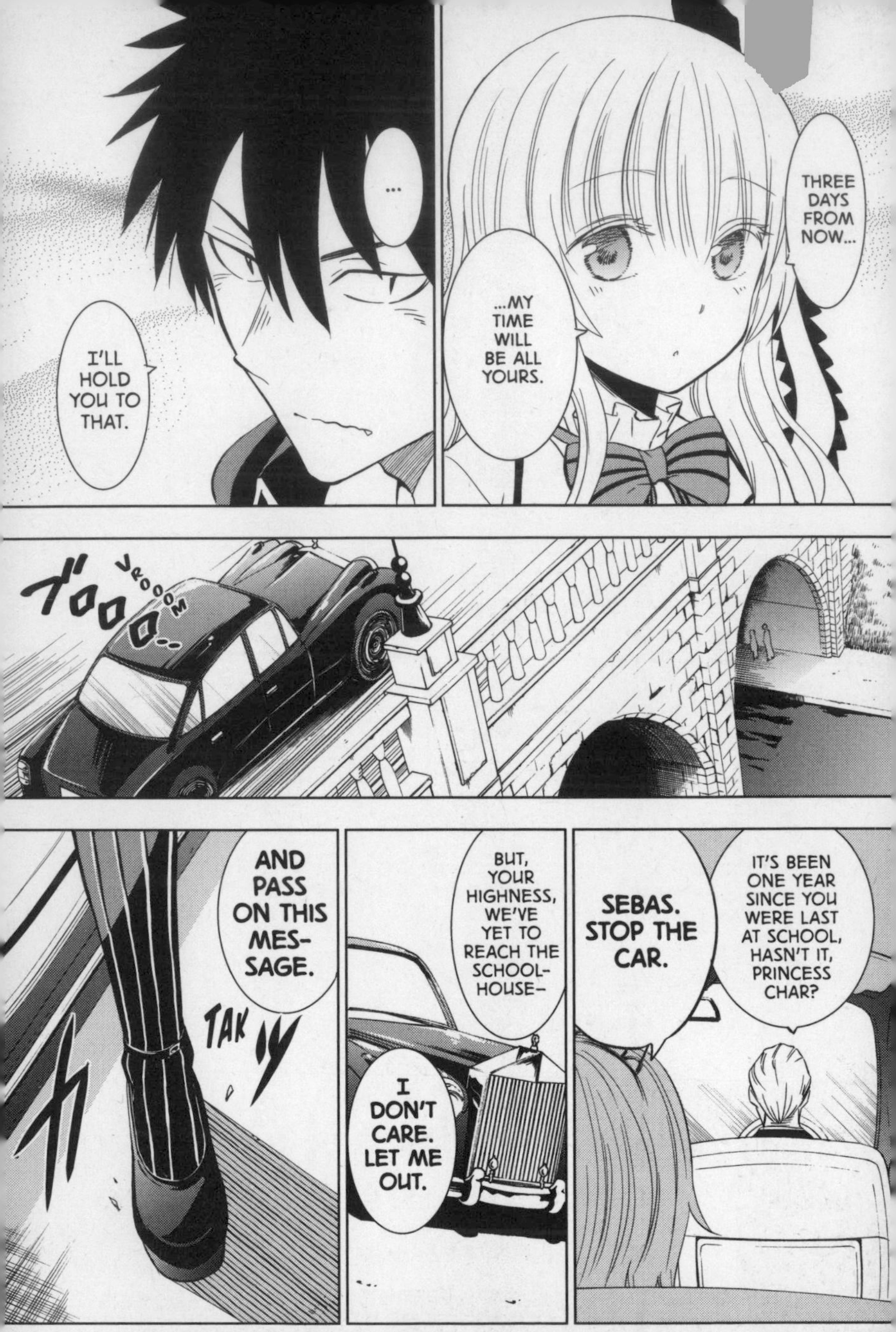
THREE DAYS FROM NOW...
...MY TIME WILL BE ALL YOURS.
...
I'LL HOLD YOU TO THAT.
VROOOOM
IT'S BEEN ONE YEAR SINCE YOU WERE LAST AT SCHOOL, HASN'T IT, PRINCESS CHAR?
SEBAS. STOP THE CAR.
BUT, YOUR HIGHNESS, WE'VE YET TO REACH THE SCHOOL-HOUSE–
I DON'T CARE. LET ME OUT.
AND PASS ON THIS MES-SAGE.
TAK

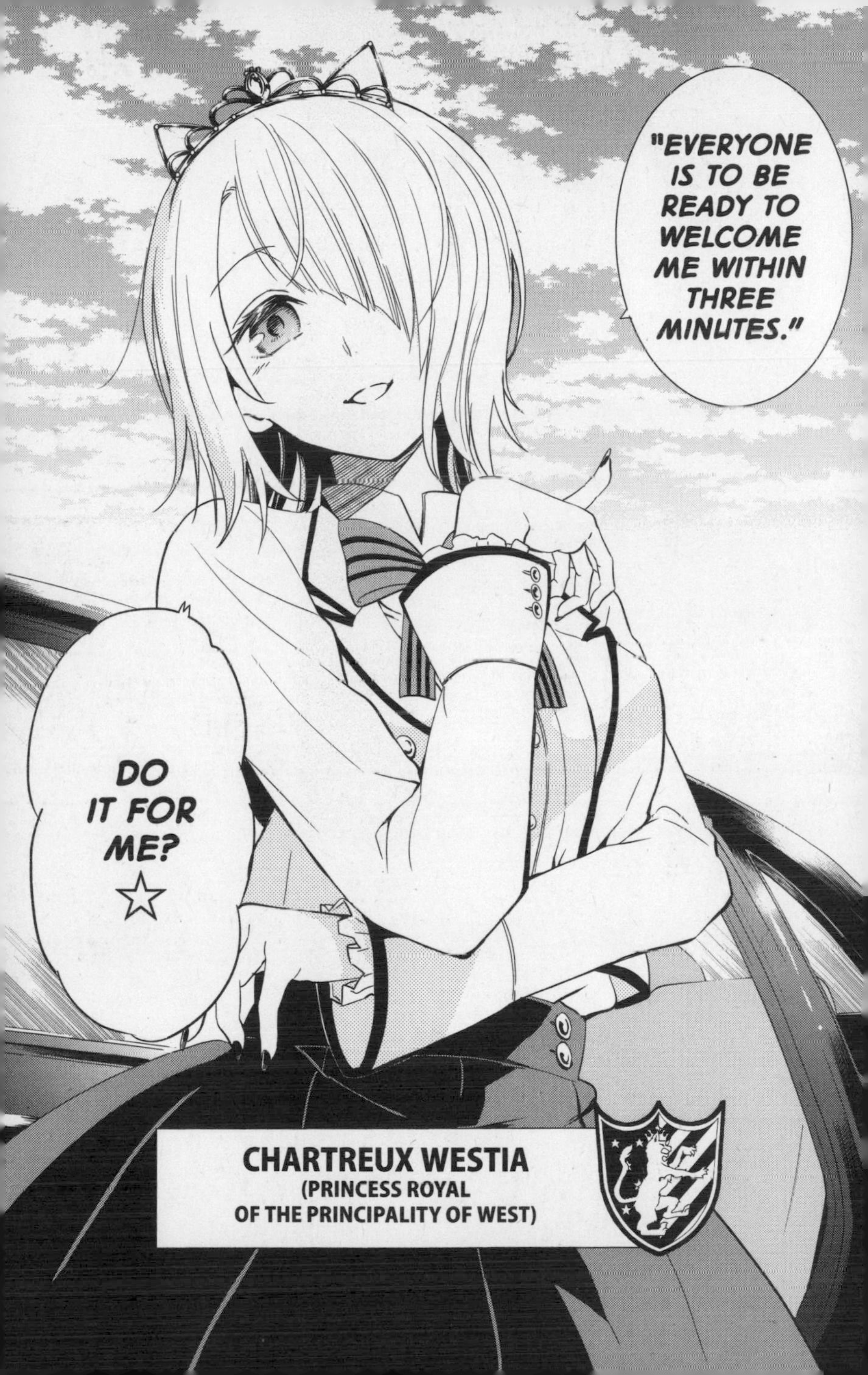
"EVERYONE IS TO BE READY TO WELCOME ME WITHIN THREE MINUTES."
DO IT FOR ME? ☆
CHARTREUX WESTIA
(PRINCESS ROYAL OF THE PRINCIPALITY OF WEST)

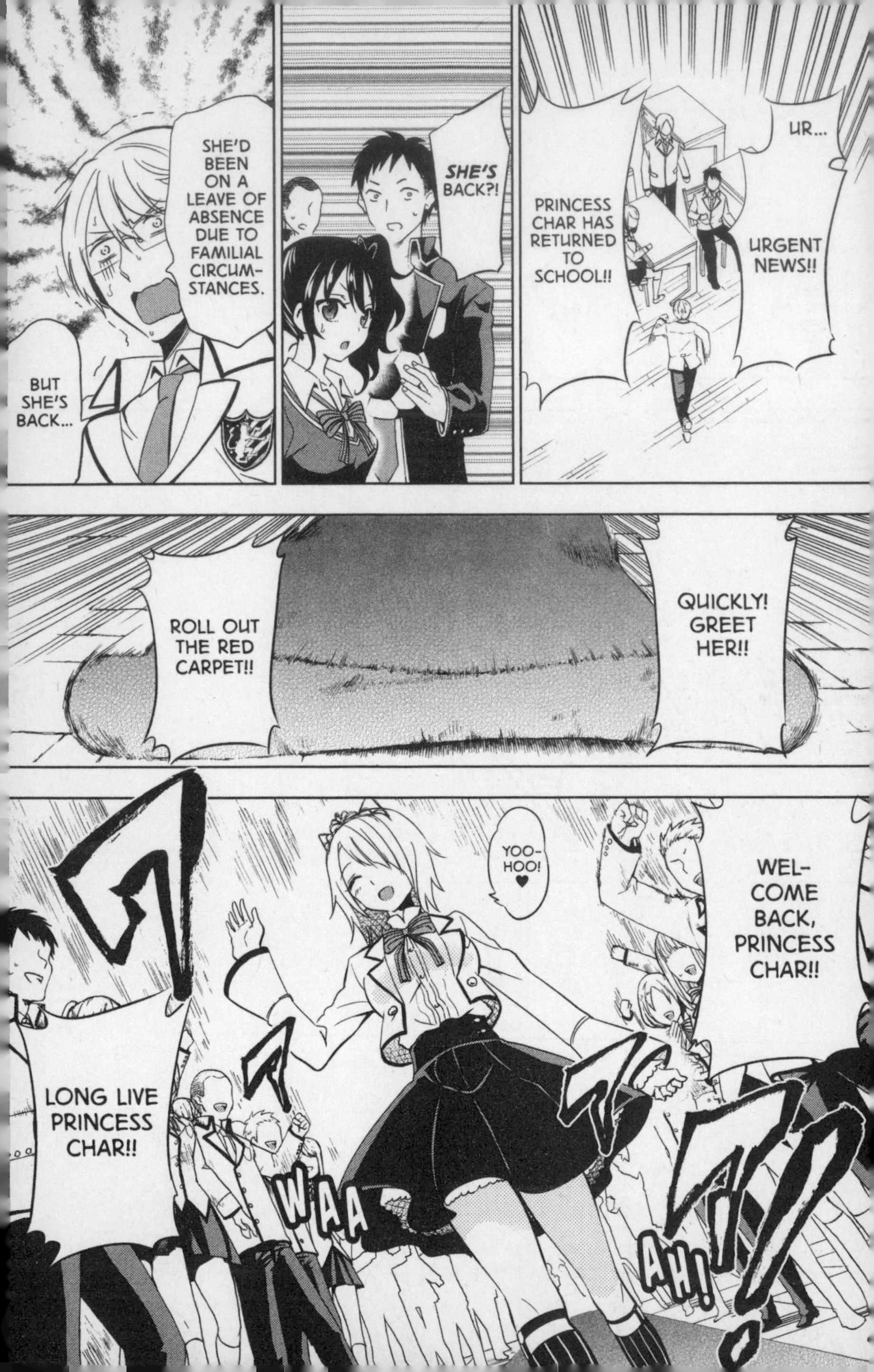
UR...
URGENT NEWS!!
PRINCESS CHAR HAS RETURNED TO SCHOOL!!
SHE'S BACK?!
SHE'D BEEN ON A LEAVE OF ABSENCE DUE TO FAMILIAL CIRCUM-STANCES.
BUT SHE'S BACK...
QUICKLY! GREET HER!!
ROLL OUT THE RED CARPET!!
WEL-COME BACK, PRINCESS CHAR!!
YOO-HOO! ♥
LONG LIVE PRINCESS CHAR!!
WAA
AH!

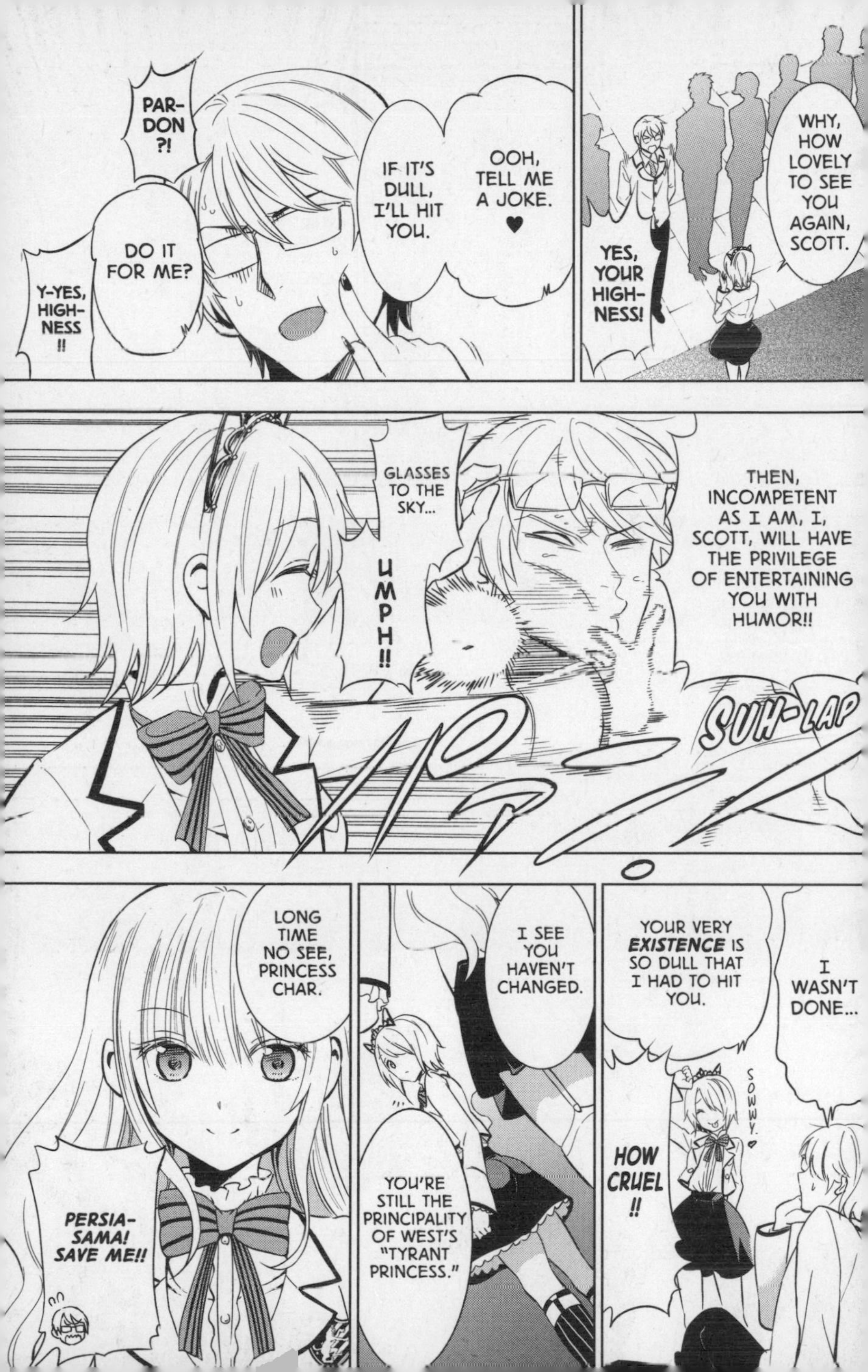
WHY, HOW LOVELY TO SEE YOU AGAIN, SCOTT.
YES, YOUR HIGHNESS!
OOH, TELL ME A JOKE. ♥
IF IT'S DULL, I'LL HIT YOU.
PARDON?!
DO IT FOR ME?
Y-YES, HIGHNESS!!
THEN, INCOMPETENT AS I AM, I, SCOTT, WILL HAVE THE PRIVILEGE OF ENTERTAINING YOU WITH HUMOR!!
SUH-LAP
GLASSES TO THE SKY...
UMPH!!
I WASN'T DONE...
YOUR VERY EXISTENCE IS SO DULL THAT I HAD TO HIT YOU.
SOWWY. ♥
HOW CRUEL!!
I SEE YOU HAVEN'T CHANGED.
YOU'RE STILL THE PRINCIPALITY OF WEST'S "TYRANT PRINCESS."
LONG TIME NO SEE, PRINCESS CHAR.
PERSIA-SAMA! SAVE ME!!

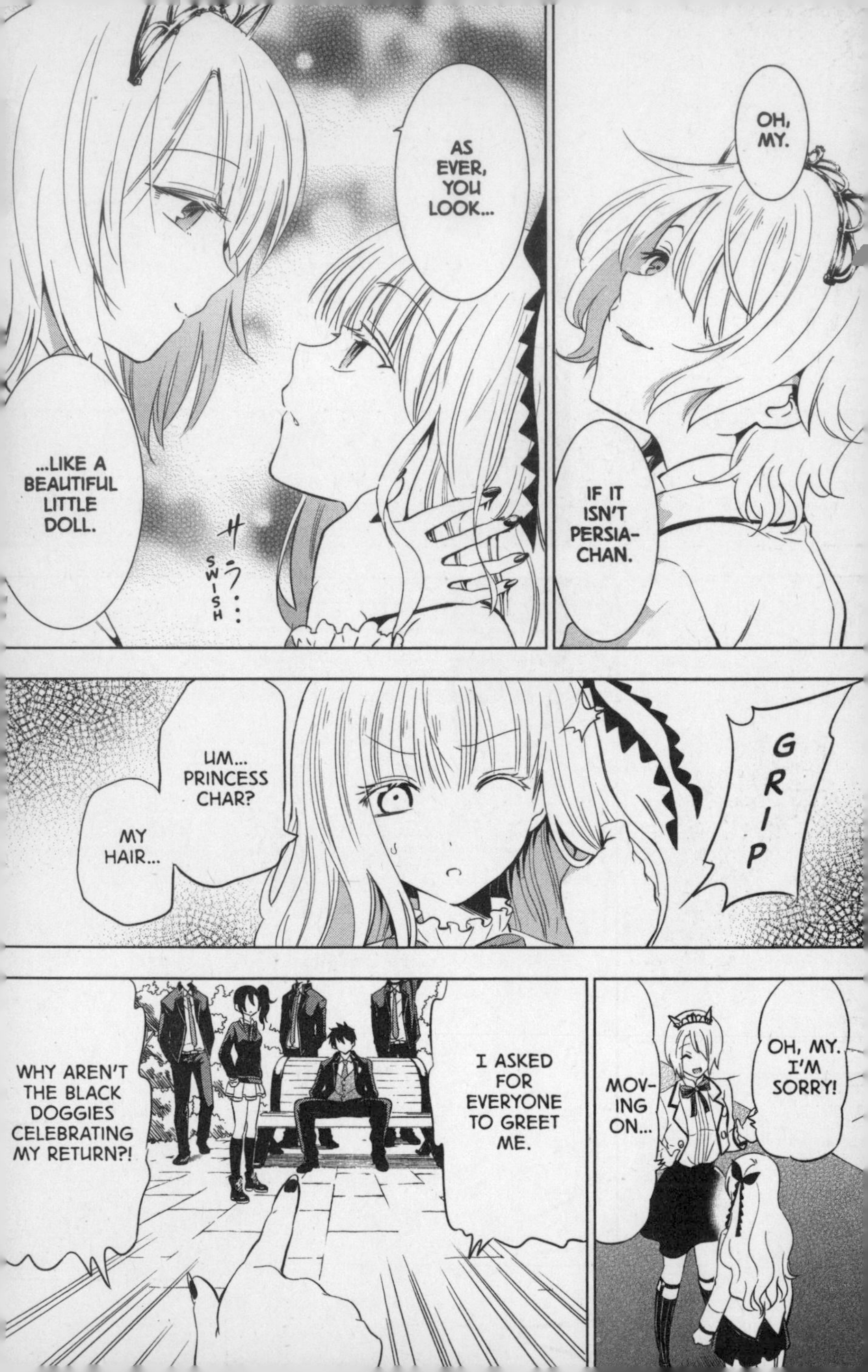
OH, MY.
IF IT ISN'T PERSIA-CHAN.
AS EVER, YOU LOOK...
...LIKE A BEAUTIFUL LITTLE DOLL.
SWISH
GRIP
UM... PRINCESS CHAR?
MY HAIR...
OH, MY. I'M SORRY!
MOV-ING ON...
I ASKED FOR EVERYONE TO GREET ME.
WHY AREN'T THE BLACK DOGGIES CELEBRATING MY RETURN?!

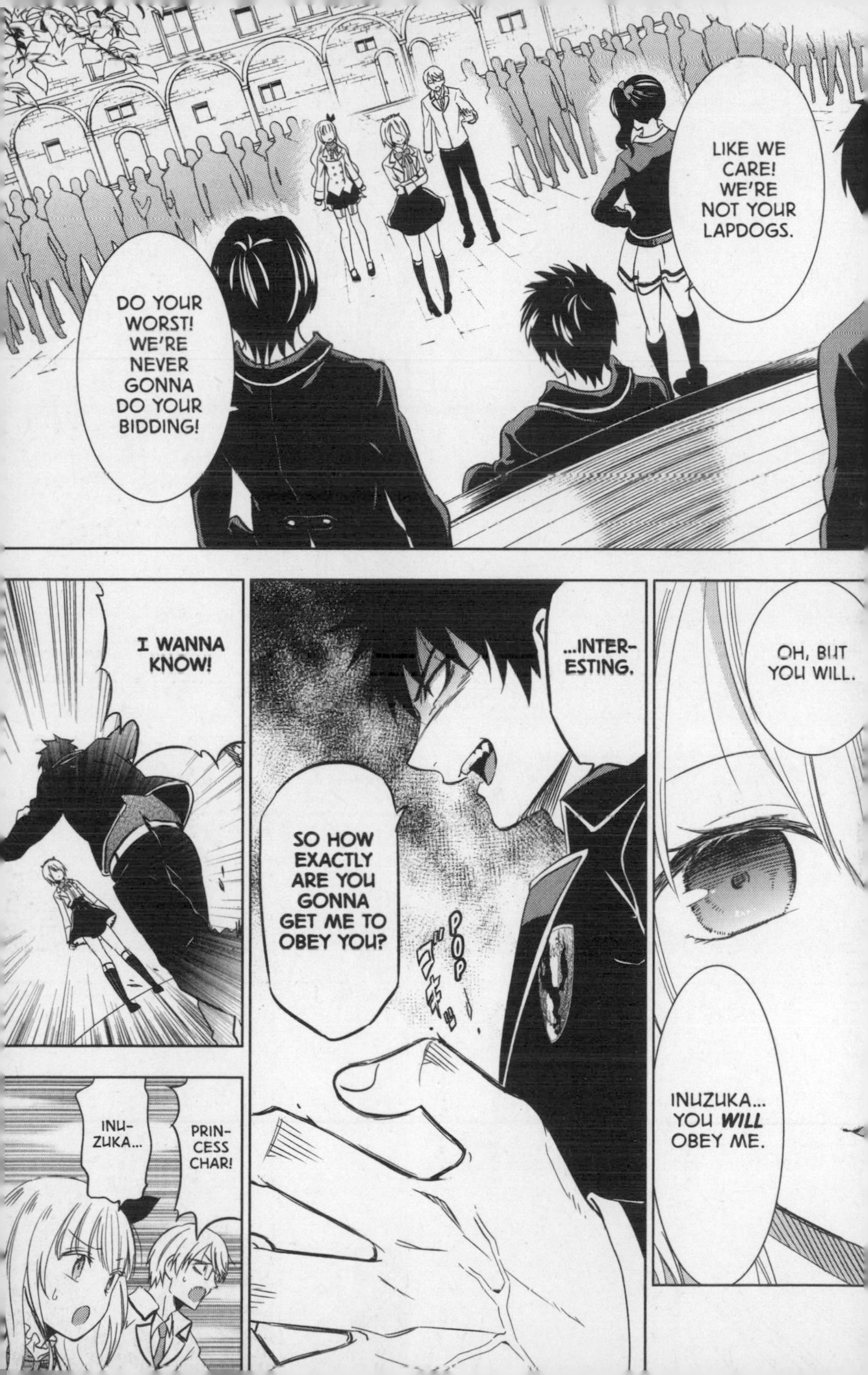
LIKE WE CARE! WE'RE NOT YOUR LAPDOGS.
DO YOUR WORST! WE'RE NEVER GONNA DO YOUR BIDDING!
...INTER-ESTING.
SO HOW EXACTLY ARE YOU GONNA GET ME TO OBEY YOU?
POP
ゴキッ
OH, BUT YOU WILL.
INUZUKA... YOU ***WILL*** OBEY ME.
I WANNA KNOW!
PRIN-CESS CHAR!
INU-ZUKA...

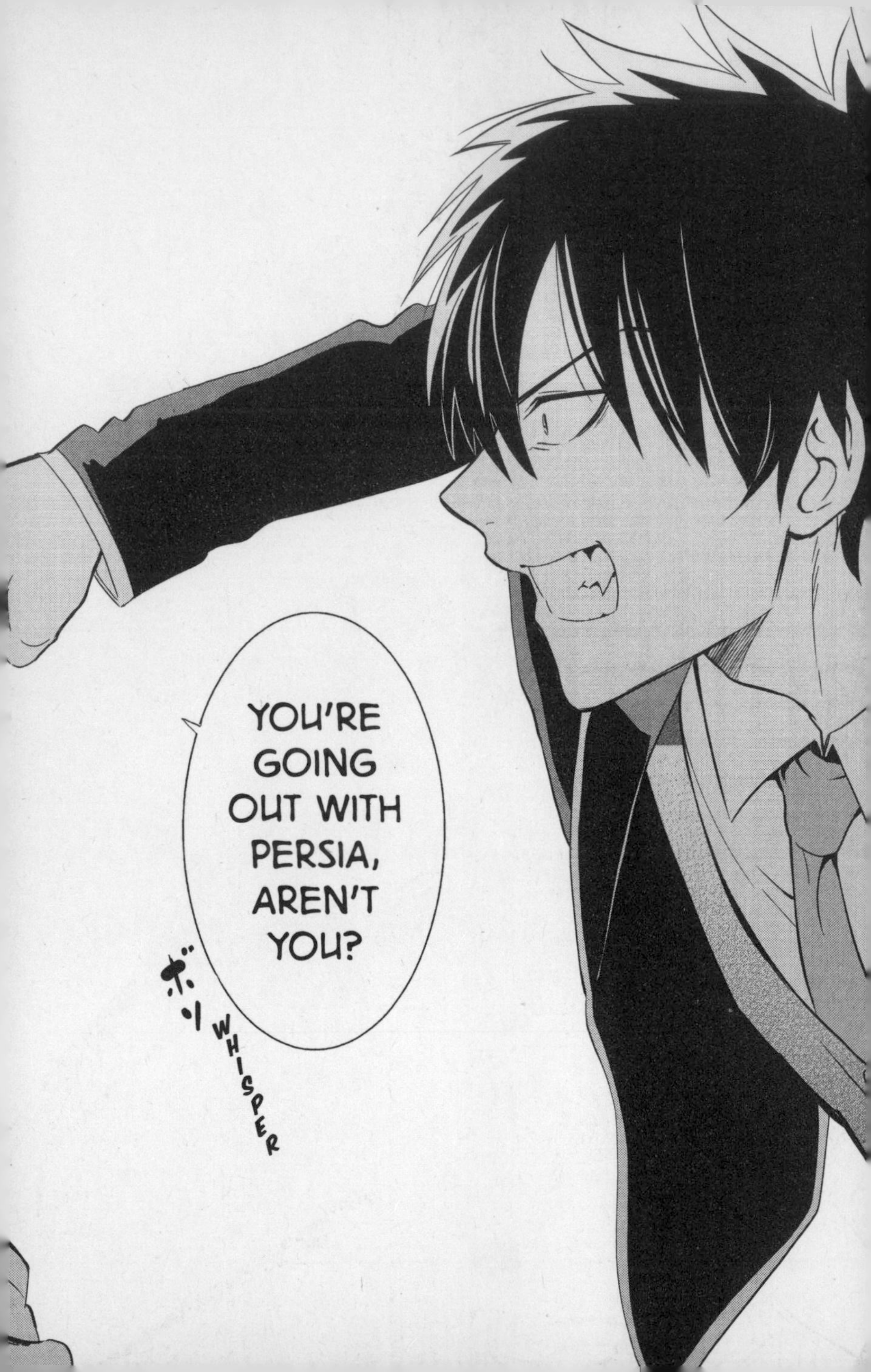
YOU'RE GOING OUT WITH PERSIA, AREN'T YOU?
WHISPER

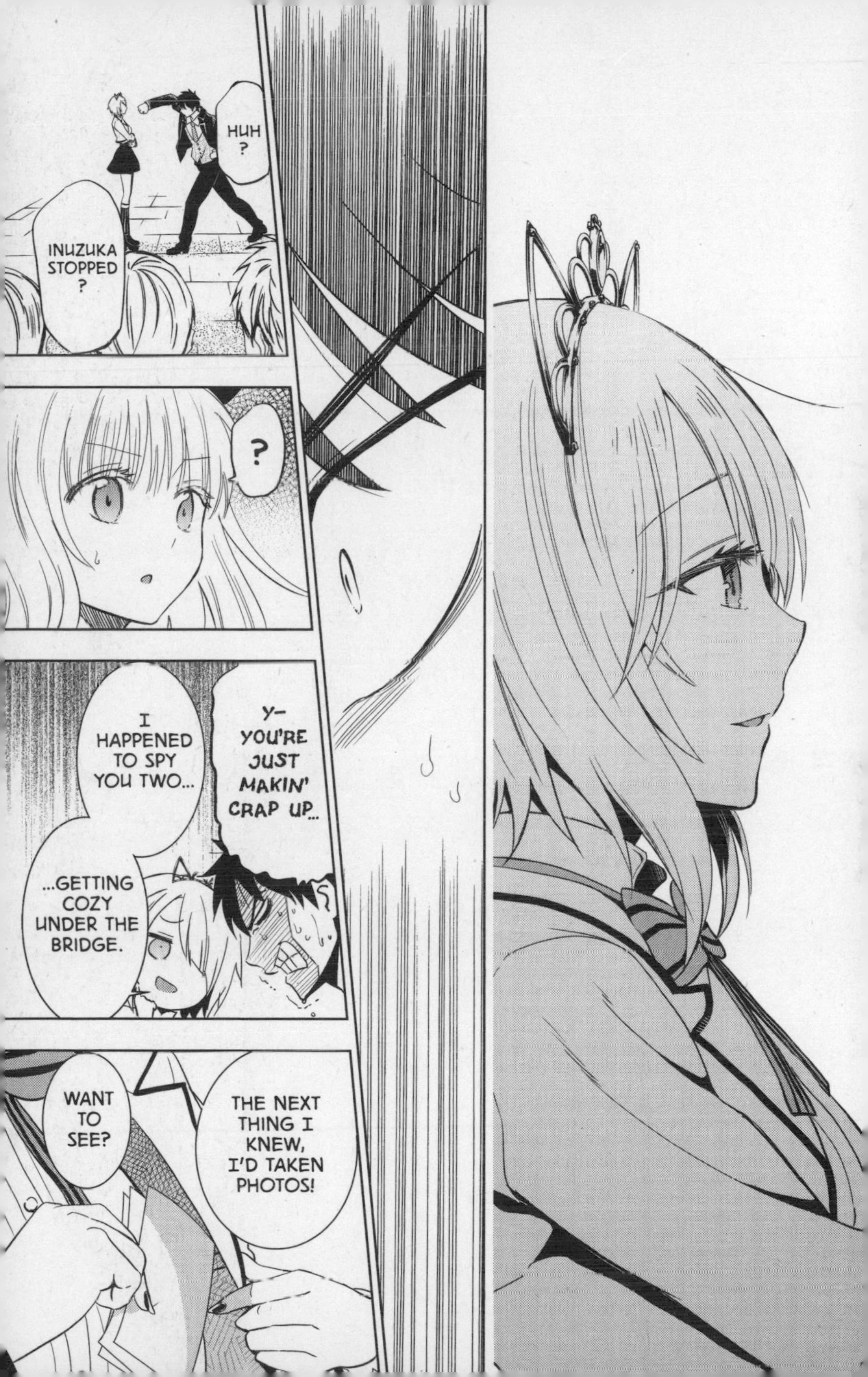
HUH ?
INUZUKA STOPPED ?
?
Y- YOU'RE JUST MAKIN' CRAP UP...
I HAPPENED TO SPY YOU TWO...
...GETTING COZY UNDER THE BRIDGE.
THE NEXT THING I KNEW, I'D TAKEN PHOTOS!
WANT TO SEE?

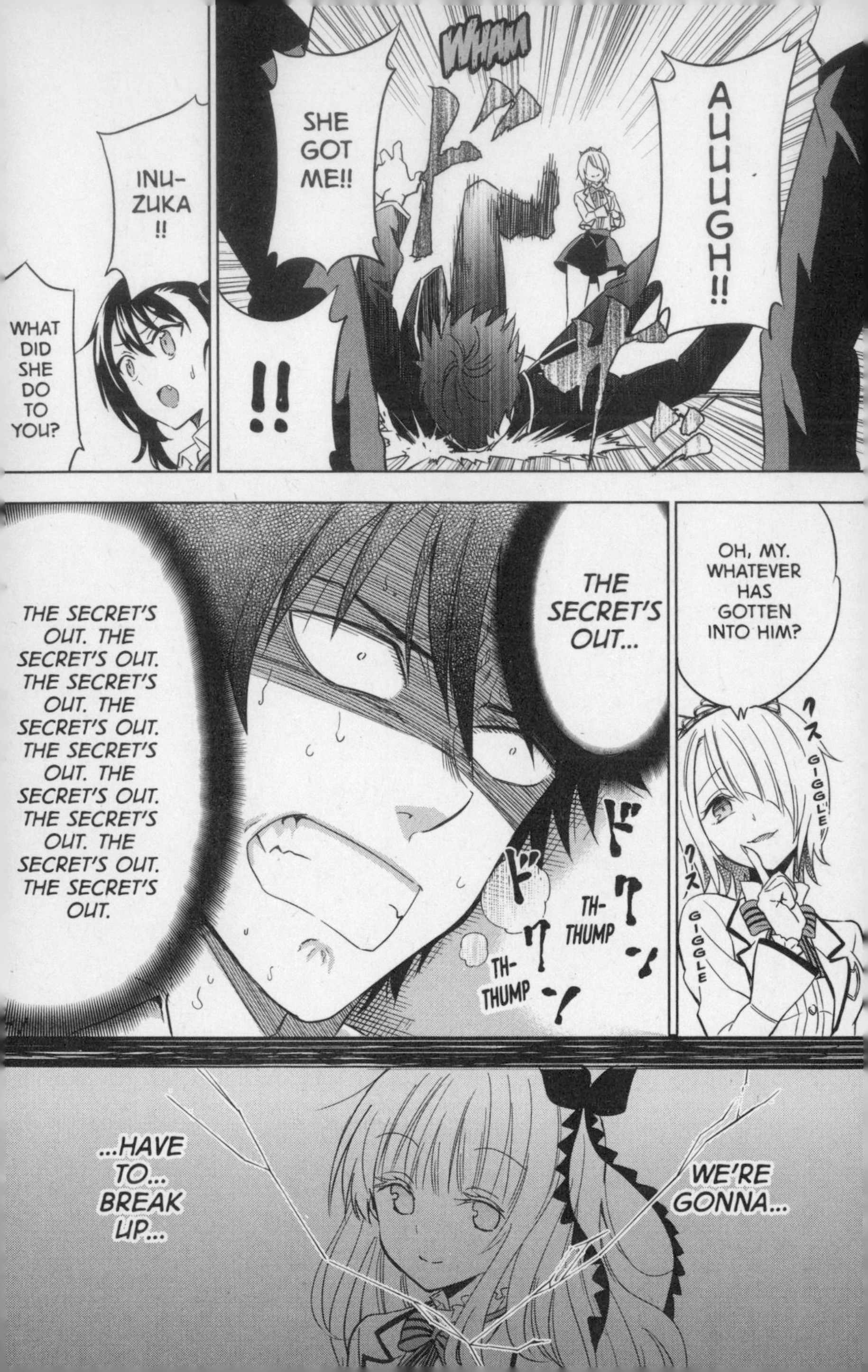
WHAM
AUUUGH!!
SHE GOT ME!!
!!
INU-ZUKA!!
WHAT DID SHE DO TO YOU?
OH, MY. WHATEVER HAS GOTTEN INTO HIM?
GIGGLE
GIGGLE
THE SECRET'S OUT...
TH-THUMP
TH-THUMP
THE SECRET'S OUT. THE SECRET'S OUT. THE SECRET'S OUT. THE SECRET'S OUT. THE SECRET'S OUT. THE SECRET'S OUT. THE SECRET'S OUT. THE SECRET'S OUT. THE SECRET'S OUT. THE SECRET'S OUT.
WE'RE GONNA...
...HAVE TO... BREAK UP...

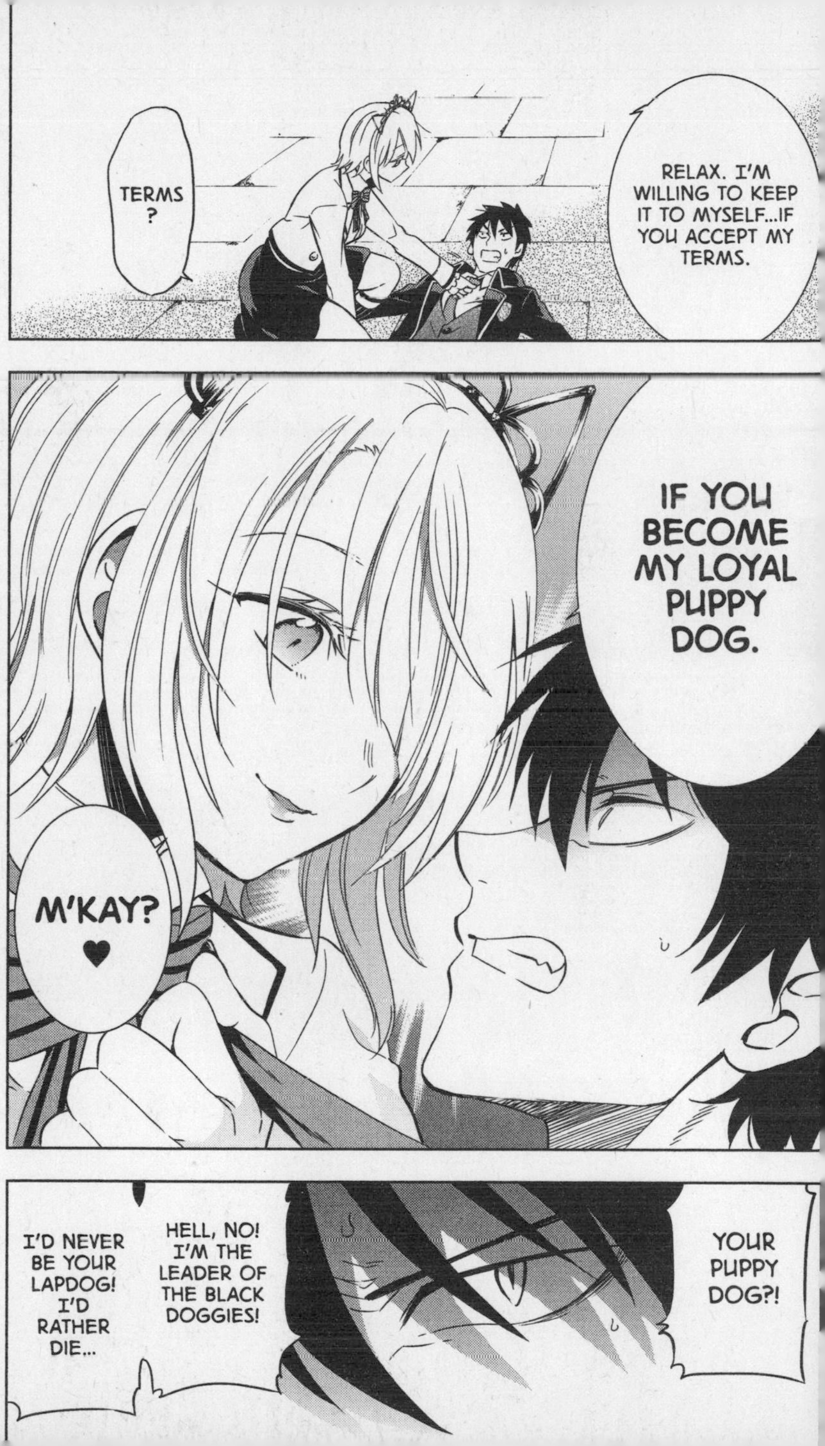
RELAX. I'M WILLING TO KEEP IT TO MYSELF...IF YOU ACCEPT MY TERMS.
TERMS?
IF YOU BECOME MY LOYAL PUPPY DOG.
M'KAY? ♥
YOUR PUPPY DOG?!
HELL, NO! I'M THE LEADER OF THE BLACK DOGGIES!
I'D NEVER BE YOUR LAPDOG! I'D RATHER DIE...

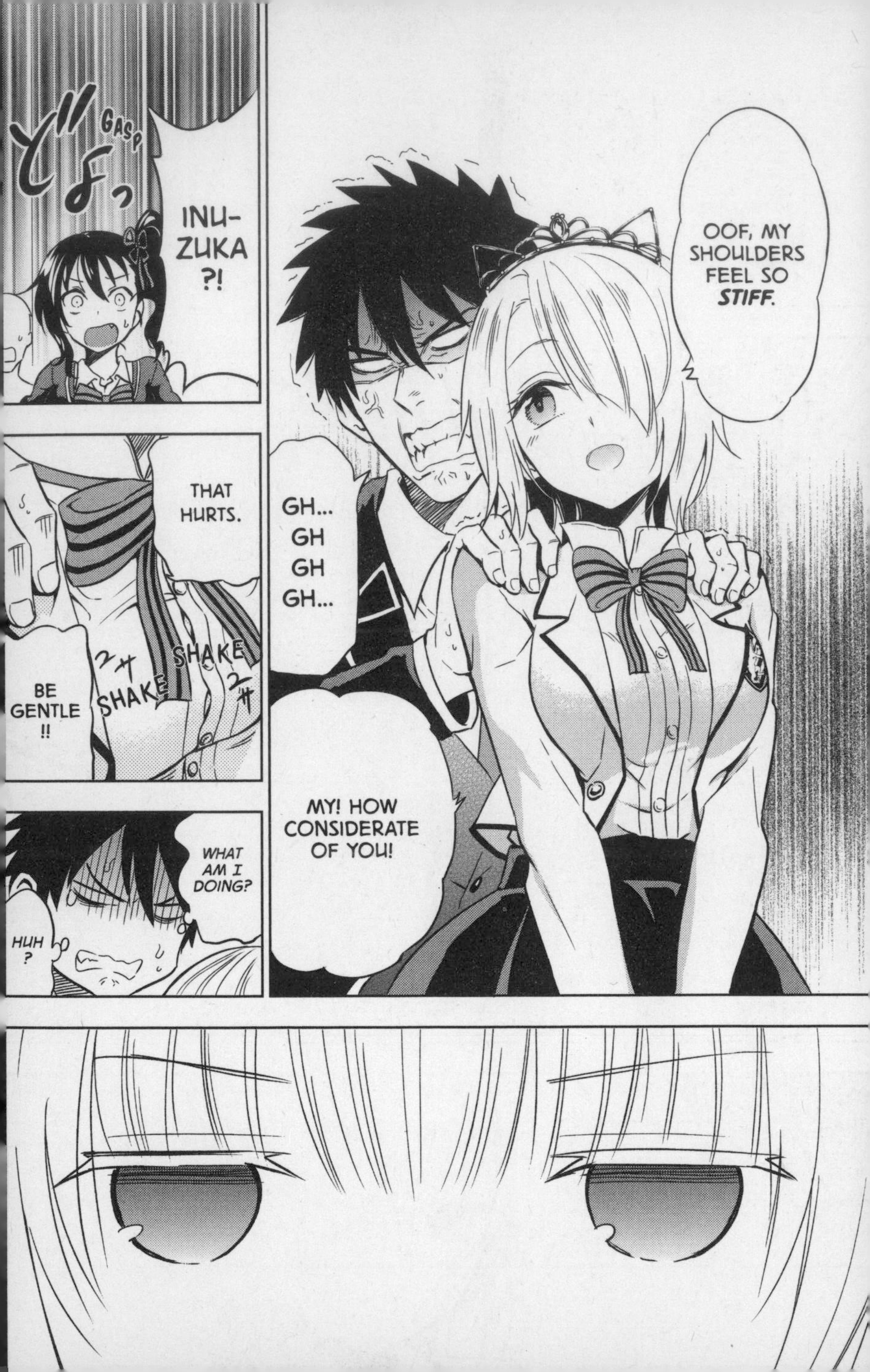
OOF, MY SHOULDERS FEEL SO *STIFF*.
GH... GH GH GH...
MY! HOW CONSIDERATE OF YOU!
GASP
INU-ZUKA ?!
THAT HURTS.
SHAKE SHAKE
BE GENTLE !!
WHAT AM I DOING?
HUH?

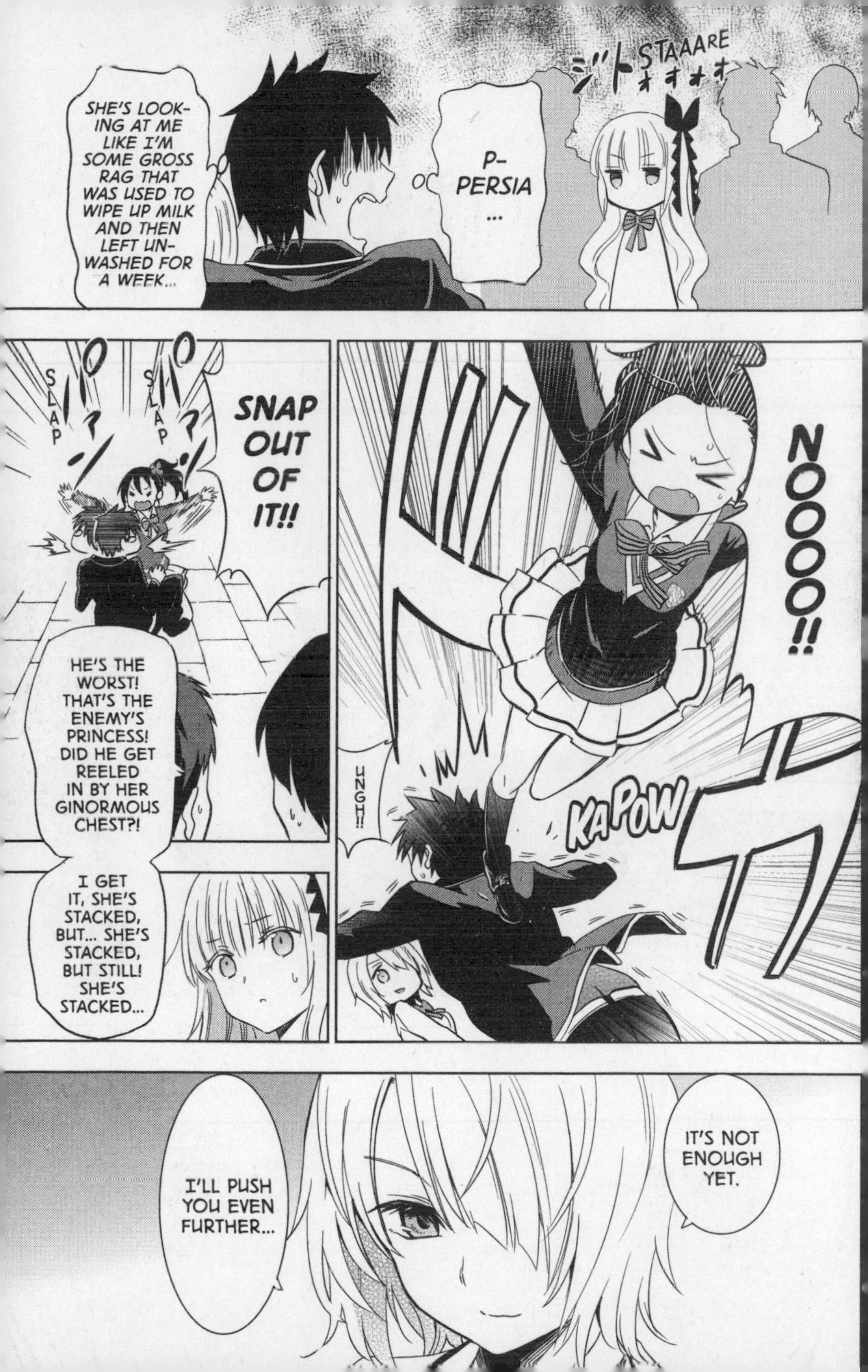
ジトオオオ STAAARE
P-PERSIA ...
SHE'S LOOKING AT ME LIKE I'M SOME GROSS RAG THAT WAS USED TO WIPE UP MILK AND THEN LEFT UNWASHED FOR A WEEK...
NOOOOO!!
KAPOW
UNGH!!
SLAP
SLAP
SNAP OUT OF IT!!
HE'S THE WORST! THAT'S THE ENEMY'S PRINCESS! DID HE GET REELED IN BY HER GINORMOUS CHEST?!
I GET IT, SHE'S STACKED, BUT... SHE'S STACKED, BUT STILL! SHE'S STACKED...
IT'S NOT ENOUGH YET.
I'LL PUSH YOU EVEN FURTHER...

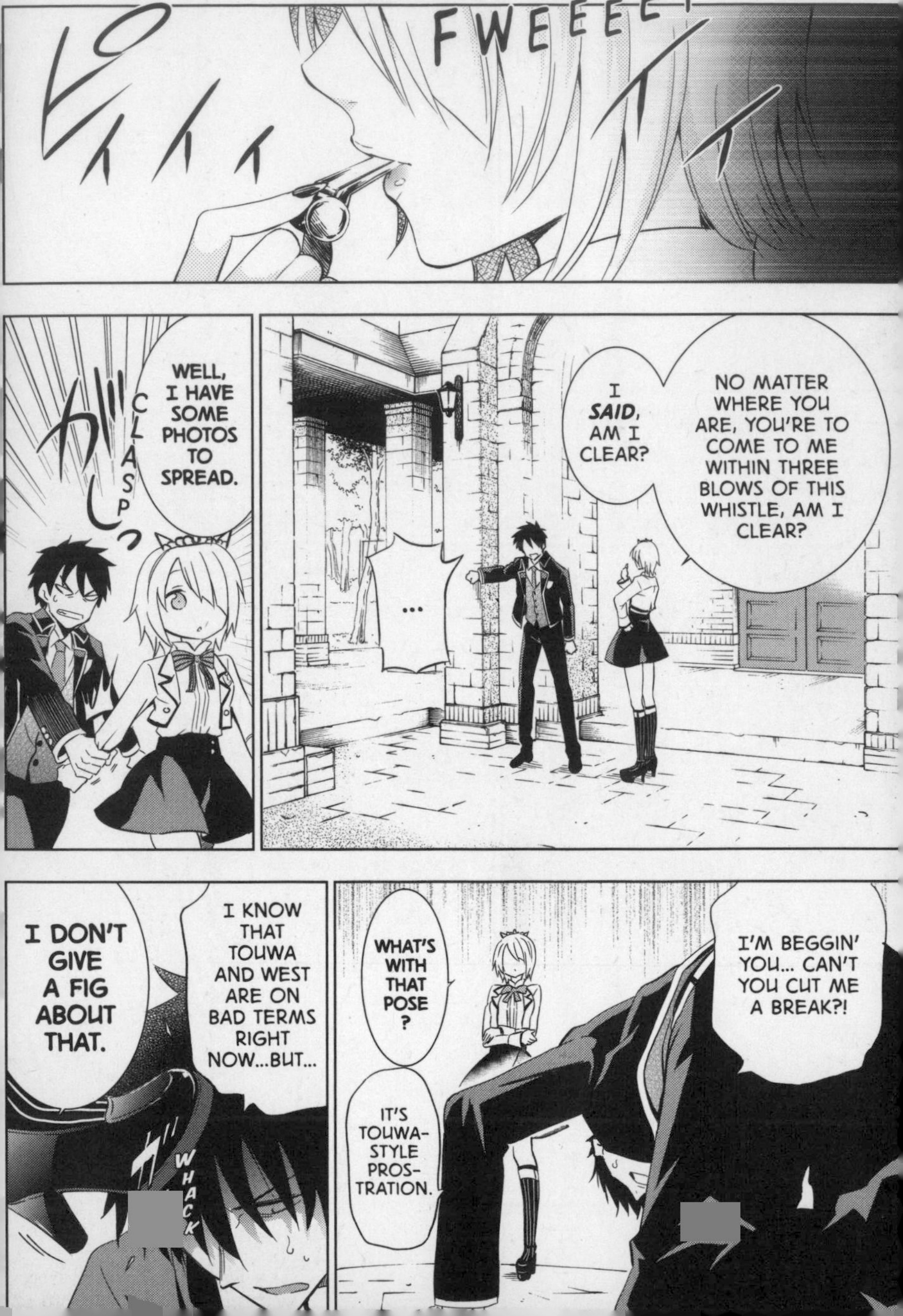
FWEEEET
NO MATTER WHERE YOU ARE, YOU'RE TO COME TO ME WITHIN THREE BLOWS OF THIS WHISTLE, AM I CLEAR?
I *SAID*, AM I CLEAR?
...
CLASP
WELL, I HAVE SOME PHOTOS TO SPREAD.
I'M BEGGIN' YOU... CAN'T YOU CUT ME A BREAK?!
WHAT'S WITH THAT POSE?
IT'S TOUWA-STYLE PROSTRATION.
I KNOW THAT TOUWA AND WEST ARE ON BAD TERMS RIGHT NOW...BUT...
I DON'T GIVE A FIG ABOUT THAT.
WHACK

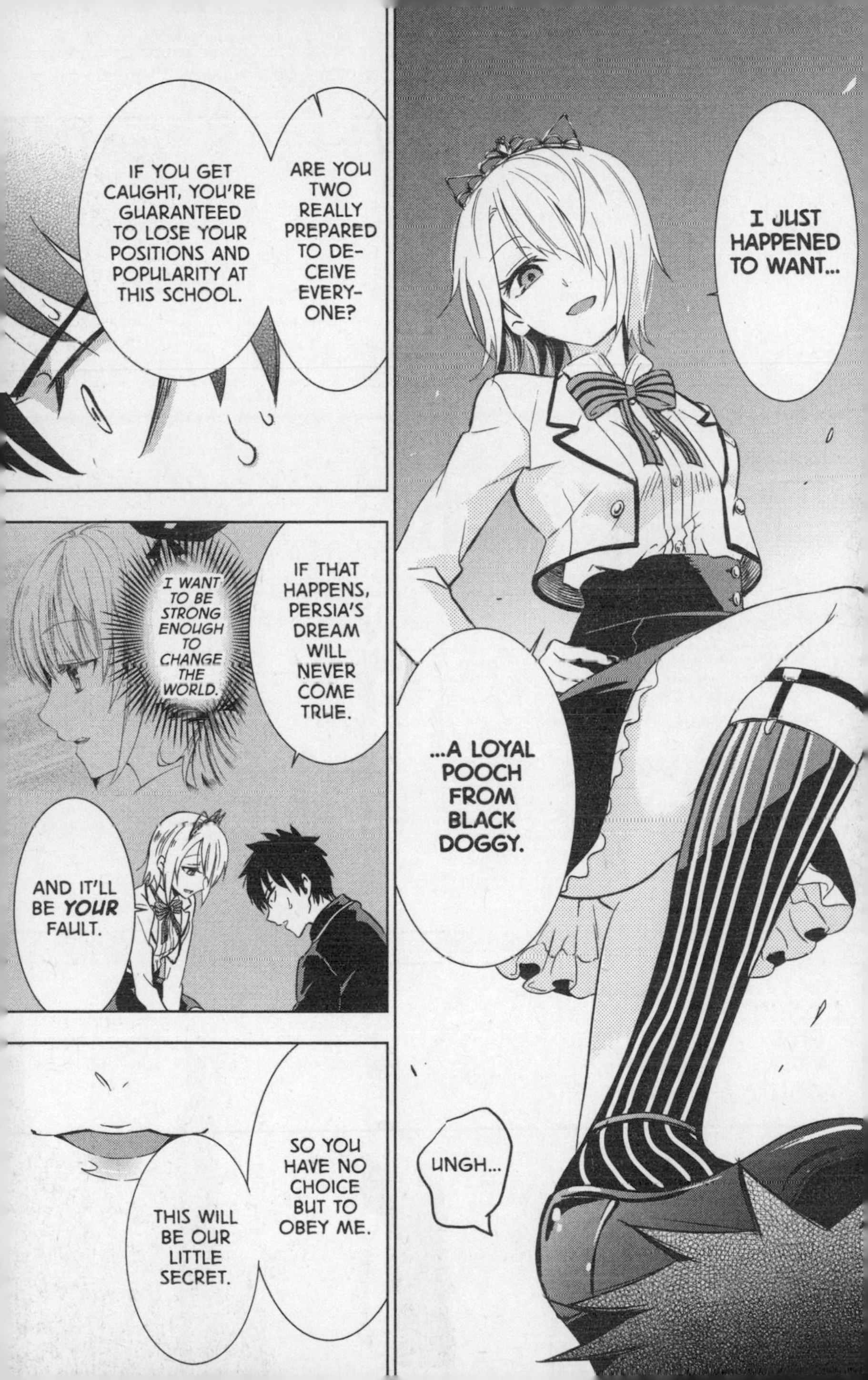
I JUST HAPPENED TO WANT...
...A LOYAL POOCH FROM BLACK DOGGY.
UNGH...
ARE YOU TWO REALLY PREPARED TO DE-CEIVE EVERY-ONE?
IF YOU GET CAUGHT, YOU'RE GUARANTEED TO LOSE YOUR POSITIONS AND POPULARITY AT THIS SCHOOL.
IF THAT HAPPENS, PERSIA'S DREAM WILL NEVER COME TRUE.
I WANT TO BE STRONG ENOUGH TO CHANGE THE WORLD.
AND IT'LL BE ***YOUR*** FAULT.
SO YOU HAVE NO CHOICE BUT TO OBEY ME.
THIS WILL BE OUR LITTLE SECRET.

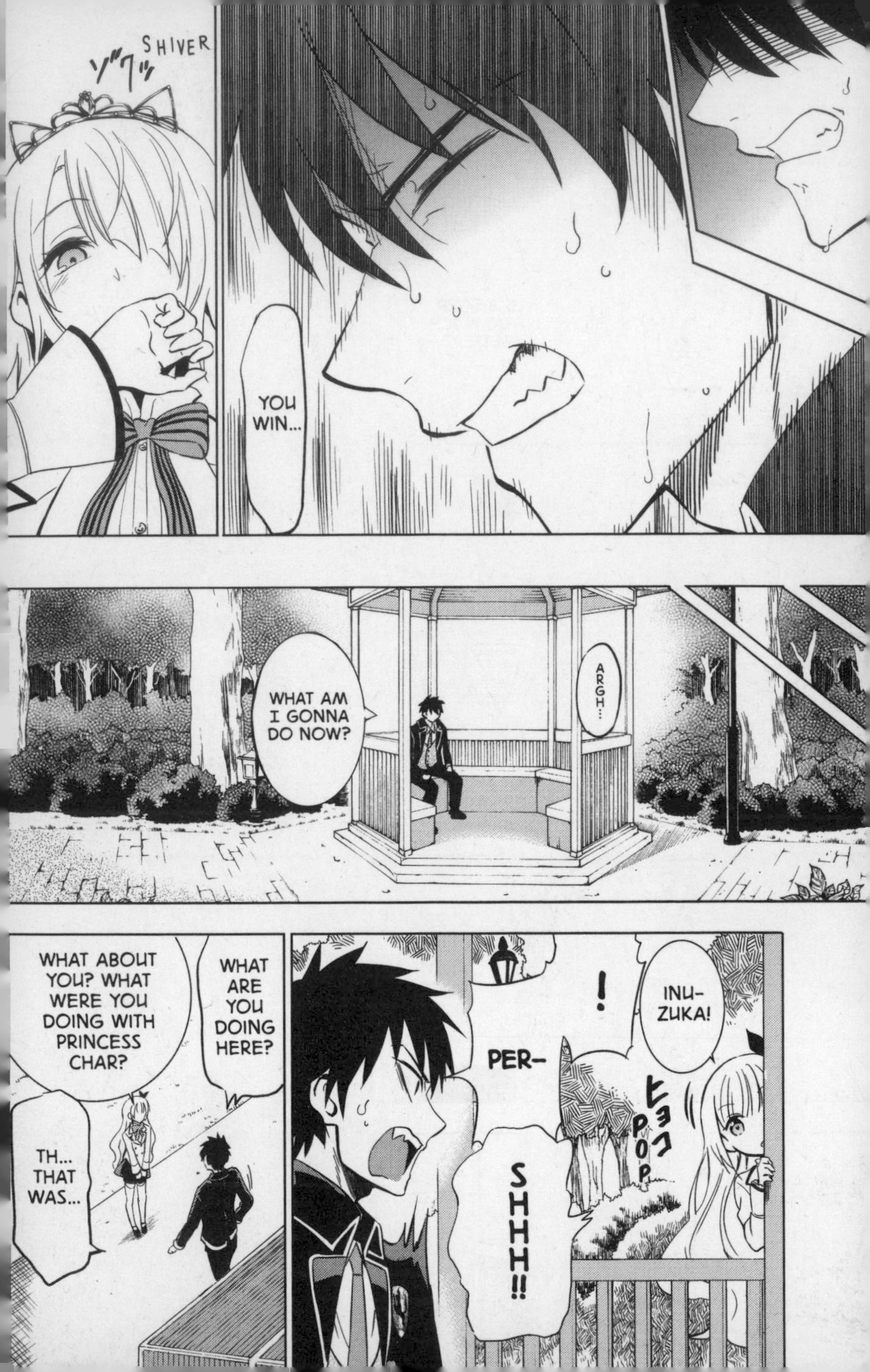
YOU WIN...
ゾクッ
SHIVER
ARGH...
WHAT AM I GONNA DO NOW?
INU-ZUKA!
!
PER-
ヒョコ
POP
SHHH!!
WHAT ARE YOU DOING HERE?
WHAT ABOUT YOU? WHAT WERE YOU DOING WITH PRINCESS CHAR?
TH... THAT WAS...

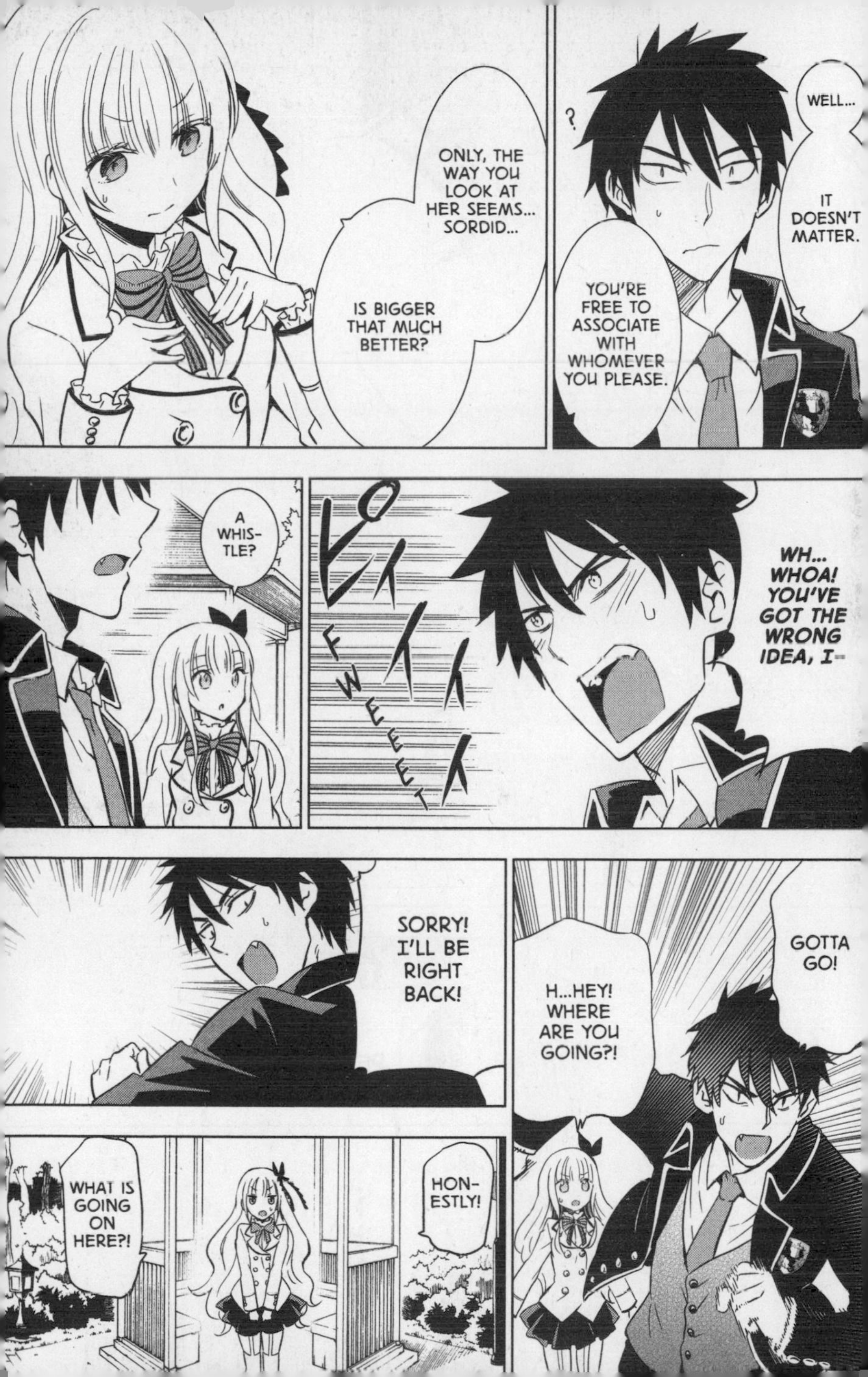
WELL...
IT DOESN'T MATTER.
YOU'RE FREE TO ASSOCIATE WITH WHOMEVER YOU PLEASE.
?
ONLY, THE WAY YOU LOOK AT HER SEEMS... SORDID...
IS BIGGER THAT MUCH BETTER?
WH... WHOA! YOU'VE GOT THE WRONG IDEA, I—
FWEEEET
A WHIS-TLE?
GOTTA GO!
H...HEY! WHERE ARE YOU GOING?!
SORRY! I'LL BE RIGHT BACK!
HON-ESTLY!
WHAT IS GOING ON HERE?!

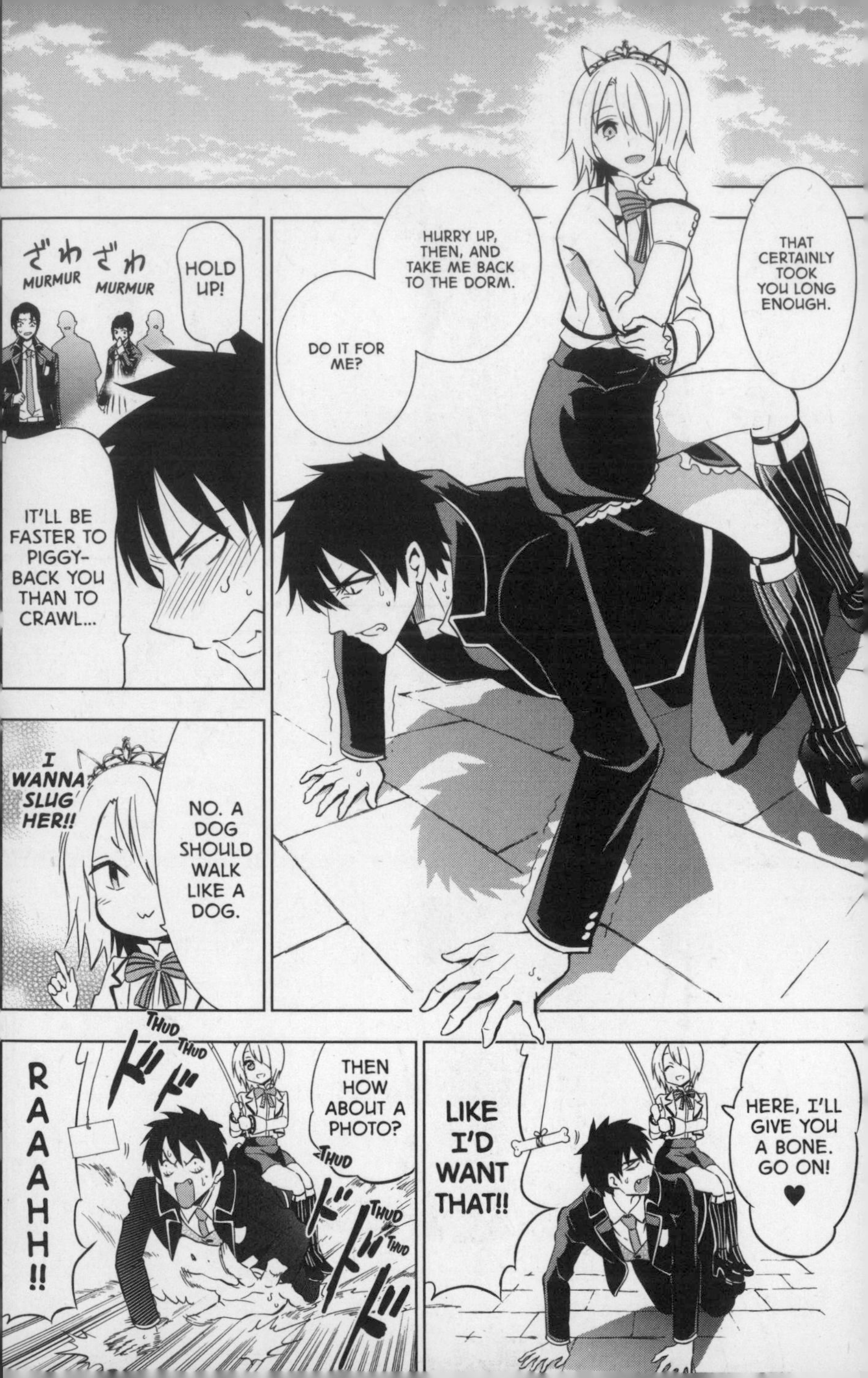
THAT CERTAINLY TOOK YOU LONG ENOUGH.
HURRY UP, THEN, AND TAKE ME BACK TO THE DORM.
DO IT FOR ME?
HOLD UP!
ざわざわ MURMUR MURMUR
IT'LL BE FASTER TO PIGGY-BACK YOU THAN TO CRAWL...
NO. A DOG SHOULD WALK LIKE A DOG.
I WANNA SLUG HER!!
HERE, I'LL GIVE YOU A BONE. GO ON! ♥
LIKE I'D WANT THAT!!
THEN HOW ABOUT A PHOTO?
THUD THUD THUD THUD THUD
RAAAAHH!!

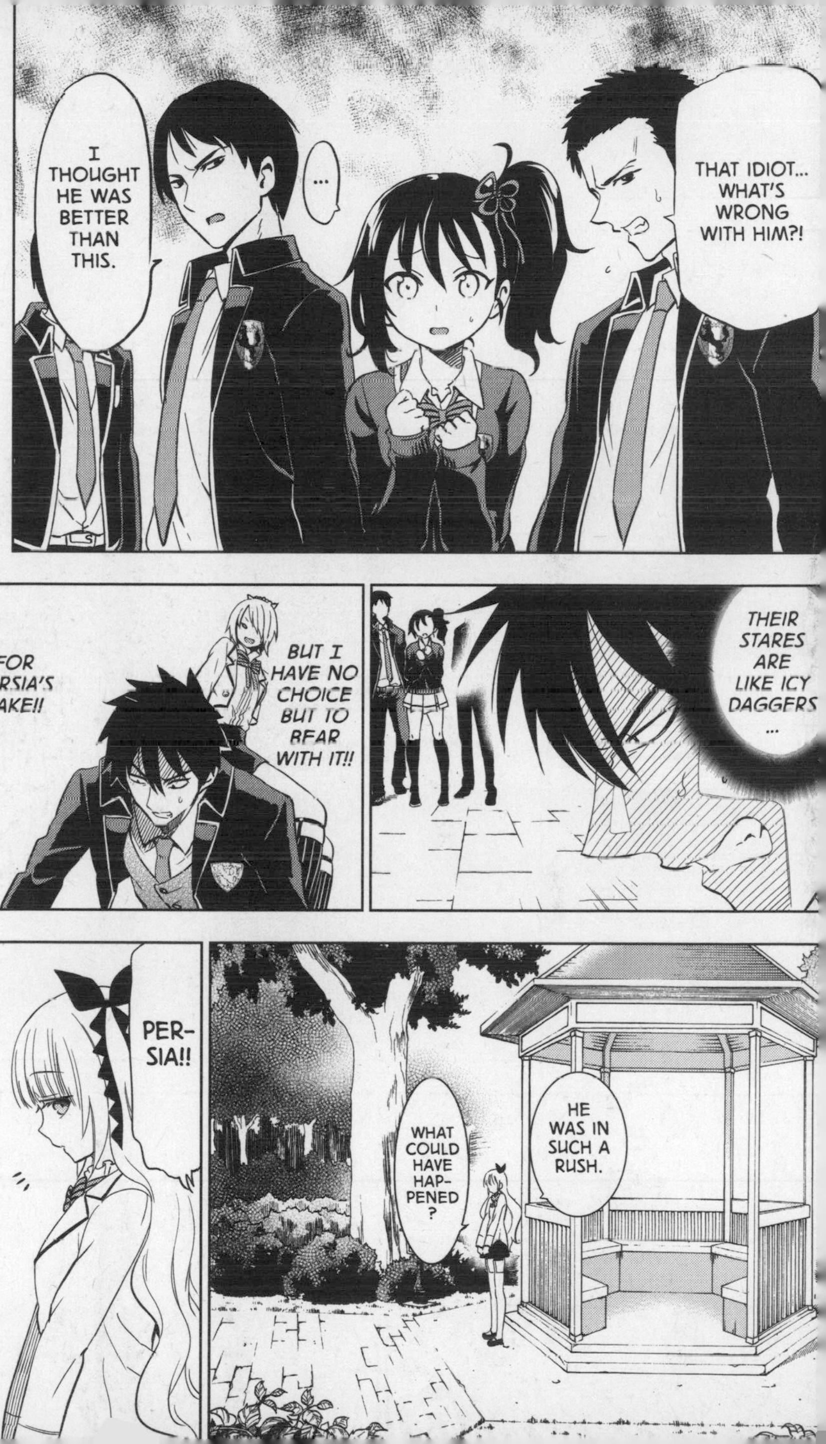
THAT IDIOT... WHAT'S WRONG WITH HIM?!
...
I THOUGHT HE WAS BETTER THAN THIS.
THEIR STARES ARE LIKE ICY DAGGERS...
BUT I HAVE NO CHOICE BUT TO BEAR WITH IT!!
FOR PERSIA'S SAKE!!
HE WAS IN SUCH A RUSH.
WHAT COULD HAVE HAP-PENED?
PER-SIA!!

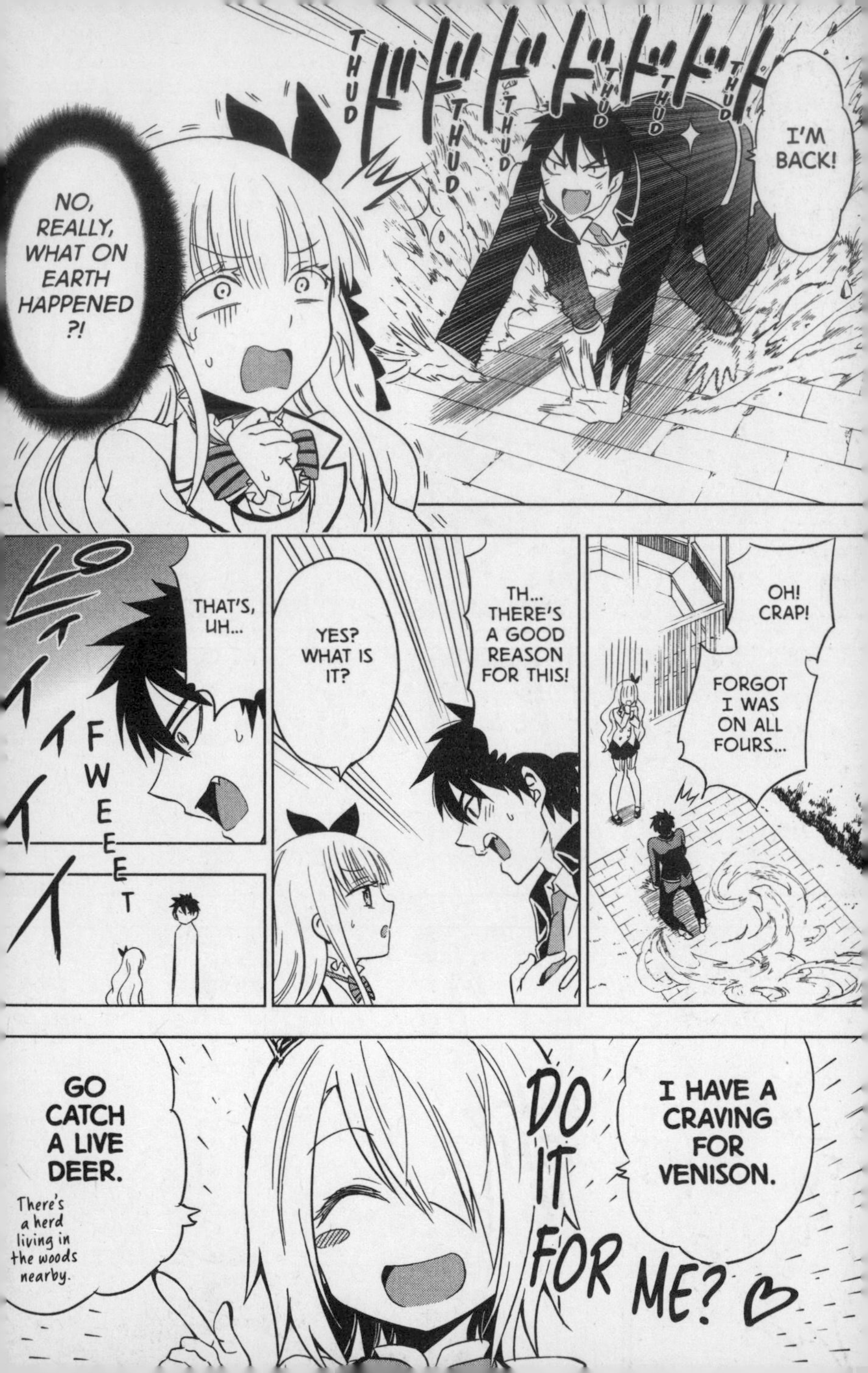
THUD
THUD
THUD
THUD
THUD
THUD
I'M BACK!
NO, REALLY, WHAT ON EARTH HAPPENED?!
OH! CRAP!
FORGOT I WAS ON ALL FOURS...
TH... THERE'S A GOOD REASON FOR THIS!
YES? WHAT IS IT?
THAT'S, UH...
FWEEEET
I HAVE A CRAVING FOR VENISON.
DO IT FOR ME? ♡
GO CATCH A LIVE DEER.
There's a herd living in the woods nearby.

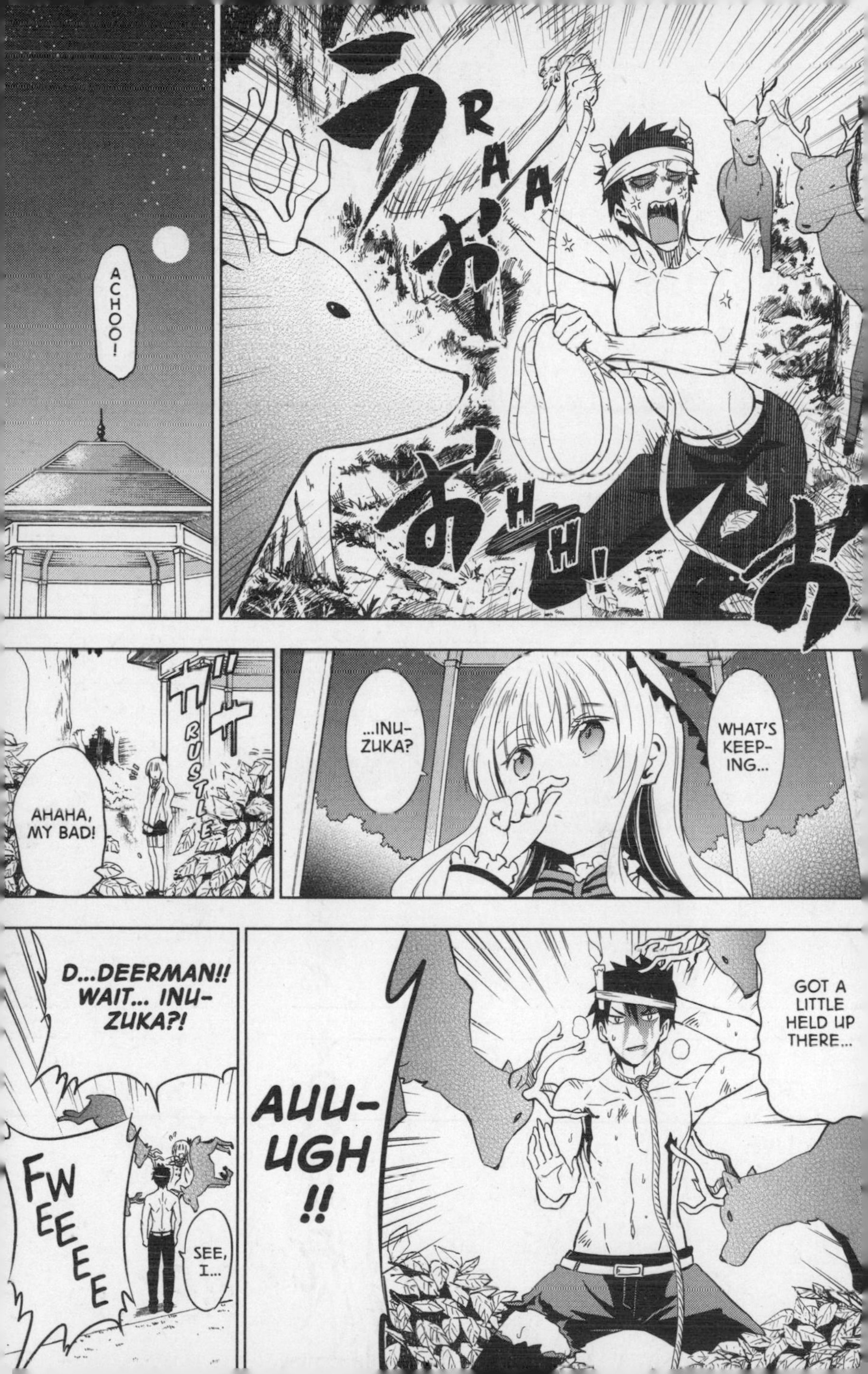
うおおお
RAAHH!
ACHOO!
WHAT'S KEEP-ING...
...INU-ZUKA?
ガサ
RUSTLE
AHAHA, MY BAD!
GOT A LITTLE HELD UP THERE...
AUU-UGH!!
D...DEERMAN!! WAIT... INU-ZUKA?!
FWEEEEE
SEE, I...

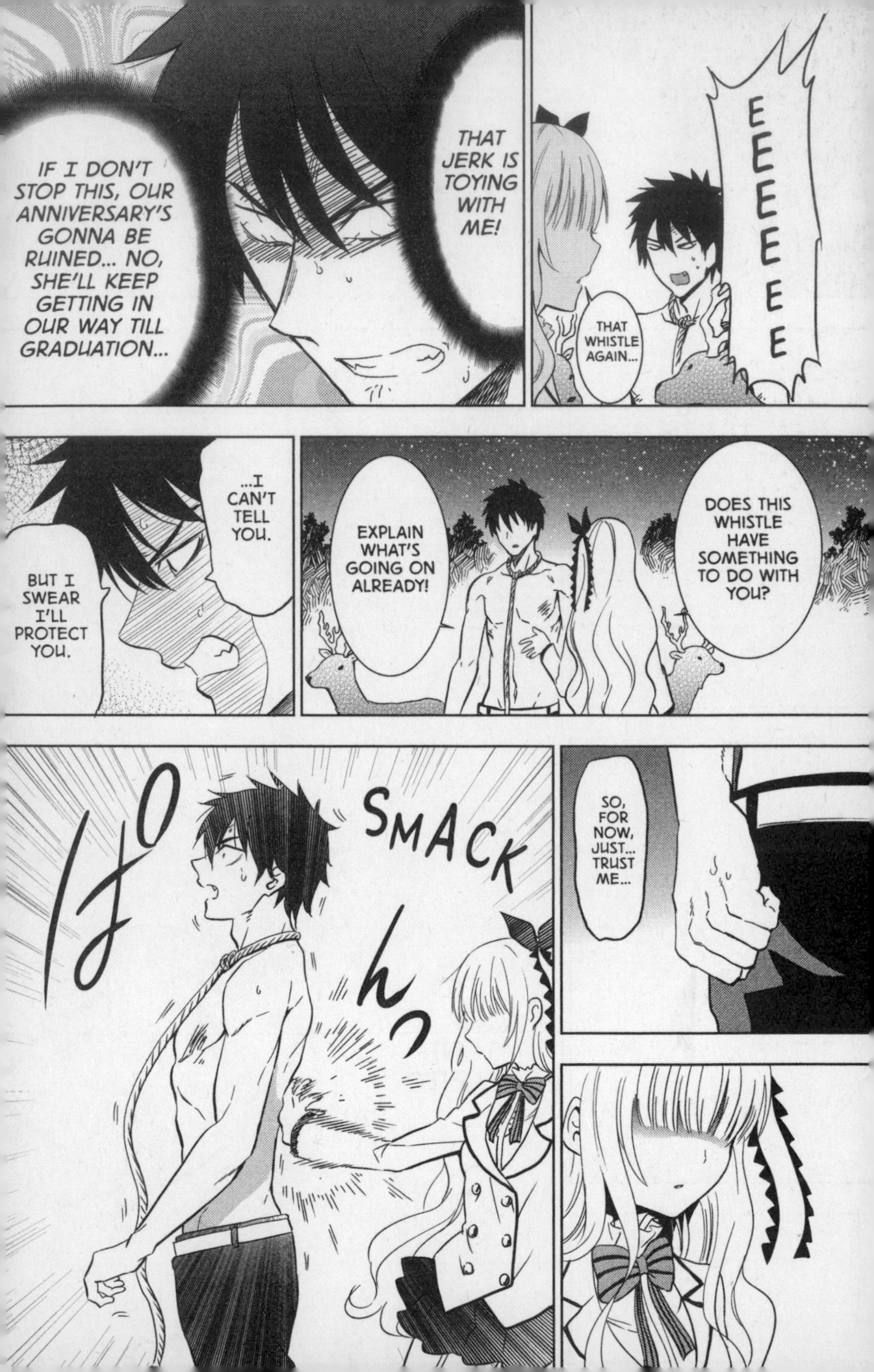
EEEEEEE
THAT WHISTLE AGAIN...
THAT JERK IS TOYING WITH ME!
IF I DON'T STOP THIS, OUR ANNIVERSARY'S GONNA BE RUINED... NO, SHE'LL KEEP GETTING IN OUR WAY TILL GRADUATION...
DOES THIS WHISTLE HAVE SOMETHING TO DO WITH YOU?
EXPLAIN WHAT'S GOING ON ALREADY!
...I CAN'T TELL YOU.
BUT I SWEAR I'LL PROTECT YOU.
SO, FOR NOW, JUST... TRUST ME...
SMACK

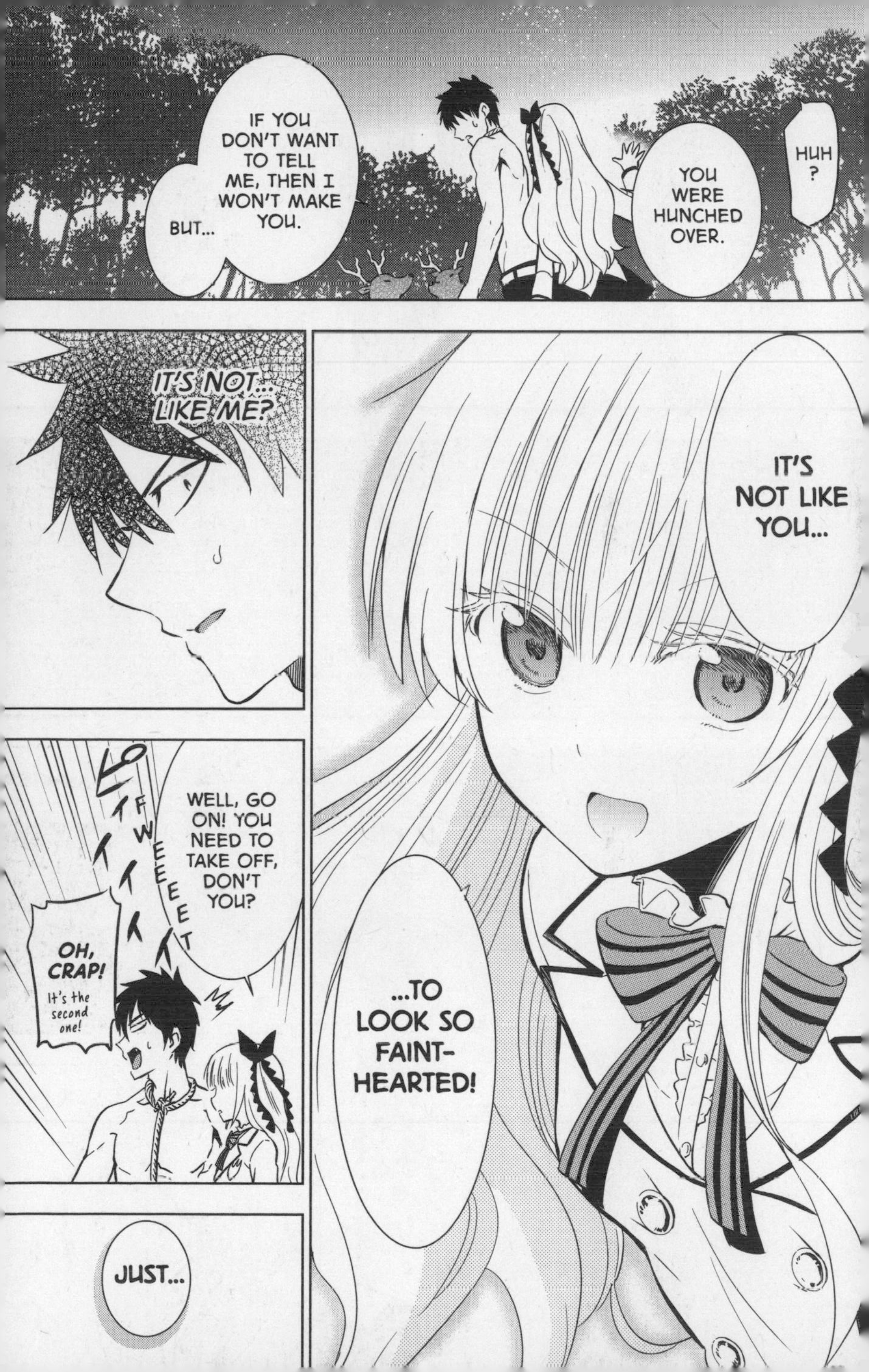
HUH?
YOU WERE HUNCHED OVER.
IF YOU DON'T WANT TO TELL ME, THEN I WON'T MAKE YOU.
BUT...
IT'S NOT LIKE YOU...
...TO LOOK SO FAINT-HEARTED!
IT'S NOT... LIKE ME?
WELL, GO ON! YOU NEED TO TAKE OFF, DON'T YOU?
FWEEEEET
OH, CRAP!
It's the second one!
JUST...

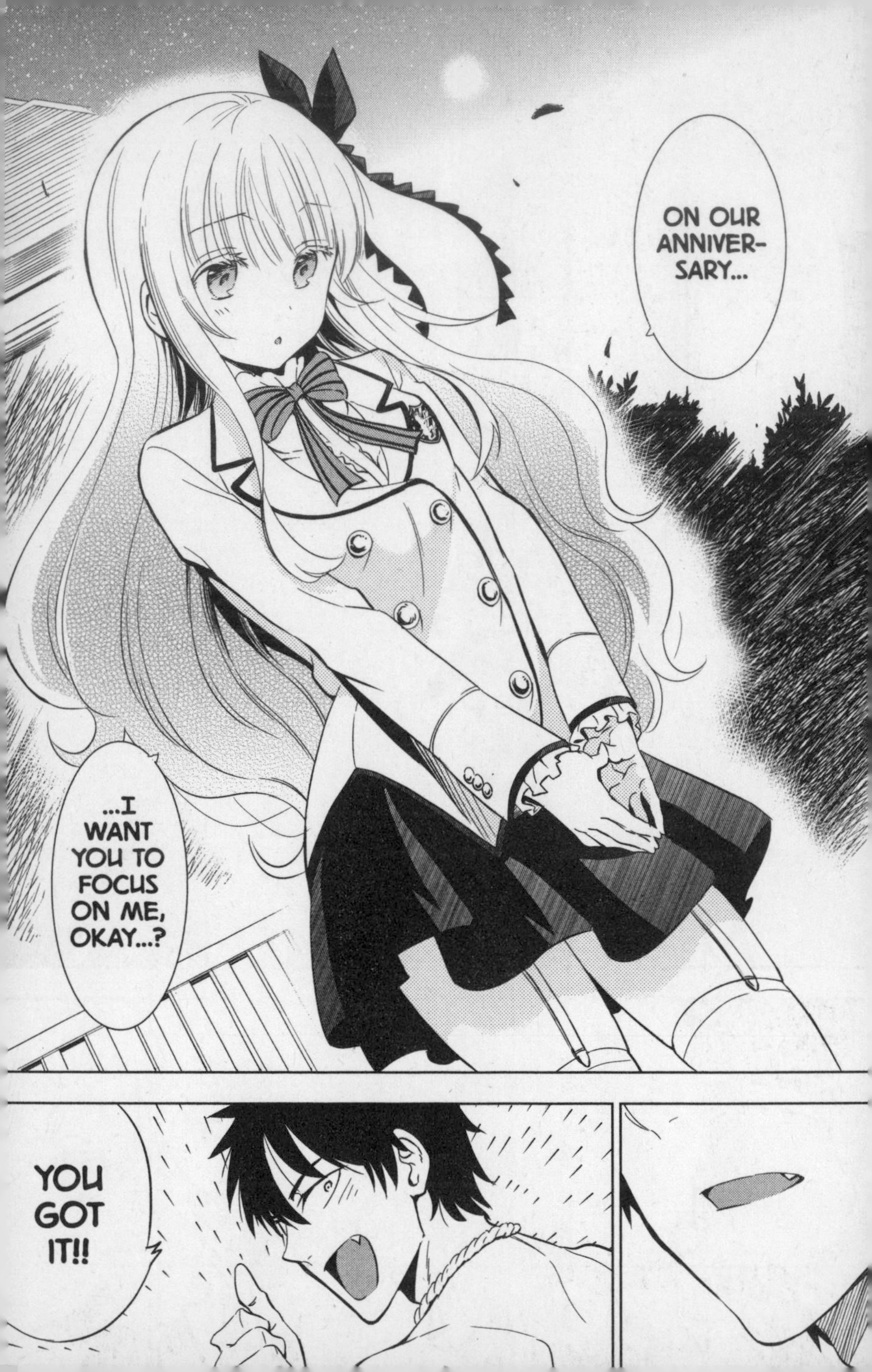
ON OUR ANNIVER-SARY...
...I WANT YOU TO FOCUS ON ME, OKAY...?
YOU GOT IT!!

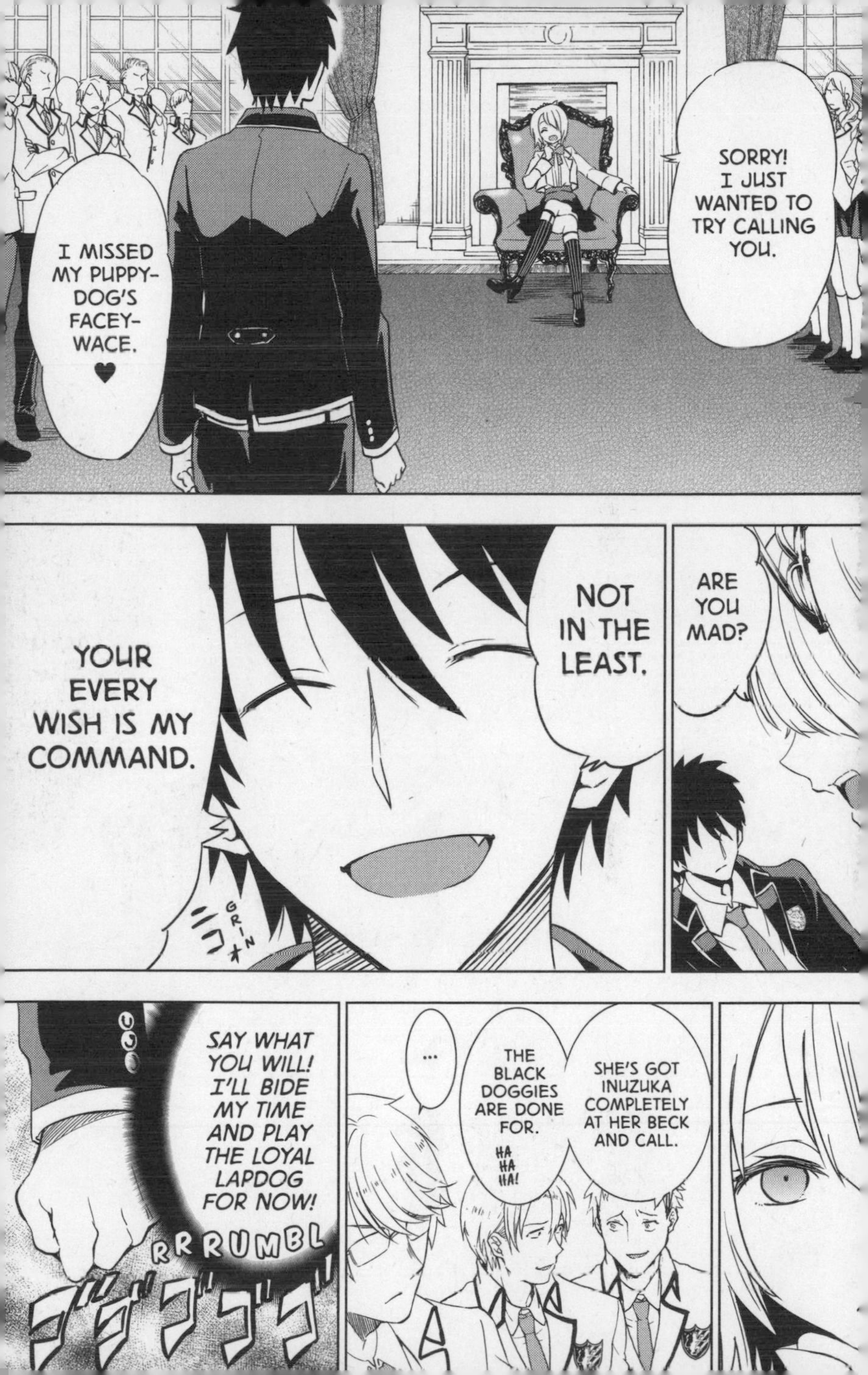
SORRY! I JUST WANTED TO TRY CALLING YOU.
I MISSED MY PUPPY-DOG'S FACEY-WACE. ♥
ARE YOU MAD?
NOT IN THE LEAST.
YOUR EVERY WISH IS MY COMMAND.
GRIN
SHE'S GOT INUZUKA COMPLETELY AT HER BECK AND CALL.
THE BLACK DOGGIES ARE DONE FOR.
HA HA HA!
...
SAY WHAT YOU WILL! I'LL BIDE MY TIME AND PLAY THE LOYAL LAPDOG FOR NOW!
RRRUMBL

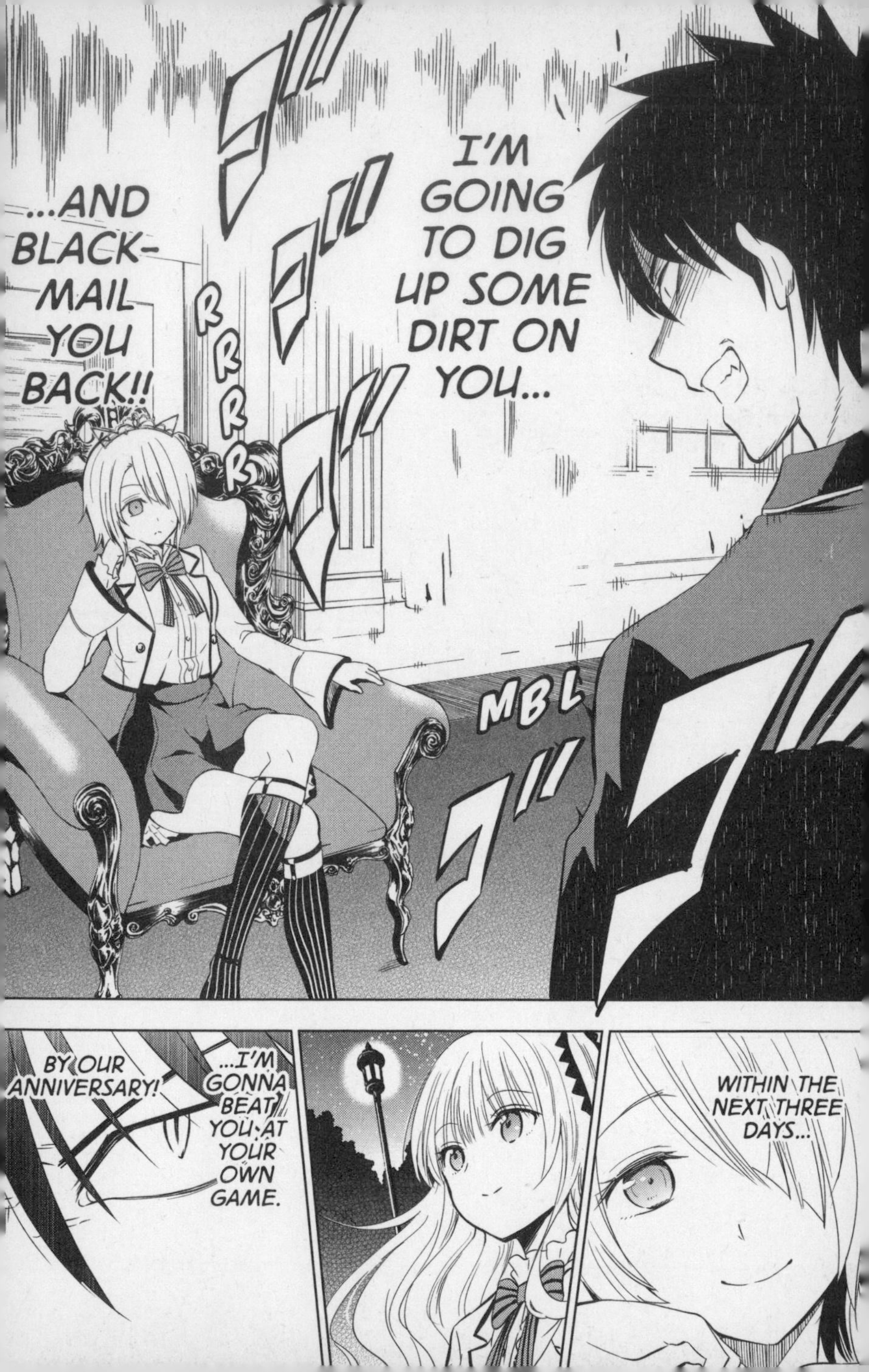
I'M GOING TO DIG UP SOME DIRT ON YOU...
...AND BLACK-MAIL YOU BACK!!
RRRRR
MBL
WITHIN THE NEXT THREE DAYS...
...I'M GONNA BEAT YOU AT YOUR OWN GAME.
BY OUR ANNIVERSARY!

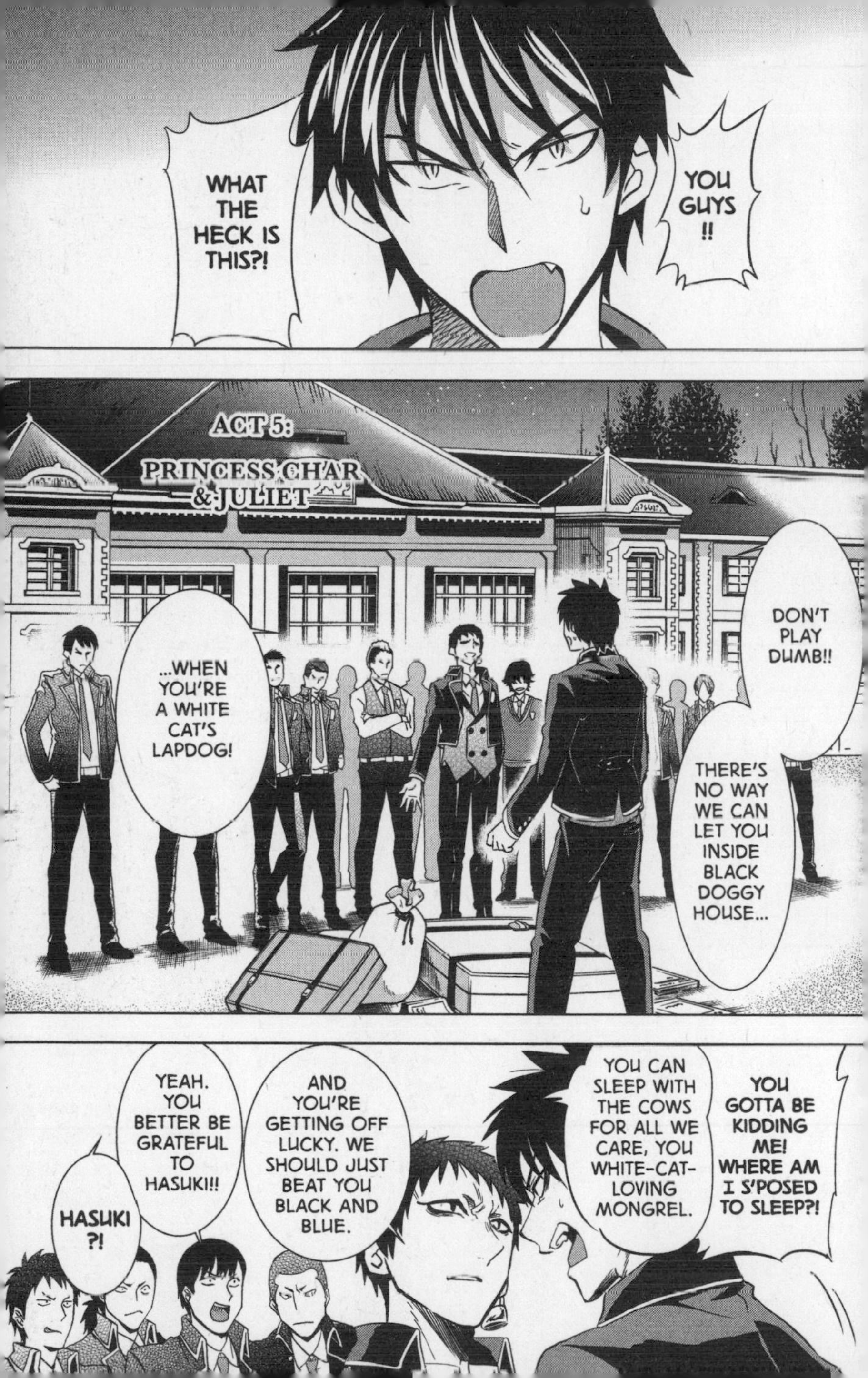
YOU GUYS!!
WHAT THE HECK IS THIS?!
ACT 5: PRINCESS CHAR & JULIET
DON'T PLAY DUMB!!
THERE'S NO WAY WE CAN LET YOU INSIDE BLACK DOGGY HOUSE...
...WHEN YOU'RE A WHITE CAT'S LAPDOG!
YOU GOTTA BE KIDDING ME! WHERE AM I S'POSED TO SLEEP?!
YOU CAN SLEEP WITH THE COWS FOR ALL WE CARE, YOU WHITE-CAT-LOVING MONGREL.
AND YOU'RE GETTING OFF LUCKY. WE SHOULD JUST BEAT YOU BLACK AND BLUE.
YEAH. YOU BETTER BE GRATEFUL TO HASUKI!!
HASUKI?!

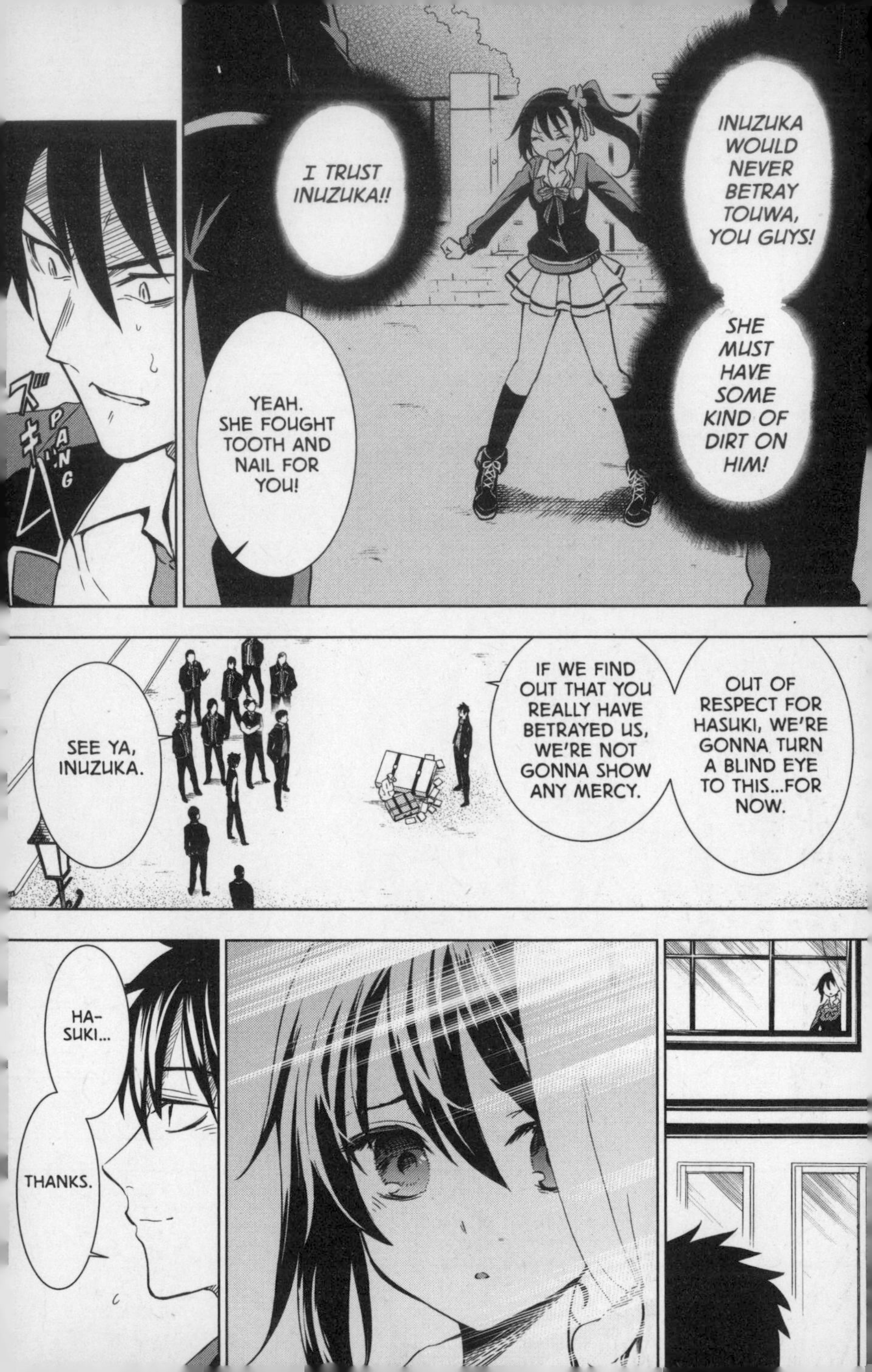
INUZUKA WOULD NEVER BETRAY TOUWA, YOU GUYS!
I TRUST INUZUKA!!
SHE MUST HAVE SOME KIND OF DIRT ON HIM!
YEAH. SHE FOUGHT TOOTH AND NAIL FOR YOU!
ズキ
PANG
OUT OF RESPECT FOR HASUKI, WE'RE GONNA TURN A BLIND EYE TO THIS...FOR NOW.
IF WE FIND OUT THAT YOU REALLY HAVE BETRAYED US, WE'RE NOT GONNA SHOW ANY MERCY.
SEE YA, INUZUKA.
HA-SUKI...
THANKS.

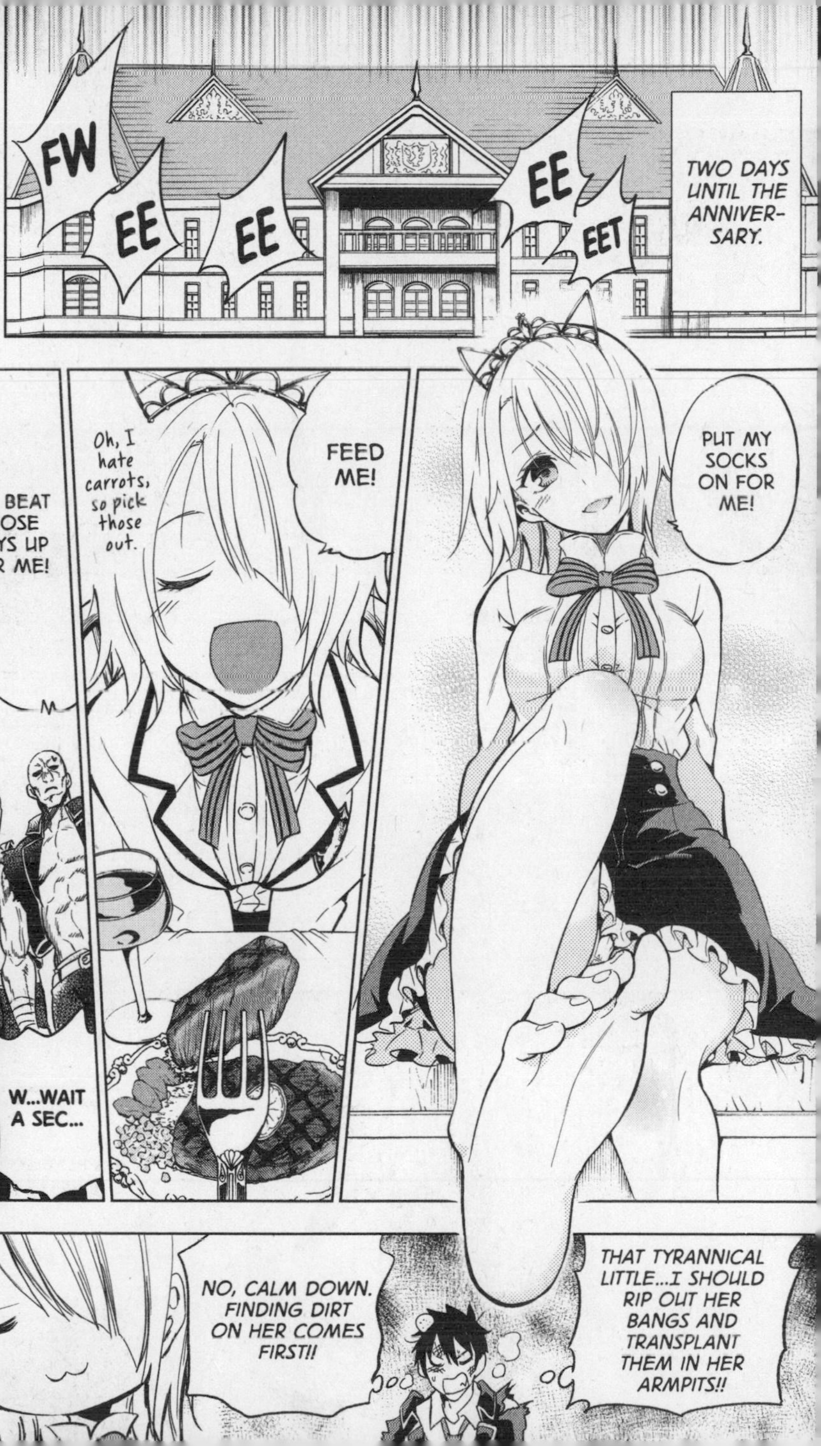
TWO DAYS UNTIL THE ANNIVERSARY.
FW EE EE EE EET
PUT MY SOCKS ON FOR ME!
FEED ME!
Oh, I hate carrots, so pick those out.
GO BEAT THOSE GUYS UP FOR ME!
W...WAIT A SEC...
THAT TYRANNICAL LITTLE...I SHOULD RIP OUT HER BANGS AND TRANSPLANT THEM IN HER ARMPITS!!
NO, CALM DOWN. FINDING DIRT ON HER COMES FIRST!!

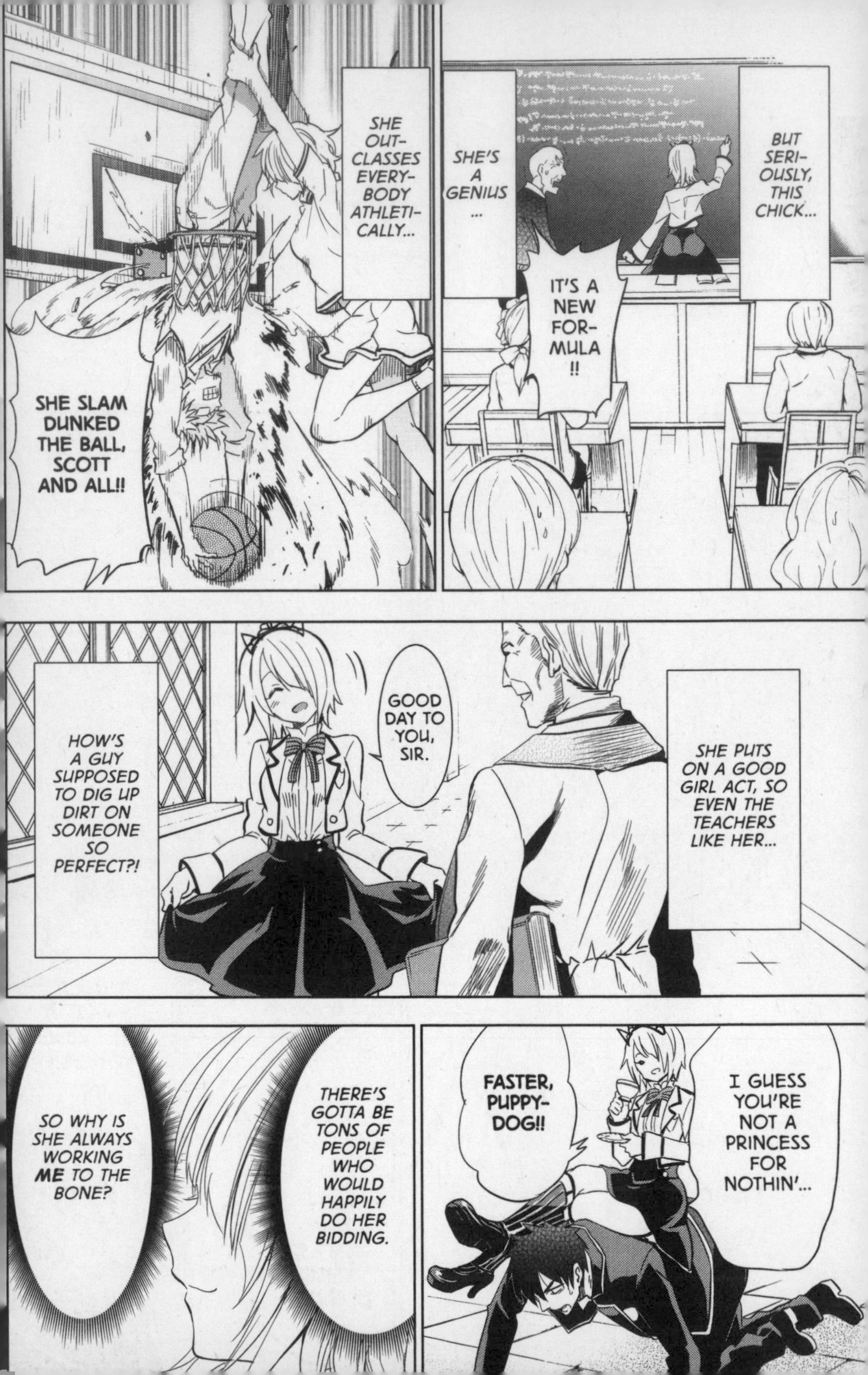
BUT SERIOUSLY, THIS CHICK...
SHE'S A GENIUS...
IT'S A NEW FORMULA!!
SHE OUTCLASSES EVERYBODY ATHLETICALLY...
SHE SLAM DUNKED THE BALL, SCOTT AND ALL!!
SHE PUTS ON A GOOD GIRL ACT, SO EVEN THE TEACHERS LIKE HER...
GOOD DAY TO YOU, SIR.
HOW'S A GUY SUPPOSED TO DIG UP DIRT ON SOMEONE SO PERFECT?!
I GUESS YOU'RE NOT A PRINCESS FOR NOTHIN'...
FASTER, PUPPY-DOG!!
THERE'S GOTTA BE TONS OF PEOPLE WHO WOULD HAPPILY DO HER BIDDING.
SO WHY IS SHE ALWAYS WORKING **ME** TO THE BONE?

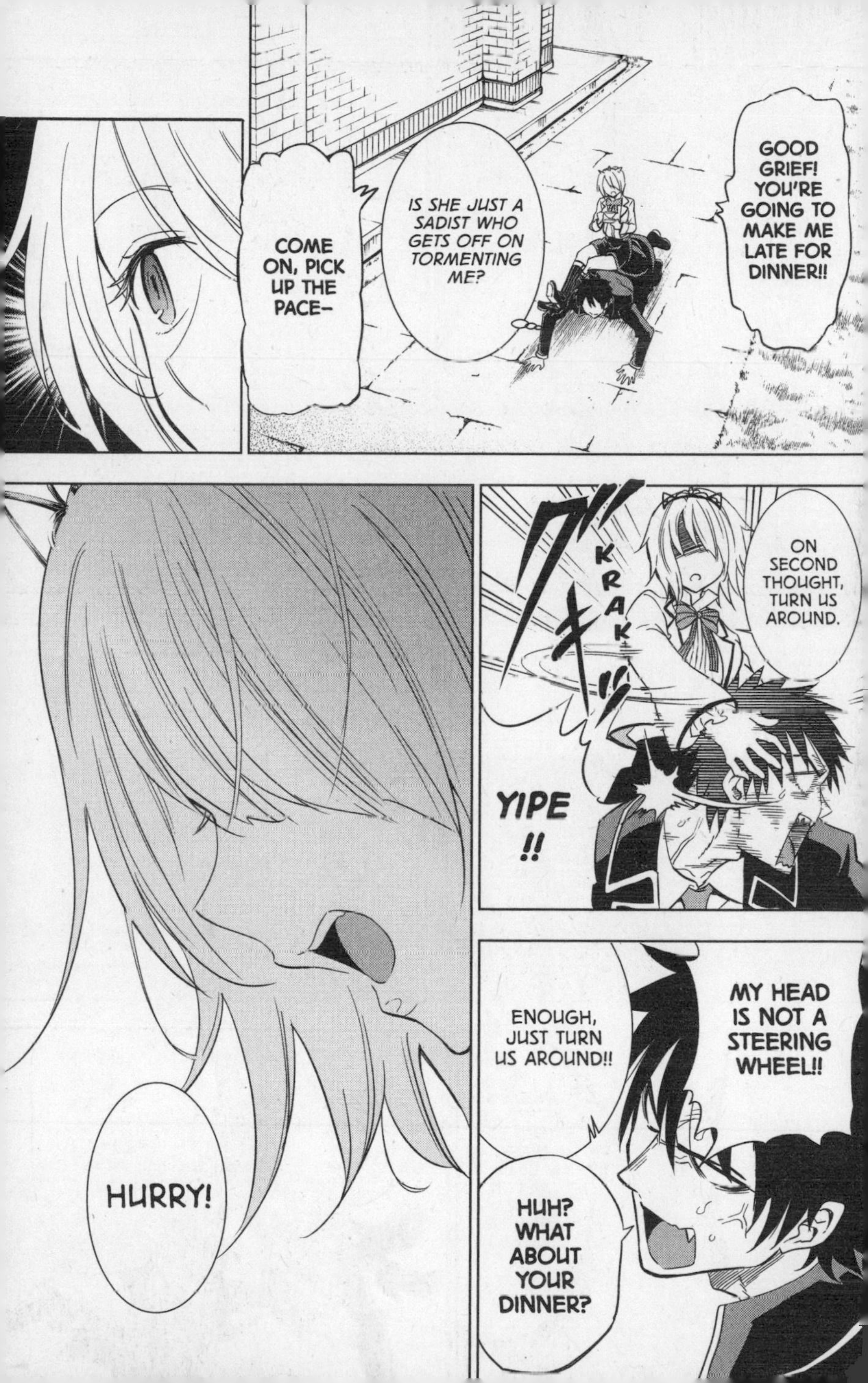
GOOD GRIEF! YOU'RE GOING TO MAKE ME LATE FOR DINNER!!
IS SHE JUST A SADIST WHO GETS OFF ON TORMENTING ME?
COME ON, PICK UP THE PACE–
ON SECOND THOUGHT, TURN US AROUND.
KRAK
YIPE!!
MY HEAD IS NOT A STEERING WHEEL!!
ENOUGH, JUST TURN US AROUND!!
HUH? WHAT ABOUT YOUR DINNER?
HURRY!

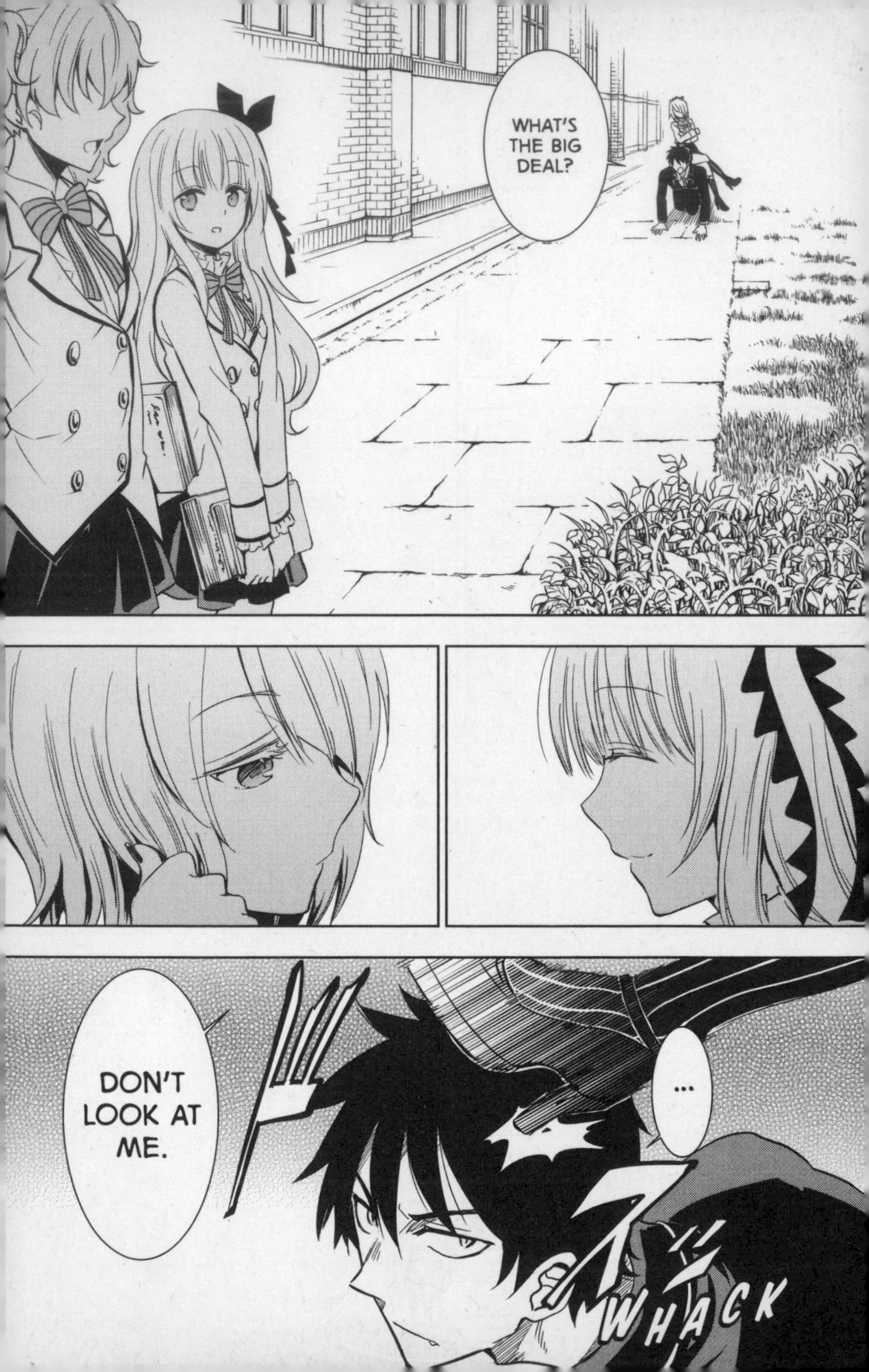
WHAT'S THE BIG DEAL?
...
DON'T LOOK AT ME.
WHACK

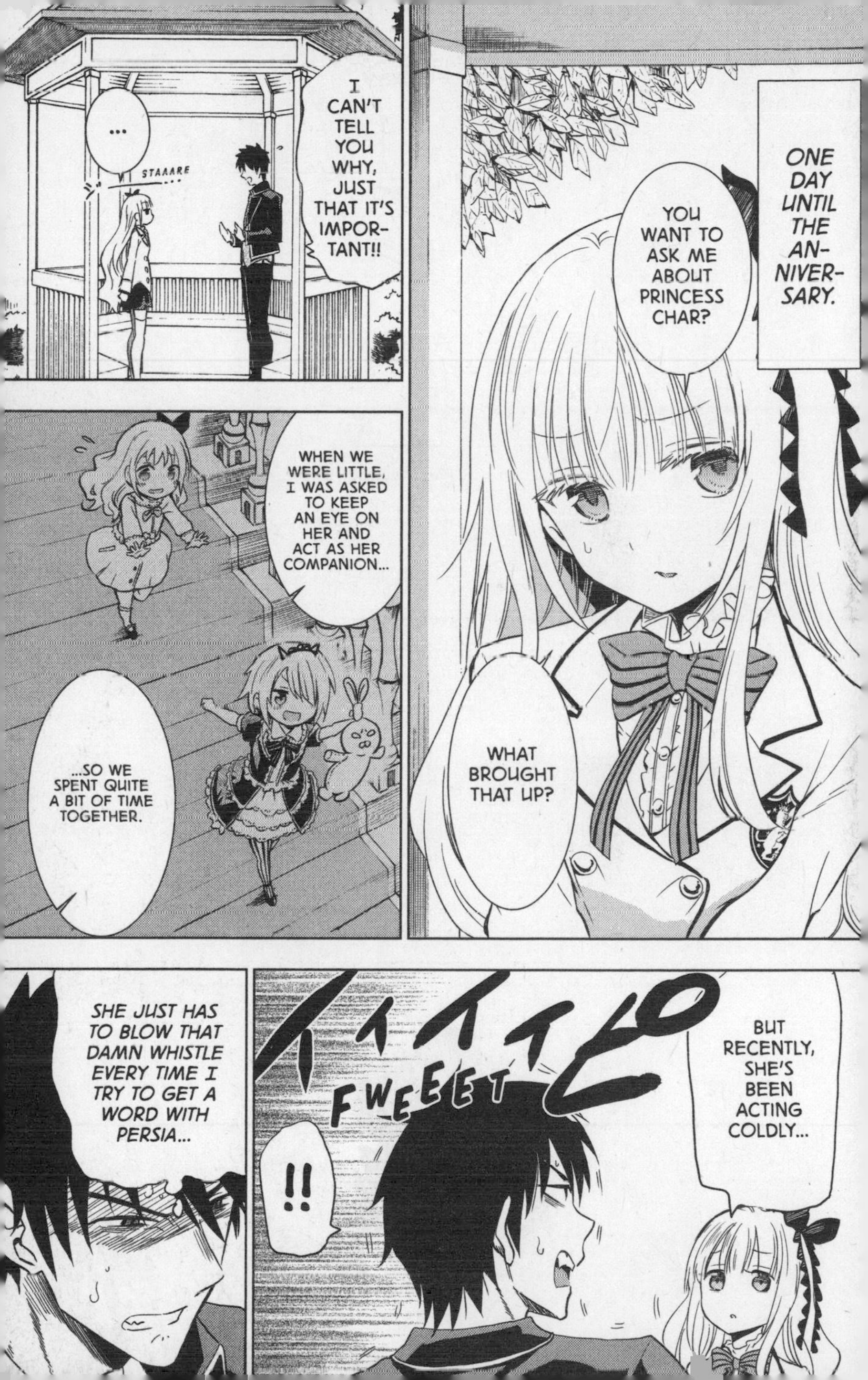
ONE DAY UNTIL THE ANNIVERSARY.
YOU WANT TO ASK ME ABOUT PRINCESS CHAR?
WHAT BROUGHT THAT UP?
I CAN'T TELL YOU WHY, JUST THAT IT'S IMPORTANT!!
...
STAAARE...
WHEN WE WERE LITTLE, I WAS ASKED TO KEEP AN EYE ON HER AND ACT AS HER COMPANION...
...SO WE SPENT QUITE A BIT OF TIME TOGETHER.
BUT RECENTLY, SHE'S BEEN ACTING COLDLY...
FWEEET
!!
SHE JUST HAS TO BLOW THAT DAMN WHISTLE EVERY TIME I TRY TO GET A WORD WITH PERSIA...

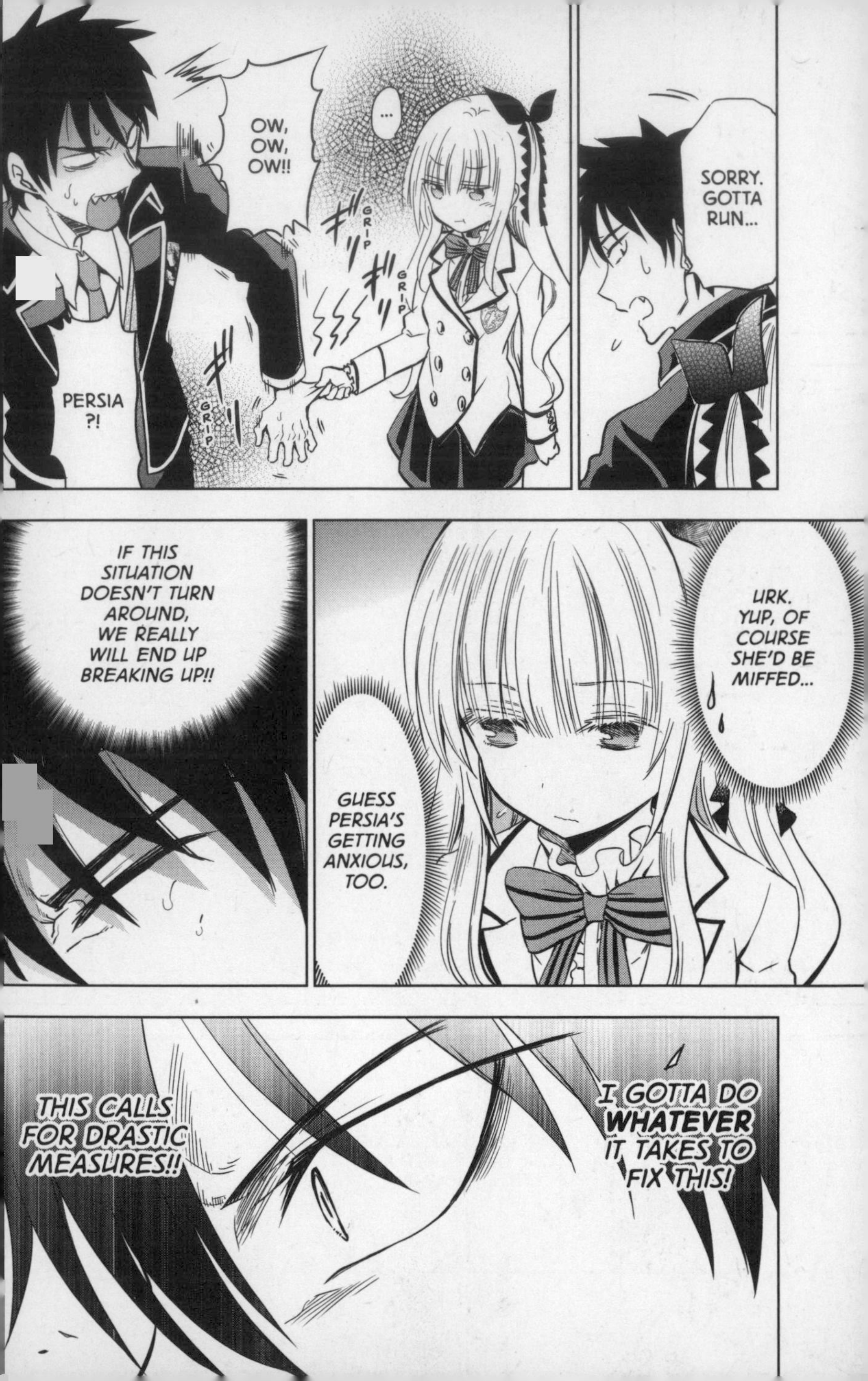
SORRY. GOTTA RUN...
...
OW, OW, OW!!
GRIP
GRIP
GRIP
PERSIA ?!
URK. YUP, OF COURSE SHE'D BE MIFFED...
GUESS PERSIA'S GETTING ANXIOUS, TOO.
IF THIS SITUATION DOESN'T TURN AROUND, WE REALLY WILL END UP BREAKING UP!!
I GOTTA DO WHATEVER IT TAKES TO FIX THIS!
THIS CALLS FOR DRASTIC MEASURES!!

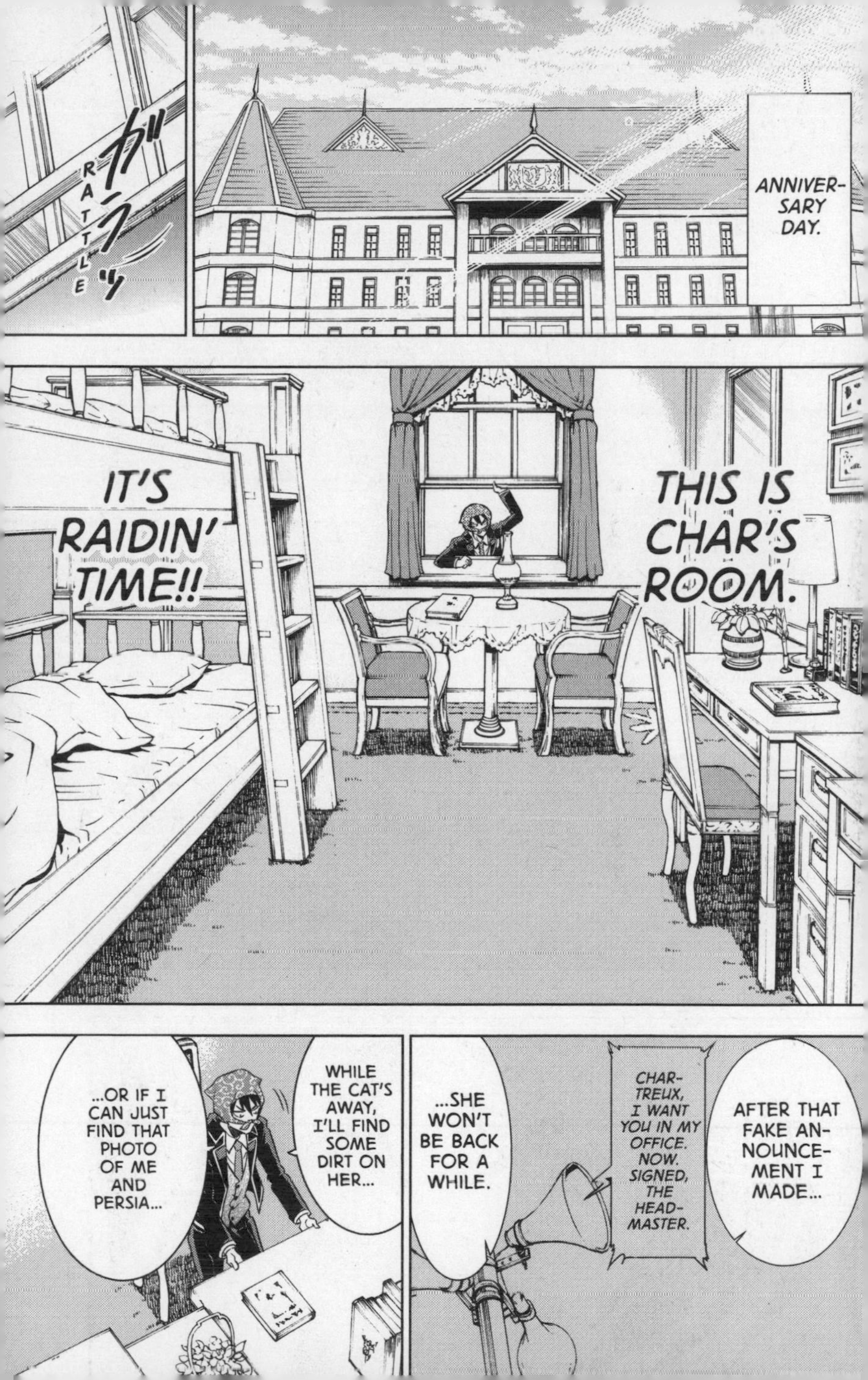
ANNIVERSARY DAY.
ガラッ
RATTLE
THIS IS CHAR'S ROOM.
IT'S RAIDIN' TIME!!
AFTER THAT FAKE ANNOUNCEMENT I MADE...
CHARTREUX, I WANT YOU IN MY OFFICE. NOW. SIGNED, THE HEADMASTER.
...SHE WON'T BE BACK FOR A WHILE.
WHILE THE CAT'S AWAY, I'LL FIND SOME DIRT ON HER...
...OR IF I CAN JUST FIND THAT PHOTO OF ME AND PERSIA...

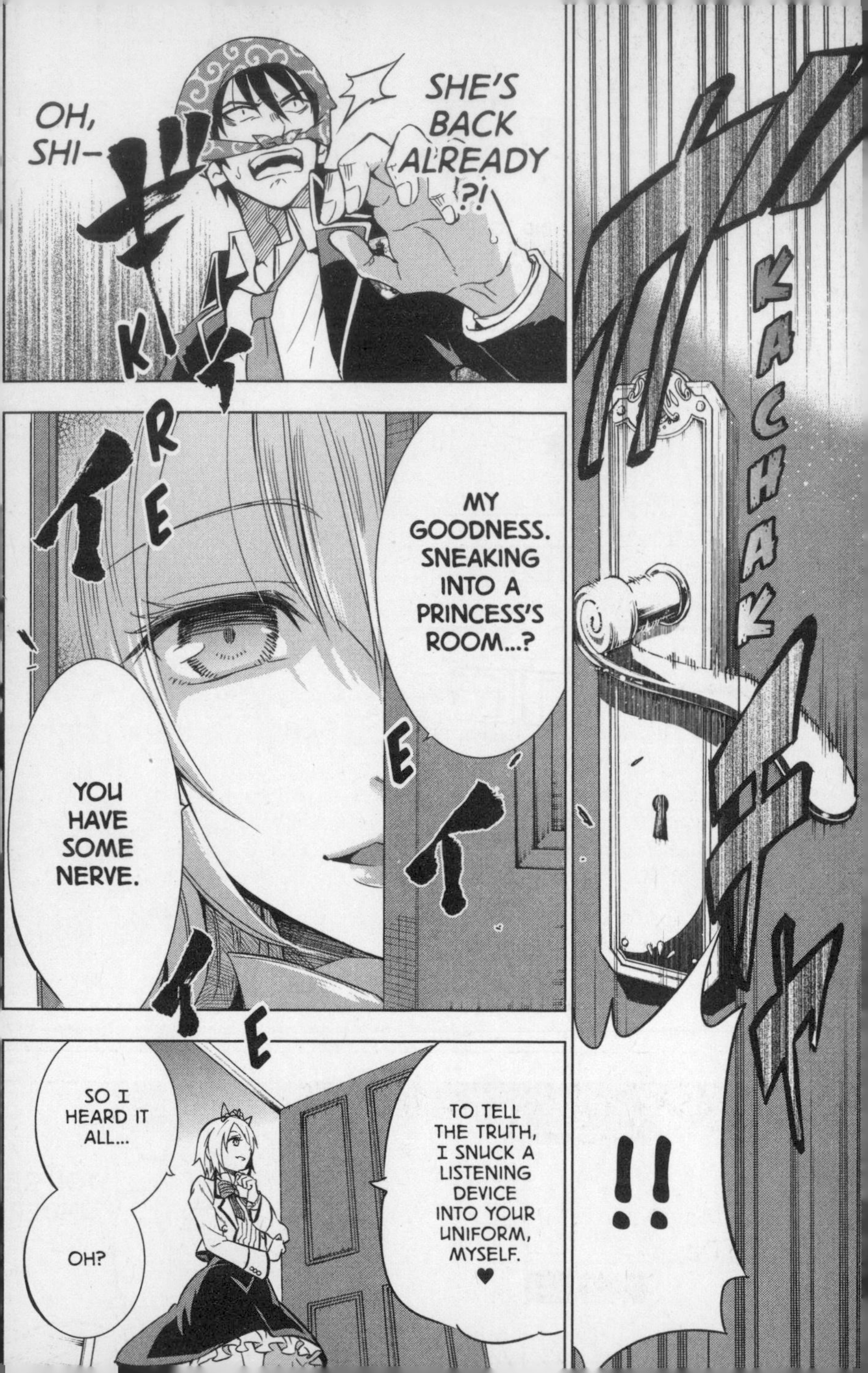
KACHAK
!!
SHE'S BACK ALREADY?!
OH, SHI–
KREEE
MY GOODNESS. SNEAKING INTO A PRINCESS'S ROOM...?
YOU HAVE SOME NERVE.
TO TELL THE TRUTH, I SNUCK A LISTENING DEVICE INTO YOUR UNIFORM, MYSELF. ♥
SO I HEARD IT ALL...
OH?

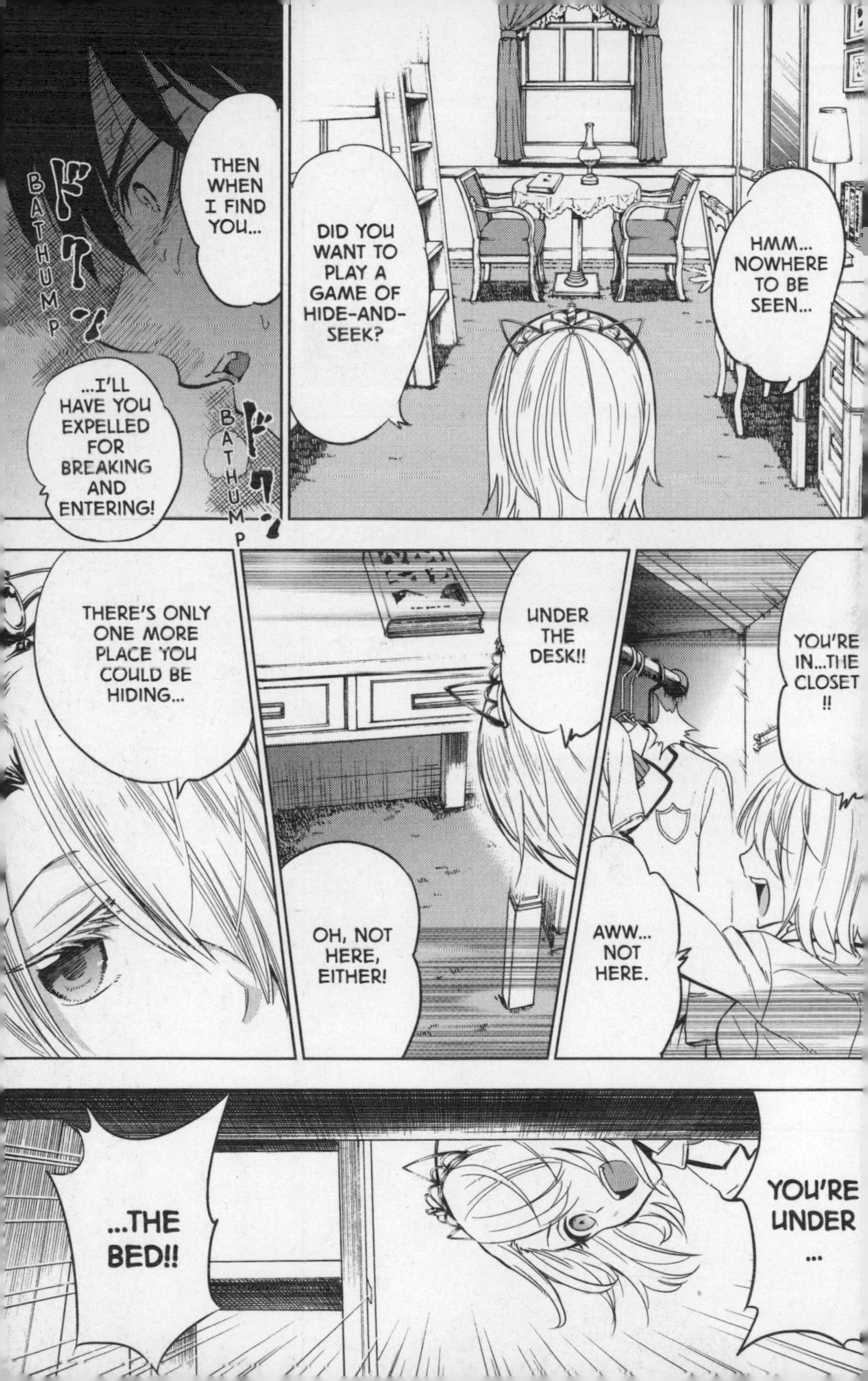
HMM... NOWHERE TO BE SEEN...
DID YOU WANT TO PLAY A GAME OF HIDE-AND-SEEK?
THEN WHEN I FIND YOU...
BATHUMP
...I'LL HAVE YOU EXPELLED FOR BREAKING AND ENTERING!
BATHUMP
YOU'RE IN...THE CLOSET !!
AWW... NOT HERE.
UNDER THE DESK!!
OH, NOT HERE, EITHER!
THERE'S ONLY ONE MORE PLACE YOU COULD BE HIDING...
YOU'RE UNDER ...
...THE BED!!

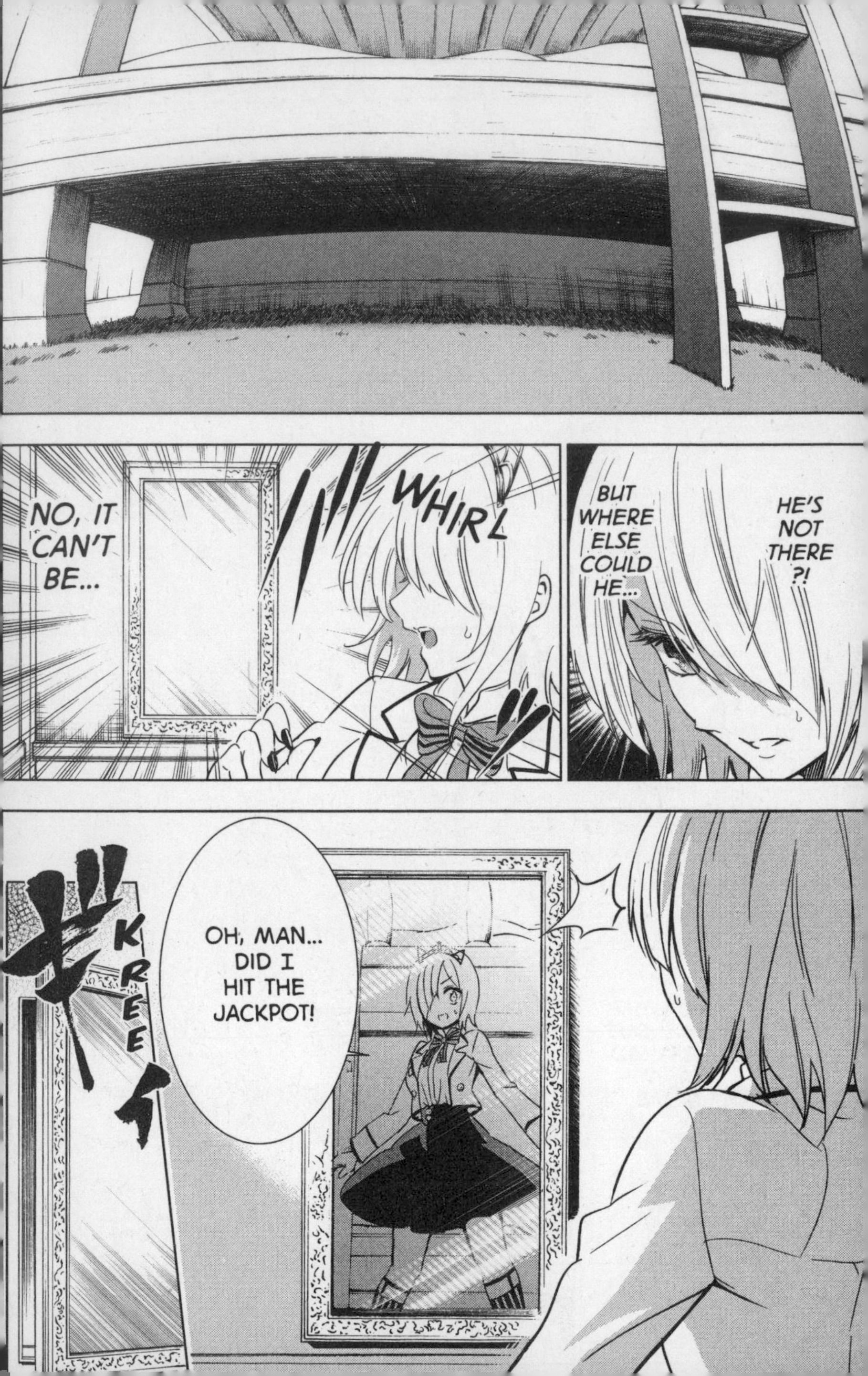
HE'S NOT THERE?!
BUT WHERE ELSE COULD HE...
WHIRL
NO, IT CAN'T BE...
OH, MAN... DID I HIT THE JACKPOT!
KREEE

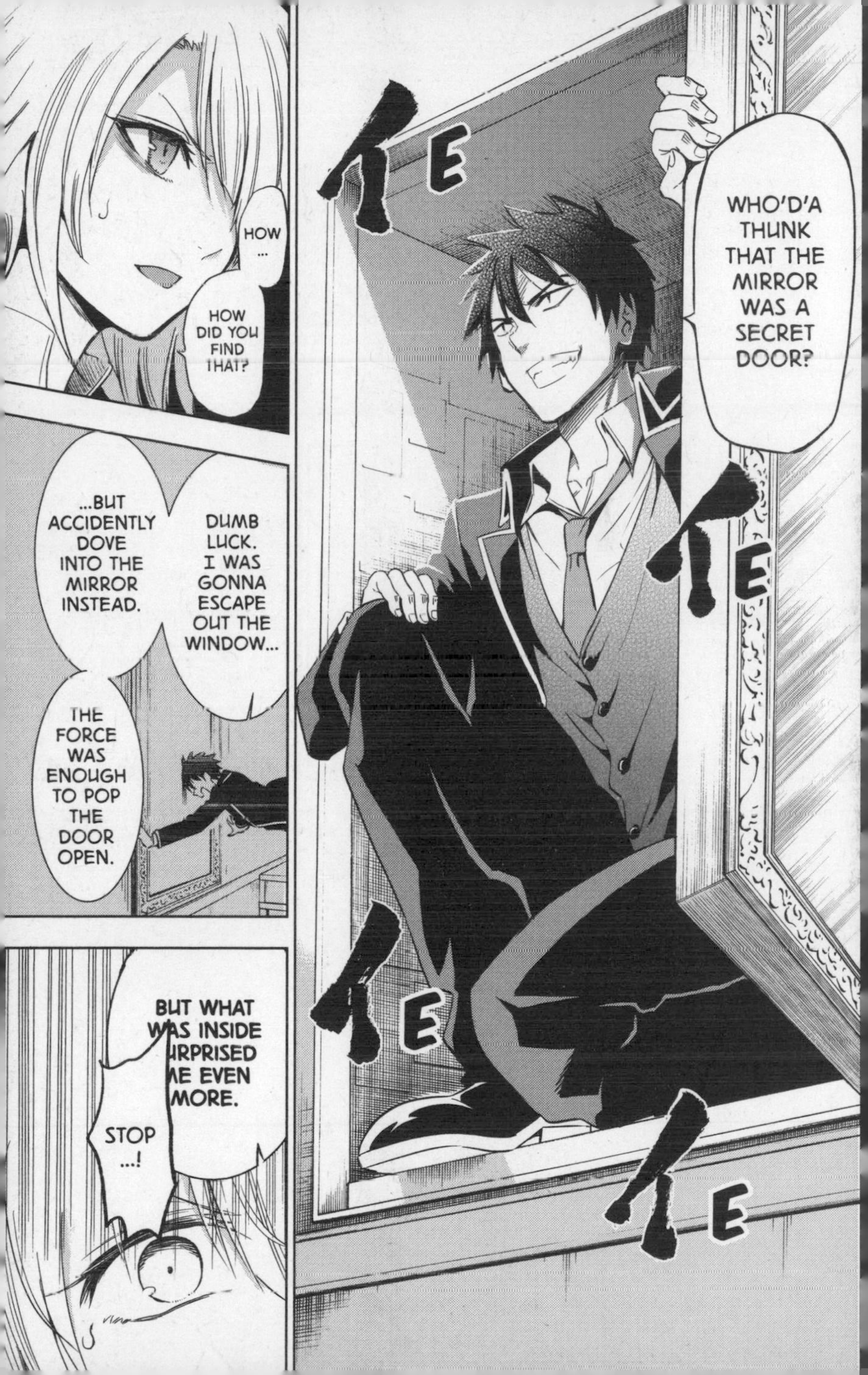
WHO'D'A THUNK THAT THE MIRROR WAS A SECRET DOOR?
HOW ...
HOW DID YOU FIND THAT?
DUMB LUCK. I WAS GONNA ESCAPE OUT THE WINDOW...
...BUT ACCIDENTLY DOVE INTO THE MIRROR INSTEAD.
THE FORCE WAS ENOUGH TO POP THE DOOR OPEN.
BUT WHAT WAS INSIDE URPRISED ME EVEN MORE.
STOP ...!

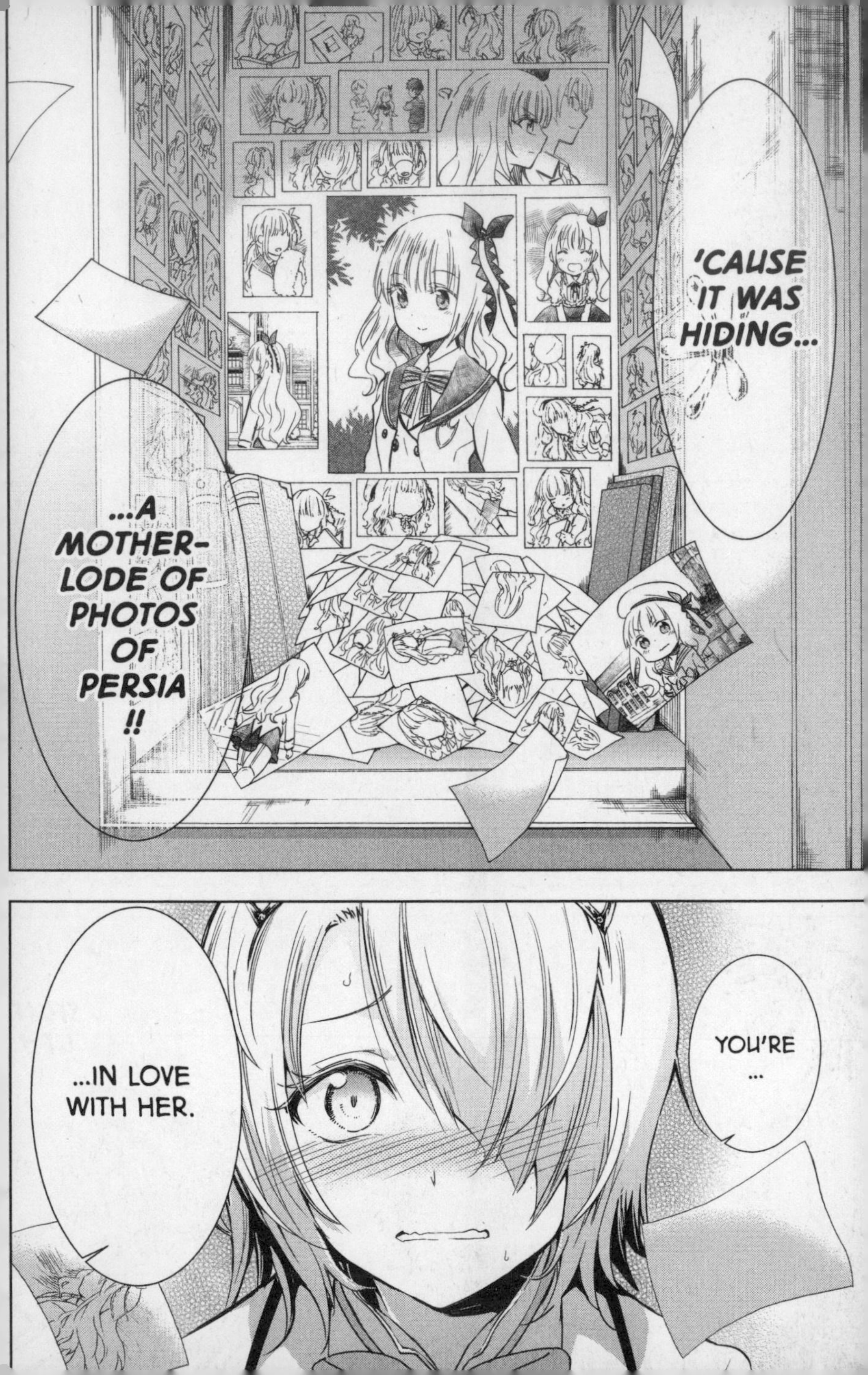
'CAUSE IT WAS HIDING...
...A MOTHER-LODE OF PHOTOS OF PERSIA !!
YOU'RE ...
...IN LOVE WITH HER.

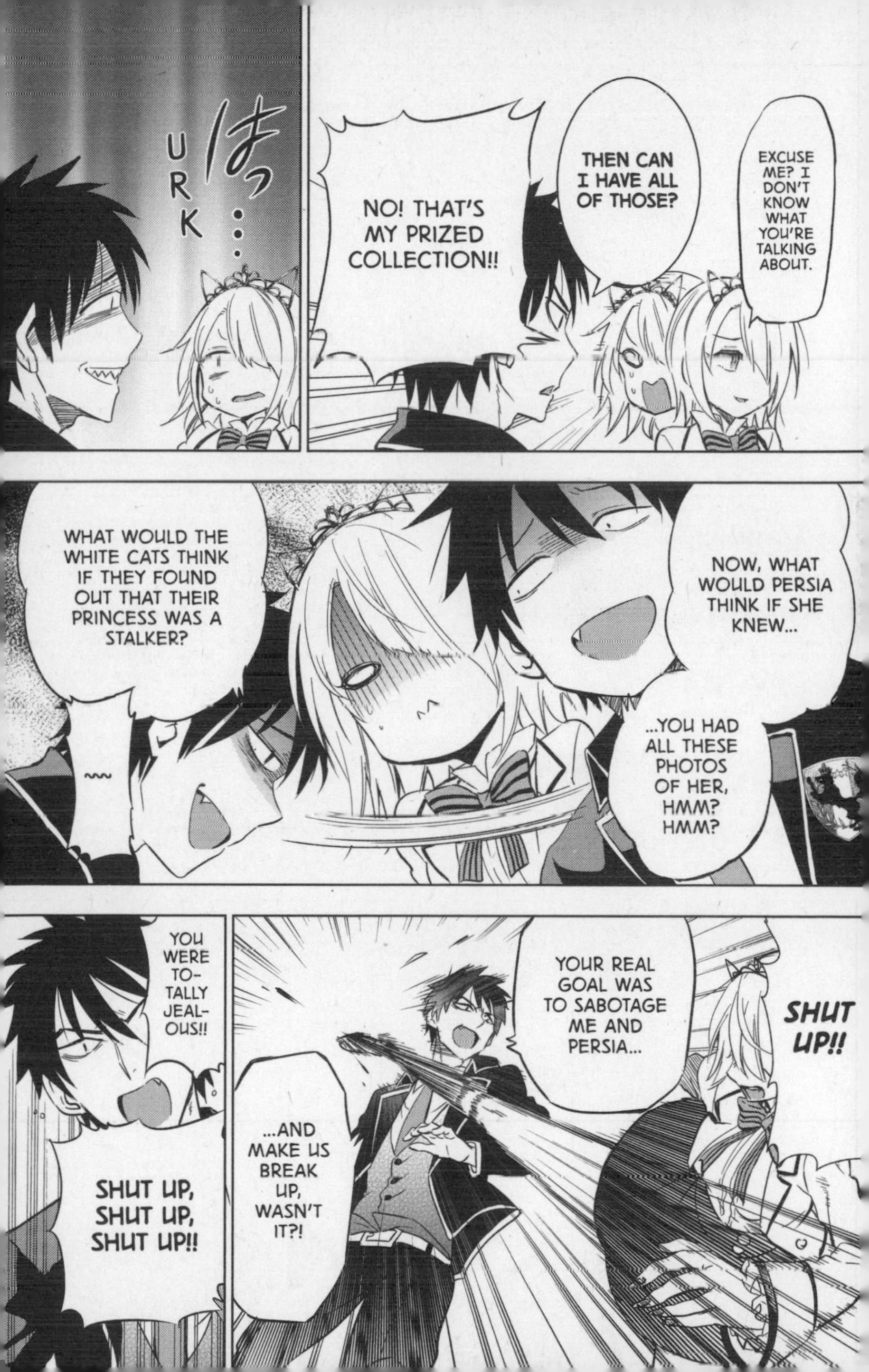
EXCUSE ME? I DON'T KNOW WHAT YOU'RE TALKING ABOUT.
THEN CAN I HAVE ALL OF THOSE?
NO! THAT'S MY PRIZED COLLECTION!!
はっ
URK...
NOW, WHAT WOULD PERSIA THINK IF SHE KNEW...
...YOU HAD ALL THESE PHOTOS OF HER, HMM? HMM?
WHAT WOULD THE WHITE CATS THINK IF THEY FOUND OUT THAT THEIR PRINCESS WAS A STALKER?
YOUR REAL GOAL WAS TO SABOTAGE ME AND PERSIA...
...AND MAKE US BREAK UP, WASN'T IT?!
SHUT UP!!
YOU WERE TO-TALLY JEAL-OUS!!
SHUT UP, SHUT UP, SHUT UP!!

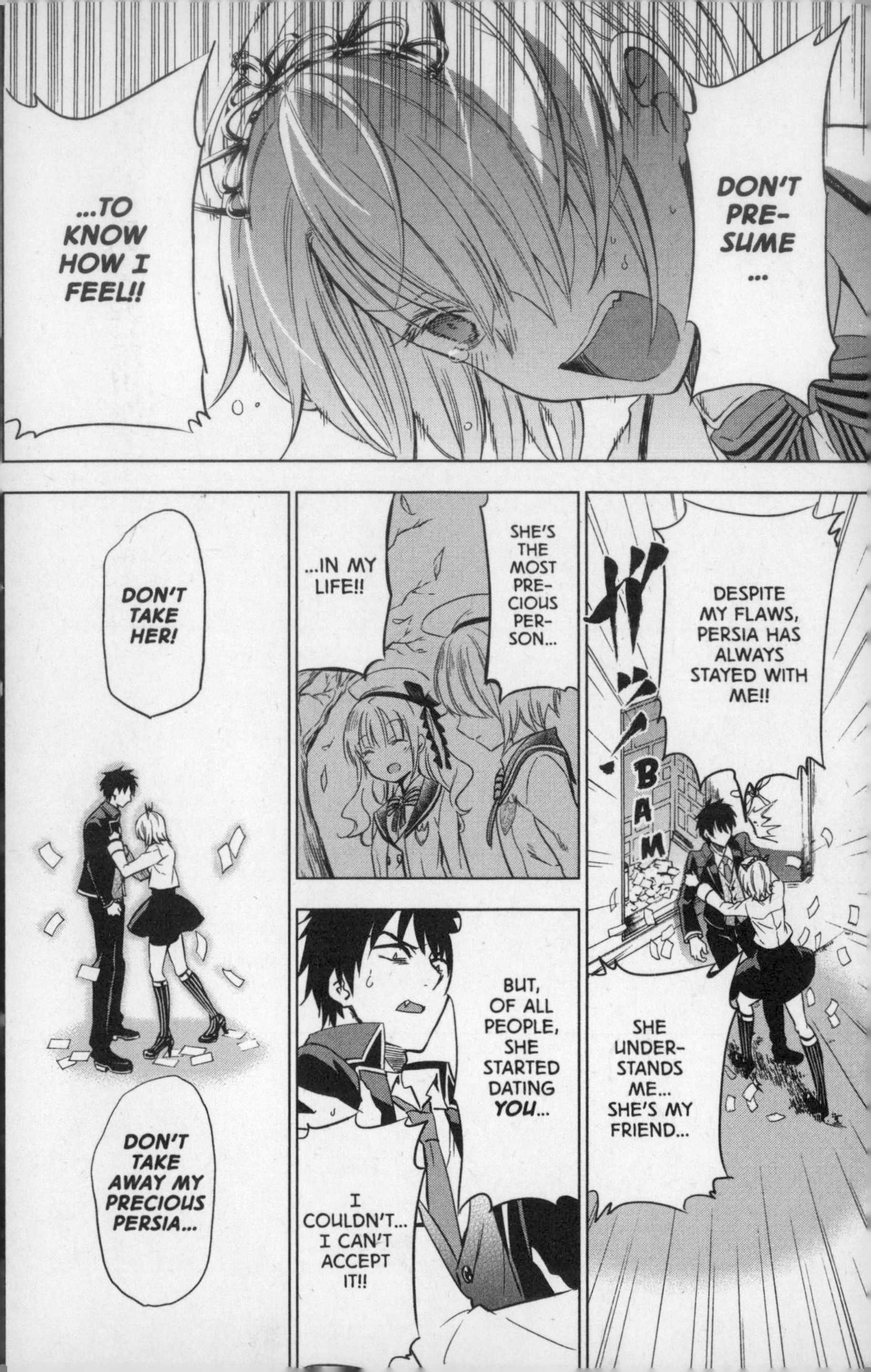
DON'T PRE-SUME ...
...TO KNOW HOW I FEEL!!
DESPITE MY FLAWS, PERSIA HAS ALWAYS STAYED WITH ME!!
BAM
SHE UNDER-STANDS ME... SHE'S MY FRIEND...
SHE'S THE MOST PRE-CIOUS PER-SON...
...IN MY LIFE!!
BUT, OF ALL PEOPLE, SHE STARTED DATING *YOU*...
I COULDN'T... I CAN'T ACCEPT IT!!
DON'T TAKE HER!
DON'T TAKE AWAY MY PRECIOUS PERSIA...

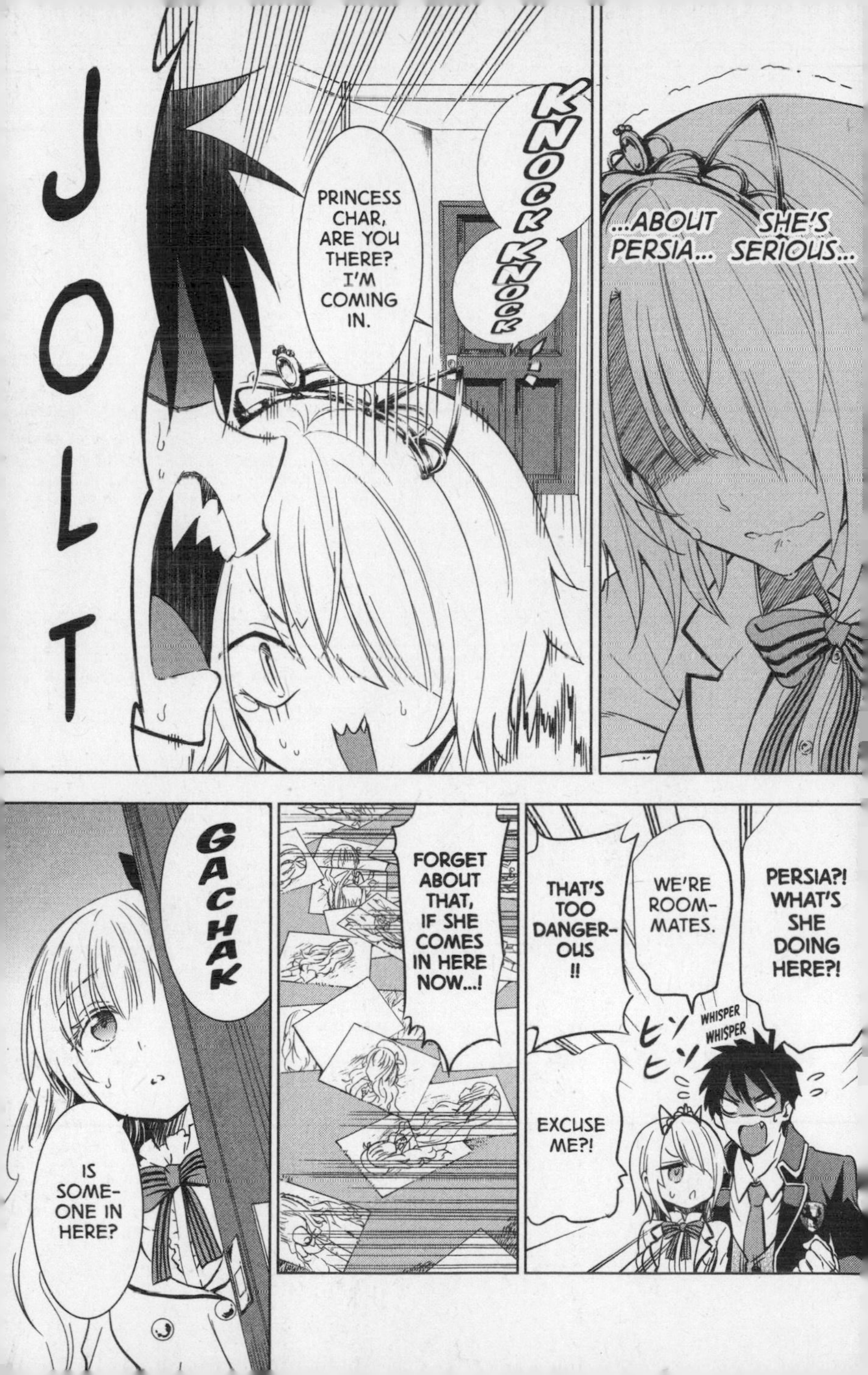
SHE'S SERIOUS...
...ABOUT PERSIA...
KNOCK KNOCK
PRINCESS CHAR, ARE YOU THERE? I'M COMING IN.
JOLT
PERSIA?! WHAT'S SHE DOING HERE?!
WE'RE ROOM-MATES.
WHISPER WHISPER
EXCUSE ME?!
THAT'S TOO DANGER-OUS!!
FORGET ABOUT THAT, IF SHE COMES IN HERE NOW...!
GACHAK
IS SOME-ONE IN HERE?

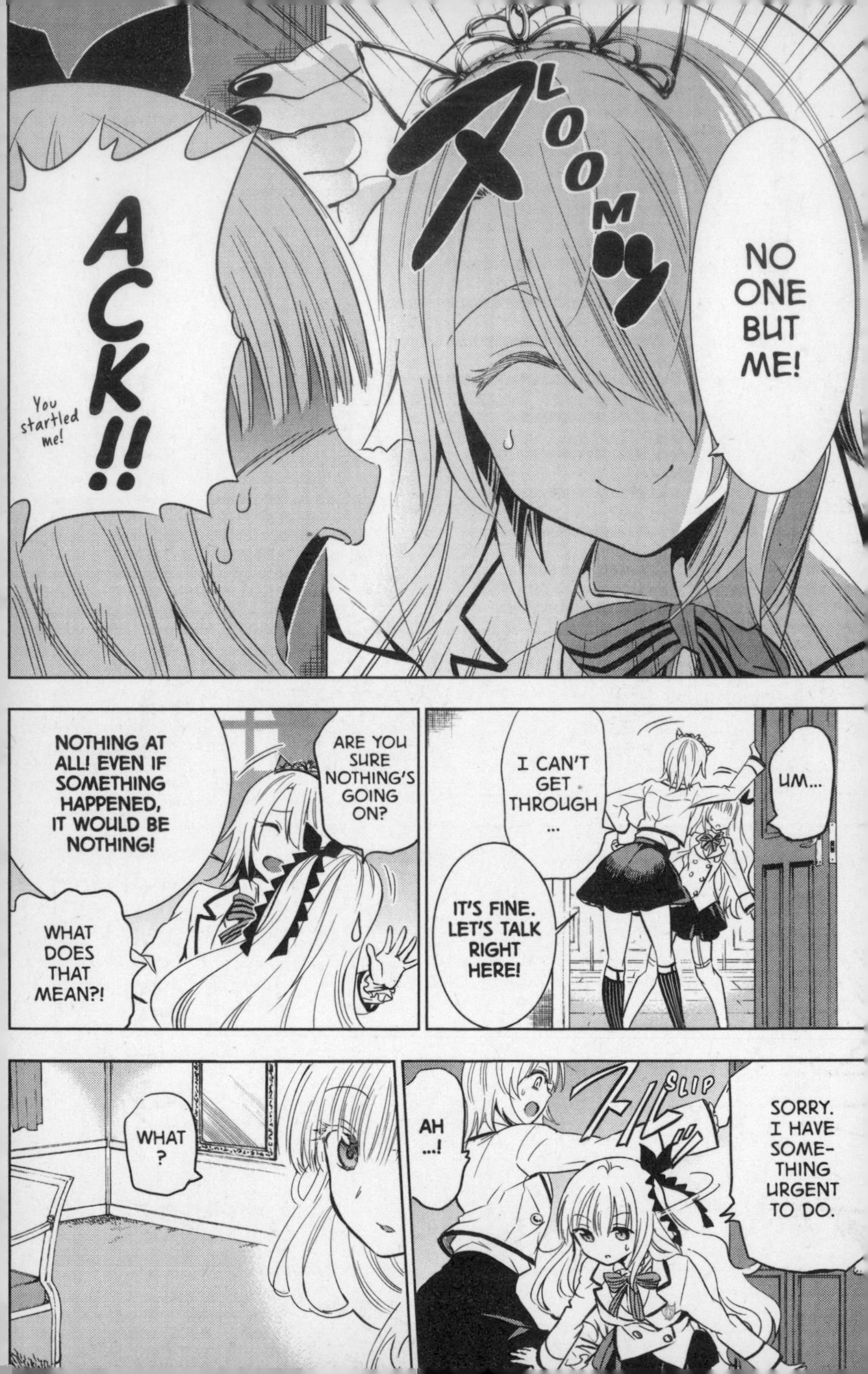
NO ONE BUT ME!
LOOM
ACK!!
You startled me!
UM...
I CAN'T GET THROUGH ...
IT'S FINE. LET'S TALK RIGHT HERE!
ARE YOU SURE NOTHING'S GOING ON?
NOTHING AT ALL! EVEN IF SOMETHING HAPPENED, IT WOULD BE NOTHING!
WHAT DOES THAT MEAN?!
SORRY. I HAVE SOME-THING URGENT TO DO.
SLIP
AH ...!
WHAT ?

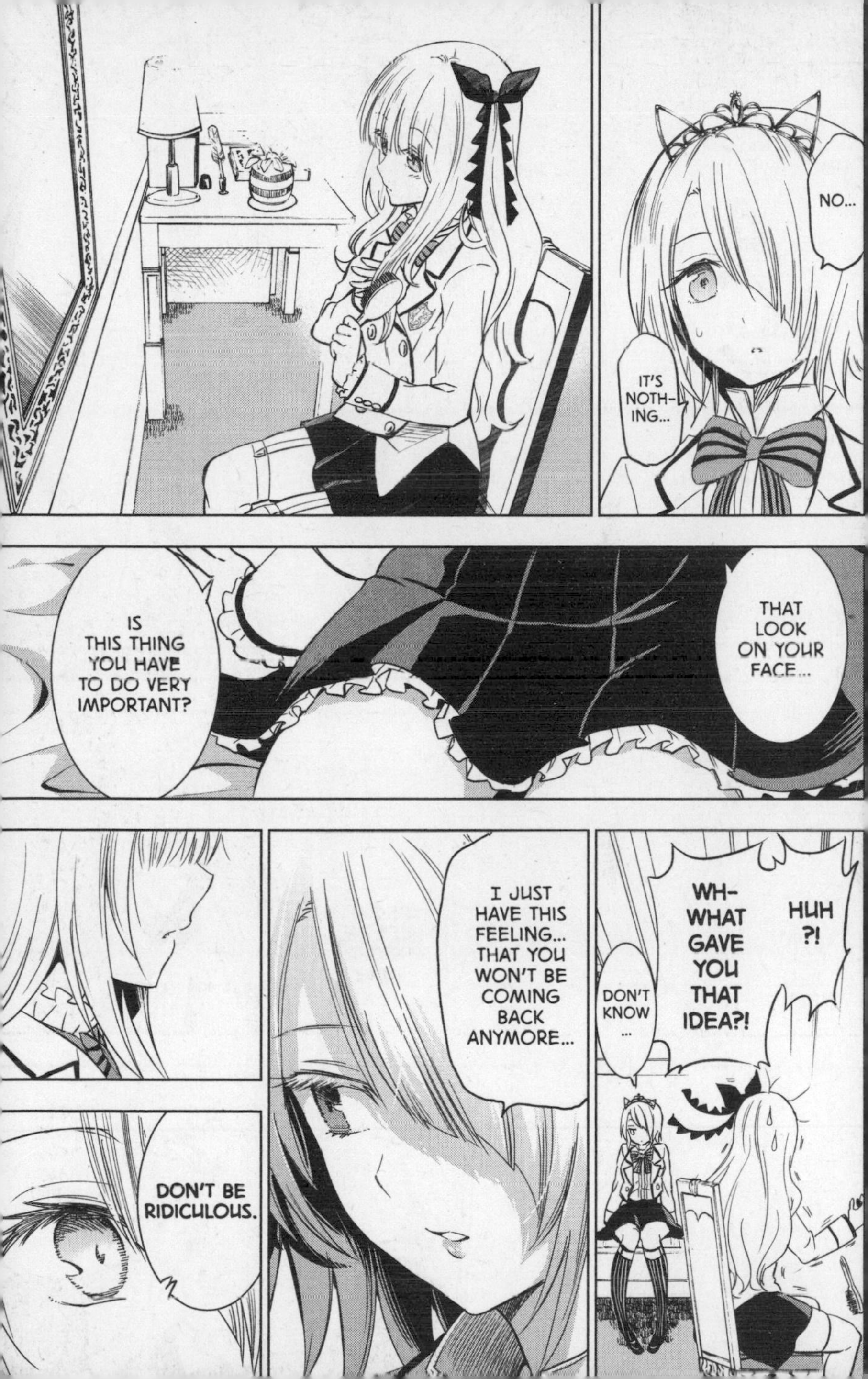
NO...
IT'S NOTHING-ING...
THAT LOOK ON YOUR FACE...
IS THIS THING YOU HAVE TO DO VERY IMPORTANT?
HUH?!
WH-WHAT GAVE YOU THAT IDEA?!
DON'T KNOW...
I JUST HAVE THIS FEELING... THAT YOU WON'T BE COMING BACK ANYMORE...
DON'T BE RIDICULOUS.

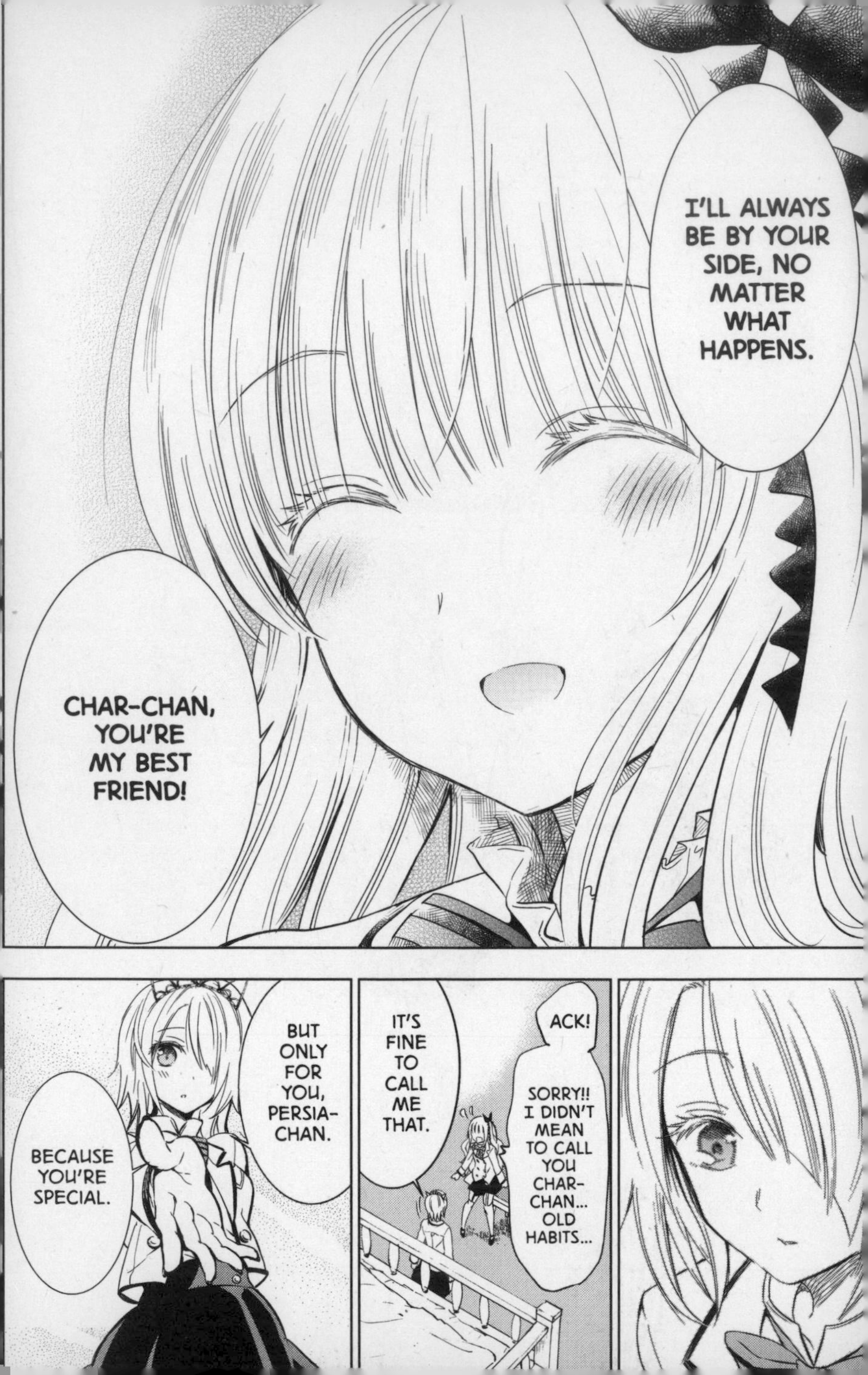
I'LL ALWAYS BE BY YOUR SIDE, NO MATTER WHAT HAPPENS.
CHAR-CHAN, YOU'RE MY BEST FRIEND!
ACK!
SORRY!! I DIDN'T MEAN TO CALL YOU CHAR-CHAN... OLD HABITS...
IT'S FINE TO CALL ME THAT.
BUT ONLY FOR YOU, PERSIA-CHAN.
BECAUSE YOU'RE SPECIAL.

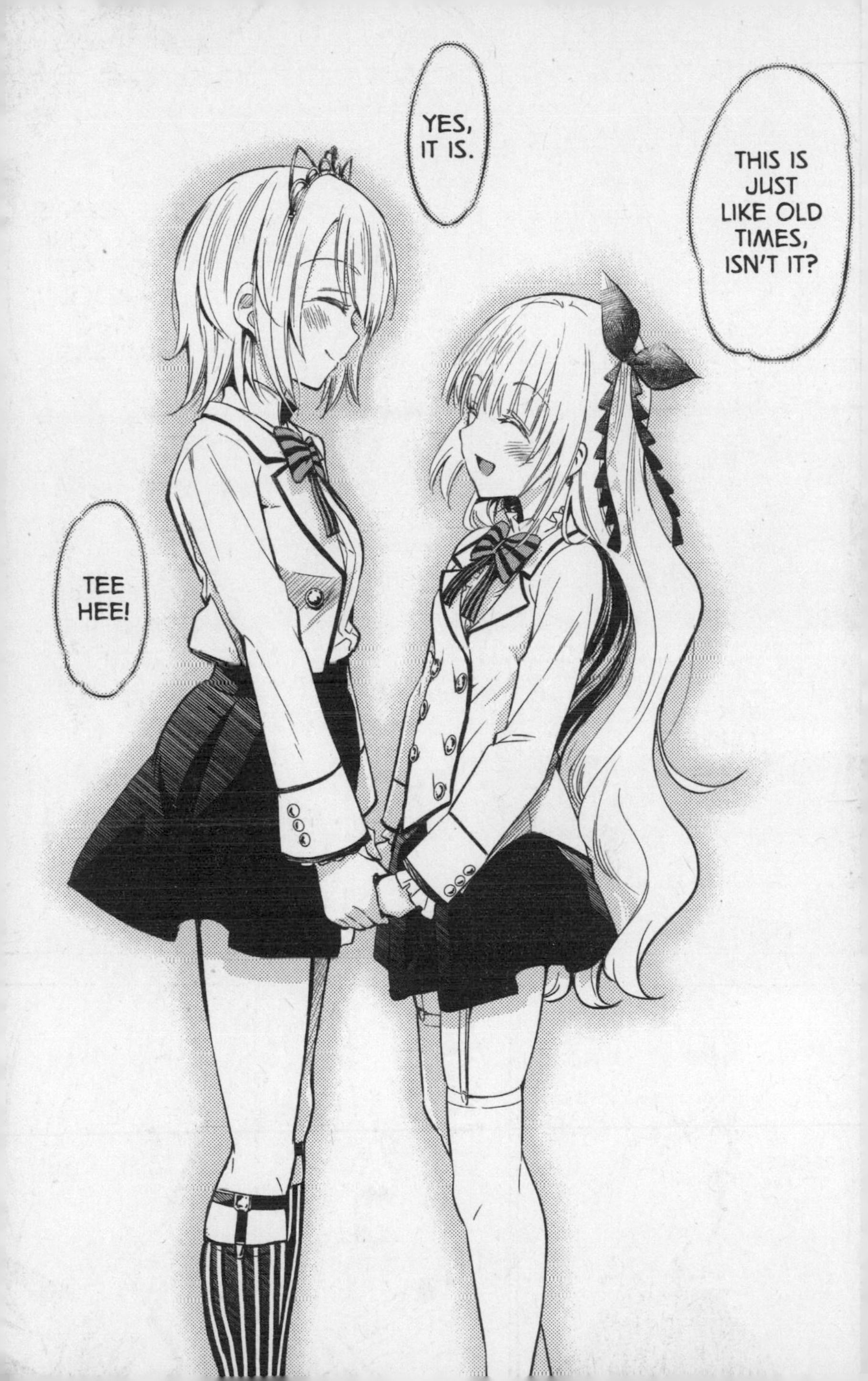
THIS IS JUST LIKE OLD TIMES, ISN'T IT?
YES, IT IS.
TEE HEE!

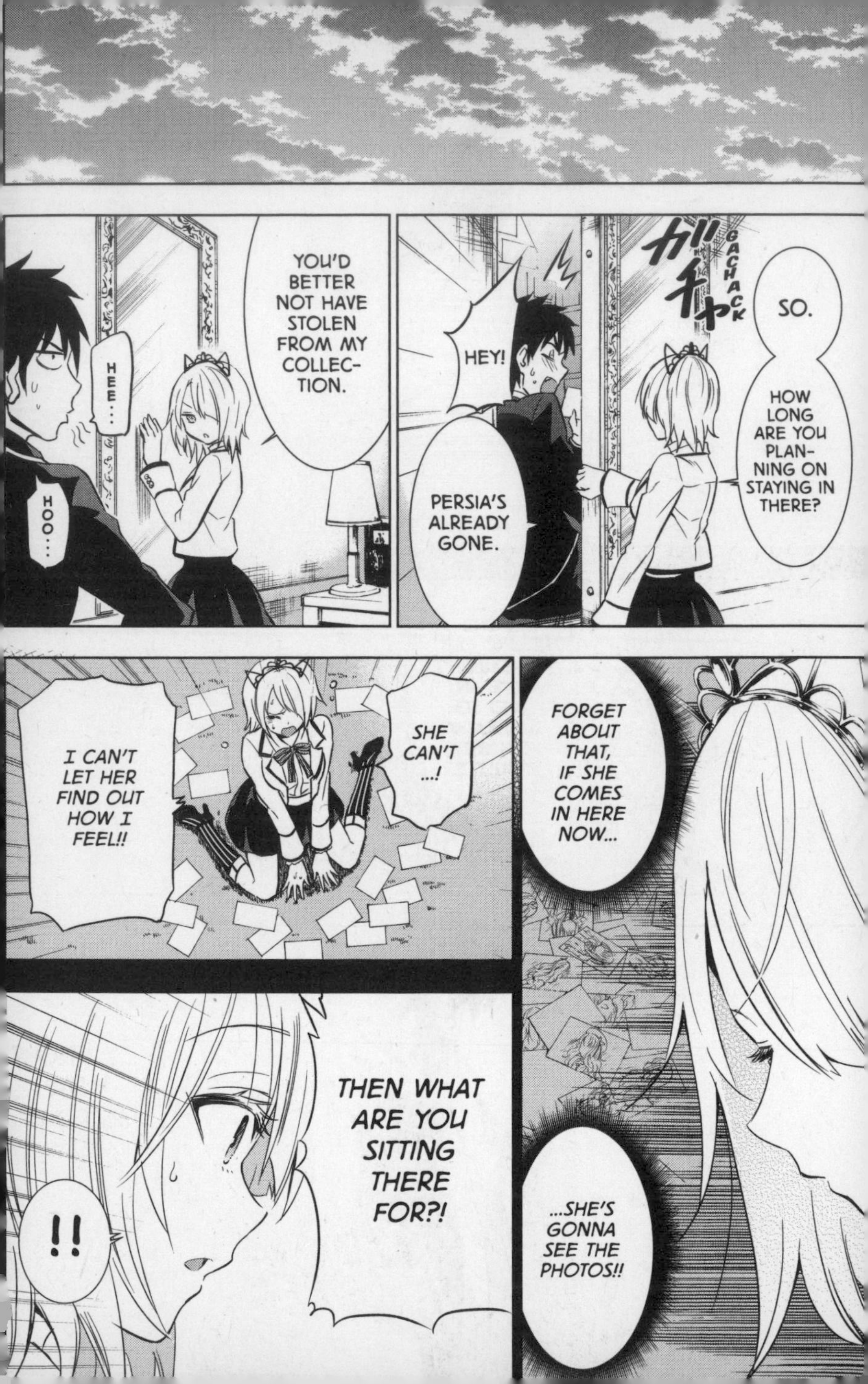

ガチャ
GACHACK
SO.
HOW LONG ARE YOU PLANNING ON STAYING IN THERE?
HEY!
PERSIA'S ALREADY GONE.
YOU'D BETTER NOT HAVE STOLEN FROM MY COLLECTION.
HEE...
HOO...
FORGET ABOUT THAT, IF SHE COMES IN HERE NOW...
...SHE'S GONNA SEE THE PHOTOS!!
SHE CAN'T ...!
I CAN'T LET HER FIND OUT HOW I FEEL!!
THEN WHAT ARE YOU SITTING THERE FOR?!
!!

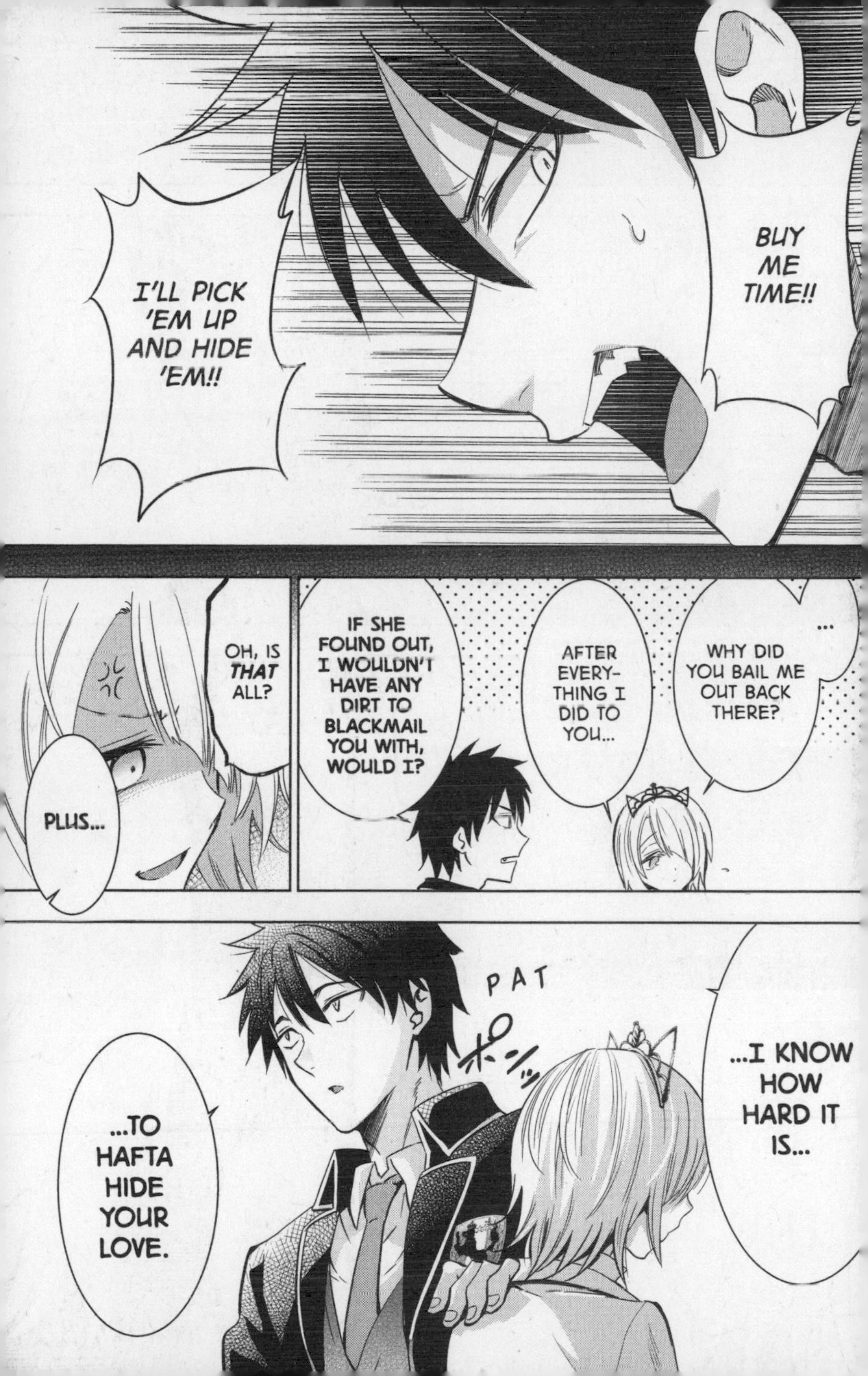
BUY ME TIME!!
I'LL PICK 'EM UP AND HIDE 'EM!!
...
WHY DID YOU BAIL ME OUT BACK THERE?
AFTER EVERY-THING I DID TO YOU...
IF SHE FOUND OUT, I WOULDN'T HAVE ANY DIRT TO BLACKMAIL YOU WITH, WOULD I?
OH, IS *THAT* ALL?
PLUS...
PAT
ポンッ
...I KNOW HOW HARD IT IS...
...TO HAFTA HIDE YOUR LOVE.

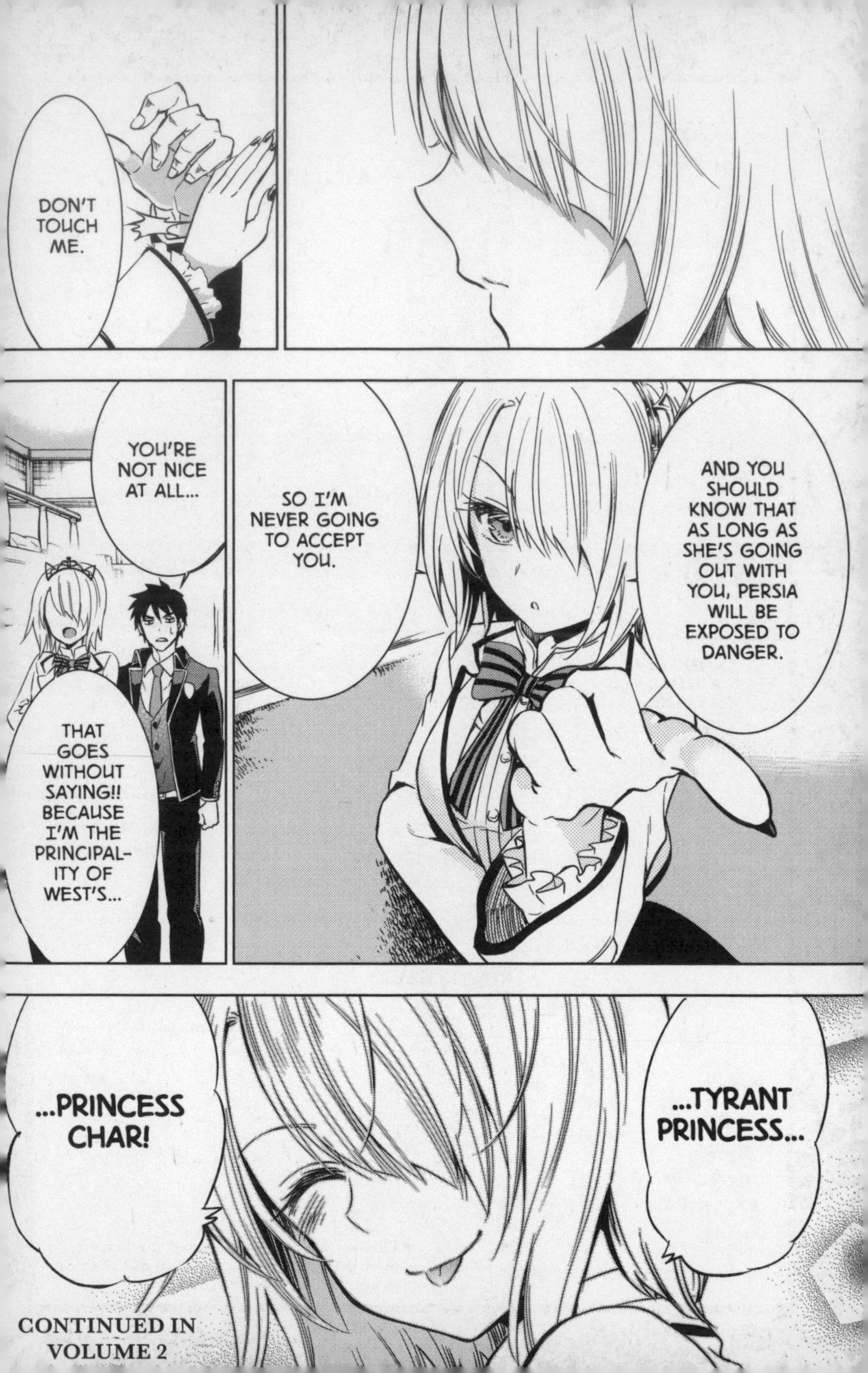
DON'T TOUCH ME.
AND YOU SHOULD KNOW THAT AS LONG AS SHE'S GOING OUT WITH YOU, PERSIA WILL BE EXPOSED TO DANGER.
SO I'M NEVER GOING TO ACCEPT YOU.
YOU'RE NOT NICE AT ALL...
THAT GOES WITHOUT SAYING!! BECAUSE I'M THE PRINCIPAL-ITY OF WEST'S...
...TYRANT PRINCESS...
...PRINCESS CHAR!

CONTINUED IN VOLUME 2

Boarding School Juliet

~EARLY DESIGN WORK~

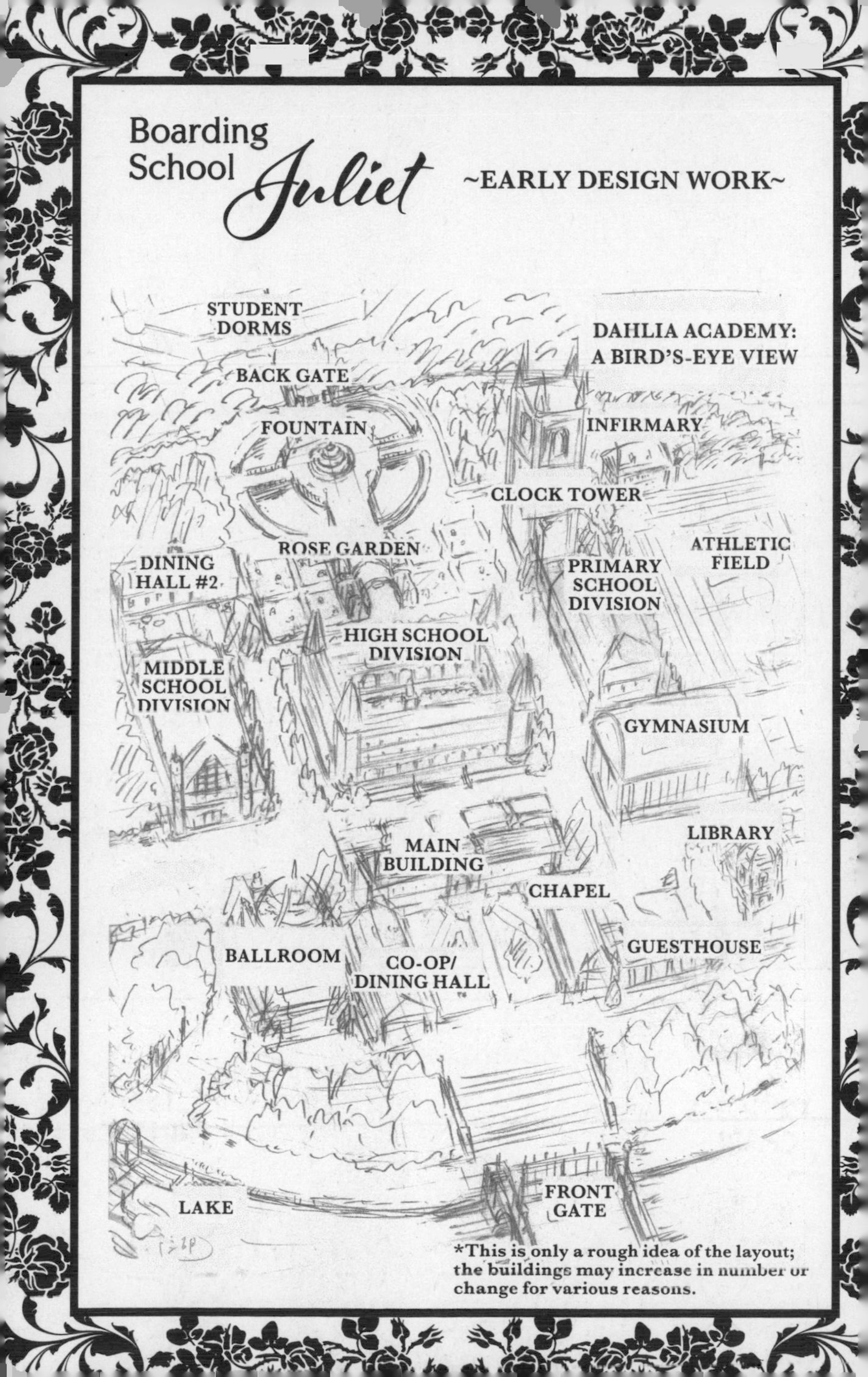
DAHLIA ACADEMY:
A BIRD'S-EYE VIEW
STUDENT DORMS
BACK GATE
FOUNTAIN
INFIRMARY
CLOCK TOWER
ROSE GARDEN
DINING HALL #2
ATHLETIC FIELD
PRIMARY SCHOOL DIVISION
HIGH SCHOOL DIVISION
MIDDLE SCHOOL DIVISION
GYMNASIUM
LIBRARY
MAIN BUILDING
CHAPEL
GUESTHOUSE
BALLROOM
CO-OP/ DINING HALL
LAKE
FRONT GATE

*This is only a rough idea of the layout; the buildings may increase in number or change for various reasons.

~ SCHOOL UNIFORM: BOYS ~
(BLACK DOGGY VER.)

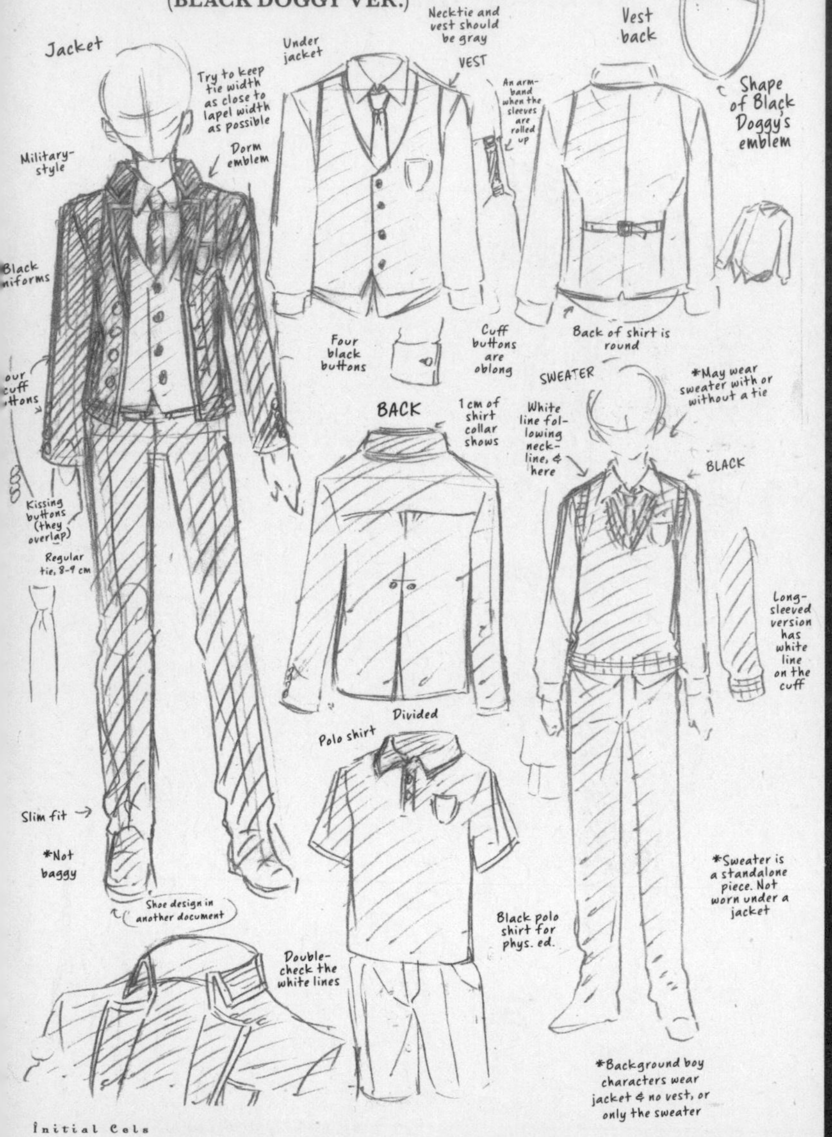
Jacket
Try to keep tie width as close to lapel width as possible
Military-style
Dorm emblem
Black uniforms
our cuff ttons
Kissing buttons (they overlap)
Regular tie, 8-9 cm
Slim fit
*Not baggy
Shoe design in another document
Under jacket
Necktie and vest should be gray
VEST
An arm-band when the sleeves are rolled up
Four black buttons
Cuff buttons are oblong
Vest back
Shape of Black Doggy's emblem
Back of shirt is round
BACK
1 cm of shirt collar shows
Divided
Polo shirt
Double-check the white lines
Black polo shirt for phys. ed.
SWEATER
White line fol-lowing neck-line, & here
*May wear sweater with or without a tie
BLACK
Long-sleeved version has white line on the cuff
*Sweater is a standalone piece. Not worn under a jacket
*Background boy characters wear jacket & no vest, or only the sweater

~ SCHOOL UNIFORM: GIRLS ~
(BLACK DOGGY VER.)

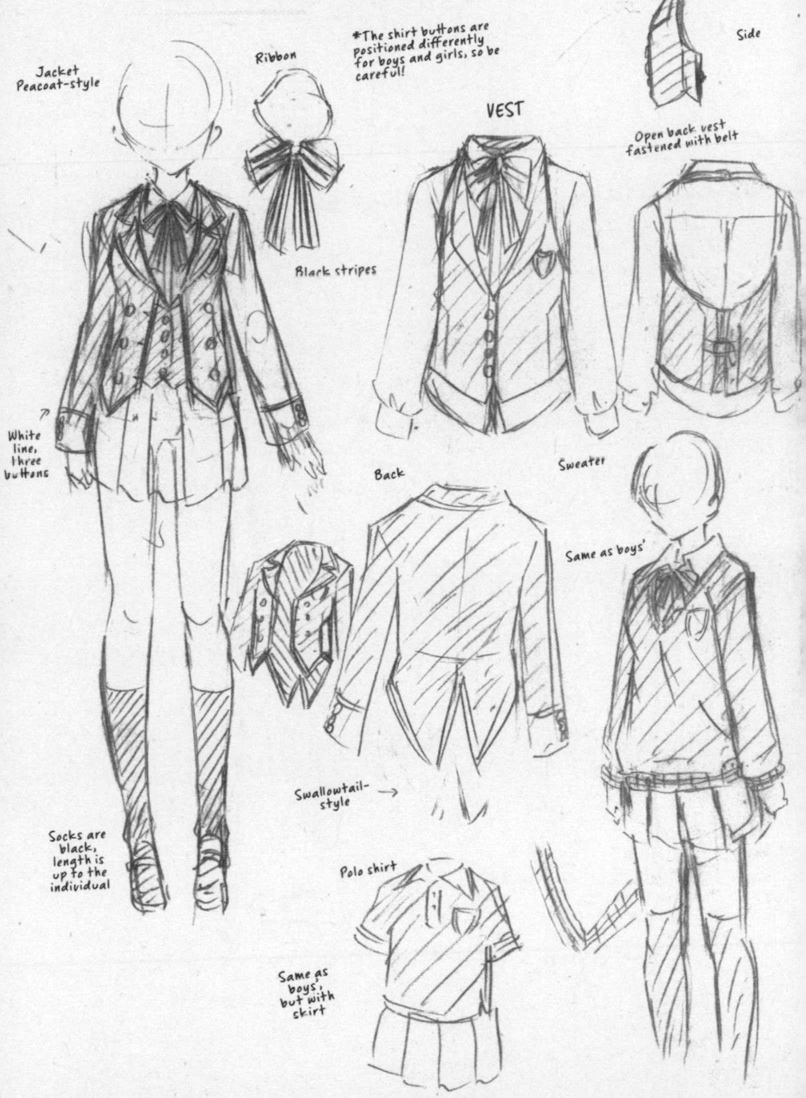
Jacket
Peacoat-style
Ribbon
*The shirt buttons are positioned differently for boys and girls, so be careful!
Side
VEST
Open back vest fastened with belt
Black stripes
White line, three buttons
Back
Sweater
Same as boys'
Swallowtail-style
Socks are black, length is up to the individual
Polo shirt
Same as boys', but with skirt

~EMBLEMS~

WHITE CAT HOUSE

BLACK DOGGY HOUSE

SCHOOL EMBLEM

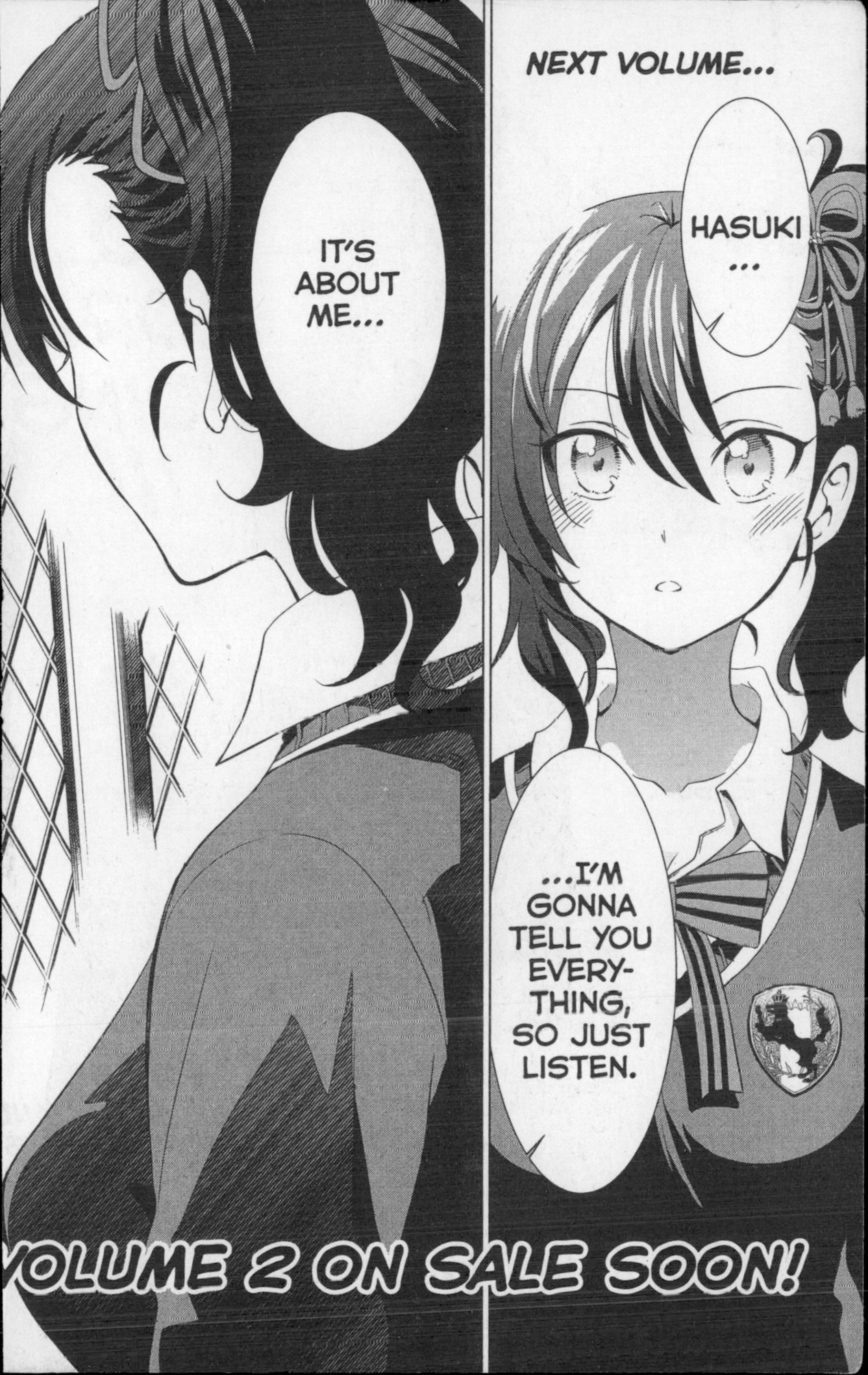
NEXT VOLUME...
HASUKI ...
...I'M GONNA TELL YOU EVERY-THING, SO JUST LISTEN.
IT'S ABOUT ME...
VOLUME 2 ON SALE SOON!

SUPPLEMENTAL CORNER

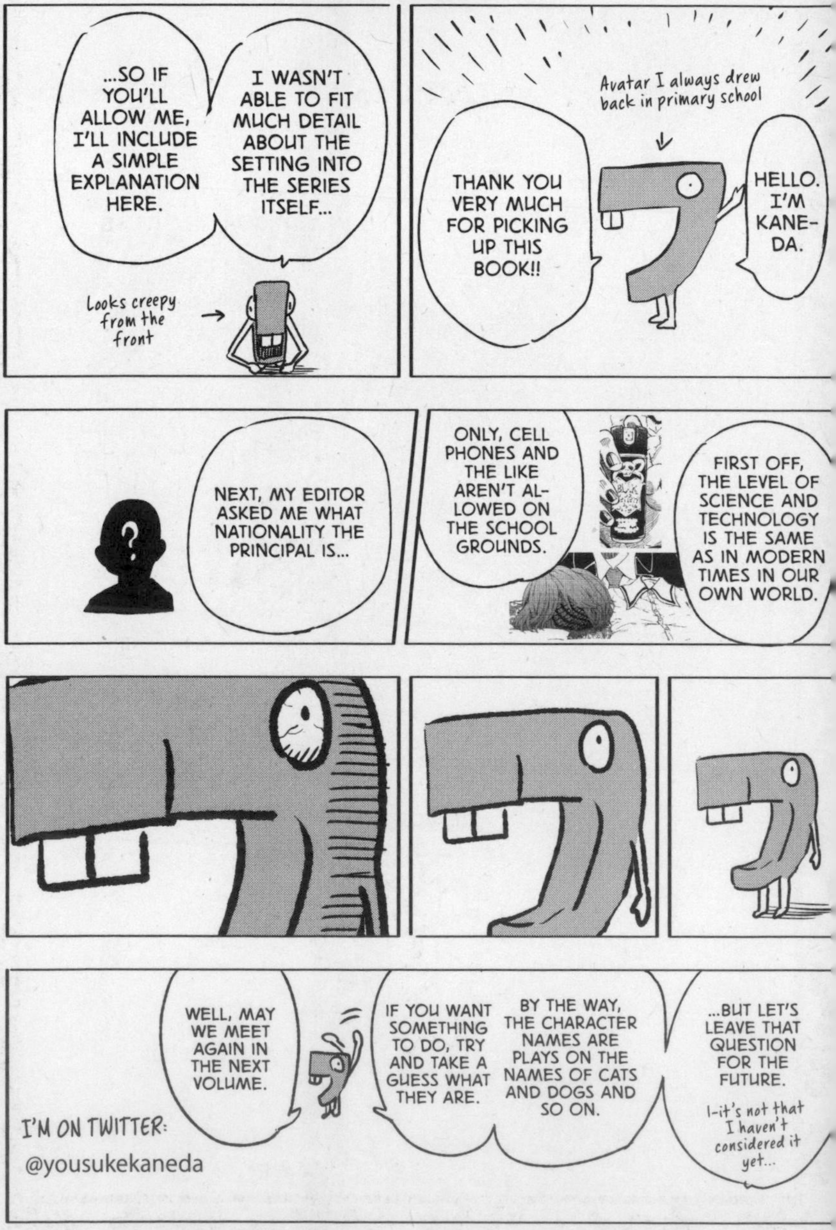
HELLO. I'M KANE-DA.
Avatar I always drew back in primary school
THANK YOU VERY MUCH FOR PICKING UP THIS BOOK!!
I WASN'T ABLE TO FIT MUCH DETAIL ABOUT THE SETTING INTO THE SERIES ITSELF...
...SO IF YOU'LL ALLOW ME, I'LL INCLUDE A SIMPLE EXPLANATION HERE.
Looks creepy from the front
FIRST OFF, THE LEVEL OF SCIENCE AND TECHNOLOGY IS THE SAME AS IN MODERN TIMES IN OUR OWN WORLD.
ONLY, CELL PHONES AND THE LIKE AREN'T AL-LOWED ON THE SCHOOL GROUNDS.
NEXT, MY EDITOR ASKED ME WHAT NATIONALITY THE PRINCIPAL IS...
...BUT LET'S LEAVE THAT QUESTION FOR THE FUTURE.
I-it's not that I haven't considered it yet...
BY THE WAY, THE CHARACTER NAMES ARE PLAYS ON THE NAMES OF CATS AND DOGS AND SO ON.
IF YOU WANT SOMETHING TO DO, TRY AND TAKE A GUESS WHAT THEY ARE.
WELL, MAY WE MEET AGAIN IN THE NEXT VOLUME.
I'M ON TWITTER:
@yousukekaneda

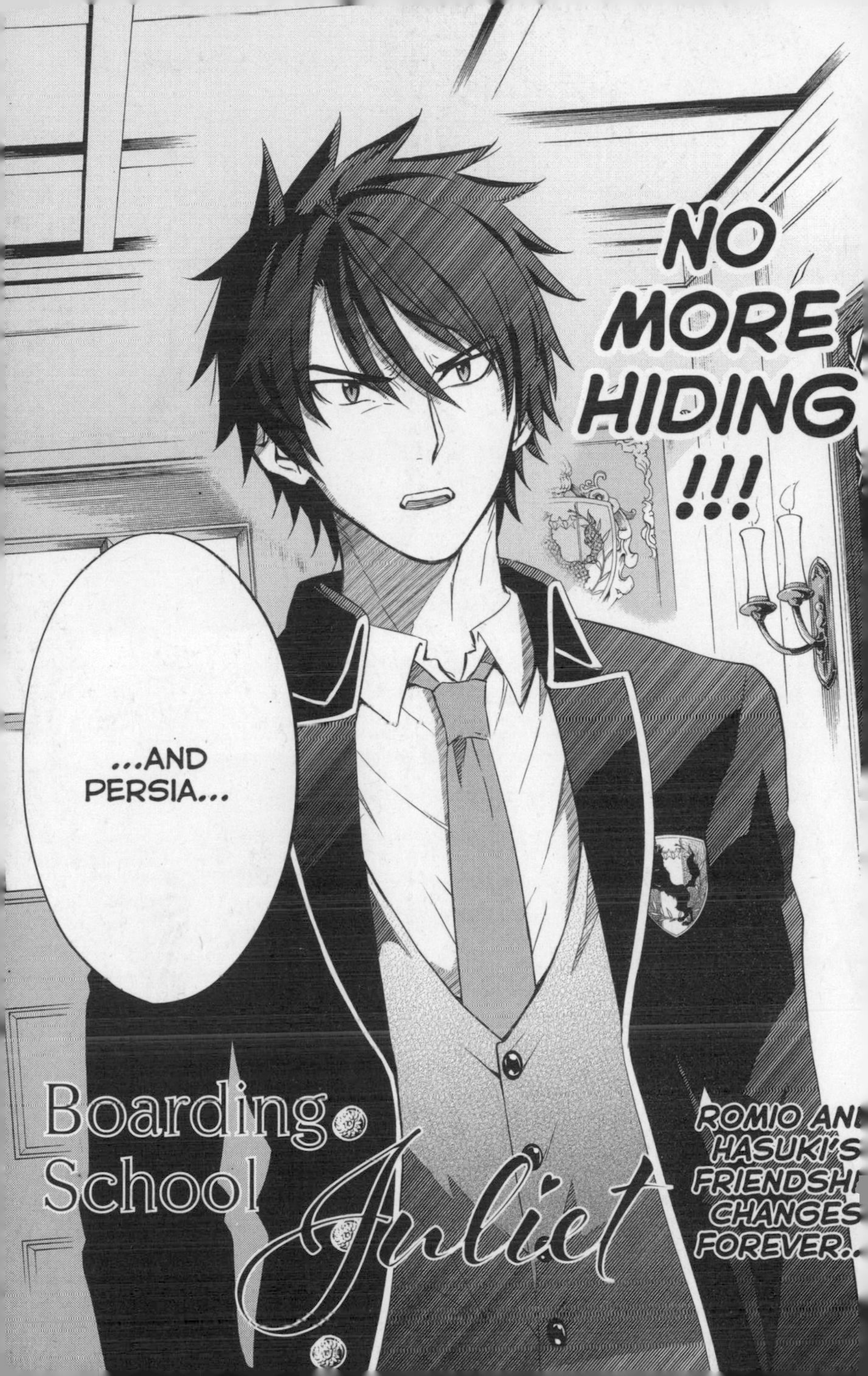
NO MORE HIDING !!!
...AND PERSIA...
ROMIO AN
HASUKI'S
FRIENDSH
CHANGES
FOREVER..
Boarding School Juliet

Boarding School Juliet volume 1 is a work of fiction. Names, characters, places, and incidents are the products of the author's imagination or are used fictitiously. Any resemblance to actual events, locales, or persons, living or dead, is entirely coincidental.

A Kodansha Comics Trade Paperback Original.

Boarding School Juliet volume 1 copyright © 2015 Yousuke Kaneda
English translation copyright © 2018 Yousuke Kaneda

Published in the United States by Kodansha Comics,
an imprint of Kodansha USA Publishing, LLC, New York.

Publication rights for this English edition arranged through
Kodansha Ltd., Tokyo.

First published in Japan in 2015 by Kodansha Ltd., Tokyo, as
Kishuku Gakkou no Juliette volume 1.

ISBN 978-1-63236-750-1

Printed in the United States of America.

www.kodanshacomics.com

9 8 7 6 5 4 3 2 1

Translation: Amanda Haley
Lettering: James Dashiell
Editing: Erin Subramanian and Paul Starr
Kodansha Comics edition cover design: Phil Balsman